CASS LIBRARY OF SCIENCE CLASSICS

No. 16

General Editor: Dr. L. L. LAUDAN, University of Pittsburgh

THE USEFULNESS OF MATHEMATICAL LEARNING

THE USEFULNESS OF MATHEMATICAL LEARNING

Explained and Demonstrated:

BEING

Mathematical Lectures
Read in the Publick Schools at the
University of Cambridge

BY

Isaac Barrow

FRANK CASS & CO. LTD.

1970

Published by
FRANK CASS AND COMPANY LIMITED
67 Great Russell Street, London WC1B 3BT

First edition	1734
New impression	1970

ISBN 0 7146 1591 9

Printed in Great Britain by Clarke, Doble & Brendon Ltd.
Plymouth and London

Printed for Stephen Austen at the Angel and Bible in S.t Paul's Church Yard

The Usefulness of Mathematical Learning explained and demonstrated:

BEING

MATHEMATICAL LECTURES

READ IN THE

PUBLICK SCHOOLS

AT THE

University of CAMBRIDGE.

By *ISAAC BARROW*, D.D. Professor of the MATHEMATICS, and Master of *Trinity-College*, &c.

To which is prefixed,

The ORATORICAL PREFACE of Our Learned AUTHOR, spoke before the University on his being elected *LUCASIAN* Professor of the Mathematics.

Translated by the Revd. Mr. *JOHN KIRKBY*, of *Egremond* in *Cumberland*.

LONDON:

Printed for STEPHEN AUSTEN, at the *Angel* and *Bible* in St. *Paul's Church-yard*. MDCCXXXIV.

THE CONTENTS.

Lecture I.

Lecture II.

Lecture III.

Lecture IV.

Lecture V.

Lecture VI.

Lecture

LECTURE

LECTURE XV.

LECTURE XVI.

LECTURE XVII.

LECTURE XVIII.

LECTURE XIX.

LECTURE XX.

LECTURE XXI.

ERRATA.

PAGE 12. l. 28. read *Spherics.* p. 18. l. 11. r. *Isorrhopics. ibid.* l. 13. r. *Automatopoëtics.* p. 20. l. 3. r. *Blancanus.* p. 25. l. 29. r. *Isorrhopics.* p. 42. l. 25. r. *composed of.* p. 43. l. 6. r. *Root* (√2.) p. 53. l. 19. r. *perused. ibid.* l. 33. r. *the Senses.* p. 83. l. 9. r. *hence.* p. 103. l. penult. r. *indemonstrable.* p. 126. l. 6. r. *Rivaltus.* p. 133. l. 36. dele *by.* p. 134. l. 20. r. Hypotheses. p. 139. l. 10. r. *Hypotheses.* p. 141. l. 5. r. *acquiring another Coincidence.* p. 167. l. 3. r. *coexist.* p. 194. l. 24. r. *varied.* p. 197. l. 9. r. *Cavallerius.* p. 242. l. 35. r. *Cavallerius.* p. 217. l. 24. r. *effect it.* p. 221. l. 21. r. *occupable.* p. 240. l. 25, *&c.* r. *Asymmetry.* p. 245. l. 3. r. *by receding.* p. 252. l. 1. r. *which respect.* p. 265. l. 16. r. *Euthymetry.* p. 271. l. 29. r. *Right Sine.* p. 293. l. 5. r. *most candid.* p. 314. l. 23. dele *in.* p. 326. l. 28. r. *As if in.* p. 331. l. 34. r. *of it to others.* p. 332. l. 30. dele *Country Man the.* p. 349. l. 25. r. *cannot.* p. 354. l. 30. dele *very often,* r. *are differently.* p. 366. l. 27, 28. for *or* r. *and.* p. 385. l. 26. dele *tho' it.* Pages 386, 387, 390, 391, 394, 395, 398, 399, are wrong number'd. p. 387. l. ult. r. *sagacious Person.* p. 388. l. 7. dele *wherefore.* p. 392. l. 1. r. *Property.* ibid. l. 3. for *any four* r. *several Fours of.* ibid. l. 20. for *Equality* r. *Proportionality.* ibid. l. 22. r. *Reason.* p. 393. l. 23. dele *Use.* p. 394. l. 21. dele *and.* p. 396. l. 22. dele *also.* p. 397. l. 3. dele *there.* p. 404. l. 31. dele *some.* p. 409. l. 36. for *Things,* r. *Verity of the Theorems.* ibid. l. 37. dele *concerning the, &c.* p. 411. l. 16. r. *by which.* p. 419. l. 22. r. *against* Euclid's. p. 421. l. 26. r. *I enquire.* p. 423. l. 14. r. *He should not then make.* ibid. l. 15. r. *infinite Comparisons.* ibid. l. 16. r. *But he.*

THE

THE

Prefatory ORATION.

SINCE ſome Reſpite has been given to the Hurry of your ordinary Employments, and the Tranquillity which in the mean Time is reſtored to your Affairs, has prepared your Minds and opened your Ears for the telling and hearing new Things; if it may be acceptable to you, pray give your Attention, while I ſatisfy myſelf with imparting ſomething ſtrange, and not unlike a Prodigy. Fortune has ſmiled of late: Why are ye diſquieted? Do we gaze upon the dire Comet that now ſhews itſelf, as the Harbinger of the Miſchances that daily encreaſe upon us, or upon the Armies of Fanaticks bent againſt the Will of Heaven? Rather let us turn our Eyes upon a new but beneficial Star, ſparkling with a true as well as auſpicious Luſtre, never the like of which for many Years paſt has appeared above the Horizon of this Univerſity; to compute whoſe Magnitude, explain its Motions, and preſage its Events, I am come hither, not as a vain Aſtrologer.

Would you have me ſpeak more plainly? No Body then, who has either turned his Eyes upon the calamitous State of Literature, or not been altogether deaf to the frequent Complaints of learned Men, can be ignorant how unequally the preſent Age behaves againſt the one, how maliciouſly and ungratefully towards the other. Wherefore we may the more wonder that a noble *Mecænas* has at laſt appeared,

appeared, a *Mecœnas* not in Name, but in Fact; not one who has made a ſhew of bare Favour towards Learning, but who has ſpent much real Labour in it; not who has embraced it with a good Will only, but who has obliged it with a Munificent Hand; by regarding its preſent Melancholy State, wiping the Stain of Infamy from off the Age, inſpiring Vigour into theſe languiſhing Studies, and clearing the Path of doing Benefits which lay covered through long diſuſe without the leaſt Sign of Footſteps. To declare the Praiſes and publiſh the Virtues of which Man, I wiſh I had Words ſuitable to ſuch great Merits and Eloquence equal to the Matter, and that it were not as difficult to ſpeak worthily upon ſuch an illuſtrious Argument, as it is unpardonable, that it ſhould be altogether paſſed by in Silence. However ſince publick Gratitude, and eſpecially the Reaſon of my own private Office, requires it, though I have not the Faculty to grace the Memory of our Benefactor with a ſuitable Eulogy, yet I will ſhew my good Will to do it, at leaſt in ſome, though imperfect and diſagreeable Manner.

Henry Lucas, then, was the Perſon (to whoſe great Name you of this Univerſity owe the higheſt Reverence and Eſteem) *Lucas*, I ſay, a Name at once thundering forth the Prowеſs of *Mars*, and breathing the Wiſdom of *Minerva*; which will fill both Pages of Hiſtory with the Glories of War and Peace, and be equally celebrated by Poſterity, for the Examples of Heroic Fortitude, and Godlike Munificence. *Henry Lucas*, a Man much to be honoured for the Dignity of his Deſcent, as being related to very noble Families by the neareſt Kindred of Blood; but the Greatneſs of his Mind rather detracted from the Nobleneſs of his Stock, and darkened the Splendor of his Parentage with the Excellence of his Virtues. He was born to

a moderate

a moderate Fortune, which by a thriving Injuſtice, the Importunity of a litigious Court, and the Unlawfulneſs of the Law bereft him of, while an Orphan; leſt either his Ability of living honourably himſelf, or the glorious Faculty of benefiting others, ſhould be imputed to a fooliſh Fortune, rather than to a laudable Induſtry. For to be poſſeſſed of Riches tranſmitted from Parents is a Matter of pure Felicity, but to acquire them honourably of ones ſelf is perfectly Praiſe-worthy: to impart of the Things a Man has received has the Appearance of juſt Reſtitution; but courteouſly to beſtow the Fruits of his own Labour deſervedly obtains the Title of Liberality. It is from hence the Caſe reaps the greateſt Glory, from hence the Virtue becomes compleat. Such is our Benefactor, the Maker of his own Fortune, the Heir of his own Virtue, the Iſſue of his own private Induſtry: He ſtruggled from Poverty to Abundance, from a low Eſtate to a Degree of Eminence. Perhaps you will enquire by what Means, or on what Helps he did rely. Was it by proceeding in Rapines, by fomenting Quarrels, by trucking Commodities, or practiſing unlawful Gain? None of theſe, but by the moſt harmleſs Method, the moſt approved Arts and ſacred Inſtruments, whereby Nature has inſtructed Men to keep off the Inconveniences of Life; by Politeneſs of Judgment, Eloquence of Speech, and Probity of Manners. Being entered into the moſt honourable College of *St. John* (which among all that vaſt Number of famous Men it has afforded to the Church, and very many to the Commonwealth, and I think has not brought up a Scholar more profitable to the Univerſity;) I ſay, being entered into this fruitful Seminary, he profited ſo well, ſo cultivated his Underſtanding with the liberal Arts, and ſeaſoned his Mind with the Principles of Virtue; that when there was no Office

Office for which he was not qualified, no Promotion of which he seemed not worthy, he quickly reached at least so far as to gain Admittance into the Family of the most illustrious Earl of *Holland*, a Man of singular Favour with his most Serene Majesty, and your Chancellor (an Honour then coveted by the chiefest of the Nobility) by whom he was removed to his more secret Councils (the principal and most honourable Place in the Gift of a Nobleman;) which he discharged with such singular Dexterity, Sincerity, and Diligence, that it is not to be wondered at, while he managed the Affairs of his Patron so well, that he did not look badly to his own; but stored up some Fruit into his own Barn from so plentiful a Harvest.

Thus having enlarged his Estate by an honest Industry, he determined to use it with equal Prudence, and suffered not the Fruit of such commendable Labour to be spent dishonourably, or unhappily to miscarry. He laid it not out in splendid Superfluities, nor wasted it in filthy Pleasures; he did not (as is now the Custom of wealthy People) environ himself with a Guard of idle Companions, nor prepare magnificent Entertainments; he did not vainly catch the Breath of popular Applause, nor immersed himself in Factions of State: But loving a kind of Life frugal, modest, and peaceable, being only at leisure for Piety and Study, he was sparing of his Time towards himself, that he might exercise a perpetual Liberality towards others: and being not solicitous to have Issue of his own, or enlarge his Family, he afforded himself a Father to the Needy, chose the University for his Habitation, and as it were all Mankind for his Posterity. He thought it not a Duty incumbent upon him to make some one Person rich without Pains, nor furnish his own House with Abundance, but his Care was to supply the Neces-

sities

ſities and reward the Induſtry of all in his Power; and eſpecially to illuminate all Mankind with Knowledge. Though it ought by no Means to be thought that he either neglected the Honour of his Family, or any Way obſcured his Reputation by erecting to them ſuch durable Monuments, and committing their Memory to the immortal Muſes. For let us but nicely weigh the Matter, and we will find that the Glory of a Family can no way ſpread itſelf wider, or fix its Roots deeper into Eternity, than by conciliating to itſelf the Favour of Letters, whereby it is wont to make Time itſelf the Keeper and Witneſs of its Affairs; and with whoſe unwearied Breath the loud Trumpet of Fame is always full. Learning muſt have an End, the Light of all Memory be extinguiſhed, and the Face of Things overcaſt with a moſt diffuſive Barbarity, when the Name of *Lucas* ceaſes to be famous, when it ceaſes continually to reſound with ſolemn Praiſes in this illuſtrious Theatre of Glory.

But we have here alſo an Example of Juſtice no leſs noble than that of Prudence. He received ſome Splendor from his Family, and he reflected back much more upon it; he had a ſmall Patrimony from his Anceſtors, and he reſtored back large Gifts to his Relations; he returned ample Intereſt for the Benevolence of his Friends, and there was none that deſerved well of him, whom he did not oblige in his Turn with Benefits. But if he acquired both the chief Subſtance of his Fortune and Ornament of his Mind, eſpecially from the Benefit of Letters; if the Univerſity was the Parent to which he owed the Beginning of his better Life; the Miſtreſs who trained him in thoſe Principles of Virtue and Improvements of Learning, which made him ſhine with ſo bright a Luſtre; and laſtly the Benefactreſs which added moſt to the Increaſe of his Dignity; why ought he not in all Juſtice to make a grate-

a grateful Return for thoſe Benefits, and oblige her with mutual good Offices? For to be appointed once or twice to the ſupreme Court of the Kingdom in the Name of the Univerſity, there to plead the Cauſe, undertake the Defence, and ſuſtain the Part of a learned Community; to repreſent your Body, *i. e.* the very Body of Learning itſelf; and to be approved, elected, and preferred before other worthy Competitors by your moſt grave Judgment; is this a ſlight Honour? Nay is it not to be eſteemed beyond any Price, and preferred above all proud Titles? And I heartily wiſh your Judgments may be always ſo fortunately aimed, your Benefits ſo rightly placed, that they whoſe Education has raiſed them to a more exalted Degree, and who have had a like Teſtimony of your Benevolence, may become the ſame way minded to you: And thus the liberal Sciences would not be ſo impoveriſhed, ſo ſhareleſs of Honour; nor would our Studies languiſh being deſtitute not only of due Rewards, but alſo of neceſſary Supports. He indeed alone for many Years paſt has protected Letters from Injury, he has reſcued the Sciences from Contempt, delivered them from Want, aſſiſted them with his Endeavours, and enlarged them with his Intereſt. For in theſe wicked and unhappy Times, when a covetous Barbarity gaped after the Profits of the Univerſity, impoſing Burthens upon all, and every where exacting the moſt unreaſonable Taxes; ſtoutly defended your Cauſe and maintained your Immunities; he ſtrenuouſly exerted all his Power, and effected much, what through Advice, what through Perſuaſion, that the Gown might not be made tributary to the Cloth; that the Fury of *Mars* might not prey upon the Property of *Minerva*; that the Wealth dedicated to the Nurture of the liberal Arts might not be perverted to maintain the worſt of Tyrants, and to promote the Enterprizes of of wicked Men. Thus he at that Time made himſelf your Shield againſt a dangerous Indolence, that he might afterwards become your Sword againſt Ignorance; he took from you a pernicious Loſs, that he might enrich you with an advantageous Gain. For when he perceived himſelf to have arrived at the laſt Stage of his mortal Courſe, that he might at leaſt ſurvive for your Benefit, and not ceaſe to be profitable to you, even when he ceaſed to live; he began to conſider with himſelf and adviſe with his Friends, by what Means he might beſt ſuit your Studies; reſolving to ſtrengthen that Part with ſuitable Helps, where you were weakeſt, to apply fit Remedies to your Wounds, ſupply your Wants and retrieve your Loſſes.

While he had an Eye upon all Things, the Subject of *Mathematical Learning* offered itſelf as moſt worthy of his Beneficence: Which, being recommended by a ſingular advantageous Profit, joined with an entertaining Pleaſure, by its peculiar Difficulty that required no ſmall Aſſiſtance, the exceeding Care with which it was cultivated among the ancient Philoſophers, the extraordinary Applauſe it received among Men of all Ages, and eſpecially the ſurprizing Honours paid to it by the preſent Age, I know not whether it is more to be accounted a Matter of Wonder, or of Grief, that it had hitherto obtained no Place, no aſſigned Reward, no allowed Privilege in the Univerſity, the fruitful Mother of all Diſciplines, and benign Nurſe of all Studies. Being deſirous to remove ſo great a Diſhonour, and reſtore this neglected Science, he lent to his helping Hand, ſo that the Profeſſion of *Mathematics* was introduced by his Management, and endowed with a liberal Stipend from his Subſtance. Moreover when the *Lambeth* Books taken from your Library had given you ſo grievous a Wound, he in Part healed, at leaſt very much

much mitigated it, by substituting his own; indeed a Library less stately and magnificent, but equally choice and precious; a remarkable Monument of his own Learning, and a Help to yours. Which Benefits, since they cannot be amplified with Words, nor illustrated with Colours, and since it is altogether the same to relate them simply, as to celebrate them at large, I will rather commit them to you to be cultivated with a grateful Remembrance, than be violated by me with a rude Encomium. However we may briefly take Notice by the by, that though many have testified their good Affection to several Colleges, and contributed large Gifts (the Mother, as is usually done, being neglected that the Daughters may have better Treatment) yet hitherto no Son has been equally dutiful, no Scholar equally grateful, no Patron equally liberal to the University in general: Their Gifts were of as much narrower a Mind, as much slighter a Merit than his, as the Sun in the Firmament outshines the Candle in the House; or as it is more noble to diffuse a beneficial Influence upon all, than only to derive it upon a few. In like manner though others might afford greater Gifts, yet our Benefactor dispensed his more prudently, if that was the most fitting Season, when your too long neglected Affairs required a conspicuous Favour, and when the melancholy Condition of Letters implored a powerful Assistance to Uses necessary in the highest Degree; the want whereof it is hard to say, whether it was more dishonourable, or more detrimental to you. Lastly others have deserved very much of you for the Benefits they have done, but no Body so much for the Examples they have shewn. Those cried up Learning while it was in Vogue, according to the Disposition of the Times, complying with the Manners of the Age they lived in; but he opposing the contrary Genius of his Age durſt favour Learning while it ſtruggled with Envy, and was expoſed to Reproach, and therefore is worthy to be had in the greater Eſteem: Thoſe adjoined themſelves Companions, or rather Foot-men, to them that travelled in the beaten Path; he walked through an impervious Solitude, a Guide to himſelf, a Companion to none: Thoſe cheriſhed the Hopes of Studies while quick and lively; he raiſed them when fallen, reſtored them when depreſſed, and revived them when almoſt buried: Thoſe in ſome meaſure ſuſtained, or a little promoted the Fame of their own Times, while flouriſhing; but he not only very much honoured the Age he lived in, but delivered it from the greateſt Infamy. Laſtly, thoſe obtained a vulgar Praiſe from ſuch vulgar Benefits; but our Benefactor acquired, nay merited, a ſingular Glory from a ſingular Beneficence. He indeed far outwent the Merits of them that went before him, and has ſnatched away the Palm from them that are to follow him: We are beholden to him for what he has done himſelf, and hereafter ſhall be beholden to him, for what others ſhall do in Imitation of him; to whom he has before afforded a happy Omen, carried a ſhining Light, and ſhewn them an open way to promote Learning under his Patronage; that none hereafter may be aſhamed of Liberality beſtowed upon Literature, but that all ought rather to be aſhamed of not following the Authority of ſuch a Man, of not walking in the Footſteps of ſo great a Guide.

But I am carried unawares too far into the Sea of a boundleſs Oration, and do plainly perceive how very eaſy it is for one who is engaged in an Argument ſo noble, ſo ſplendid, ſo generous, to ſay more than enough: Therefore humbly begging your Pardon, I will contract my Diſcourſe, yet ſo (moſt worthy Man) as rather to cover thy

private

private Praises with a modest Silence, than disgrace them with an unseasonable Publication. Thy extraordinary Piety towards God, Regard towards Friends, Benignity to all; thy unspotted Candor of Mind, blameless Probity of Manners, singular Courtesy in Conversation, Skilfulness in Action, Perspicuity of Judgment and Eloquence of Speech; thy Faithfulness in performing Obligations, Equity in Deeds, Modesty in Words, and Constancy in Purpose; finally thy sincere Love of Truth, ardent Study after Knowledge, generous Disposition, consummate Learning, and thy innumerable other God-like Virtues of Mind, noble Endowments of Understanding, and remarkable Actions of Life; these Things indeed I have received, as Rays conveyed in a Course not direct but broken and weakened with the Interposition of a thicker Medium; I have not known them by my own Experience, but relying upon the Credit of others have had them from Fame alone; yet a Fame certain and undoubted, supported by the united Suffrages of many good and wise Men; so that if I attempted to go through with this Subject, it would be like a blind Man's undertaking to paint the brightest Lustre, or a deaf Man to sing the sweetest Melody. O that I could behold thy living Countenance encompassed round with so delightful a Splendor, that I could contemplate thy Demeanor mingled with that gentle Severity, could taste thy Speeches seasoned with such a sweet Salubrity, and draw some few Drops from that inexhaustible Sea of Eloquence: Perhaps a Breast impregnated with thy Breathings might conceive something like thee, and a Mouth moistened with thy Nectar might express something worthy of thee. But I think it better for me not at all to meddle with so great Virtues, than do them Injury by handling them unworthily, or fully them with an unpolite Speech.

There

There only remains one Commendation more (and that not to be reckoned among the laſt) which I ought in no Reaſon to paſs by; I mean the Commendation of a moſt happy Prudence ſhewn in chuſing and deputing thoſe to whom he deſigned to commend the chief Care of executing his Will, or rather of diſpenſing his Charity. For ſince Things the beſt deſigned, either by the baſe Diſhoneſty, ſlothful Negligence, or ſtupid Folly of thoſe to whom they are committed, do often fail and miſcarry of their hoped for Succeſs; he took abundant Care that this might not be his own Lot, and appointed two Men for his Adminiſtrators of ſincere Honeſty, unwearied Diligence, and approved Prudence; whoſe Names it would be the moſt unpardonable Thing in me not to mention with all grateful Remembrance, their great Regard towards you, and ſingular Humanity to my ſelf being ſufficiently experienced. The one who is perhaps not ſo well known (yet worthy to be known and honoured by all) is that moſt excellent and accompliſhed Perſon, *Robert Raworth*, a Man ſingularly diſcreet and prudent, who to his remarkable Skill in Law adjoined an equal Love of Juſtice, to his great Experience an uncommon Integrity of Mind; eſpecially wonderful and happy in this, that while he manages all Things according to the ſtrict Rules of Equity, never perferring the Pleaſure of hearing well before the Inclination of doing well, yet has been able to obtain the Opinion of the beſt of Men among all, and to preſerve an unſpotted Character together with a ſound Conſcience: A Man perfectly juſt, and unſhaken in that Situation, wherein Reaſon has affixed him, of a worthy Behaviour, a free and ingenuous Diſpoſition, involved in no Cloud, covered over with no Daubing, quick and ſagacious in diſcerning the Importance of Things, mature and

and circumſpect in taking Advice, conſtant and ſteady in retaining his Purpoſe ; one who attempts nothing raſhly, nor eaſily ſuffers himſelf to be removed from a promiſing Undertaking. Laſtly a Man in whom the greateſt Truſt may be ſafely repoſed, and weightieſt Affairs aptly committed, having behaved himſelf in this Province ſo faithfully, dexterouſly and wiſely, that not only I myſelf, with all that ſhall hereafter ſucceed me in this Office, but alſo the whole Univerſity, and all good Literature ſhall owe him immortal Thanks. But the other, *Thomas Buck*, is perfectly known to every one of you from the honourable Place which he has ſuſtained among you for ſo many Years, being ſufficiently recommended by his Virtues, and highly to be reverenced for his excellent Merits towards you: The very ſame whoſe auguſt Appearance and venerable Dignity of Countenance is daily ſeen with your Eyes, whoſe moſt courteous Civility you always perceive, and whoſe active, truſty and fortunate Endeavours in manageing your moſt important Affairs, vindicating your Honour and promoting your Intereſt, you have ſo often experienced. A Man endowed in no mean Degree in all the Parts of good Literature, who yields the Preheminence to none in Prudence and Faithfulneſs (Things approved and demonſtrated in him, after a moſt remarkable Manner) and leaves moſt, I had almoſt ſaid all, Mortals a long Space behind him in a laudable Induſtry. It would be difficult, nay altogether impoſſible for me to expreſs what Labours he has undergone, what Troubles he has endured, how much Pains he has taken for your Sakes, or that my Diligence in ſaying ſhould come up to his Diligence in doing. I was a Witneſs, I ſay a Witneſs, as far as Admiration permitted, how much he provided for your Honour, how ſerviceable he was to your Intereſt, while

while he pushed forward your Business of Printing at the Expence of his own Health and Substance, the Praise of which will endure to the most distant Posterity imprinted on shining Characters, and consecrated to Eternity with the sacred Writings themselves, whose Value and Excellence he has in some sort advanced. But while I am speaking of this, I cannot observe without great Astonishment, a Man grown up in Years, and in a bad State of Health, to have been able if he was willing, or willing if he was able, to use such Vigilance over the Affairs of others, as perhaps none else, even in the Prime of his Strength and Vigour, would have used over his own. So great an Ardour inflamed him of meriting well of you, such a Desire of finishing the great Work he had begun, that the Strength of his Body and Vigour of his Mind, seemed to encrease with his Years, and the nearer he approached to the End of his Life the more vigorously he seemed to be carried. But why do I commemorate his Diligence in this Performance, rather than mention the unwearied Study wherewith he undertook it, and his great Benevolence shewn towards you? For indeed you owe the first Fruits of this huge Benefit, in Part to him: our great Benefactor being excited by his Admonition, persuaded by his Advice, and drawn by his Exhortation, both to institute this Mathematical Profession, and to endow and adorn your Library with a most choice Treasure of Books. For is not he to be accounted the Author of a Benefit who hath gained and as it were given you the Benefactor himself, who hath as well profited for you out of another Person's Wealth, as out of his own Wisdom, his own Good-Will; and who hath derived upon your Grounds the overflowing Streams of another's Munificence? Without whom indeed it had not been, it could not be to Day that I could congratulate you upon the Ac-

cess

ceſs of ſuch a Help to your Studies, ſuch an Ornament to the Univerſity, ſuch an Example to the Age: Here my Tongue falters, my Invention fails, and my Mind ceaſes to furniſh me with Words in any wiſe ſuitable to ſo vaſt a Benefit, the Greatneſs of which is eaſier to be conceived than expreſſed. I will therefore forbear attempting ſo inſuperable a Difficulty, only give me leave to declare this one Thing, that the laſt Gentleman's remarkable Kindneſs towards me has merited a far greater Teſtimony of Gratitude.

What then can be ſaid of theſe two worthy Perſons appointed for this Office? Did they violate the Truſt committed to them, or delude the Hope conceived of them? Were they too intent upon their own private Advantage, or did they delay the hoped for Benefit for many Years? Nay, did they permit even one Year to paſs, without being a Witneſs of the Diſcharge of their Truſt, of the Anſwer of their Appointment? They apply themſelves quickly to the Work, take ſpeedy Care of procuring you Books, purchaſe Lands for the Profeſſor's Salary, preſcribe Laws for determining the Office; in ſum, leave nothing undone to prevent the Corruption of the Meaning of ſo great a Benefit by Delays; ſo that your Hope was even anticipated by its Expedition, and you ſcarcely ſooner knew what you had to expect, than you perceived yourſelves in the actual Poſſeſſion: I ſaid they preſcribed Laws, but I will not preſume to declare your Judgment of them, nor arrogate ſo weighty a Cenſure to myſelf, how juſt they are in themſelves, how profitable to your Studies, and how ſuitable to your Circumſtances. At leaſt I dare affirm this for certain, that of ſeveral able and unprejudiced Judges, Men of Worth and Honour who have ſeen them (I ſpeak within compaſs, for a great many ſaw them who were no leſs eminent

nent for their high Dignity than their remarkable Wiſdom) the moſt approved well of them; and their Number was not ſmall that judged them worthy of all Commendations, however, ſo far worthy, that when ſeen, no Body oppoſed their Eſtabliſhment by the King's Authority. And having thus effectually performed their Parts, they were not yet content to proceed no farther, but ſuch was their Good-Will, that in ſome Meaſure they out-went the Limits of their Power, obtaining to this Place a good many Privileges farther from the King's Clemency, which themſelves could not bring about, ſuch as were either very profitable or altogether neceſſary: By which Means, whoſoever ſhall hereafter obtain the Office of this Profeſſion will be obliged in Gratitude to acknowledge and confeſs them its ſecond Founders, at leaſt principal Fautors. I will venture to ſpeak no farther of thoſe Reverend Heads of Colleges, by whoſe Advice this Affair was chiefly carried on, who are as much ſuperior to me in Judgment and Eloquence, as in Years and Dignity; I only beg leave to make this one Remark, that as to what relates to the common Good, they have acted wiſely and moderately, as it became ſuch Men; but all of them have laid no ſmall Obligations upon me, and above all I am in the higheſt Degree bound to the two moſt worthy Vice-Chancellors of the laſt and the preſent Year, for their ſingular Kindneſs and Benevolence towards me.

Thus the Debt of a grateful Remembrance being in ſome ſort diſcharged, it will perhaps be expected that I ſhould declare ſome out of the way Things, as particularly to ſhew what Reaſon induced me to deſert my former Office for undertaking a new one, which it may be will make me look in the Eyes of ſome, as a Man of a wavering or unconſtant Diſpoſition, too negligent of my own

Credit,

Credit, and careleſs of yours: Which Perſons, if any ſuch there are, would do better to moderate the Acrimony of their Judgment with a more deliberate Advice, and not raſhly meaſure the State of another Perſon's Mind by their own Meaſure. The firmeſt Rocks do now and then bear the Surges of contrary Tides, and the moſt conſtant Men are oftentimes moved with the various Changes of Things. As to what belongs to the Matter; I who upon Conſtraint had engaged my ſelf in the Province of Greek Profeſſor, then deſireable to none by reaſon of the ſmall or even no Reward for the vaſt Labour attending it, when I conjectured there were many both very willing to undertake and able to diſcharge that Office, as being for their Intereſt ſo to do, I conceived there was nothing to hinder me from entirely following my own Inclination, when it was no Inconvenience to you, and from changing a heavy Labour with a very light Gain, by withdrawing myſelf from the Drudgery of *Grammar* to the more deſireable Exerciſe of *Mathematics*. For though I was never wholly averſe to *Philology*, yet not to diſſemble, I was always more deeply in Love with *Philoſophy*; tho' I did not moroſely deſpiſe the ſportive Diverſion about Words, yet I had a more hearty Inclination for the ſerious Enquiry into Things; I am not impatient of all kind of Labour, yet I am more deſirous of a moderate Eaſe; I would ſo far refrain from all Injury towards others, as to preſerve my own Freedom over myſelf: In ſhort, though I engaged myſelf to be moſt obedient to your Pleaſure, and moſt mindful of your Authority; yet did I never altogether renounce my Liberty: I did not enſlave myſelf to Grammar Learning, nor ſuffered my Ears to be bored through with the Languages, ſo as to make it ever after unlawful for me to lay hold on an honeſt Opportunity of deliver-
ing

ing myſelf; much leſs to diſoblige my Friends, while they invited me to an Office indeed leſs honourable, but much more convenient, more acceptable to my Inclination, and which abounds with much more Freedom and Leiſure. What needs more? I uſed my own Right and did not invade that of others; I left my own Profeſſion, and did not thruſt others out of theirs; I ſtripped myſelf of an Honour beyond my Deſert, without degrading any one from his; much leſs did I ſeek to diſhonour you, who are moſt beloved and reverenced by me; for whom I have always had the deepeſt Affection and moſt profound Eſteem, and for whoſe Honour, if any one, ſurely I, did ever according to my ſmall Ability ſhew myſelf the moſt obſequious, the moſt reſpectful, with Heart and Hand, with Word and Deed. Nor did I ever in the leaſt depart from your Converſation, but when driven by ſome juſt Neceſſity, when conſtrained by hard need. No Device could compel, no Condition entice me from you, or make me altogether deſert your Camp; nor did I ever fight under any other Colours, but your own. But I have not indeed ſo much forſaken your Confines as enlarged your Juriſdiction, I have not diſhonoured your Name, but have extended it; nor do I ſeem to be carried ſo much by my own Head, as by a certain Fate careful and apprehenſive of your future Advantage; that the Prelude I am now making to the Exerciſe I am about to enter upon, in this celebrated Circus, might ſerve alſo in ſome other more obſcure Place. Whoſoever then ungenerouſly reproaches me for this, as a faithleſs Deſerter, or fugitive Servant, let him look what juſt and likely Reaſons he has for ſo doing.

However I cannot but joyfully congratulate myſelf, that after having eſcaped ſo many Errors, been delivered from ſo many Diſquietudes, experienced ſo many Changes; I have at length arrived at this ſtill Port, and am repoſed in ſo ſafe a Station. For nothing could ever have happened more agreeable to my Wiſhes, than to be placed in the Boſom of our gracious Mother the Univerſity, which abounds with all Manner of innocent Delights; even in your Society (conſiſting of Men endowed with the moſt ingenuous Diſpoſition, ſincere Affection, ſublime Underſtanding, and unparallel'd Learning) which in my Opinion is to be envied by Kings themſelves; in the moſt beautiful Palace of the Muſes, the moſt ſacred Temple of Virtue, the moſt noble School of Wiſdom, and illuſtrious Theatre of great Examples: Here to cultivate my Underſtanding, form my Manners, compoſe my Affections, and learn the Liberal Sciences along with you (being bound to you in a ſufficiently honourable and eaſy Servitude, and enjoying a Condition by no means to be deſpiſed) is what, might I have my free Choice, I would a hundred Times ſooner always chuſe, than to live in the Pomps of a Court, the Tumults of a City, or Solitudes of a Country; did I fare ever ſo delicately, abound with the greateſt Plenty, flow with all kind of bodily Pleaſures, and were honoured with the higheſt Titles. Which Happineſs granted me by the ſingular Kindneſs of a benign Providence, favourably regarding my Affairs while diſtreſſed in the higheſt Degree by theſe late Calamities, I look upon with that humble Reverence and pious Devotion of Mind, which is meet towards the Divine Majeſty. And I alſo do gratefully acknowledge and embrace the Benevolence of good Men given me of their own moſt free Choice, without the leaſt Entreaty or Solicitation of mine; to whom, becauſe I am not able to make any ſuitable Return, I will however do what in me lies in the Diſcharge of my Office, that they may neither re-

pent

pent of their Benefits conferred upon me, nor be aſhamed of their Sentiments conceived of me. Which I do not ſpeak, as if I were inſenſible of my own Meanneſs, or did arrogate any Thing to myſelf (for I openly confeſs that Weakneſs and Unworthineſs, which I inwardly perceive) but to be a Spur to my Diligence, a Support to my tottering Underſtanding, that I deſpair not of ſupplying what is wanting in me with Induſtry, and recompenſing my Inability with Care. But from you, who are liberally educated, I hope for, nay I promiſe to myſelf every Thing worthy your Candor and Humanity; nor do I in the leaſt doubt, but as you have hitherto favoured me with your good Wiſhes, you will alſo now receive me with Kindneſs; being not unmindful of the Good-Will which I have ſhewn heretofore of recalling theſe Mathematical Studies from their Exile, and bringing them out of Darkneſs into Light.

And if, while I was a private Perſon nor otherwiſe obliged, being enamoured only with the Lovelineſs of the Thing, I ſhewed ſuch hearty Deſires and Endeavours to have theſe Sciences in the higheſt Degree recommended to you; it cannot now be doubted but by Reaſon of my publick Office, and more ſolemn Engagement, I will more diligently apply myſelf to their Promotion according to my ſlender Ability; ſince what was then an Inclination becomes now a Duty. But what the Laws do ſtrictly require of me, that I have always ſhewed the greateſt Readineſs to perform, ſo that I did not only willingly admit, but earneſtly invited you of my own Accord, to familiar Meetings, ſo that I not only once or twice every Week opened the Doors of my private Chamber, but daily publiſh'd the inward Secrets of my Heart, and unfolded my Breaſt to all Comers.

If

If it be then your Pleaſure, ye Lovers of Study, come always; be not reſtrained through any Fear, or retarded by too much Modeſty, what you may do by your Right, you ſhall make me do willingly, nay gladly and joyfully. Aſk your Queſtions, make your Enquiries, bid and command; you ſhall neither find me averſe nor refractory to your Commands, but officious and obedient. If you meet with any Obſtacles or Difficulties, or are retarded with any Doubts while you are walking in the cumberſome Road of this Study of *Mathematics*, I beg you to impart them, and I ſhall endeavour to remove every Hindrance out of your Way to the beſt of my Knowledge and Ability. But if nothing elſe can compel you to apply yourſelves vigorouſly to theſe Diſciplines, and labour diligently in this Exerciſe, at leaſt that Spur of noble Minds, the Thirſt of following all great Examples, which always ſinks deep into generous Diſpoſitions, ſhould the more ſtrongly provoke and enflame you.

For to paſs by thoſe Ancients, the wonderful *Pythagoras*, the ſagacious *Democritus*, the divine *Plato*, the moſt ſubtle and very learned *Ariſtotle*, Men whom every Age has hitherto acknowledged and deſervedly honoured, as the greateſt Philoſophers, the Ring-leaders of Arts; in whoſe Judgments how much theſe Studies were eſteemed, is abundantly proclaimed in Hiſtory and confirmed by their famous Monuments, which are every where interſperſed and beſpangled with Mathematical Reaſonings and Examples, as with ſo many Stars; and conſequently any one not in ſome Degree converſant in theſe Studies will in vain expect to underſtand, or unlock their hidden Meanings, without the Help of a Mathematical Key: For who can play well on *Ariſtotle*'s Inſtrument but with a Mathematical Quill; or not be altogether deaf to the Leſſons of natural *Philoſophy*, while ignorant

rant of *Geometry?* Who void of (*Geometry* ſhall I ſay, or) *Arithmetic* can apprehend *Plato*'s *Socrates* liſping with Children concerning Square Numbers; or can conceive *Plato* himſelf treating not only of the Univerſe, but the Polity of Commonwealths regulated by the Laws of Geometry, and formed according to a Mathematical Plan? Nor to mention thoſe Moderns reſembling and nearly equalling the Ancients in Sagacity, viz. *Galileus*, *Gaſſendus*, *Gilbertus*, *Mercennus*, *Carteſius*, and ſuch others of the preſent Age as were famous for having extended the Circuits of Natural Science beyond its ancient Bounds, depending only on the Mathematics; the Sight of whoſe Writings every where ſhining with the Rays of Geometrical Diagrams, the Unſkilful in theſe Things are afraid of, as ſo many Owls at the bright Splendor of the Sun: Let us rather take a View of theſe Sciences, ſuch as this Day they are preſented to you, dignified in the Robes of Nobles, glorying in the Titles of Princes, and ſitting upon the Thrones of Kings themſelves: All whom it would yet be unmannerly to compare, and moſt unjuſt to prefer to you, in any Kind of ingenious Literature: Eſpecially ſince you cannot merit the Name or ſuſtain the Dignity of an Univerſity upon any other Account, than by preſerving to yourſelves a Knowledge more than common in all Kinds of Science becoming a generous Mind; and by taking away every Occaſion of Calumny from all who either envy your Happineſs, or emulate your Fame; not ſpending your Time like Infants in learning the Languages, nor neglecting the Care of ſearching after Truth for digging up fooliſh Fables out of the Rubbiſh of obſolete Antiquity; not affecting the vain Trappings of Words, and the Deluſions of a painted Speech, while the Nature of Things lies unregarded, and the Uſe of plain Reaſon is ſet aſide;

not

not laſtly abuſing your Leiſure, playing away your Time, and miſerably wreſting and torturing your Wits with ſophiſtical Trifles and empty Jargon, engaging yourſelves in barren Diſputes, inſiſting upon uncertain Conjectures, and venting of doubtful Opinions.

Theſe Reproaches (which I confeſs are thrown upon you by way of Banter and without Cauſe) you may either eaſily wipe off, or entirely avoid, by only applying yourſelves to the Study of the *Mathematics* with that Diligence which is requiſite: The *Mathematics*, I ſay, which effectually exerciſes, not vainly deludes nor vexatiouſly torments ſtudious Minds with obſcure Subtilties, perplexed Difficulties, or contentious Diſquiſitions; which overcomes without Oppoſition, triumphs without Pomp, compels without Force, and rules abſolutely without the Loſs of Liberty; which does not privately over-reach a weak Faith, but openly aſſaults an armed Reaſon, obtains a total Victory, and puts on inevitable Chains; whoſe Words are ſo many Oracles, and Works as many Miracles; which blabs out nothing raſhly, nor deſigns any Thing from the Purpoſe, but plainly demonſtrates and readily performs all Things within its Verge; which obtrudes no falſe Shadows of Science, but the very Science itſelf, the Mind firmly adhering to it, as ſoon as poſſeſſed of it, and can never after deſert it of its own Accord, or be deprived of it by any Force of others: Laſtly the Mathematics, which depends upon Principles clear to the Mind, and agreeable to Experience; which draws certain Concluſions, inſtructs by profitable Rules, unfolds pleaſant Queſtions; and produces wonderful Effects; which is the fruitful Parent of, I had almoſt ſaid all, Arts, the unſhaken Foundation of Sciences, and the plentiful Fountain of Advantage to Human Affairs. In which laſt Reſpect, we may be ſaid

to

to receive from the *Mathematics*, the principal Delights of Life, Securities of Health, Increaſe of Fortune, and Conveniences of Labour : That we dwell elegantly and commodiouſly, build decent Houſes for ourſelves, erect ſtately Temples to God, and leave wonderful Monuments to Poſterity : That we are protected by thoſe Rampires from the Incurſions of the Enemy ; rightly uſe Arms, ſkilfully range an Army, and manage War by Art, and not by the Madneſs of wild Beaſts : That we have ſafe Traffick through the deceitful Billows, paſs in a direct Road through the tractleſs Ways of the Sea, and come to the deſigned Ports by the uncertain Impulſe of the Winds : That we rightly caſt up our Accounts, do Buſineſs expeditiouſly, diſpoſe, tabulate, and calculate ſcattered Ranks of Numbers, and eaſily compute them, though expreſſive of huge Heaps of Sand, nay immenſe Hills of Atoms : That we make pacifick Separations of the Bounds of Lands, examine the Moments of Weights in an equal Balance, and diſtribute every one his own by a juſt Meaſure: That with a light Touch we thruſt forward vaſt Bodies which way we will, and ſtop a huge Reſiſtance with a very ſmall Force : That we accurately delineate the Face of this Earthly Orb, and ſubject the Œconomy of the Univerſe to our Sight : That we aptly digeſt the flowing Series of Time, diſtinguiſh what is acted by due Intervals, rightly account and diſcern the various Returns of the Seaſons, the ſtated Periods of Years and Months, the alternate Increments of Days and Nights, the doubtful Limits of Light and Shadow, and the exact Differences of Hours and Minutes : That we derive the ſubtle Virtue of the Solar Rays to our Uſes, infinitely extend the Sphere of Sight, enlarge the near Appearances of Things, bring to Hand Things remote, diſcover Things hidden, ſearch

Nature

Nature out of her Concealments, and unfold her dark Myſteries: That we delight our Eyes with beautiful Images, cunningly imitate the Devices and portray the Works of Nature; imitate did I ſay? nay excel, while we form to ourſelves Things not in being, exhibit Things abſent, and repreſent Things paſt: That we recreate our Minds and delight our Ears with melodious Sounds, attemperate the inconſtant Undulations of the Air to muſical Tunes, add a pleaſant Voice to a ſapleſs Log and draw a ſweet Eloquence from a rigid Metal; celebrate our Maker with an harmonious Praiſe, and not unaptly imitate the bleſſed Choirs of Heaven: That we approach and examine the inacceſſible Seats of the Clouds, the diſtant Tracts of Land, unfrequented Paths of the Sea; lofty Tops of the Mountains, low Bottoms of the Valleys, and deep Gulphs of the Ocean: That in Heart we advance to the Saints themſelves above, yea draw them to us, ſcale the etherial Towers, freely range through the celeſtial Fields, meaſure the Magnitudes, and determine the Interſtices of the Stars, preſcribe inviolable Laws to the Heavens themſelves, and confine the wandering Circuits of the Stars within ſtrict Bounds: Laſtly, that we comprehend the huge Fabrick of the Univerſe, admire and contemplate the wonderful Beauty of the Divine Workmanſhip, and ſo learn the incredible Force and Sagacity of our own Minds, by certain Experiments, as to acknowledge the Bleſſings of Heaven with a pious Affection.

I omit the advantageous Spur to our Reaſon which accrues from this Mathematical Exerciſe, both effectually to turn aſide the Strokes of true Arguments, and warily decline the Blows of falſe ones; to diſpute ſtrenuouſly as well as judge ſolidly with a Readineſs of Invention, a Juſtneſs of Method, and Clearneſs of Expreſſion.

In

In like manner theſe Diſciplines ſerve to inure and corroborate the Mind to a conſtant Diligence in Study, to undergo the Trouble of an attentive Meditation, and cheerfully contend with ſuch Difficulties as lie in the Way. They wholly deliver us from a credulous Simplicity, moſt ſtrongly fortify us againſt the Vanity of Scepticiſm, effectually reſtrain us from a raſh Preſumption, moſt eaſily incline us to a due Aſſent, perfectly ſubject us to the Government of right Reaſon, and inſpire us with Reſolution to wreſtle againſt the unjuſt Tyranny of falſe Prejudices. If the Fancy be unſtable and fluctuating it is as it were poized by this Ballaſt, and ſteadied by this Anchor; if the Wit be blunt it is ſharpened upon this Whetſtone; if luxuriant it is pared by this Knife; if headſtrong it is reſtrained by this Bridle; and if dull it is rouzed by this Spur. The Steps are guided by no Lamp more clearly through the dark Mazes of Nature, by no Thread more ſurely through the intricate Turnings of the Labyrinths of Philoſophy; nor laſtly is the Bottom of Truth ſounded more happily by any other Line. I will not mention with how plentiful a Stock of Knowledge the Mind is furniſhed from theſe, with what wholeſome Food it is nouriſhed, and what ſincere Pleaſure it enjoys. But if I ſpeak farther, I ſhall neither be the only Perſon, nor the firſt, who affirms it; that while the Mind is abſtracted and elevated from ſenſible Matter, diſtinctly views pure Forms, conceives the Beauty of Ideas, and inveſtigates the Harmony of Proportions; the Manners themſelves are ſenſibly corrected and improved, the Affections compoſed and rectified, the Fancy calmed and ſettled, and the Underſtanding raiſed and excited to more divine Contemplations. All which I might defend by the Authority, and confirm by the Suffrages of the greateſt Philoſophers.

My

My Time, my Speech, my Breath, would fail me, even but lightly to run over the principal Heads of theſe Things. For no Words can juſtly deſcribe the Limits, can fully contain the Advantages, can perfectly exhauſt the Praiſes of that Science, which wanders through and encompaſſes the Heavens, the Earth, and the Seas. I ſhould therefore be very unwiſe either to give myſelf much Trouble, or tire your Patience in a Matter ſo much ſpoke of by all, and by you, I imagine, ſufficiently underſtood. Though methinks I have neither wandered from the Purpoſe, nor out of my Sphere, in thus exerciſing your Patience; ſince there can be no Introduction more ſuitable, or more profitable to the Mathematics than Patience itſelf; nor is any Perſon well qualified for theſe Diſciplines, but he whoſe Ears have learned patiently to bear an inſipid and empty Oration of leſs than two Hours long without Loathing or Wearineſs. I rightly named it an empty Oration, and therefore the more ſeaſonable (for who can become eloquent or abound with Speech free from Blame with the Diet of dumb Fiſhes?) But if I find it to have been very diſagreeable to you, I ſhall eaſily comfort, yea congratulate myſelf with this ſtrong Argument and certain Augury, that I have to Day performed the Part of an accompliſhed Mathematician, *i. e.* a moſt wretched Orator. I have done.

Mar. 14. 1664.

ISAAC BARROW.

MATHEMATICAL LECTURES.

LECTURE I.

Of the Name and general Division of the Mathematical Sciences.

BEING about to treat upon the *Mathematical Sciences*, according to my Office, before I enter into the inner Parts of the Edifice I chuſe to tarry a little at the Entrance; and that I may humour, or rather oblige thoſe who come leſs prepared to ſuch Studies, ſhall firſt of all touch upon certain *general Things* belonging thereto (*a*). This, to paſs by all unneceſſary Circumſtances, I ſhall cloſely aſſay to do in the following Method. Firſt, I ſhall diſcourſe a few things of the *Name* of theſe Sciences; then of their *Object* and the Diviſion ariſing from thence; next of the manner of handling the *Object*, or inveſtigating and demonſtrating its *Properties*; (where an occaſion will offer itſelf of enquiring into the Principles theſe Sciences aſſume, the Differences of the Propoſitions they exhibit, the twofold Method of demonſtrating by *Analyſis* and *Syntheſis*, and other Matters of like kind) laſtly, I ſhall perhaps ſubjoin ſomething hiſtorical concerning their *Riſe*, *Progreſs*, and *Increaſe*.

(*a*) Ἐξωτερικά.

In

In the firſt Place, as to the *Name*; The word *Mathematics*, (*i. e. Diſciplines*) in its proper and primary Signification ſeems common to every acquired Science, and vulgarly means no more than to attain to the Knowledge of ſomething we have hitherto been ignorant of; in which Senſe *Sextus Empiricus* diſputing againſt all the Arts made publick, (*viz. Grammar*, *Rhetoric*, *Logic*, &c.) inſcribes his Book againſt the *Mathematicians*: alſo the chief Authors of Antiquity uſe the word *Mathematics* for any kind of Learning whatſoever; ſo *Plato*: (*b*) *They*, ſays he, *who are by nature Arithmeticians, do ſhew themſelves ready to learn the whole Mathematics*, i. e. *every thing, which is capable of being learned.* In like manner (*c*) *Ariſtotle*; *Every kind of Learning and mental Mathematics* (or *Diſcipline*) *is made from a previous Knowledge*: Among which he reckons his (*d*) *Culinary Mathematics*, or *Diſcipline of preparing Victuals.* But what are theſe, when many hundred ſuch Inſtances occur here and there?

Whence theſe Sciences are after a peculiar manner ſtiled *Mathematical*, i. e. *Diſciplinal*; and the (*e*) *Mathematics*, or Sciences acquired by *Diſcipline.* Sometimes they are called in the ſingular Number the *Mathematic*, as by (*f*) *Ariſtotle. It is the part of an Optician to ſhew the Reaſon of the Rainbow, either ſimply or according to the Mathematic*, meaning *Geometry*, from whence the *Optician* draws his Concluſions. Laſtly, by a certain *Metonymy* of the Action for the Object, they are frequently called *Matheſis*, the *Diſcipline.* For all which Names many different Reaſons are aſſigned by different Perſons.

(*b*) Plat. 7. de Rep. (*c*) Ariſt. 2. Poſt. Anal. Initio.
(*d*) Lib. 1. Polit. cap. 7. (*e*) Τὰ μαθήματα.
(*f*) Οἷον τὸ περὶ τῆς ἴριδος· τὸ μὲν γὰρ ὅτι φυσικοῦ εἰδέναι, τὸ δὲ διότι Ὀπτικοῦ, ἢ ἁπλῶς, ἢ κατὰ τὸ μάθημα. 1. Anal. Poſt. c. 13.

Some

Some think they have this Name from their extraordinary *Evidence*, *Certitude*, and Conſtancy, becauſe no other Knowledge deſtitute of theſe Qualities ſeems to deſerve the Name of *Diſcipline*, neither ought any one to imagine himſelf to have learned that, which he does not perceive clearly, embrace firmly, and retain reſolutely *(g)*. He that gropes in Darkneſs, fluctuates in his Opinion, *(h)* or may be biaſſed in his Judgment in reſpect of any thing, can by no means be ſaid to have learned that thing. And ſince theſe Conditions agree with the Sciences we are treating of, either ſolely or at leaſt in a more peculiar manner than with any other, they therefore merit the Title of *Diſciplines* or *Mathematics*, to be appropriated to them, by way of Eminence.

Others think them ſo denominated, becauſe being ſomething difficult in themſelves they require the previous help of a Maſter or Interpreter, and ought to be applied to with very great Study and Attention: according to that Saying of *Plato (i)*. *The Mathematics are no where ſet by, and are faintly applied to, by reaſon of their Difficulty, and becauſe the Students require a Guide, without which they are not to be acquired.* And *Proclus*, at the End of the firſt Commentary upon his firſt Element, ſeems to aſſign a Reaſon of this ſort; which, becauſe by ſome it is more ſeverely carped at than thoroughly underſtood, I ſhall therefore relate. According to him, the Method of attaining the Knowledge of things is threefold, *viz.* Firſt, by *Senſation*, or the Impreſſion coming from without. Secondly, by *Opinion*, or the inward Motion of the Fancy: And thirdly, by the diſcurſive Operation of the Mind ſearching out, and as it were rouſing from Sleep, the internal Images that lie

(g) Ariſt. *(h)* 1. Poſt. Anal. c. 2. *(i)* 7. de Rep.

treaſured

treaſured up in it. Which laſt may be appoſitely called *Diſcipline*, as being a kind of *(k) Remembrance*, and becauſe the word *(l) Diſcipline* may properly reſpect any Knowledge for the acquiring of which we come, not indeed perfectly, yet in ſome meaſure, prepared from a certain previous (though ſomewhat obſcure Notion) of the thing to be learned; in which Caſe the Mind executes the Office of a Miſtreſs teaching and inſtructing herſelf. And becauſe this Method of acquiring Knowledge agrees principally to the Mathematics; as being ſuch, which, to uſe the words of *Proclus*, *do promote Knowledge*, *excite Contemplation*, *purify the Thought*, *draw forth the internal Images*, *take away Forgetfulneſs and Ignorance*, *and diſſolve the Chains of Error*; alſo ſince the Followers of *Pythagoras*, who either firſt invented or firſt cultivated the *Mathematics*, do ſay the ſame Things of them; they are therefore ſo named by reaſon of the manner of inventing them, and becauſe they merit the Title of *Diſcipline*. Theſe are nearly the words of *Proclus*, which are indeed both ſubtle and ingenious.

But perhaps all theſe Things are more elegantly deviſed than truly aſſerted. For neither does this Term (with many others) ſeem ſo much taken from nice Reaſoning, as from common Uſe, depending on a probable Cauſe. Therefore I rather judge the *Mathematics* to be ſo called, becauſe when the *Grecians* firſt begun to apply themſelves to the Study of Arts, theſe only were delivered in the Schools; the other Arts being not yet invented for the Inſtruction of their Youth. They, I ſay, ſtudied theſe Arts alone, no other being known to them, except *Philoſophy*; which was not ſo much learned

(g) Ἀνάμνησις from μιμνήσκειν, to bring to mind.

(h) Μάθησις from μανθάνειν, to learn. Which words, he takes notice, may ſeem to proceed from the ſame Original, and be of near ſignification.

by

by the Youth, as anxiouſly ſought after by the Aged: for in thoſe early Times there was ſcarce found any among them, who attained to a Pitch of Learning, ſo bold as to profeſs himſelf a *(i) Philoſopher*; and thoſe wandering Sophiſts that firſt arrogated the Title, were deſervedly puniſhed by *Socrates*. But ſome time after, the other *Arts* of *Writing*, *Speaking* and *Diſputing* took their riſe: And indeed the Art of *Writing* (I mean *Grammar*) is referred by moſt to *Ariſtotle*; at leaſt it ſeems to have taken its beginning about his Time; for the mention which is made by *Plato* concerning the Invention of *(k) Grammar* by *Theuth* an *Egyptian*, I take to be only ſpoke of the bare Deſcription of Letters, (indeed a moſt uſeful and wonderful Artifice) but in no wiſe of Grammar Precepts adjuſted into the form of an Art, concerning which I am of Opinion ſcarce any thing was known to *Plato*. The Art of *Speaking* (or *Rhetoric*) *Cicero* relates to have been begun by the two *Sicilians*, *Corax* and *Tiſias*, a little before *Plato*, and was put into writing by *Ariſtotle*: But theſe two only ſeem to have drawn the firſt Draughts, or begun the Foundations of the Art, as *Ariſtotle* intimates at the End of his Book of *Sophiſtry*. Laſtly, the Art of *Diſputing* (or *Logic*) took its beginning from *Eleates Zeno*, a Cotemporary and Companion of *Socrates*, and ſcarcely was reduced by *Ariſtotle* to the Method of an Art (as himſelf teſtifies); at leaſt it was wholly unknown to the *(l) Pythagoreans*, and moſt other Philoſophers before *Plato*. It ſeems in that Infancy of Learning theſe popular Arts were not yet grown to Maturity: It had not yet come into Men's Heads that either the Faculty of writing ſkilfully, or ſpeaking eloquently, or diſputing ſub-

(i) Or *Maſter of Wiſdom*. *(k)* Plat. in Philebo.
(l) Ariſt. 1. Metap. cap. 6.

tilly were to be drawn from Precepts; which peradventure they either thought natural to every one, or believed them to be more eaſily attainable by daily Uſe than an elaborate Education; nor did they think themſelves much deceived by Experience.

In thoſe firſt Ages then Men's whole Studies were employed about theſe two Studies, *viz. Mathematics* and *Philoſophy*; the former of which was wont to be inſtilled into the Youth by ſkilful Maſters in the Schools, the latter did exerciſe the Contemplation of the more Aged in their more ſecret Retirements: the former prepared Men's Minds, and paved their Way to the latter. To which may be referred that triple Commentary writ by *Pythagoras*, which *Laertius* mentions, *(m) viz. Inſtitutive*, *Civil*, and *Natural*, in which the whole Literature of thoſe Times does ſeem to be comprehended: nor is it much to be doubted, but the *Inſtitutive* did ſignify the ſame with (*n*) *Mathematical*, by which previous Diſcipline that Prince of Philoſophers prepared the Way to both the following Parts of Philoſophy, *viz. Civil* and *Natural*. And that threefold Gradation of the Doctrine of *Pythagoras*, which *Gellius* ſpeaks of, ſeems to belong to the ſame; according to which, his Followers were called firſt (*o*) *Hearers*, next *Learners*, and laſtly *Philoſophers*; *i. e.* firſt they ſtudied to hold their Tongues and exerciſe their Ears, as ignorant of all things; then to learn ſomething, or endeavour after ſome Science; laſtly to be wiſe, *i. e.* to acquire the Knowledge of the moſt excellent things. To this alſo *Plato* refers when he calls the *Mathematics* a (*p*) *previous Education*, or as it

(*m*) Παιδευτικὸν, πολιτικὸν, φυσικόν. (*n*) Μαθηματικόν. (*o*) Ἀκουστικοὶ, μαθηματικοὶ, φυσικοί. Lib. 1. c. 9. (*p*) Προπαιδείαν. 7. de Rep.

were

were a Prelude to Philoſophy. And in the firſt Book of *Proclus* they are named *(q) The Way to Education:* Likewiſe *Xenocrates* elegantly ſtiles them *(r) The Handles of Philoſophy*; and others the *(s) Steps and Aſcents* by which Men mount up to the Knowledge of ſublime Things. Laſtly, *Theon Smyrnæus*, the ancient Expoſitor of *Plato's Mathematics*, according to the Notion of his Predeceſſors, very well repreſents the whole Method of ſearching out Wiſdom by the ſacred Knowledge of the Myſteries anciently in uſe; the Degrees or Parts of which were five in all, *viz.* *(t) Purgation*, *Initiation*, *Inſpection*, *a perfect Knowledge in the Myſteries*, and the *Dignity of Bliſs:* Where *Philoſophy* (*viz.* rational, civil, and natural) may be fitly compared to the *Initiation*, *Theology* to the Inſpection, and *Mathematics* to the preparatory *Purgation*; by which laſt the uninſtructed were driven far from the Myſteries, as profane and unqualified.

I ſuppoſe then enough has been ſaid to convince us how juſtly theſe Sciences are called by the Name of *Mathematics*, (i. e. *Diſciplines*) becauſe they alone were at firſt learned by *Diſciples* or Scholars, and not only Things but Names alſo do of right belong to them who are firſt in Poſſeſſion. The Name which they firſt obtained from the Verity of the Thing, they afterwards deſervedly retained (uſe confirming the Poſſeſſion); and may they retain it not in vain, but be ſtudiouſly learned by young Perſons with that Induſtry which is requiſite.

(q) Ἡ κατὰ παίδευσιν ὁδός. pag. 6. *(r)* Λαβὰς τῆς φιλοσοφίας. *(s)* Κλίμακας καὶ ἐπιβάθρας. Τοῦ ἀεὶ ὄντος ἡ γεωμετρικὴ γνῶσις ἐστίν· ἑλκὸν ἄρα πρὸς ἀλήθειαν ψυχὴν εἴη ἄν· καὶ ἀπεργαστικὸν φιλοσόφου διανοίας, πρὸς τὸ ἄνω σχεῖν· ἃ νῦν κάτω, οὐ δέον, ἔχομεν. Plat. 7. de Rep. *(t)* Καθαρμὸς, τελετὴ ἐποπτεία, ἱεροφαντεία, εὐδαιμονισμός.

But while I am conſidering the Name *Mathematics*, it may perchance be worth the while to take Notice of that moſt ſhameful Abuſe of it, which prevailed among the *Roman* Writers of a worſer Age, who commonly applied it to the baſeſt and moſt worthleſs kind of Men, to the *Aſtrologers*, (or rather *(u) Caſters of Nativities) Fortune-tellers*, *Cunning-Men*, *Soothſayers*, and other ſuch like paltry Knaves of that peſtilent Rabble. Whence *Tacitus* ſpeaks of the *Mathematicians* as a *Brood of Fellows treacherous to thoſe above them*, *falſe to thoſe who put their Truſt in them* ; *which* (ſays he) *in our City will be always prohibited*, *and yet always retained*. And it is recorded that the Senate paſſed a Decree for baniſhing the *(w) Mathematicians* and *Conjurers* out of *Italy*. What an unequal Pairing is here ! much like the coupling of Birds with Serpents, or Lambs with Tygers. And *Seneca* ſays of the genuine *Mathematicians*, or *Soothſayers*, *(x) that they ſometimes ſpeak Truth*. But many hundred ſuch like Inſtances are to be found in *Suetonius*, *Tacitus*, and other degenerating Hiſtorians of that Time. Whence *Gellius* ſays, (*y*) *The Vulgar call thoſe Mathematicians who are properly Soothſayers*. Which vile Abuſe of a Word ſignifying the moſt noble and honourable kind of Literature, ſhews the groſs Ignorance of thoſe Times, which were degenerating into the utmoſt Barbarity of Language : foraſmuch as a Confuſion of Names does ſometimes argue an Unſkilfulneſs of Things. But in a better Age, when Learning flouriſhed more among the *Romans*, the *Mathematicians* were

(u) ’Αϛρομαντέσι. (*w*) Annal. I. *(x)* Patere Mathematicos aliquando Verum dicere, qui illum ex quo Princeps factus eſt omnibus Annis, omnibus Menſibus efferunt. *Seneca in* ἀποκολοκυντώσει Claudiana. *(y) Gell. Lib.* I. *cap.* 9.

in

in greater Efteem, and *Cicero* carefully diftinguifhes them from that Rafcality of Jugglers that arrogated to themfelves the Foreknowledge of future Events. *(z) Do ye imagine*, fays he, *that they*, *who are faid to divine*, *can refolve whether the Sun be greater than the Earth*, *or fo great as it feems*; *and whether the Moon has an inherent Light*, *or borrows it from the Sun?* &c. *Thefe things*, as he goes on, *belong to Mathematicians and not to Soothfayers:* A Judgment indeed worthy of *Cicero*, *Dignum fapiente bonóque.* But more than enough has been fpoken concerning the Name.

Left therefore I fhould feem to act the Part of a *Philologer* rather than a *Mathematician*, to come to the Purpofe, let us in the next Place confider the *Object* of *Mathematics:* From the various Kinds, or different Confideration of which, the Science itfelf is divided into various Parts. In handling of which, we will firft, according to the Examples of others, deliver what is for the moft part agreeable to the common Opinions; then make a more curious Enquiry concerning the Thing it felf, and explain what fort of Object the *Mathematics* refpects, how far it extends itfelf, how it is limited or diftributed into Parts, and what is our own Opinion. Alfo, laying afide all Authority, we will now and then produce certain *(a) Paradoxes*, *i. e.* Things contrary to Opinion, but not perhaps (*b*) contrary to Reafon. For I defign not to follow all Things in the beaten Road, neither to undertake any thing rafhly; but will freely difcufs whatfoever offers itfelf worth the Enquiry, and not fear ftrenuoufly to avouch every thing that feems agreeable to Truth; yet fubmitting all I fay to be examined and decided by the Judgment of your Candour and Sagacity.

(z) Cic. de Divin. *(a)* Παράδοξα. *(b)* Παράλογα.

There-

Therefore, as to what pertains to the general Object of *Mathematics*, it may seem wonderful that it has no proper Name agreeing to it, either in *Greek* or *Latin*. For (*c*) *Aristotle* improperly makes τὸ ποσὸν to be the common Genus of both *Multitude*, as it is numerable, and *Magnitude* as it is mensurable; which Word properly signifies *Quotity*, and only respects *Number*. And, on the contrary, *Quantitas*, by which Word the *Latins* use to express the τὸ ποσὸν of *Aristotle*, denotes *Magnitude* only, and cannot properly be referred to *Number*. Which Defect of a common Name to *Magnitude* and *Multitude* is perhaps an Argument that the Antients had no common Conception of them: Whether they had any with respect to the Thing, we will hereafter take notice. But whatsoever becomes of the general Object, it is plain the *Mathematics* is conversant about two Things especially, *viz.* (*d*) *Quantity* strictly taken, and *Quotity*; or, if you please (*e*) *Magnitude* and (*f*) *Multitude*. By others they are called *Continued* and *Discontinued Quantity*, the Appositeness of which will be spoke to hereafter.

But because both *Magnitude* and *Multitude* may be considered in a double respect; *viz.* either as they are mentally separated, or abstracted from all Matter, material Circumstances, and Accidents; (*i. e.* are considered generally in themselves, without regard to these Things); or as they inhere in some particular Subject, and are found conjoined with certain other physical Qualities, Actions and Circumstances: Hence arises the Division of *Mathematics* into *Pure* or *Abstract*, and *Mixed* or *Concrete*. Which Division (*g*) *Plato* seems to in-

(*c*) V. Metaph. cap. 13. (*d*) In Greek, τὸ πηλίκον, and τὸ ποσὸν, strictly taken. (*e*) Τὸ μέγεθος. (*f*) Τὸ πλῆθος. (*g*) In Philebo.

timate,

timate, when he aſſerts ſome *Diſciplines* (expreſly ſignifying *Arithmetic* and *Geometry*) to be *Pure*, *Prime*, and (*h*) *Principal*; and others *Impure*, Secondary, and leſs exact. The Parts of *Pure* or *Abſtract Mathematics* do abſolutely reſpect the general Nature and proper Affections of *Magnitude* and *Number*; but the *Mixed* or *Concrete* Parts conſider the ſame as applied to certain Bodies and particular Subjects, conjunctly with the Force of Motion and other phyſical Accidents. Whence theſe latter are by *Ariſtotle* called (*i*) *Phyſical* and *Senſible*; and by others (*k*) *Phyſico-Mathematical*.

Pure *Mathematics* then is only twofold, *viz.* *Geometry*, which ſearches the Nature, diſtinguiſhes the Species, and inveſtigates the Properties of *Abſtract Magnitude*; and *Arithmetic*, which conſiders *Multitude* or *Number* with its Species and Affections after the ſame manner: But *Mixed* Mathematics is manifold according to the various Species or different *Quality* of the Matter, which is the Subject of *Magnitude* or *Multitude*; nor conſequently is it the ſame Way divided, either by the antient or modern Philoſophers, as we will ſhew by and by. In the mean time we will give a few Examples, for Illuſtration's ſake, concerning the different Method of conſidering the Things we have ſpoke of. For example, a *Right Line*, which is a Species of Magnitude, may be conceived either abſolutely and moſt univerſally, according to its Definition, as the moſt ſimple Dimenſion, deſigning the ſhorteſt Interval between any two Points; under which Conſideration it has certain general Properties either preſuppoſed or demonſtrated by the Geometrician: or it may be conſidered as being drawn from the Center of the Sun to the Center of the

(*h*) Ἡγεμονικὰς. (*i*) Φυσικοτέρας, Auſcult. Phyſ. Lib. 2. cap. 2. (*k*) Ἀισθητικὰς, Anal. Poſt. Lib. 1. cap. 13.

Earth

Earth it ſignifies the Diſtance of thoſe Bodies: or as repreſenting a Ray of Light it ſtrikes upon ſome Body, rebounds from it, paſſes through ſuch a Medium, and is turned or bent this Way and that Way: or as being fixed at one Extreme it carries about or ſuſtains a Weight made faſt to the other, and ſerves to determine the *Momentum* according to its Diſtance from the immoveable Center: or as repreſenting a muſical Scale or Rule it exhibits on its Diviſions the various Proportions of Sounds. According to each of which different Ways, the *Geometrician*, *Aſtronomer*, *Optician*, *Mechanic* and *Muſician* conſider a Right Line reſpectively. In like manner a *Sphere* may be conſidered, as a Figure produced by the Rotation of ſuch a *Plane*, bounded by ſuch a *Superficies*; diviſible in ſuch a wiſe, endued with a certain Proportion to other *Homogeneous Magnitudes*; by which means the Geometrician examines its Nature and Affections: or as placed at ſuch a Diſtance, and illuminated uniformly or ununiformly through ſuch a Medium with ſuch a Light it exhibits ſuch a Form of itſelf to the Beholder; which is the Uſe made of it by the *Optician*, and much the ſame by the *Aſtronomer:* or as immerſed in any Matter it obtains a Power of deſcending towards the Center of the Earth, called Weight or Gravity, and according to the various Diſpoſition and Situation of its Parts, its Connexion with other Matter, different Suſtentation or Suſpenſion it either entirely reſts, or is inclined to certain Parts, or moved to ſuch a Limit; in which reſpect it is conſidered by the *Mechanic*. Laſtly, the *Arithmetician* handles Numbers one Way, to diſcover their general Affections; and the *Muſician* another, that he may accommodate them to expreſs the Proportions of Sounds. And theſe Examples may ſuffice.

(l) But the mental *Abſtraction* we ſpake of is not the only Property of *Mathematics*, but is common to all Sciences. For every Science conſiders the Nature of its own Subject abſtracted from all others; forms its own general Precepts and Theorems; and ſeparates its own Properties from the Properties of others, examining the former, and diſmiſſing the latter. *(m)* For example, *Phyſics* conſiders the conſtitutive Principles, Matter, Form, *&c.* of Body in general; then the Affections common to all Bodies, *viz.* Quantity, Place, Motion, Reſt, and the like; from whence it deſcends to the next lower Species, inveſtigating their particular Natures and Properties; but meddles not with particular Bodies or Individuals, as well becauſe they are innumerable and diſtinguiſhed from one another by innumerable Differences, as becauſe being treated ſort by ſort they may be adapted accordingly. The ſame way *Geometry* propoſes Magnitude for the Subject of its Enquiry, not the peculiar Magnitude of this or that Body, but Magnitude taken univerſally; together with its general Affections, *viz.* Diviſibilty, Congruence, Proportionality, a Capacity of different Situation and Poſition, Mobility, *&c.* declaring theſe to be inherent to it, and after what manner they are ſo: Next it defines the various Species of *Magnitude*, (*viz.* a *Line*, *Superficies*, and a *Body* or *Solid*) and particularly draws forth and demonſtrates their diſtinct Properties; continually dividing theſe Species into others more contract, and ſearching and proving their Affections by univerſal Propoſitions, Rules and Theorems lawfully demonſtrated, till it has wholly exhauſted its Subject, and deſcended to the very loweſt Species. And theſe Theorems howſoever more or leſs general as to their Matter, may be

(l) Ariſt. Metaph. XI. 1. *(m)* Ariſt. Metaph. XI. 3.

truly and properly accommodated to Subjects particular to themſelves. True *Mathematical Abſtraction* then, is ſuch as agrees with all other Sciences and Diſciplines, nothing elſe being meant (whatſoever ſome do ſtrangely ſay of it) than an Abſtraction from particular Subjects, or a diſtinct Conſideration of certain things more univerſal, others leſs univerſal being omitted and as it were neglected. But enough of this.

Our next Buſineſs ſhould be to handle the Diviſion of *Mathematics* in a more diſtinct manner; but, if I am not miſtaken, the Time admoniſhes us to reſerve that for the following Lecture.

LECTURE II.

Of the particular Diviſion of the Mathematical Sciences.

THE Diſquiſition we begun in our firſt Lecture, concerning the Diviſion of the *Mathematical Sciences*, we will now aſſay to purſue more diſtinctly, as was then propoſed, delivering in the firſt place the Method of the Antients, and afterwards our own Method. *(n)* The *Pythagoreans* who, as *Ariſtotle* ſays, were the firſt among the *Greeks*, that meddled with *Mathematics*, divided them into *four Parts*, of which, two were *Pure* and *Primary*, namely *Arithmetic* and *Geometry*; and the other two *Mixed* and *Secondary*, as *Muſic* and *Spheres*, i. e. *Aſtronomy*. And the Reaſon which they gave for this Diviſion, according to *(o)* *Proclus* and *Boethius*, was, becauſe ſince the Species of

(n) 1. Met. 5. *(o)* Procl.

the

the general Object are two, to wit, *Multitude* and *Magnitude*, each of which may be two Ways considered; *viz. Multitude* either simply as subsisting in itself, or respectively with reference to the Sounds whose Proportions it expresses; and Magnitude, as it is fixed in a (*p*) Place, or is carried about with Motion; hence arise these four Parts of *Mathematics*. Thus did the *Pythagoreans* of old divide the *Mathematics*, I suppose, because they had not yet applied themselves to the other Parts, such as *Optics*, *Mechanics*, *&c.* which the curious Diligence of after Ages, and Time, the Inventor of all Things, brought forth and devised.

And that of *(q) Plato* differs not much from this most ancient Division, who distributes the *Mathematics* into *five Parts*, *Arithmetic*, *Geometry*, *Stereometry*, *Music*, and *Astronomy*, to which *Theon Smyrnæus* reduces all Things in *Plato* relating to the *Mathematical Sciences*. The Division, I say, of *Plato* differs from *Pythagoras*'s no more than this, because, according to him, *Geometry* being taken more strictly, only signifies the Doctrine of *(r) Planometry* or the Mensuration of *Planes*; whereas in the other it extends to the whole Science of *Mensuration*, and consequently also comprehends under it *Stereometry* or the Mensuration of *Solids*. But why *Plato*, a Man of so universal an Education, should confine the *Mathematics* within such narrow Limits, and add no other Disciplines to them, I think proceeds from hence; because, in his time, others were either not yet invented, or not sufficiently cultivated, or at least were not yet received into the Number of the *Mathematical Sciences*.

Nor is it a wonder to find their Number encreased by *Aristotle*, by the addition of *Optics*, *Mechanics*, and *Geodesy*; forasmuch as these Studies, a little after

(p) Boeth. Initio. Arithmetices. *(q)* 7. de Rep. *(r)* Ἐμπεδομετρία.

Plato,

Plato, eſpecially being recommended by ſo great a Man, began to grow apace, and in a ſhort time made an immenſe Progreſs. But theſe adventitious Parts are ſometimes reckoned by *Ariſtotle* among the Mathematical Sciences, and ſometimes diſjoined from them, becauſe they obtained a *(s) middle Place*, being equally Sharers of *Phyſics* as well as *Mathematics*. For inſtance, when he ſays Optics ſhews the reaſon of the Rainbow either abſolutely, or as it requires the Help of *(t) Geometry*; here he plainly ſeparates *Optics* from *Geometry*; and again he elſewhere diſtinguiſhes the *(u)* ſenſible Sciences, ſuch as *Optics*, from the *Mathematical* ones.

But afterwards, according to the Teſtimony of *Proclus*, when the *Mathematics* was farther extended, and enlarged by the more diligent Study of ſucceeding Times, being as it were compleated by its own Numbers, *Geminus*, a famous Geometrician, who flouriſhed about the Age of *Pompeius M.* (and others of the ſame Degree of Learning) diſtributed it after this manner. They ſuppoſed ſome Parts of the *Mathematics* to be converſant about *(w)* Things only perceptible to the Underſtanding; and others about *(x)* Things ſenſible: to the former belonged the principal and leading Sciences of *Arithmetic* and *Geometry*; and to the latter the ſix following Parts, *viz. Geodeſy*, *Logiſtics*, *Optics*, *Canonics*, *Mechanics*, and *Aſtrology*. Under theſe Terms they included the whole of *Mathematics*, as a Body compoſed of ſo many Members, which they again ſubdivided into other leſſer Joints or Articles. *Geometry* they diſtributed into *Planometry* and *Stereometry*, (and perhaps it would not have been amiſs to have added *Grammometry* or the Menſuration of Lines) *Arithmetic* into the Theories of *Linear*, *Plane*

(s) 1. Anal. Poſt. cap. 13. *(t)* Τὸ μάθημα. *(u)* Ἀισθητικαὶ. *(w)* Τὰ νοητὰ. *(x)* Τὰ αἰσθητὰ.

and

and *ſolid Numbers.* *Geodeſy* they diſtinguiſhed from *Geometry*, becauſe it only meaſures ſuch Figures as are perceptible to the Senſes by ſenſible Inſtruments: as when *Proclus* meaſured Heaps riſing in a Point for Cones, and Wells for Cylinders, by the help of Chords, Rules, and Plumb-lines contrived for that purpoſe. In like manner *Logiſtics* they diſtinguiſhed from *Arithmetic*, becauſe it conſiders not abſtract Numbers, but applies them to things occurring to the Senſes; as when it is ſought how many Parts of its Orbit a Star paſſes through in a given Time; how many Soldiers are required to compleat a Battalion; or for what Expences a Houſe may be erected. *Optics*, as the Offspring of *Geometry*, (borrowing from thence its Rays and viſual Angles) they ſubdivided into three Branches; *viz.* *Optics*, properly ſo called, which may not unſuitably be called *Adjſpective*, becauſe it unfolds the Reaſons of things adſpectable (*i. e.* offered to the ſight) in a direct View; as why parallel Lines proceeding to a great Diſtance do ſeem to coincide; and why a Square beheld afar off appears in the Figure of a Circle; *Catoptrics*, which examines the Appearances reſulting from Rays reflected by an opaque Body, or bent in their Tranſit through a different pellucid Medium (this they took in a more extenſive Senſe to comprehend that alſo which is now commonly called *Dioptrics*, deſigning another thing by the word *Dioptrics*, as we ſhall ſee anon: And *Sciography*, (now called *Perſpective*, *Scenography*, *Projecture* or the Art of Projection) which delineates upon any Superficies the Traces or Footſteps made by Rays emitted upon it from any adſpectable Thing, repreſenting its Figure, Poſition, Diſtance, and other Circumſtances juſtly and beautifully. Next they named that Diſcipline *Canonic*, *Harmonic* or *Muſic*, which makes a Judgment of the apparent Proportions of Sounds, meaſuring them on the Diviſions

ſions of a Canon or muſical Scale, with a regard alſo to the Aſſiſtance of the Ears. Mechanics, or the Art of diſcovering the weight and motive Power of any maſſy Body, they divided into three Kinds; *viz. Organopoëtics*, which ſhews the Structure and Uſe of Inſtruments, eſpecially military: *Thaumaſtopoëtics*, which performs things to be wondered at by the Impulſe of Winds, the Power of Weights, and Tenſion of Nerves or Strings imitating the Motions of Life (to which conſequently are referred *Pneumatics* or the Art of making Wind-Engines, *Horrhopics* or the Art of Balancing, *Centrobarycs* or the Art of the Center of Gravity, *Automatapoëtics* or the Art of making Self-movers): And (*y*) *Spheropoëtics*, which contrives material Spheres in ſuch ſort as to exhibit all the heavenly Motions upon them. Laſtly, *Aſtrology*, which conſiders the Order of the mundane Syſtem, and the Motions, Figures, Magnitudes, Diſtances and Influences of the celeſtial Bodies; this they diſtributed into *Gnomics*, which meaſures Time by the Shadow of a Gnomon or Stile; *Meteoroſcopics*, which reſolves the different Elevations of the Stars, their Diſtances from one another, *&c.* And *Dioptrics*, which examines the Stars apparent Magnitudes and Intervals by the help of *Diopters*, *i. e.* certain Inſtruments which convey and direct the viſual Rays. But *Tactics*, *i. e.* the Art of rightly diſpoſing an Army of Men, they purpoſely baniſhed out of the Number of Mathematical Diſciplines, though it computed their Legions and formed their Camps by the help of Logiſtics and Geodeſy; juſt as the Hiſtorian (according to their way of arguing) is not to be accounted a Mathematician, becauſe he relates the Climates of Countries and Circumferences of Cities. Such was the Diviſion of Mathematics inſtituted by *Geminus* and his Cotemporaries, ſomewhat more copious indeed than that of *Pythagoras*

(*y*) Σφαιροποιΐα.

and

and *Plato*, as comprehending the principal Sciences which vulgarly go by the Name of *Mathematics*, but in my Opinion far from being sufficiently just and accurate. For first of all, it is a very weak and slippery Foundation to depend upon, that the *Mathematics* are conversant about Things *intelligible* and Things *sensible*, because in reality every one of its Objects are at the same time both intelligible and sensible in a different respect; intelligible as the Mind apprehends and contemplates their universal (z) Ideas, and sensible as they agree with several particular Subjects occurring to the Sense: For who does not view with the Eye and feel with the Hand all the particular Dimensions of Bodies? But there is no reason why the Doctrine of Generals should be separated from the Consideration of Particulars, since the former entirely includes and primarily respects the latter. (a) Why *ex. gr.* should one Science treat of an intelligible Sphere, and another of a sensible one? when these, as to the Verity of the Thing, are altogether the same, and as to the Action of the Mind subordinate; nor can any thing be attributed to the intelligible Sphere (*i. e.* one understood universally) which does not perfectly agree with the sensible (*i. e.* with every particular one): Whence it is altogether amiss to disjoin *Geodesy* from *Geometry*, and *Logistics* from *Arithmetic*. But permitting the Foundation to stand, at least this Division cannot be accurate, but will be found altogether lame and imperfect; for the Multitude of sensible Things, to which Number and Magnitude may be applied, is too diffusive to be circumscribed within these Limits, and consequently, if this Supposition be admitted, the Field of Mathematics will become far too wide and extensive; as will appear more clearly anon. And so much for the Division of

(z) Arist. Met. Lib. 2. c. 3. (a) Anal. Post. Lib. 1. c. 24.

Geminus,

Geminus, which yet moſt Mathematicians of a later Date do embrace; ſaving that ſome baniſh hence Geodeſy and Logiſtics; as *Blancus* in his Book concerning the Nature of the Mathematical Sciences; *Peter Herigon* before his *Curſus*; and *Guildinus* in the *Prolegomena* to his *Centrobarycs* treating of the Diviſion of the Mathematics. Theſe conſtitute two pure and primary Parts, namely, Geometry and Arithmetic, and four mixed and ſubaltern, *viz.* Optics, Mechanics, Muſic and Aſtronomy, which they again ſubdivide various Ways into Parts more contracted. There occur alſo other Diviſions of theſe Diſciplines invented by the Moderns, ſome more compleat and accurate, others leſs; whoſe Number it would indeed be difficult to enter upon, and not very profitable; becauſe moſt an end the manifold Diviſion and Subdiviſion of things into their minuteſt Parts rather tends to breed Confuſion, than to remove it (*b*): eſpecially ſince many or all of theſe are liable to the ſame Exceptions with the forementioned Diviſion of *Geminus.* Wherefore paſſing them by, we will conſult the thing itſelf, and impart what is our own Judgment.

And this is my Opinion, firſt, that there is really no Quantity in Nature different from what is called *Magnitude* or *continued Quantity*, and conſequently that this alone ought to be accounted the Object of Mathematics; whoſe moſt general Properties it enquires into and demonſtrates in the firſt Place, next its leſs general ones, and laſtly, the Affections agreeing to each. This being ſuppoſed for the preſent, (which will hereafter be ſufficiently proved) as to what belongs to the Sciences termed *Mixed Mathematics*, I ſuppoſe they ought all to be taken as Parts of *Natural Science*, being the ſame in Number with the Branches of *Phyſics*, except thoſe that are merely (*c*) *Effective*, as many perhaps are;

(*b*) Proclus, pag. 21. (*c*) Ποιητικαὶ.

such

ſuch as *Painting*, *Sculpture*, *Statuary*, *Architecture*; to which may be adjoined all their kindred Arts taken from Phyſics. For theſe mixed Sciences are ſtiled Mathematical for no other Reaſon, but becauſe the Conſideration of Quantity intervenes with them, and becauſe they require Concluſions to be demonſtrated in Geometry, applying them to their own particular Matter. And, according to the ſame Reaſon, there is no Branch of natural Science that may not arrogate the Title to itſelf; ſince there is really none, from which the Conſideration of Quantity is wholly excluded, and conſequently to which ſome Light or Aſſiſtance may not be fetched from Geometry. For Magnitude is the common Affection of all phyſical Things, it is interwoven in the Nature of Bodies, blended with all corporeal Accidents, and well nigh bears the principal Part in the Production of every natural Effect. All Bodies obtain their own Figures, and execute their own local Motions; by which means, if not all, yet the moſt and chiefeſt Effects (whatſoever admits of a philoſophical Explication) are performed, for the determining and comparing of which the Theorems of Geometry do often conduce. But if we make our Calculation thus, and name every kind of Learning Mathematical, which either requires, or any way uſes the Help of Geometry, ſo far *Medicine* itſelf will be a Part of Mathematics; becauſe, as (*d*) *Ariſtotle* notes, the Phyſician takes the Cauſe from Geometry, why orbicular Wounds, as being more capacious than others, are more difficult to heal: and becauſe *Hippocrates*, for the ſame Reaſon, adviſed his Son to ſtudy Geometry, that he might more perfectly underſtand the Situations, Luxations, Contritions and Exemptions of the Bones. Alſo by a like Reaſon *Politics* may

(*d*) Anal. Poſt. c. 13.

be

be aſcribed to the Mathematics, becauſe it requires the aſſiſtance of Geometry, as well for Ornament in Peace, as Safeguard in War; for the elegant building of Houſes, the ſtrong Fortifications of Cities, and the commodious Conveyance of Waters; alſo for the right Diſcharge of every military Office, the pitching of Camps, diſpoſing an Army, inventing of Engines, and applying them to uſe. Whence (*e*) *Plato*; *There is indeed*, ſays he, *a vaſt Difference between a Man's being expert and inexpert in Geometry for the ſetting out of Camps, the poſſeſſing of advantageous Places, the ranging a Battalia in cloſe Order or extending it farther, and the repreſenting all other Figures of that Kind by which an Army ought to be diſpoſed in Battles or Marches.* Whence, at leaſt *Tactics* and *Poliorcetics* (*i. e.* the Art of beſieging Towns) with every kind of Architecture, ought to be numbered among the Mathematical Sciences. But to return to Phyſics, I ſay there is no Part of this which does not imply Quantity, or to which geometrical Theorems may not be applied, and conſequently which is not ſome Way dependant on Geometry; I will not except even *Zoology* itſelf, (*i. e.* the Science of living Bodies) which of all others ſeems to be moſt foreign. For does not the certain Figure, apt Proportion, and due Poſition of the Members come into Conſideration in examining the Structure of a living Body? Cannot the Walking, Flying and Swimming of Animals, the Method of moving forward, ſuſtaining and poiſing their Bodies, be examined and proved according to the Laws of Geometry? And many ſuch things will offer themſelves to him who examines any other Part of Nature. I confeſs there are ſome Parts of Phyſics where Quantity occurs more frequently than in others, and conſequently

(*e*) 7. de Rep.

where

where the Knowledge of Geometry is more needful; ſuch as thoſe *ex. gr.* which treat upon the heavenly Bodies, becauſe by reaſon of their too great Diſtance from us, we can ſcarce know any thing at all of them, beſides their apparent Figures, their Magnitudes, their Intervals, their Progreſſes, and the Periods of their Motions: whence it comes to paſs that the whole Science almoſt of the celeſtial Luminaries ſeems to be Mathematical, becauſe all the Knowledge we can attain of them reſpects or depends upon Quantity. Hence have we *Aſtronomy* with its Parts; *viz. Syſtematics*, which enquires into the Diſpoſition of the principal mundane Bodies, with their Situation in reſpect of one another: *Sphærics*, which teaches the apparent diurnal Motion common to all heavenly Bodies, with its Conjuncts and Accidents: And *Theorics*, which contemplates the Motions of the Planets and the Affections proceeding from thence. To which may be adjoined the Sciences drawn from or dependent on theſe; *viz. Chronology*, (or at leaſt that Part of it ſtiled *Technical*) which juſtly divides the Intervals of Time from the periodical Courſes of the Sun and Moon; and *Gnomics*, which diſtinguiſhes the Particles of their diurnal Motion, diſcovering in like manner their Altitudes and Declinations from the Shadows of opaque Bodies: Alſo hither are referred *Cometology*, and the Doctrine which treats of new Stars, ſometimes appearing out of the common Courſe. Moreover becauſe the ſpherical Figure of the Earth is diſcovered to be the ſole Cauſe why the Light of the heavenly Bodies, as to Continuance of Time, Species, or Situation, is different to the Inhabitants of different Places, therefore *Geography* is alſo reckoned to the Mathematics; becauſe in it the Geometrical Concluſions concerning the Sphere are entirely neceſſary to be well conſidered and underſtood. And for the ſame Reaſon *Nautics* (or the

Art of *Navigation*) is annexed, which directs a Ship's Course by Angles made with the Meridian, and determines its Place in the vast Ocean with the Time of the Day, from celestial Appearances. Again, because the Animal Vision is conceived to be performed by Rays proceeding like Right Lines from any assignable Point of the (enlightning or enlightned) Object towards its correspondent Point in the Eye, and consequently what Geometry demonstrates concerning Right Lines (and the Figures they constitute) may be adapted to these Rays; hence *Optics* is referred to the Mathematics: whose Parts are, *Catoptrics*, which considers the Appearances coming from Rays reflected by an opaque Body; and *Dioptrics*, which draws the Consequences of Radiation infracted by a different Medium: To which are annexed the effective Arts respecting Vision; *viz. Perspective*, which teaches the Method of representing justly and neatly the Species or Figures of visible Objects upon any Table, especially Planes; *Graphics* or *Painting*, which adds Colour and Shade to Perspective; *Engraving*, *Carving*, *Statuary*, and the like. And if the Figure of the Air's Undulation could be the same way discovered, by which Sound is performed, and the Sense of Hearing impelled, there would doubtless arise thence a new Part of Mathematics to be celebrated by the Name of *Accustics*, or the Science of Sounds. Also *Haptics*, *Geustics*, and *Osphrantics* (or the Sciences of Touches, Tastes and Smells) would by a similar Reason merit to be chosen into this Order: and, if these Sensations be performed by such Motions, Philosophers might smell by guess. However, as to what pertains to the Sense of Hearing, because from the certain Division of a sonorous String, or from the Length of two Strings differing according to a certain Proportion, both stretched alike, if both be struck with a Quill, there is found a deter-

minate

minate Habitude of the Sounds produced, which wonderfully anſwers to the Proportion of the Strings according to the Degrees of Sharpneſs and Flatneſs, and conſequently is explicable by Numbers (or at leaſt by Right Lines), hence ariſes that Part of Mathematics termed *Muſic*, *Harmonics* or *Canonics*, which (as ſome love to ſpeak) is ſubaltern to Arithmetic; but perhaps it would be more rightly ſubordinate to Geometry. Moreover, ſince the Power of deſcending directly towards the Earth, called Weight, which is inherent to moſt Bodies endowed with ſenſible Magnitude, from whatſoever efficient Cauſe it proceeds, may in fact be limited and obtain its Degrees from theſe things conſpiring together, *viz.* partly its own Bulk, partly the Situation of its Parts, and partly the Diſtance from the immoveable Center of its Motion about which it is turned; and by like Reaſon ſince the Power of reſiſting theſe ponderous Bodies, of ſuſtaining, elevating, or any how removing them from their Place is determined and depends on the ſame Cauſes; hence the Diſciplines concerning the Reſt or Motion of theſe Weights whether conſidered abſolutely or comparatively (*i. e.* as they mutually reſpect one another) are aſcribed to the Mathematics; becauſe they require the help of Geometry to determine their Magnitudes, Poſitions and Diſtances: of which kind are *Statics* (*i. e.* the Science of Weights) *Mechanics*, *Centrobarycs*, *Horrhopics*, and the like. And to theſe may be referred *Automatopoetics*, or the Art of making Machines moveable, not by an extrinſecal Impulſe, but from an internal Gravity, or elaſtic Virtue within themſelves. Yea, becauſe no local Motion as to its Duration, Impetus, Intention, Direction, and all kinds of Differences can be otherwiſe eſtimated in itſelf, or compared with another Motion, but from the Spaces (*i. e.* the Right or Circular Lines) it paſſes through, therefore

fore moſt Parts of Phyſics, and all their kindred Arts univerſally wherein local Motion principally obtains, are to be accounted Mathematical, ſo far as they make uſe of the Dimenſion of Lines or Spaces appropriated to Geometry: From whence accrues a plentiful Crop of Sciences to the Mathematics. For hence is the Doctrine concerning the Motion of Bodies deſcending naturally in what proportion they are accelerated: concerning the Motion of Projectiles which is compounded of a natural and acquired Motion, what Curve Line they deſcribe: concerning the throwing of Darts and the Impulſe of miſſive Weapons diſcharged from Engines of War, what Force they have, and how the Machines ſerving them are to be diſpoſed ſo as to hit the Mark aimed at with the greateſt Force and Certainty: alſo concerning the Conveyance of Waters upwards by the Force of Air or Wind, by Compreſſion, Rarefaction, Attraction, Evacuation, or whatſoever other Cauſe. Theſe particular Sciences, I ſay, treating of ſuch Things, and the like, do very much encreaſe the Parts of Mathematics: Of which kind were *Belopoëtics*, *i. e.* the Art of making Battering-Rams; *Baliſtics*, or the Art of making and uſing Engines of War wherewithal to caſt Darts or Stones; *Pneumatics*, the Art of making Machines which go by the Force of the Air or Wind; *Hydraulics*, *i. e.* the Art of making Engines to carry or raiſe Water, with all ſorts of Water-works, *&c.* Hence I conceive it appears ſufficiently plain (as I purpoſed to ſhew) that *Mathematics*, as it is vulgarly taken and called, is adequate and co-extended with *Phyſics*. Alſo I have at the ſame time ſhewn (as by the by, yet deſignedly) how far every particular Science aſpires at the Dignity and Title of *Mathematics* by its own Merit, and by what means the Compaſs of this Science has come to that vaſt Extent it now is; ſo that

that it may be ſaid of it, as once it was ſaid of the *Roman* Republick, *it ſinks under its own Weight.* Nay it is come to that paſs, that even the Learned ſeem to fall into the Error of the Vulgar, and whatſoever can be any way expreſſed by a Diagram or ſhadowed to the Senſe by a viſible Image, that is, *ipſo facto*, ſuppoſed to belong to the Mathematics. Whereas in reality thoſe which are called *Mixed* or *Concrete* Mathematical Sciences, are rather ſo many Examples only of Geometry, than ſo many diſtinct Sciences ſeparate from it: for when once they are diſrobed of particular Circumſtances, and their own fundamental and principal Hypotheſes come to be admitted (whether ſuſtained by a probable Reaſon, or aſſumed *gratis*) they become purely Geometrical. For example, ſuppoſe a Star or celeſtial Point in the Heavens (*i. e.* the indefinite Space) be carried through a right, circular, elliptic, or any other Line, with an uniform or apparently equable Motion reſpecting ſome determinate Point, in a certain Time (*i. e.* with a certain Velocity determinable by the Proportion of Numbers or Right Lines); theſe Things, I ſay, being ſuppoſed, all the conſequent Diſcourſe uſed in *Aſtronomy* becomes purely Geometrical. And how much the more ſimple and evidently poſſible the Hypotheſes are taken, ſo much the nearer do theſe Arts approach to Geometry: From whence *ex. gr.* that Part of Mechanics treating of the Center of Gravity, and that Branch of Optics vulgarly called Perſpective, are not unfitly numbered among the Parts of Geometry, becauſe they ſcarce require any thing which is not granted and proved in that Science, nor uſe any other Principles or Reaſonings than what are ſtrictly Geometrical. But enough of theſe Things for the preſent.

Perhaps ſome may wonder, that while I am endeavouring to make a perfect Enumeration of all the Parts (at leaſt the principal Parts) of Mathematics, I am wholly ſilent about that which is called *Algebra* or the *Analytic Art.* I anſwer, this was not done unadviſedly. Becauſe indeed *Analyſis*, underſtood as intimating ſomething diſtinct from the Rules and Propoſitions of *Geometry* and *Arithmetic*, ſeems to belong no more to *Mathematics* than to *Phyſics*, *Ethics*, or any other Science. For this is only a Part or Species of *Logic*, or a certain Manner of uſing Reaſon in the Solution of Queſtions, and the Invention or Probation of Concluſions, which is often made uſe of in all other Sciences. Wherefore it is not a Part or Species of, but rather an Inſtrument ſubſervient to the Mathematics: No more is *Syntheſis*, which is the manner of demonſtrating Theorems in Contradiſtinction to *Analyſis*. But of theſe we will treat more clearly hereafter, when we come purpoſely to diſcourſe of the Mathematical Ways of *Invention* and *Demonſtration.*

It was nearly for the ſame Cauſe, that I deſignedly paſſed by *Logiſtics*; for neither do I reckon this among the Parts of Mathematics, becauſe it has no Object diſtinct and proper to itſelf, but only delivers a kind of Artifice for deſigning Magnitudes and Numbers by certain Notes or Symbols, and collecting and comparing their Sums and Differences, founded in Geometry or Arithmetic: From whence it conſtitutes no Part of Mathematics diſtinct from *Geometry* or *Arithmetic*, but is entirely contained in them. But I perceive a more weighty Complaint will be brought againſt me, becauſe *Arithmetic* itſelf, hitherto accounted almoſt the chief of all Sciences, ſeems as it were baniſhed by me out of the Confines of Mathematics; at leaſt is wholly omitted. The Fact I cannot deny, but the Reaſon why I did it, having not now Opportunity, I will ſhew in the next Lecture.

LECTURE

LECTURE III.

Of the Identity of Arithmetic *and* Geometry.

WHEN I treated in the foregoing Lecture concerning the Division of the Mathematical Sciences, I affirmed the Whole of Mathematics to be in ſome ſort contained and circumſcribed within the Bounds of Geometry. And indeed concerning the other Sciences then mentioned, I imagine no Body will much deny, but they are conveniently enough reduced to Geometry. But now I have brought a harder Taſk upon myſelf, to ſhew allowable and fit Cauſes for expunging *Arithmetic* out of the Liſt of Mathematical Sciences, and as it were degrading the moſt noble Science from the Degree which it has been ſo long poſſeſſed of. Albeit I am conſcious to myſelf that I have committed no ſuch Fault. Be it far from me to take away or ſeclude a Science ſo excellent and profitable as that of Numbers from the Mathematics. I will rather reſtore *it* into its lawful Place, as being removed out of its proper Seat, and ingraff and unite it again into its native Geometry, the Stock from whence it has been plucked. Nay, my Conſcience would not permit me to oppoſe ſo illuſtrious and venerable an Authority, and obtrude ſuch a monſtrous Paradox upon you, if I did not put great Confidence in the Cauſe I have undertaken, and thought it very much to the Purpoſe of Mathematics, that Arithmetic be accounted not only like and of kin to Geometry in Nature (or, according to the Saying of (*f*) *Archytas* of *Tarentum*, that antient *Pythagorean* Philoſopher,

(*f*) Nicomachum 1. Arith.

its

its Sister) but more nearly conjoined, yea altogether the same, and wholly indistinct from it. For I am convinced that Number really differs nothing from what is called Continued Quantity, but is only formed to express and declare it; and consequently that Arithmetic and Geometry are not conversant about different Matters, but do both equally demonstrate Properties common to one and the same Subject; and very many, and very great Improvements will appear to be derived from hence upon the Republic of Mathematics.

I. For first of all it appears that there is neither any general Axiom nor particular Conclusion agreeing with Geometry (which respects Magnitudes not taken absolutely, but in Comparison with one another according to certain Proportions of Equality or Inequality, *i. e.* as they are capable of being designed and compared together by Measures) but what by the same Reason also agrees with Arithmetic: And on the other hand that nothing can be affirmed, concluded, or demonstrated, concerning Numbers which may not in like manner be accommodated to Magnitudes; whence accrues a remarkable Light and vast Improvement to both Sciences; the Cause being removed of superfluously repeating and demonstrating Theorems by Nature altogether the same, also of often solving the same Problems. For the Confirmation of which, innumerable Examples as well as Arguments may be produced, and the whole Doctrine of Proportions is a most remarkable Instance.

II. This Coalition of Numbers and Magnitudes being admitted, a plentiful Accession accrues to each Discipline. For it will be a very easy thing to discover and demonstrate very many Theorems concerning Numbers by the Assistance of Geometry, which, by keeping within the common Limits of Arithmetic would scarcely, if at all, be capable

either

either of Inveſtigation or Demonſtration: Alſo very many Things may be more briefly and clearly found out and demonſtrated from hence. And reciprocally, the Ratio's or Reaſons of Numbers being well underſtood will communicate not a little to the more evident Explication and ſtrong Confirmation of many Geometrical Theorems. We will illuſtrate the Matter with an Example or two. It is an Arithmetical Theorem, that *the Sum of an infinite* (or *indefinite*) *Series of Numbers increaſing from Nothing to a certain Term, which is the greateſt according to the Ratio of the ſquare Roots of Numbers continually exceeding one another by Unity, (i. e. as* 0, 1, $\surd$ 2, $\surd$ 3, *&c.* ad infinitum) *is ſubſeſquialter the Sum of as many equal to the ſaid greateſt Term*; Which Theorem I am of Opinion can never be exactly demonſtrated by any Method in Arithmetic itſelf: but it is plainly deduced from Geometry. For if the Diameter of any Parabola be conceived to be divided indefinitely into many equal Parts, then the Right Lines which are ordinately applied to the Diameter, through the Points of the Diviſions, will proceed in the ſame Ratio, as is ſhewn in Geometry: But the Parabola which is conſtituted of theſe, whether Right Lines or Parallelograms, is there alſo demonſtrated to be Subſeſquialter to the Parallelogram, upon the ſame Baſe and of the ſame Height, or which is the ſame thing, to the Sum compoſed of as many Right Lines or Parallelograms equal to the greateſt: From whence, the Agreement of Arithmetic with Geometry being ſuppoſed which we deſire to advance, it plainly follows, that a Series of Numbers of this ſort is Subſeſquialter the Sum of as many equal to the greateſt.

But we will propoſe an eaſier Example, not much unlike the former. *The Sum of a Series of Numbers infinitely decreaſing in a triple Ratio*

(i. e. *as*

as 1, $\frac{1}{3}$, $\frac{1}{9}$, $\frac{1}{27}$, &c.) *till the laſt or leaſt Term be nothing is to Unity as* 3 *to* 2; or *the ſame Sum excluding Unity is equal to* $\frac{1}{2}$; This Theorem (which for Eaſineſs and Perſpicuity's ſake, I have propoſed in a determinate, *viz.* a triple Ratio) although it may be demonſtrated Univerſally (*g*); yet I think, by making Uſe of a continued Quantity, it will be ſhewn much more clearly and expeditiouſly, at leaſt more handſomely and elegantly (FIG. I.) *Ex. gr.* Suppoſe the moveable Point A to be carried through the Right Line A Z, with an uniform Motion: Alſo imagine the Point E to be moved uniformly through the ſame, but with a Velocity ſubtriple the Velocity wherewith the Point A is carried; then, in whatſoever time the Point A runs through the Right Line A E in the ſame time will the Point E run through a third Part of A E, ſuppoſe E F. Alſo in whatſoever time the former Point runs through the Right Line E F, in the ſame time will the latter run through the third Part of E F, ſuppoſe F G, and ſo on, *ad infinitum*, till the Point A overtake E in Æ. Now if we ſuppoſe the Line A E to be Unity, then will E F be $\frac{1}{3}$; F G $\frac{1}{9}$, and G H $\frac{1}{27}$, *&c. ad infinitum*, according to the Hypotheſis; but it appears that the Line A E run through by A is triple the Line E Æ which is run through by E in the ſame time, becauſe A is ſuppoſed to move with three times the Velocity of E. Therefore E Æ is to A E (*i. e.* the decreaſing Series including Unity is to Unity) as 3 to 2. Q. E. D. This Theorem univerſally is as follows. *The Sum of any Series of Numbers continually de-*

(*g*) *Thus*;

$$Z - 0 \,.\, Z - \alpha :: \alpha \,.\, \beta.$$
$$Z\beta = Z\alpha - \alpha\alpha.$$
$$\alpha\alpha = Z\alpha - Z\beta.$$
$$\therefore \frac{\alpha\alpha}{\alpha - \beta} = Z.$$

creaſing

creasing from Unity infinitely, or to Nothing, in any Proportion, will be to Unity, as the Antecedent, or greater Term of the Proportion, is to the Excess of the Antecedent above the Consequent. Or *the same Sum, excluding Unity, will be to Unity, as the Consequent, or lesser Term of the Proportion, is to the Excess of the Antecedent above the Consequent.* For the foregoing Premisses being supposed, let the Ratio be given between R and S, and let A E represent Unity, as above; then because A Æ (*i. e.* A E + E Æ) : E Æ : : R : S. therefore (by dividing the Proportion) A E : E Æ : : R--S : S, *i. e.* Unity is to the Sum of the proposed Series, as the Excess of the Terms of the Proportion is to the lesser Term : And again, because A E . E Æ : : R-S : S. therefore A Æ. A E : : R : R-S, by Conversion, *i. e.* the proposed Sum including Unity is to Unity, as the greater Term of the Proportion is to its Excess above the lesser. So easily are Arithmetical Conclusions, (otherwise sufficiently intricate and difficult to be investigated) drawn from the Consideration of Geometry. Thus doth the one Science require the help of the other, and after a friendly sort conspire together.

(b) III. Moreover another Convenience arises from this Conjunction, because (contrary to what one not long ago of a great but mistaken Genius ventured to assert, that he might veil his Mistakes in Geometry, and decline the easy Confutation of his Errors) no Geometrical Argument is of Force, which agrees not exactly with an Arithmetical Calculus, and consequently all false Reasonings committed in Geometry may be examined and refuted most easily,

(b) Quoniam Arithmetica instrumentum est omnis supputationis, & numeri sunt termini, quibus quælibet magnitudo significatur, non dubium est, quin per numeros fieri possit omnis magnitudinis calculus. *Maurolycus* in Prolegom. ad Lib. II. Arithmet.

certainly,

certainly, and juſtly, by Arithmetical Computation: Alſo all true Concluſions, and lawful Demonſtrations in Geometry may be confirmed and illuſtrated by Help of an Arithmetical Calculus: Which Conſideration being preſuppoſed and eſtabliſhed, the Method of treating Geometry will be found no where to differ from the Calculations of Arithmetic.

Theſe Conveniences, not to mention more at this time, will flow to the Mathematics by taking away the Difference between Geometry and Arithmetic, or by conſtituting and aſſerting their Identity. But that they are the ſame, the very Name of Geometry (which ſignifies meaſuring the Earth) does confirm, at leaſt it creates a ſtrong Suſpicion: And much more ſo, that more general Name *Metrices* (*i. e.* The Science of *Meaſure*) which *Plato* prefers before the Name *Geometry.* For what, I beſeech you, is meant by *Meaſure*, but the Notification or Expreſſion of Magnitude by Number? *Meaſure*, (*i*) ſays *Ariſtotle*, *is that whereby Quantity is known*; *but Quantity is known as Quantity*, *either by Unity*, *or by Number.* If then Geometry include Number in its Name, why ought it not to comprehend it in the Thing? Moreover, becauſe τὸ ποσὸν includes a peculiar Reſpect unto Number (by which one Word the general Object of Mathematics is wont to be deſigned) this may diſcover that becauſe the Conceptions of Magnitude and Number could ſcarce be ſeparated in the Name, they can therefore hardly be ſo in the Mind. But this will appear plainer by weighing and examining the Nature of Number a little more circumſpectly. Wherefore

1. I remark that no Number of itſelf ſignifies any thing diſtinctly, or agrees to any determinate Subject, or certainly denominates any thing. For every

(*h*) X. Metaph. cap. 1.

Number may with equal Right denominate any Quantity: and in like manner any Number may be attributed to every Quantity. For inſtance, Any Line A may be indifferently called *One*, *Two*, *Three*, *Four*, or any other Number, (or if you pleaſe, *Simple*, *Double*, *Triple*, *Quadruple*, or howſoever it may be termed *Multiple*) as it remains undivided, may be cut into, or compounded of, two, three, four, or any other Number of Parts. In like manner any Number *ex. gr.* 5. may be attributed to all the Quantities A, B, C, and an Infinity of others, as they are conceived to conſiſt of 5 Parts. Whence it appears that no Number can deſign any thing certain and abſolute, but may be applied to any Quantity at Pleaſure.

2. I obſerve, that as no particular Number taken ſeparately and abſolutely can ſignify any thing certain, ſo no two or more Numbers compared together can indicate any Habitude or Proportion determinate of itſelf. For example, the Number 3 compared with the Number 2 does neither of itſelf denote a Seſquialter, nor any other Proportion. For let the Line A be of 3 *Palms*, from whence it is denominated *Three*, and ſuppoſe the Line B to be of 2 *Feet*, from whence it is named *Two*; it is evident that the former Number 3 is not in a ſeſquialter Proportion to the latter Number 2 (for 3 *Palms* is not to 2 *Feet*, as 3 to 2) much leſs is any other Proportion here expreſſed by theſe Numbers, albeit otherwiſe they may be in a ſeſquialter Proportion; it being apparent that this Number 2 by which a Line is denominated *two Palms*, can never be equal to that Number 2 whereby a Line is ſaid to be *two Feet*.

3. I note that Numbers of themſelves can neither be added to nor ſubtracted from one another, ſo as in the one Caſe to compoſe a Sum, or in the other to leave a Difference or Exceſs. As in the preceding

preceding Example, the Number 3 expreſſing *three Palms* cannot be added to the Number 2 repreſenting *two Feet* ſo as to make a Sum of 5 Palms or Feet, or 5 of any other Meaſure notified according to the ſignification of theſe Numbers. Nor if the latter Number 2 be ſubducted from the former Number 3 will there ariſe any explicit Difference, or knowable Exceſs. And in like manner if 3 Angles be adjoined to 4 Right Lines, the Sum will be Nothing: Or if the Number 3 of Horſes be ſubtracted from the Number 5 of Angels will reſult any Difference. How then (you will ſay) comes the Determination of Numbers to certain Uſes? Are they not uſed to denote a definite Ratio and be added to and ſubtracted from one another? I anſwer, that theſe things do only now and then agree with Numbers, according to the Condition of the things to which they are attributed. If the things which the Numbers are brought to denote be homogeneous, of the ſame Name, and when compared have a mutual Proportion to one another, and conſequently the one can be increaſed by the Addition or diminiſhed by the Subtraction of the other; then they impart the ſame Attributes, Proportions, and Increments or Decrements to the Numbers by which they are denominated. As *ex. gr.* becauſe a Line of two Feet obtains a like *Nature* and *Denomination* with a Line of three Feet, therefore the Number 2 by which the one is ſignified denotes a certain ſeſquialter Proportion to the Number 3 by which the other is denominated; the ſame indeed which the Lines themſelves have that they denominate: and conſequently the former Number 2 added to the other Number 3 makes the Number 5 (*i. e.* five Feet) for the Sum, and that ſubtracted from this leaves Unity for the Exceſs or Difference: And by almoſt the ſame Method, whatſoever Attributes among Arithmeticians are proved to agree with Numbers,

Numbers, they agree not with Numbers taken abstractly and of themselves, but concretely according to the Condition of the Things they are attributed to. But a certain most learned Man, and famous Mathematician of our own Nation, asserts Geometry to be subordinate to Arithmetic, applying the Universal Propositions of Arithmetic to its self; and so making Arithmetic to be of a deeper and more abstract Nature than Geometry: for which he chiefly gives this Reason. *(i) Since,* says he, *a Line of two Feet added to a Line of two Feet makes a Line of four Feet, it does not follow that two and two make four, but rather the former follows from the latter.* To this I answer by asking the following Question; Whence comes it to pass that a Line of two Feet added to a Line of two Palms cannot make a Line of four Feet, four Palms, or four of any Denomination, if it be abstractedly, *i. e.* universally and absolutely true that 2+2 makes 4? You will say, that these Numbers are not applied to the same Matter or Measure; and so say I too; from whence I infer that 2+2 makes 4, not from the abstract Reason of the Numbers, but from the Condition of the Matter to which they are applied, *i. e.* because any Magnitude called by the Name of *Two* added to a Magnitude which is denominated by *Two* of the same Kind will make a Magnitude whose Denomination shall be *Four:* Nor indeed can any thing be imagined more absurd than to affirm that the Proportions of Magnitudes to one another depend upon the Habitude of the Numbers whereby they may be expressed.

Though otherwise it is not so much owing to any Arithmetic that 2+2 make 4, when these Numbers are applied to homogeneous Measures, as to the commonly received Signification of the

(i) D. *Wallis* Arith. p. 69.

Words

Words themſelves, whereby 4 either in Name or Character ſignifies the ſame with twice 2. And indeed the whole Artifice of Vulgar Arithmetic is the ſame Way deduced or demonſtrated; for who can prove that 3+5 equals 8, or 8—3 leaves 5 otherwiſe than from the arbitrary Signification of theſe Words? But

4. That theſe Things may appear plainer I take Notice that the Condition of the Things to which Numbers are attributed are very different. For Numbers are one way attributed to Things ſignifying a certain Meaſure (*i. e.* ſome determinate Magnitude to which other Things of the ſame Kind may be referred) and another to Things agreeing together no otherwiſe than by a certain generical Ratio. *Ex. gr.* When I ſay *Three Yards*, here the ſeveral Units whereof the *Three* is compoſed are mutually equal and ſimilar to the ſeveral other Units conſtituting every Number whereby any Length of Yards is denominated. Whence ſuch Numbers do always keep the ſame Proportion to one another with the Magnitudes they denominate, and conſequently do appoſitely ſerve to expreſs thoſe Magnitudes. But when I ſay *Three Mountains*, *Three Angels*, *Three Lines*, or *Three Numbers*, it is plain the ſeveral Units whereof the *Three* is compoſed have no neceſſary Equality to one another, but only a certain general Agreement or Similitude in the common Notion of a *Mountain*, an *Angel*, a *Line*, or a *Number*. *Ex. gr.* When I call 5, 7, 9, three Numbers, here the ſeveral Numbers, as they are Three, have the Ratio or Notion of Unity, and it is evident they are unequal, but yet all agree in the Notion of Number. Alſo if any other *Three* of Numbers be ſuppoſed, *viz.* 10, 15, 20, the former *Three* will not be equal to this *Three*. From which Conſideration there ariſes a twofold Kind of Number: The former may be called *Mathematical*,

tical, becauſe it is chiefly in uſe among Mathematicians to expreſs, and compare together the Dimenſions of Magnitudes, and becauſe to it the Properties of Magnitudes agree, and Mathematical Concluſions are applied: The latter *Tranſcendental* or *Metaphyſical*, becauſe it is indifferently attributed to all Things, even to Things heterogeneous, imaginary and privative; (for we ſay 2 *Points*, 3 *Dimenſions*, 4 *Chimeras*, 5 *Predicables*, 10 *Blindneſſes)* and becauſe ſome Notion of this Sort of Numbers may be found not only previous to Geometry but to Arithmetic itſelf: As when we define a Triangle to be included within Three Sides, alſo a Plane Number to conſiſt of two, and a Solid of three Numbers multiplied together. Whence appears a Solution of the Argument, whereby *Nicomachus* endeavours to make Arithmetic by Nature prior to Geometry; becauſe Geometry is wont to uſe Numbers, and require the Definitions, Compariſons, and mutual Proportions of Figures to be in the firſt Place explained; as when a *Triangle*, *Square*, *Pyramid*, *Cube*, and other Figures are defined from the Number of their *Sides* or *Angles*; and when the Square of a *Diameter* is demonſtrated to be double the Square of its Side, a *Cylinder* triple the *Cone* of the ſame Height ſtanding upon an equal Baſe, &c. For it will hence be eaſy to anſwer, that Geometry as well as Arithmetic borrows thoſe tranſcendental Numbers it uſes in framing its Definitions and delivering its Argumentations either from *Vulgar Uſe*, which has the Right of affixing Names to Numbers as well as other Things, or elſe from *Metaphyſics*, which conſiders and defines the moſt general Notions of Things: Whence we ſee that very many Things relating to Numbers are treated of in Metaphyſics. Though on the other Hand it muſt be confeſſed that perfect Geometry compleated in all its Parts ſtands in need of Arith-

Arithmetic, yet not as a Science in itſelf entirely different and foreign, but (which we ſhall ſee anon) as a Part of it: juſt as *Empedometry* (or the Doctrine of Planes) a Part of Geometry by Nature prior and more ſimple, is to be previous to *Streometry*, or the Doctrine of Solids, which is a Part more complex.

Nor is it hence leſs eaſy to anſwer the foreſaid learned Man arguing thus. (*k*) *That Aſſertion* (ſays he) *concerning the Equality of the Number Five with the Numbers Two and Three taken together, is a general Aſſertion, which is applicable to all other Things as well as thoſe of Geometry; for alſo two Angels and three Angels are five Angels.* I anſwer briefly: Firſt, as before, I ſay it proceeds not from the abſtract Notion of the Numbers that 2 *Angels* + 3 *Angels* make 5 *Angels*, but becauſe the Numbers *Two* and *Three* are here attributed to Beings of the ſame *Kind* and *Name*: Moreover theſe Numbers, as they are attributed to *Angels*, are *tranſcendental*, intimating no Equality of the *Angels* to one another properly ſo called, but only a *Similitude* of *Nature*; and therefore they belong not to a Mathematical Conſideration. But *Plato* perfectly underſtood, and expreſsly delivered this Diſtinction of Numbers that I have taken Notice of: Whoſe Words are worth the recital. (*l*) *Ought we not* (ſays he) *to attribute one Kind of Arithmetic to the Vulgar, and another to Philoſophers, ſince their Difference is not a little? For the Vulgar do number unequal Units of thoſe Things which are expreſſed by Numbers, as two Caſtles, two Oxen, two of any Thing, as well the leaſt, as the greateſt of all Things. But Philoſophers never reach ſo far, unleſs a Man ſuppoſe one particular Unit to conſiſt of Parts equal to another particular Unit.* Thus *Plato* refers Num-

(*k*) Pag. 73. Arith. (*l*) Pag. 399. Fic.

bers

bers consisting of unequal Units to the *Vulgar*, and others to *Philosophers*, i. e. *Mathematicians:* And this perhaps he had from the more antient *Pythagoreans*, as *Aristotle* seems to intimate, when he says in a *Mathematical Number* no one Unit differs from another. But to come still nearer the Matter and reach the principal Point of the Controversy.

5. I observe and assert that a *Mathematical Number* (such as we have been just now describing, and concerning which we have been chiefly speaking, though what we shall hereafter say, may also in Part be applied to a transcendental Number by a just Analogy, as far as a *Similitude* of *Nature* is a kind of Equality) I say that a *Mathematical Number* has no Existence proper to itself, and really distinct from the Magnitude it denominates, but is only a kind of *Note* or *Sign* of Magnitude considered after a certain Manner; *viz.* as we conceive it either as altogether incomplex, or as compounded of certain homogeneous equal Parts, every one of which is taken simply, and denominated an Unit; or lastly as intimating the Ratio it has to other Magnitudes, in like manner composed by a certain Method. For in order to expound and declare our Conception of a Magnitude, we design it by the *Name* or *Character* of a certain Number, which consequently is nothing else but the *Note* or *Symbol* of such Magnitude so taken. This is the general Nature, Import, and Notion of a Mathematical Number: But more particularly, every Number (which they call *Explicable* or *Rational*) is known and distinguished from another, consequent to the Actions of the Mind composing (or supposing to be composed) different Magnitudes from some one Magnitude which it conceives to be incomposed, by the successive Repetition of it, or the Addition of its equal. Which Repetition at

first

first performed in the Mind, and then expressed in Words is called *Numeration.*

(*m*) *Aristotle* speaks very much to the Purpose. *There is*, says he, *a Necessity of computing Number by Addition, as of Two by the Addition of one Unit to another, of Three by the Addition of One to Two, and of Four, after the same manner.* As when I repeat the Magnitude A once in my Mind, or conceive another equal to it, that Magnitude, which is conceived to be so compounded, I design by the Name or Character of *Two*; but if I still repeat the same Magnitude A, or superadd it to the before conceived Magnitude designed by the Note Two, then the Conception of another compound Magnitude is formed, which I in like manner signify by the Name or Character of *Three.* And so for the rest. But we will illustrate by an Example what we have said above concerning the general Notion of Number. Suppose *ex. gr.* any Line A; it is plain that no Number peculiarly agrees to this, on the Part of the Thing: But if we imagine it composed of some Line by the triple Repetition of itself, as is already explained; or which comes to the same Thing, that it is divisible into three Parts (for it is all one to be composed and to be resoluble into three equal Things) we will therefore call it *Three* or *three Thirds* of A, and denote it with a suitable Character. But if we conceive the same A to be an Aggregate of (or divisible into) seven equal Lines, of which same equal Parts another Line B makes (or is resoluble into) Ten, hence the Line A will be called *Seven* or *seven Tenth* Parts ($\frac{7}{10}$) of the Line B. And if the same Line A be supposed no way compounded or divided, it will obtain the Name and Character of *Unity.* Again, if the aforesaid A be apprehended as

(*m*) Met. 13. cap. 9.

a Mean Proportional between any Line B consisting of (or divided into) two equal Lines, and one of those Lines, *i. e.* between the whole of B and its half, or between any Right Line and its Double; then the Line A will be designed by the Name or Character of the Square Root ($\sqrt[2]{}$) of the Number $\frac{1}{2}$, or 2 respectively; as the Square Root of $\frac{1}{2}$ B ($\sqrt[2]{\frac{1}{2}}$ B) or the Root of 2 C ($\sqrt[2]{}$ 2 C.)

6. Whence consequently it follows that there are three Differences or Species of Numbers, (besides *Unity* which is as it were the Fountain and Original of Numbers) *i. e. Integers*, *Fractions*, and *Radicals* or *Surds*. Of which *Integers* are the *Names* or *Symbols* of Magnitudes, shewing their Composition from certain equal Parts, every single one of which is named Unity, as if the Magnitude A consist of six equal Parts or of one Part six times repeated, A will be termed six. But *Fractions* (among which I reckon *Mixed Numbers* consisting of an *Integer* and a *Fraction*) are the *Notes* of any Magnitude intimating its Composition of equal Parts, not indeed absolutely but by comparing it with some other Magnitude composed of Parts equal and of the same Name with the Parts of the former: Or *Fracted Numbers* are the *Symbols* of any Magnitude equally composed by a certain Method, exhibiting its Proportion to another Magnitude, which is composed of the same equal Parts. As if A be composed of six equal Parts, and B of nine of the same, then will A be six ninth Parts of B ($\frac{6}{9}$ B), or A will be to B as six to nine; *i. e.* the same Magnitude, which is here stiled Unity, if taken six Times composes A, if nine times, B. Lastly, *Radical* or *Surd Numbers* are Notes shewing a Magnitude to be any way in a *Mean Proportion* between some assumed homogeneous Magnitude equally composed according to the Exigence of the Number applied, whether

whether *Integer* or *Fracted*, and its Part ſupplying the Place of Unity; or which is the ſame, between any Magnitude taken ſimply and undivided and conſequently holding the Places of Unity, and another ſo multiplied as the adjoined Number requires: *ex. gr.* the *Square* or *Second Root* of the Number 3 denotes a *Mean Proportional* between any aſſumed Magnitude, and its Triple. And the *Cubic* or *Third Root* of Three deſigns the firſt of two *Mean Proportionals* between any aſſumed Magnitude, and its Triple. Alſo the Biquadratic or fourth Root of the Number 5 ſignifies the firſt of three Mean Proportionals between any Magnitude and its Quintuple; and ſo in like manner for others.

Now as to what pertains to theſe *Surd Numbers* (which, as it were by way of Reproach and Calumny, having no Merit of their own are alſo ſtiled *Irrational*, *Irregular*, and *Inexplicable*) they are by many denied to be Numbers properly ſpeaking, and are wont to be baniſhed from Arithmetic to another Science, (which yet is no Science) *viz.* *Algebra*. And by this means they demutilate Arithmetic of its nobleſt and moſt profitable Member; for while we are meaſuring Magnitudes and comparing them together, we oftner in our Computations light upon theſe *Surds* than upon *Rationals*, which they call Numbers. But with me it is beyond all Doubt, that theſe have the ſame Right to be accounted Numbers, and equally belong to the Science of Numbers, with any other *Integer* or *Fraction*, ſince they are equally apt and neceſſary, for expreſſing, comparing and determining Magnitudes, (wherein as we have already hinted the whole Ratio, Import, and Uſe of Number conſiſts) and ſince there is no general Property or Operation conſonant to *Integers* or *Fractions*, which does not alſo equally agree with theſe. *Ex.gr.* I as readily conceive

ceive what is meant by the *Square Root* of 3 Yards as what is denoted by three Yards itſelf or $\frac{1}{3}$ of a Yard, and can as truly repreſent it from the Force of its Signification. For if a Right Line A be aſſumed equal to a Yard, and another B equal to three Yards, and a *Mean Proportional* be found between theſe, as is ſhewn in Geometry, then the Right Line found will be that which is deſigned by the *Square Root* of 3 Yards. And theſe Numbers by the Direction of moſt certain Rules may be mutually added to and ſubtracted from one another, drawn into and applied to, or divided by, one another, and any way computed, meaſured, or brought to expreſs the Proportions of Magnitudes.

Wherefore there is no Reaſon, why they ought not to be taken for Numbers or be excluded from Arithmetic. But theſe Numbers, ſince they cannot even in thought itſelf be abſtracted from all Magnitude, do make it ſufficiently evident that Number differs nothing in reality from Magnitude: and therefore *Stevinus* does not incongruouſly term them *Geometrical*. For what does $\surd$ 2 ſignify abſtractly? Does it ſignify the Root of the abſtract Number 2? But this Number in that Reſpect has no Root, *i. e.* there is no Number, Integer, or Fracted, which being drawn into itſelf produces 2. Nor is it a Mean Proportional between 1 and 2, for there is no ſuch Mean Number to be found. We muſt therefore have recourſe to Magnitude, to conceive what is deſigned by this Number. For though there be no Mean Proportional to be found between the Number 1 and the Number 2, yet there is a Mean Magnitude between the Magnitude ſignified by the Name *One*, and that denominated by *Two*, which may fitly be deſigned by the Name of *the Square Root of Two*. And the ſame of Fractions, which do well nigh conſtitute the principal Part of Arithmetic, as intimately denoting

noting and implying *Composition* and *Division*, the proper Affections of Magnitude which agree with all Things elſe only ſecondarily, and for the ſake of Magnitude adjoined. He *ex. gr.* who ſays or conceives $\frac{2}{3}$, ſays or conceives nothing at all but that ſome Magnitude is compoſed of two Parts, of which another Magnitude makes three; or that ſome Magnitude is divided into three equal Parts, two of which he conceives or ſays to be aſſumed. Nor do Integers otherwiſe expreſs and repreſent Magnitudes, becauſe theſe alſo include Compoſition or Diviſion in their Notion.

Whence by the by we may know how to judge concerning the Opinion of that great Man we have ſometimes mentioned, who to ſhew that Arithmetic is much more extenſive than Geometry, entirely transfers the whole of *Algebra* from Geometry to Arithmetic, determining Algebraical Equations to aſcend higher than Geometrical ones, and denying that Geometry affords as many *Dimenſions* as Arithmetic exhibits *Degrees*; with more to the ſame Purpoſe. All which Things notwithſtanding may be very eaſily diſcuſſed, by ſaying that by theſe Algebraical Equations or Dimenſions, or Arithmetical Degrees, either nothing at all is underſtood and really ſignified, but all are imaginary Chimeras and mere Monſters; or elſe they have ſomething anſwering to them in Geometry, which they do ſignify and repreſent. As in Reality there is no Number, no Algebraical Power, no Arithmetical Degree, to which innumerable Magnitudes may not anſwer, in every Kind; ſuch Magnitudes being appoſitely repreſented and expreſſed by theſe Numbers. For inſtance, let the *Biquadrate* or *fourth Power* of the Number *Three* be ſuppoſed. To repreſent this Power Geometrically aſſume any Magnitude, it's all one whether it be Line, Superficies, or Solid, but it will be more ſimple if you take a Right Line, ſuppoſe

ſuppoſe A. Let B be the *Triple* of this, and let the Ratio of A to B be ſo continued, that 5 Right Lines A, B, C, D, E, are continued Proportionals; and E will be a Right Line to be denoted by the fourth Power of *Three*. For if A be called 1; B muſt be 3; C, 9; D, 27; and E, 81; or the Biquadrate of *Three*. We have therefore a Geometrical Biquadrate of the Number 3, or the Line B, which that Number deſigns. And by a like Reaſon any Arithmetical Degree or Algebraical Power may be exhibited Geometrically. Therefore Arguments of this Sort contain nothing of Strength. I could produce many more Things to this Purpoſe, but I am weary of dwelling out of the Way any longer, upon a Thing ſo apparent.

Notwithſtanding (*n*) *Ariſtotle* pronounces Arithmetic to be more accurate than Geometry. *For Things*, ſays he, *conſiſting of fewer Principles are more accurate, than thoſe underſtood by Addition, as Arithmetic is more accurate than Geometry*. And elſewhere more expreſly. (*o*) *That Science is more accurate which conſiſts of fewer Principles, than what is only to be underſtood by Addition, as Arithmetic is more accurate than Geometry. I ſay by Addition, as Unity is a Being underſtood without Poſition, but a Point is to be underſtood only by Poſition*: Which is thus explained by *Proclus*; *Arithmetic is indeed more accurate than Geometry, for its Principles reſpect Simplicity. Unity implies no Poſition, a Point does, and a Point requiring Poſition is the Principle of Geometry, Unity of Arithmetic.* Theſe Things are neither all agreeable to the Truth nor depend upon a good Foundation. For what Science can be more accurate than Geometry? What Science can afford Principles more evident, more certain, yea I will add, more ſimple, than Geometrical

(*n*) I. Metaph. cap. 2. (*o*) I. Anal. Poſt. c. 24.

metrical Axioms, or exercifes a more ftrictly accurate Logic in drawing its Conclufions? But *Ariftotle* and *Proclus* affirm that *Unity* (they had more rightly faid Numbers) the Principle of Arithmetic, is more fimple than a *Point* which is the Principle of Geometry, or rather of Magnitude. Becaufe a Point implies Pofition, but Unity does not. *A Point*, fays *Ariftotle*, *and Unity are not to be divided, as Quantity: Unity requires no Pofition, a Point does.* But this Comparifon of a *Point* in Geometry with *Unity* in Arithmetic is of all the moft unfufferable, and derives the worft Confequences upon Mathematical Learning. For *Unity* anfwers really to fome Part of every Magnitude, but not to a *Point*: Thus if a Line be divided into fix equal Parts, as the whole Line anfwers to the Number fix, fo every fixth Part anfwers to *Unity*, but not to a *Point* which is no Part of this Right Line. A *Point* is rightly termed Indivifible, not *Unity*. (For how *ex. gr.* can $\frac{2}{6} + \frac{4}{6}$ equal *Unity*, if *Unity* be indivifible, and incompofed, and reprefent a Point) but rather only *Unity* is properly divifible, and Numbers arife from the Divifion of *Unity*. A Geometrical Point is much better compared to a *Cypher* or *Arithmetical Nothing*, which is really the Bound of every Number, coming between it and the Numbers next following, but not as a Part. A *Cypher* being added to or taken from a Number does neither encreafe nor diminifh it; from it is taken the Beginning of Computation, while itfelf is not computed; and it bears a manifeft Relation to the principal Properties of a Geometrical Point. Nor is that altogether unexceptionable, which is faid of *Pofition*; for a *Point* taken univerfally is not lefs indeterminate, and void of *Pofition*, than *Unity* taken the fame Way: But *Unity* taken particularly implies a definite *Pofition*, and all other particular Circumftances, as well as

a partia particular *Point*. Laſtly, the Accuracy of Arithmetic and Geometry is ſo far from being different that it is altogether the ſame, drawn from the ſame Principles, and employed about the ſame Things. I might here annex many Obſervations and Conſequences drawn from hence ; but

Not to be too tedious and prolix, I judge it will appear plain enough to every one who duly weighs what I have ſuggeſted, that, in reality, *Number* (at leaſt that treated of by Mathematicians) differs nothing from *continued Magnitude* it ſelf, nor ſeems to have any other Properties (Compoſition, Diviſion, Proportion, and the like) than either from, or in reſpect to it, as it repreſents, or ſupplies its Place ; nor conſequently that it is any Species of Quantity diſtinct from Magnitude, or the Object of any Science but Geometry (which is converſant about Magnitude in general) : In ſum, that Number includes in it every Conſideration pertaining to Geometry. Therefore the *Element Writer* (whatſoever *Ramus* can object, who taunts him with that Name) did not unadviſedly, in inſerting Arithmetical Speculations among the Elements of Geometry, nay rather he did great Service to the Mathematics, and merited highly in not permitting theſe Sciences to be ſeparated from one another, as if they were ſeparate in Nature, but aſſigning to Arithmetic a ſuitable Place in Geometry. (*p*)

(*p*) Qualem certè videtur antiquitùs obtinuiſſe ; ſiquidem vel ipſe magnus Orator de Geometria obiter tractans, de recepto opinor Uſu potius quam ex Ingenio ſuo dicat, *Geometriam in Numeros atque Formas eſſe diviſam*. Quintil. *T.* 10.

LECTURE

LECTURE IV.

Of the Unfitneſs of the common Diviſion of Mathematics into Speculative *and* Practical, *and of the Excellence of Mathematical* Demonſtration.

I Have now propoſed what I thought to be of Uſe concerning the Diviſion of the Mathematical Sciences; but have purpoſely omitted their Diſtribution into *Speculative* and *Practical*, as leſs juſt and neceſſary; ſince this does not ſo much intimate Sciences as different Reſpects of the ſame Science. For, in my Opinion, every Science is both Speculative and Practical: *Speculative*, as it *ſpeculates*, *i. e.* ſeeks, inveſtigates and demonſtrates Truths (or true Propoſitions) agreeable to its Object: and *Practical*, as thoſe Truths when found and demonſtrated, may be referred to Uſe, and reduced into Practice. *Ex. gr.* The *Politician* ſpeculates and infers, from well weighed Reaſons, what Form of Government, and what Laws will beſt conduce for the public Welfare: The *Moraliſt* conſiders and pronounces (*i. e.* invents and preſcribes ſome certain Theorem or univerſal Rule) what is the Duty of a good Man in ſuch and ſuch Circumſtances: The *Phyſician* examines and determines, from Reaſon or Experience, the Nature, Virtues, and Temperaments of what they call Simples, whether they be in Faculty Cool or Hot, Dry or Moiſt, Healthful or Noxious: And ſo far theſe Sciences are *Speculative*. But if any one do uſe theſe Concluſions for the directing of his Practice, and attemperate his Actions accordingly: If he manage Affairs of State according to the Preſcript of this *Political Theorem*; if he live according

ing to that *Moral Precept*; if he take or refuse such a Plant for the sake of his Health; then do these Sciences and Conclusions become Practical. And the same happens in our Case. The Geometrician demonstrates universally *That every* Triangle *is equal to one half a* Parallelogram *upon the same Base and of equal Height: That a* Cone *is equal to one third Part of a* Cylinder *upon the same Base and of equal Height.* Which Propositions and Rules being universally true, the Geometrician finds and approves by Speculation, and they may be always used for determining the Measure of any Triangular Area, or for comparing any Conical Vessel with its circumscribed Cylinder. Both these *Theorems* therefore may be called *Practical* as they relate to Use and Practice, but they would for that Reason be very unfitly divided into *Speculative* and *Practical.* Geometry is one simple Science which may be considered in two Respects, *viz.* it is stiled *Speculative* as it is true, and *Practical* as it is useful. The Absurdity then of this Division is clear. Notwithstanding I shall not very much oppose him who urges that such Geometrical Rules are more useful, which shew the Dimensions of particular Magnitudes, or are accommodated to some certain material Subject; though that perhaps may prejudice the main Science, and it would be better to find them no where, but affixed to their proper Fundamentals in Geometry, along with their Demonstrations, *i. e.* in their proper Place and native Order: But it ought not therefore to be thought that a Collection of Rules of this Sort do constitute a Part or Species of Geometry distinct from *Speculative.* Consequently *Trigonometry*, or the Doctrine concerning the Dimension of Rectangular and Spherical Triangles; *Altimetry*, which shews the Way of finding Distances; *Planimetry*, which teaches to describe and measure

measure plain Surfaces; and *Stereometry*, which compares the Measures of solid Bodies: these are not Parts of *Speculative* more than *Practical* Geometry, but belong to the same Science, which in a different Respect may be called, either *Speculative* or *Practical.*

Hitherto we have treated concerning the general Object of the Mathematical Sciences and their Division. It remains in the next Place to consider the *Mode* or *Manner* whereby they are conversant about their Object; which is certainly the same with what obtains in all other Sciences properly so called: Forasmuch as it is the Design of all Sciences to investigate the particular *Properties*, *Affections* and *Passions* of their Object together with its Essence, either as they flow immediately or mediately from it; and to shew that they do necessarily agree with it by a certain and evident *Discursus* Though as *(q) Aristotle* takes notice, in more Places than one, this is in fact performed by some more *(r) closely* and *validly*, and by others more *loosely* and *faintly*, according to the Condition of the Matter. And this kind of *Discursus* is wont to be called *(s) Demonstration.* But it is neither my Office nor Intention to handle this Matter at large, since it properly belongs to *Logic*. He therefore that would have a more intimate Knowledge of it, and desires to taste of the Original Fountains themselves, let him consult *Aristotle* its famous Inventor and Author in his Books of *Analysis*, the posterior Books especially, where he explains the Nature of Demonstration, and prefixes Laws to it. But it may suffice for my Purpose

(q) V. Metaph. cap. 2. *(r)* XI. Metaph. cap. 7.

(s) Ἀπόδειξις, so called perhaps, because the Conclusion drawn by it appears as plainly to the Understanding, as a Thing shewn by the Pointing of the Finger appears to the Sense. For δεικνύειν signifies as much as to shew by the Pointing of the Finger, (δακτυλοδεικτεῖν) Whence δάκτυλος, as it were δείκτυλος.

only

only to take Notice of his Sayings and Prescripts as they accord with the Mathematical Way of Reasoning. But if we weigh the Matter more nicely, we shall find that Demonstration agrees properly and peculiarly with these Sciences only, and cannot with equal Justice be supposed to agree with other Disciplines. Whence *Aristotle* in the Beginning of his Ethics excuses himself why he could not strictly demonstrate *moral Truths*; because the Rigour of Demonstration is only to be found in the Mathematical Sciences, and not in that Kind of Learning; alledging it to be equally out of the Way *(t) to require persuasive Arguments from a Mathematician, as Demonstrations from an Orator.* And for the same Reason he denies that *a Mathematical Exactness* should be required from a natural Philosopher: Which when that excellent Logician *Jac. Zabarella* had considered, as he somewhere testifies of himself, he diligently pursued *Euclid*'s Elements over and over, that he might the better understand and explain the Nature of Demonstration. But it will perhaps be worth the Trouble, briefly to enquire into the Causes from whence this Difference proceeds; why Demonstration which is every where found in the Mathematics, should occur so seldom, or rather never in other Disciplines. And I know no other Way by which the Nature of Mathematical Demonstration will appear more easily and clearly, than by such a Comparison. And that

I. Because we do clearly conceive, and readily obtain distinct Ideas of the Things which these Sciences contemplate; they being Things the most simple and common, such as lie exposed to Senses, capable to be represented by the most familiar Examples, and therefore most easy to be understood, as containing in them nothing abstruse, intricate or unusual. What *ex. gr.* is a *Right Line?* What,

(t) I. Metaph. cap. ult.

a *plain*

a *plain Superficies*, a *Triangle*, a *Square*, a *Circle*, a *Pyramid*, a *Cube*, a *Sphere?* These are Things which we perceive clearly and distinctly, where very few Things are required, and which may be expressed in the fewest Terms, and represented by the clearest Examples. Whence it comes to pass that concerning Things so evidently and accurately perceptible it is no hard Matter to demonstrate some Truths, *viz.* such as agree with these Ideas, or are immediately inferred from them. But in other Sciences it generally falls out otherwise, because the Things which they consider are of a Nature more recondite and abstracted from the Senses, more intricate and complex, and more dark and confused to the Apprehension. *Ex. gr.* It is hard to imagine distinctly, and define exactly what is *Colour* in *Physics*, *Happiness* in *Ethics*, or the *Law of Nations* in *Politics*, because we have seldom any clear Notion of these Things; and if we have, it is so complex, that perhaps no two Persons have entirely the same, or we are not able to make it out to those with whom we converse. Whence it falls out, that there are almost as many different Conceptions and Explications of such Things, as there are Authors and Interpreters.

II. A second Reason is, because Mathematicians do use such Words as make their Definitions perspicuous, and without the least Ambiguity: or to speak more fully, they express their Conceptions with more adequate Terms, such as are of a certain and invariable Signification; so that, as soon as ever the Term for the Thing proposed is heard, the Conception answering to it immediately occurs to the Mind. Nor does there arise any Doubt or Controversy, about whatsoever is affirmed or denied of such Things, but every Thing apparently tends to the Certitude of the Propositions.

Propoſitions. But in other Diſciplines, as the Obſcurity, Perplexity, and Confuſion of the Notions, ſo alſo the Ambiguity and Inconſtancy of the Words by which thoſe Notions are ſignified, do neceſſarily produce much Darkneſs and Uncertainty in their Concluſions. For in general, they neglect the Definition of their Terms, oftentimes admit Speeches improper and metaphorical, and accept the ſame Word in different Senſes; at leaſt different Authors do variouſly take and differently deſcribe one and the ſame Thing, every one accommodating his Concluſions to his own Signification or Deſcription: From whence there neceſſarily ariſes not only an Uncertainty, but alſo a Contrariety of their Propoſitions; the Contemplation of the Truth degenerating into Diſputation, and that Diſputation ending in mere Logomachy; the principal Part of the Controverſy being ſpent in the indefinite Signification of the Terms. And the Definitions and Deſcriptions, which they bring, do not only for the moſt Part leave theſe Faults unremedied, but do very often involve the Queſtion in Obſcurities and Trifles. For what Light can be had from ſuch Definitions as theſe? *Motion is the Action of a Being in Power, as it is in Power. Light is the Action of a Thing perſpicuous, as it is perſpicuous. The Soul is mere Action or Perfection*, or *it is Number moving itſelf.* Which Explications do rather ſerve to perplex and confound, than enlighten or inſtruct us. So that that jeſting Definition of a Man, which was uſed by *Democritus*, is better and more uſeful than theſe: *A Man is what all of us know.* In ſhort, if the Matter of the Propoſitions to be demonſtrated which are Words, (*i. e.* the Symbols of the Things conceived in the Mind) have no certain Signification, it will be impoſſible to come at any Certainty concerning the Truth of the Propoſitions.

III. A

III. A third Reaſon why Demonſtration is ſo peculiar to Mathematicians is, becauſe they admit no Principles or Axioms which are not univerſally true, which are not proved by a continued Induction, not granted by common Suffrage, and laſtly which are not ſupported by their own Strength, and conſpicuous from their own Light; ſo that what Concluſions are drawn from hence do neceſſarily compel the Aſſent of the Hearer. For who does not eaſily underſtand ſuch Propoſitions as theſe as ſoon as he hears them; and readily acknowledge them as Things moſt true, moſt plain, and agreeable to conſtant Experience? *viz. That Things equal to the ſame Third are equal to one another: That if equal Magnitudes be added to or taken from equal Magnitudes, the Sums or Remainders will be equal: That the Whole is greater than its Part, &c.* which are Truths that ſuffer no Exception, and require no Proof or further Explication. But in other Diſciplines, the Principles on which the Superſtructure is to be raiſed, either for the moſt part may be weakened, as to their Univerſality, by contrary Inſtances, and conſequently require ſome Exceptions, Limitations, or Diſtinctions, to avoid the Imputation of Falſity; or elſe they are only admitted precariouſly, and do not force the Aſſent of the Hearer; or laſtly, they require farther Confirmation, or a more prolix Explication; whence it happens, that no Concluſion, which is univerſally true, evident, indubitable and irrefragable can be inferred from them, nor can any ſtable irreſiſtible Demonſtration be erected upon Foundations ſo wavering and inconſtant. For what Certainty, pray, can be deduced from ſuch Principles as theſe? *Nature does nothing in vain: All Things aim at good: Nothing gives what it has not: and the like.* How many contradictory Propoſitions by uſing a little Subtilty, both may

and

and are wont to be inferred from theſe by ſuch as delight in Querks? For extricating and reconciling which to one another, they are forced to invent ſuch a vaſt Number of little Diſtinctions, as is indeed wonderful; from whence reſults much Diſputation, but no Demonſtration.

IV. Like to the laſt is a fourth Reaſon, *viz.* That Mathematicians admit no *Poſtulates*, nor ſuppoſe any *Hypotheſes* but ſuch as are evidently poſſible, and moſt eaſy to the Imagination: ſuch as according to *Proclus*, are *Eaſy*, *Helpful*, *Simple* and *Ready:* Such as none can refuſe to grant howſoever prejudiced, unlearned, and untractable. *Ex. gr.* When 'tis ſuppoſed or required *that a Right Line may be either drawn, or conceived to be drawn through any two Parts aſſignable: That aſſuming any Point as a Center, the Circumference of a Circle may either paſs or be underſtood to paſs through any other given Point: That any Body may be cut with a Plane: That a Semicircle may be turned about its Axis.* Who will deny that theſe Things may be done or conceived to be done; or object againſt any one for ſuppoſing Things ſo evidently poſſible: Things which he ſees and experiences to be done daily? But in other Sciences the Matter is far otherwiſe. Theſe ſeem not any Way to explain the Cauſes of Things, nor do their Profeſſors ſtick at coining *Hypotheſes* ſuitable to their Arguments, and requiring *Poſtulata* which are altogether arbitrary, hard to be digeſted, and monſtrouſly immodeſt: Things which are not only difficult to be believed, but oftentimes hard to be conceived. As *ex. gr.* When in Phyſics, it is required to be granted for the Explication of Viſion, *That I don't know what kind of intentional Species are diſperſed around from every Appearance of the viſible Object.* Or according to others, *That certain corporeal Effluvia, or thin Skins, peeled from the*

the Thing objected, more fine than Thought itself, are every where carried in a direct Course towards whatsoever is placed in View: Or lastly, which is the Opinion of some, *That certain Motions, Actions, or Endeavours are directed and derived with the utmost Ease and Speed from every Point of the illuminating or illuminated Object to every Point of the circumscribed Medium.* No Body surely is so simple or credulous, as immediately to agree or force himself to acquiesce with any of these *Hypotheses* (though ingeniously devised) not only as true, but as at all possible, or in any Degree probable; because so many Difficulties occur to prevent or destroy his Faith, who does but a little attend to them. And who would not make him ashamed of his Unreasonableness that has the Forehead obstinately to require many such Things granted him? At least, who can imagine that a solid Demonstration can stand upon so loose and sandy a Foundation?

V. Moreover fifthly Mathematicians being a Sort of Men, in the highest Degree modest, and patient of Labour, do not only go upon Principles *(u)* manifestly true, and assume such Hypotheses as are apparently possible, but do beyond Measure affect a strict Paucity in both. They had rather take any Pains to demonstrate their Assertions, than beg the Assent *gratis*, or make too free with the Hearers Liberality. They desire that the Evidence and Validity of their Conclusions may be owing to the Force of their proper Reasons, and not to another's Easiness. They esteem it worth all their Diligence and Pains to grow exorbitantly rich out of a small Stock, to encrease to an immense Height of Knowledge from a little Root, and to build a vast, and no

(u) Arist. I. Post. cap. 25.

leſs firm, Structure upon a narrow Foundation. They therefore uſe a great deal of Labour and tedious Prolixity in deducing ſome Propoſitions, otherwiſe moſt eaſy, becauſe they hate a Multiplicity of Poſtulates and Axioms. Upon which Account that great (*v*) Cenſurer (or rather Carper) *Ramus* ſharply reproves *Euclid*, becauſe he undertook to demonſtrate many Propoſitions, which in his Opinion were ſufficiently evident from their own Light, and therefore ſhould have been paſſed by undemonſtrated, and been reckoned among the Number of Axioms. But he might as well have gone through the whole Troop of ancient Geometricians, who were all guilty of the ſame Fault; and among them accuſe the *divine Archimedes* himſelf, becauſe he refuſed the Liberty of aſſuming more Axioms or Poſtulates than were neceſſary; and, arrogating ſuch a Licence to himſelf, rather choſe to propoſe and demonſtrate his admirable Theorems with ſomething more of Intricacy and Prolixity, which might have been done otherwiſe, with more Shortneſs and Perſpicuity. But in my Thoughts their Method ſeems by no means Blame-worthy, but ought rather to be very much commended and embraced. For no Diligence or Solicitude ſhould be thought too much, which is ſpent in eſtabliſhing the firſt Principles of Sciences. It is far better that many Demonſtrations be redundant, than for one to ſeem defective. Every Handle for cavilling or refuſing the Aſſent to the Principle of any Argument as uncertain or leſs notorious is to be taken away from *Epicurean* Diſpoſitions. All Suſpicion, all Dread, all Heſitation is to be removed from theſe Diſciplines, as much as may be. Nor is the Faith of Learners to be put to too much Trial, nor

(*v*) Schol. Mathem. Lib. 3.

their

their Minds too far ſtrained and blunted with the Multitude of Hypotheſes, nor too much accuſtomed to a raſh Preſumption. Howſoever it may not be either unprofitable or unpleaſant to ſhew the Coherence and Affinity of the firſt Propoſitions one with another by a Syllogiſtical Operation: And as it is more great and glorious to ſubdue an Enemy with a ſmall Force, ſo to erect innumerable Truths upon a few Principles procures more Admiration, and merits a greater Praiſe to conquering Reaſon. Wherefore neither do I think that curious, but ingenious, Sedulity of the great *Apollonius* at all to be blamed, much leſs with ſome to be accuſed of Ambition or Madneſs, who attempted to demonſtrate that famous Axiom *of the Equality of Things equal to the ſame third.* Nor do I carp at the needleſs Study of *Regiomontanus*, who, as it is ſaid, undertook to deduce the firſt Rules of vulgar Arithmetic from *Euclid*'s Elements. In Imitation of whom, one of our own Philoſophers, well known to all, attempted the Demonſtration of that moſt remarkable Principle, *That the Whole is greater than its Part.*

But however what I purpoſed to ſhew appears from what has been ſaid, it is plain, that where ſo much Labour is taken, and ſuch Care uſed to prevent any Propoſition from aſpiring at the Dignity of an Axiom, and the Number of Hypotheſes from encreaſing to a Multitude; there it can be no Wonder, if every Concluſion be moſt validly demonſtrated. But in other Kinds of Learning, the Reaſon and Method of Proceeding is different. In thoſe do grow an infinite Crop of Axioms, which, if tranſcribed, would make well repleniſhed Store-houſes of Volumes. Every probable Propoſition aſpires at the Degree of an Axiom; and however it be aſſumed *gratis*, it works

all

all that is requisite for the Proof of a Conclusion. And for the Dispatch of every Question, or the Explication of a Phænomenon, a new and distinct Hypothesis is invented. From whence it happens that in what is called and accounted the same Science are found Hypotheses without Number; even as many as there are Subjects to be handled, which not only overcome the Faith of the Hearers, but confound the Memory itself; so that they can scarce by any Means be made consistent, nay do often oppose and contradict one another. And every one sees what a System of Demonstrations must proceed from hence.

VI. But again sixthly, the *Generations* of Magnitudes, by which Mathematicians do sometimes define them, and deduce their Properties are most easily perceived by the Imagination as highly possible and to the utmost Degree reasonable. *Ex. gr.* When a Circle is described from the carrying about of a Right Line one of whose Extremes is fixed; a *Cone* is formed from the Rotation of a Rectangular Triangle about one of its immoveable Legs; a *Sphere* is generated from the turning of a Semi-circle about its Diameter, as an Axis: In like manner, when a *Right Line* is made from the shortest direct Motion of a Point; a *Parallelogram* from the transverse Passage of a Right Line keeping a perpetual Parallelism through the same Plane; a *Prism* or *Cylinder* from the like parallel Transit of a Rectilineal Plane Figure or a Circle; when a *Spiral* and *Quadratrix* (two *Curve Lines*) are described from a twofold uniform Motion, the one right or parallel, the other circular; a *Parabola* from a twofold Motion, the one uniform, and the other uniformly accelerated. Now no Body, who will but attend a little can deny, or in the least doubt, but such Motions may be performed; and that such Effects must necessarily

result

result from them. Our Understandings cannot but clearly perceive what will follow from supposing such Generations. Therefore the Properties of Magnitudes may be easily drawn and demonstrated from such Causes.

But the Production of natural or other Things are not so manifest; neither can the Properties of the Effects proceeding from any such supposed Causes be thus deduced. *Ex. gr.* Supposing such a Complexion or Temperament of elementary Things, or so great a scorching of Sulphur, or that the Rotation of some subtle Matter prevails over its direct Passage; who dare boldly and peremptorily assert that such an Appearance will necessarily be produced to the Sight as is wont to constitute or accompany a *Red Colour?* Consequently none can demonstrate the Passions and Affections of Things from such feigned Generations.

VII. Hither also we may refer, seventhly, the accurate *Order* in which Mathematicians handle their Subjects, investigate their Truths and dispose their Propositions. (*w*) *Aristotle* takes Notice that the *Order* used amongst Mathematicians *is helpful to the Memory*; and consequently to the reasoning Faculty. In the *Order* of the Mathematics, it may be especially observed, that those first self-evident Propositions which are requisite for the Demonstration of others, *viz. Definitions*, *Axioms*, and *Postulates*, are wont to be carefully ranged in the Front, the Nature of our Way of Arguing so requiring: Next to these are placed the more simple Propositions which are immediately deduced from the former; then follow those that are drawn from these latter, and thus an indissoluble Chain of Arguments is carried on in an uninterrupted Series, the

(*w*) Tract. de Memoria & Reminisc. cap. 2.

the latter ſtill receiving Light and Strength from the former. Whence it alſo happens, that the Original of every Propoſition may be derived even from its firſt Principles, its Dependance upon and Connection with them perceived, and conſequently its Verity diſcovered by a certain and infallible Ratiocination. Again we may obſerve with the Mathematicians, that if any Propoſitions found and demonſtrated be of more remarkable Note or univerſal Nature, if they excel either in Point of Elegance or Uſefulneſs, theſe being approved and eſtabliſhed by the Examination of ſkilful Perſons are reſerved as a Treaſure, and laid up in a kind of publick Storehouſe, from whence they may be drawn forth, as Uſe ſhall require, to ſerve for the Inveſtigation and Demonſtration of others. Of which Kind are moſt of the Propoſitions of the ancient Geometricians, which do exhibit the particular Properties of certain Magnitudes more remarkably obvious to the Mind; as the *Elements* of *Euclid*, the *Spherics* of *Theodoſius*, the *Conics* of *Apollonius*, *Archimedes* of the *Sphere* and *Cylinder*, with others. Theſe are as ſo many Seminaries or Storehouſes of Geometrical Truths upon various Subjects, from whence innumerable Concluſions are eaſily deduced; or as ſo many Principles leading to the Invention and Probation of almoſt all other Propoſitions; or laſtly, as ſo many *Criteria* or Touchſtones by which other Truths are to be tried and examined.

In other Diſciplines it for the moſt part falls out otherwiſe. For if you ſeek for Principles you will no where find them, or at leaſt you will find them mingled and confounded with their Concluſions without Diſtinction; and like the Ships of *Æneas* diſperſed through the wide Ocean; which muſt needs very much diſturb and impede the

the Progreſs of the Student: For, as (*x*) *Proclus* ſays, *The mingling of Principles hinders all Knowledge, and compares together Things that have no Relation to one another.* Nor will you obſerve in them any Order, or almoſt any Connection of the Propoſitions themſelves; ſo that you cannot trace the Origin of any particular Propoſition whatſoever to its firſt Principles, nor can it certainly appear to you whether it is true or falſe; but according to the Saying of *Hierocles*, *the Miſplacing of Things deceives and perverts the Judgment.* By Reaſon of which, no Principles are at Liberty to be known by all or confirmed by the common Suffrage, to which every Diſcurſus is to be referred, from which the Invention of Theorems and Reſolution of Queſtions is to be fetched, and laſtly by which the Truth of Propoſitions is to be examined.

VIII. Eighthly and laſtly; It may be obſerved of Mathematicians that they only meddle with ſuch Things as are certain, paſſing by thoſe that are doubtful and unknown. They profeſs not to know all Things, neither do they affect to ſpeak of all Things. What they know to be true, and can make good by invincible Arguments, that they publiſh and inſert among their Theorems. Of other Things they are ſilent and paſs no Judgment at all, chuſing rather to acknowledge their Ignorance, than affirm any Thing raſhly. They affirm nothing among their Arguments or Aſſertions which is not moſt manifeſtly known and examined with the utmoſt Rigour, rejecting all probable Conjectures and little Witticiſms. They ſubmit nothing to Authority, indulge no Affection, deteſt the Subterfuges of Words, and declare their Sentiments, as in a Court of Judicature, *without Paſſion*, *without Apology*; knowing that their Rea-

(*w*) Lib. 2. pag. 22.

ſons,

ſons, as (*x*) *Seneca* teſtifies of them, are not brought *to perſuade, but to compel.* And by this means they preſerve their Sciences pure and free from the leaſt Stain either of Error or Doubt. In others, which are called Sciences, Things doubtful are promiſcuouſly mingled with Things certain, Things taken upon Preſumption with Things found by Experiment, Things obſcure with ſuch as are manifeſt, and true Things with falſe. Their Profeſſors propoſe all Things to themſelves to be examined, explained, and decided, according to what they know and what they do not know: And when they cannot bring certain Reaſons, they produce any Kind of Conjecture, diſguiſed under beautiful Colours, oftner divining than demonſtrating. In fine, they plead with all their Eloquence, as for their Properties; and what they can't prove, they endeavour to perſuade.

But I am afraid you will begin to grow weary with the Length and Prolixity of this Compariſon. From whence notwithſtanding it may in ſome Sort appear what Method of *Demonſtration* is uſed by Mathematicians; which is ſuch, that they only take thoſe Things into Conſideration, of which they have clear and diſtinct Ideas, deſigning them by proper, adequate and invariable Names, and premiſing only a few Axioms which are moſt noted and certain to inveſtigate their Affections and draw Concluſions from them, and agreeably laying down a very few Hypotheſes, ſuch as are in the higheſt Degree conſonant to Reaſon and not to be denied by any one in his right Mind. In like manner they aſſign Generations or Cauſes eaſy to be underſtood and readily admitted by all; they preſerve a moſt accurate Order, every Propoſition immediately following from what is ſuppoſed and

(*x*) Sen. I. Qu. Nat.

proved

proved before, and reject all Things howſoever ſpecious and probable which cannot be inferred and deduced after the ſame manner.

And this Kind of Argumentation is properly *Demonſtrative*, and produces the moſt certain Knowledge which the Mind of Man is capable of: Such as none can either deny or doubt. For if the Premiſes be ſuch as no Body can contradict or make the leaſt Scruple of, and if the Method of drawing the Concluſion be alſo lawful, ſuited according to the infallible Rules of *Logic*; what can hinder the Inferences from being neceſſarily true, the *Diſcurſus* from being juſtly called *Demonſtration*, and its *Effects*, (*i. e.* the habitual Knowledge remaining in the Mind) to merit the Name of *Science?* But yet ſome both have been, and ſtill are ſo ſubtle as to deny that the Mathematics are truly Sciences, and that they afford true *Demonſtrations:* whoſe Reaſons we will conſider in the following Lecture.

LECTURE V.

Containing Anſwers to the Objections which are uſually brought againſt Mathematical Demonſtration.

HAVING gone thorough what I had to ſay concerning the *Object* and *Diviſion* of the Mathematics, I began in my laſt Lecture to ſpeak of the Mode or Manner whereby they are converſant about their Object. To illuſtrate which in ſome meaſure I thought it would not be amiſs to underſake a Compariſon of theſe with other Diſciplines. And hence I have not obſcurely inſinuated from what

what Fountains the Efficacy of a Mathematical Discursus flows, asserting its Validity *by way of Confirmation.* It now remains on the other Hand to treat *by way of Confutation, i. e.* to bear against the Assaults, oppose the Cavils, and remove the Trifles of such as impugn the Certitude and Excellence of the Mathematical Way of Reasoning.

(y) Aristotle stiles the Mathematics the most *Accurate Sciences.* He ascribes to them an *Exact Method* as their peculiar, and every where intimates and supposes the like; so that I do not doubt but he had a View chiefly to these, when he formed the Doctrine of Demonstration which he first delivered: at least he drew most of his Examples hence, for its Illustration and Confirmation. Nevertheless there formerly have been such, and that not long ago, (and what is most to be wondred at, among the *Peripatetics* themselves who subscribe to the *Aristotelian* Philosophy, and would be thought to have drawn their Opinions from *Aristotle* himself, however opposite he be to their Sentiments) who have not stuck to deny the Mathematics to be truly Sciences, or that they afford true Demonstrations. Among the Antients indeed, besides the *Pyrrhonians* and the *Ephectici* (who equally exploded all Science, and hardly would be brought to affirm, nay feared not flatly to deny that there could be any *Certainty* in any Thing) besides these, I say, the *Epicureans*, a Sect especially spiteful against the Mathematicians, endeavoured to overthrow their Principles, and weaken their Demonstrations: *Posidonius* is said to have writ a whole Volume in Confutation of one *(z) Zeno* a *Sidonian* of this Sect. And some of the Moderns tread in the same Footsteps.

(y) II. de Cœlo cap. 7. Metap. I. cap. ult. *(z)* Proclus, p. 55.

Though

Though I think it not worth the while to ſpend much Subtilty in refuting the Cavils of thoſe who ſport with other Men's Arguments and put no Confidence in their own (who are truly Heretics, or Perſons ſelf-condemned) yet however I will examine one or two of their principal Reaſons. *Firſt* then they urge that there can be no Demonſtration, but what proceeds from Principles univerſally true; which kind of Principles, as *Ariſtotle* himſelf teſtifies, can be known no otherwiſe than by an Induction of Particulars. But the univerſal Truth of Propoſitions cannot be gathered by Induction, both becauſe all the Particulars cannot be reckoned over (as being infinite or indefinite in Number) and becauſe Induction depends upon a Senſe, which in moſt Caſes is deceitful and liable to Error. Therefore there is no firm Foundation at all for Demonſtration. To this principal Argument (which yet ſtrikes not againſt the Certitude of the Mathematics only, but of all Science in general) I anſwer by aſking this ſerious Queſtion of the Objectors, and preſſing it home to their Conſciences; whether they cannot clearly perceive, and are not moſt fully perſuaded, *that if equal Quantities be ſubtracted from equal Quantities, the Remainders will be equal.* If they ſay, they can't firmly aſſent to the Truth of this Propoſition, but are doubtful, and afraid of being deceived by truſting to it, they muſt ſeem to all, and even to themſelves, whether they will or no, as Fools or Madmen. But if they cannot refuſe or avoid giving their Aſſent to this Truth, then they muſt needs have a certain Knowledge of it; for what elſe ſignifies a Certainty of Knowledge, but that the Thing known ſeems evidently true to the Mind of the Knower, ſo that all dread of the contrary is entirely excluded? It may be, you will enquire by what Means this Certitude comes, or how

how it is gotten. I anſwer, by whatſoever Way the certain Knowledge of Axioms is acquired, whether by Induction and manifold Experience, or it ariſes from the natural Notions of the Mind, or whatſoever other Way it is attained; it is ſufficient that we are intimately conſcious of it, and find it impreſſed upon the Mind in an indelible Character: For we are not diſputing about the manner of acquiring Knowledge, or the Origin of Certitude; but about the Thing itſelf, whether or no it be had. Perhaps I am ignorant of the Manner of perceiving by my Senſes, but do I not therefore ſee what is before mine Eyes? Do not I hear what ſtrikes my Ears, nor touch what is in my Hands? So certain am I of the Truth of this Propoſition; certain, I ſay, by the irrefragable Teſtimony of my own Breaſt: and in like manner you are alſo certain, whatever you may pretend to the contrary: *(a) It does not follow* (ſays *Ariſtotle*) *that what a Man ſays, he alſo thinks:* But how, or by what Means this *Certainty* comes is not equally known, nor does it matter much whether it be known or no. The certain Knowledge of the Thing may however be ſome Diſcovery, while we are enquiring and contending about the Manner of attaining that *Certainty.*

Nevertheleſs in ſome Sort to gratify theſe Objectors Importunity, let us conſider a little the Manner of arriving at this *Certainty.* About which in the firſt Place, I will affirm nothing of *Connate Notions*, a Queſtion that would require a larger Diſſertation, and carry me farther from my Deſign, than I am willing to go: I only take Notice that if it be true which many Philoſophers of no ſmall Note do earneſtly contend for,

(a) Ariſt. adv. Heraclit. in Met.

(*viz.* the *Platonists* and *Stoicks*) that ſuch natural Thoughts, original Notions, or, as (*b*) *Maximus Tyrius* calls them, *Seeds of Truth* are implanted in our Minds by Nature; againſt whoſe Light we cannot ſhut our Eyes, nor reſiſt their Force: I ſay, if this be ſuppoſed, then the Thing is done, and the Method whereby we arrive at *Certainty* will eaſily appear, ſince all the *Certainty* we have is by the infallible Guide and Inſtinct of Nature alone: The Author of our Being gives us the Principles of Knowledge all at once, as ſoon as we exiſt; ſo that we yield our Aſſent to theſe *Primary Notions* no otherwiſe than as a Stone drops to the Ground, as the Sun darts forth its Light, and the Fire feeds upon its Fewel. But paſſing by this Method of attaining *Certainty*, let us proceed to others, if any there be.

The *Senſe* then, when right and perfect, as it is naturally in moſt Men of a ſound Conſtitution, diſcerns many Objects *certainly*. *Ex. gr.* ſuch as theſe, *The Sun now ſhines*; *This Man is ſtanding by*: to doubt which would rather ſeem the Part of an impertinent Trifler than a ſage Philoſopher; of one playing both with himſelf and others, or of one who both wrongs his own Conſcience and oppoſes the Authority of all beſides (for every one gives a moſt firm Aſſent, and full Acquieſcence of Mind to the Perceptions of *Senſe*); nay I may ſay of one unjuſt and ungrateful to Nature, derogating either from its Goodneſs or Power; as if it either would not, or could not make us capable of certainly comprehending the Truth, but had rather keep us involved in perpetual Darkneſs, Uncertainty and Error. *Ariſtotle* on the contrary will have it to be the Property of *Senſe*, *That it is*

(*b*) Diſſert. 28.

always

always true, and is inherent to all living Creatures (c). Neverthelefs I cannot wholly deny, but *Senfe* is fometimes deceitful and the Caufe of falfe Judgment (indeed fometimes neceffarily and inevitably), when it is either ill difpofed and contrary to Nature, or when the Objects are not fuitably reprefented. But for a Perfon ferioufly to grant, that the *Senfe* never certainly attains its End, that it never exhibits to the Mind the Species of the Things objected, fo as to take away all Poffibility of judging falfly by relying upon its Teftimony; What is this, but as was juft now faid, to be gravely mad, to offer Violence to ourfelves, and difparage our Nature? He argues much better in (d) *Cicero*, who fays, *The Judgments of the Senfes are fo clear and certain, that were it in our Choice, and God demanded of us whether we were content with Senfes perfect and uncorrupt, or we required fomething better, I can't fee what we can feek farther.* ——*The greateft Truth is in the Senfes, when they are found and perfect, and all Obftacles and Impediments removed out of the Way.* To which Sentiment every one agrees in Thoughts, whatfoever he may profefs in Words.

But you will fay, How fhall I know, how fhall I diftinguifh whether all Things be rightly fuited for *Senfation* or no? I anfwer, there is no need for you to know or diftinguifh thefe (e) Things, fince you will be neceffarily convinced by the Evidence of the Thing itfelf, and forced to yield your Affent whether you will or no, by the Impulfe of Nature. But you will return, I am oftentimes deceived by my Senfes; (f) as when I fenfibly

(c) Lib. 3. de Anima. cap. 3.

(d) In Lucullo.

(e) Ἀεὶ γάρ ἐστιν ἐνιστῆναι πρὸς τὸν ἔξω λόγον· ἀλλὰ πρὸς τὸν ἔσω λόγον οὐκ ἀεί. I. Poft. cap. 10.

(f) Ἡ γλῶττα τέτω φιλονεικεῖ κατ' Εὐριπίδην, ἡ φρὴν οὐδαμῶς οὐδ' ἡ ψυχή.

perceive

perceive that the Colours of the Rainbow are real, that an Oar is bent in the Water, that the Sun is a little Thing nigh at hand, and that a Square Figure placed at a Diſtance is round. Be it ſo, notwithſtanding abſolutely ſpeaking you have a right Perception of ſuch Things, *viz.* that the Rainbow appears, that an Oar is in the Water, that the Sun ſhines upon you, and that a Thing appears round; but it does not belong to *Senſe*, but to *Reaſon*, to diſcern the relative Determinations of Magnitude, Diſtance and Figure: Your Error therefore in theſe Things, whatſoever it be, ought to be imputed to this, and not to that. I might explain theſe Things better, and more fully, but I am unwilling to immerſe my ſelf deeper, and wander farther from my Purpoſe in a Queſtion altogether Philoſophical. Let it ſuffice that it may be taken as a fixed and eſtabliſhed Truth, a Truth granted and ſincerely embraced on all Hands, that ſome Things, though not all, are perceived and judged of rightly by *Senſe*.

But what if I aſſert, that the *Mind* of Man, if rightly diſpoſed (and not out of Tune, as in Ideots and Mad People), is by its native Faculty able to diſcern *univerſal* Propoſitions, in the ſame manner, as the *Senſe* does *particular* ones? *i. e.* as the Truth of theſe Propoſitions, *Socrates exiſts*, *An Eagle flies*, *Bucephalus runs*, is immediately perceived and judged of by the Senſe; ſo theſe, *Contradictory Propoſitions cannot be both true*, *What begins to exiſt has its Riſe from another*; *Action argues that a Thing exiſts*, (or as it is vulgarly expreſſed, *A Thing that is not*, *acts not*) and ſuch like Propoſitions, which the *Mind* directly contemplates, and finds to be true by its native Force, without any previous Notion or applied Reaſoning: Which Method of attaining Truth is by a peculiar Name ſtiled *Intellection*, and the Faculty of attaining it the

the *Intellect*. And what hinders but the Principles of Mathematical Demonſtration may be perceived by ſuch a Faculty? But you will ſay, *Ariſtotle* teaches, that the Truth of all *univerſal* Propoſitions, even of *firſt Principles* themſelves are no otherwiſe had than from Induction. For thus he, *(g) It is manifeſt that firſt Principles are known to us by Induction; for the Senſe operates thus univerſally.* And again more expreſly in his (*h*) *Ethics to Nicomachus, There are ſome Principles from whence a Ratiocination proceeds, of which there is no Ratiocination; theſe are therefore had by Induction.* To which agree thoſe Expreſſions taken from the ſame Author, *That nothing is in the Intellect which was not firſt in the Senſe. The Intellect is as a ſmooth or unwritten Table.* To which may be referred ſuch Sayings as theſe found in him, *(i) Nothing can be known without Imagination. He that has no Senſation can neither learn nor know any Thing.* From which it appears that according to *Ariſtotle*, the Principles of all Science depend wholly upon the Teſtimony of the Senſes and particular Experiments: Which, if granted to be true, then ſcarce any human Reaſon can be ſuppoſed to come up to ſtrict Certainty, or even ariſe above a probable Conjecture. But where any Propoſition is found agreeable to conſtant Experience, eſpecially where it ſeems not to be converſant about the Accidents of Things, but pertains to their principal Properties and intimate Conſtitution, it will at leaſt be moſt ſafe and prudent to yield a ready Aſſent to it. For as we are juſtly accuſed of a raſh Temerity, by ſuffering ourſelves to be ſo much as once deceived by our Faith, ſo are we guilty of the greateſt Imprudence, if we ſhew the leaſt Diſtruſt, and

(g) II. Anal. Poſt. cap. ult. *(h)* Lib. VI. cap. 3.
(i) Lib. de Mem. c. 1. Lib. III. de Anima, c. 8.

do

do not yield our stedfast Assent and obstinately adhere, when we still find our Expectations most accurately answered, after a thousand Researches; and especially when we have the constant Agreement of Nature to confirm our Assent, and the immutable Wisdom of the first Cause forming all Things according to simple Ideas, and directing them to certain Ends: Which Consideration alone is almost sufficient to make us look upon any Proposition confirmed with frequent Experiments, as universally true, and not suspect that Nature is inconstant, and the great Author of the Universe unlike himself. Nay sometimes, from the Constancy of Nature, we may prudently infer an universal Proposition even by one Experiment alone, as (*k*) *Aristotle* observes and confirms by a most apposite Instance. *For might we* (says he) *discern some Things with our Eyes, all Doubt would be taken away; not that to perceive a Thing with the Eyes is to know it, but because the Conformity of the whole Kind arises from the Sense of Seeing. Thus could we discern the very small Pores of Glass, and the Light passing through them, it would be manifest to us why Glass is transparent, because seeing the like in different Glass, we would immediately conclude the same of all.* Whence, to apply these Things to our Purpose, he that withholds his Assent from the Principles of Mathematics, even in this Respect, cannot avoid the Imputation of extream Folly and Madness: And surely there is no farther need of any Thing to demonstrate the Efficacy of a Mathematical Discursus, than the Conviction of all but Fools and Madmen.

But setting aside all Authority, after a due Examination, we have no Reason to own, that the Principles of Mathematics depend only upon In-

(*k*) I. Post Anal. c. 25.

duction

duction or the conſtant Teſtimony of *Senſe.* For firſt it may be noted, that if we aſk any one, why he believes any Mathematical Axiom to be true, I imagine he will not anſwer, becauſe he has often ſeen and obſerved it to have happened ſo; but he will profeſs himſelf ignorant of the Cauſe why he believes it, and yet that he firmly does believe it: Which is a plain Diſcovery that the Aſſent given to the Mathematical Axioms is ſome other Way derived than from the Senſe. *Secondly*, It may be noted, that moſt Things in Mathematics, though the Occaſion of contemplating them be taken from *Senſe*, yet do not immediately and directly occur to the *Senſes*, but their Exiſtence and Quality is inferred and underſtood from the *Reaſon* alone. For who did ever ſee or perceive by the Senſe an *exact Right Line* or a *perfect Circle?* Who at any time has had the Senſe of any two Things compleatly agreeable or equal to one another? So far are we from finding the Attributes of theſe Things by Senſe, or gathering the univerſal Propoſitions from thence wherein the Attributes are annexed to the Things. By Senſation indeed (*i. e.* by one, not many) may be deduced the Poſſibility of Mathematical Hypotheſes: Thus *ex. gr.* we know that a Right Line can be drawn between two aſſigned Points; becauſe we perceive by the Senſe, how a Progreſs may be made from one Point to another, wherein if there be any Unevenneſs or Deflection, it can be ſo far rectified by the Hand as to make a Line *ſenſibly Right*; from whence we infer by our Reaſon, there being no Repugnance on the Part of the Thing, that all other Roughneſs and Exorbitances may be pared off and corrected, and ſo the Line become *perfectly Right*. And by the ſame Reaſon, one ſenſible Obſervation alone may ſufficiently atteſt that every Magnitude treated of by Mathematicians is capable

capable of a real Exiſtence; and there is no need of a long Day to teach, but one only Diſcovery of Senſe will abundantly evince, that all Mathematical Hypotheſes are poſſible, that Magnitudes can be compoſed, divided, moved, fill Space, *&c.*

And here by the Way we may take notice of their Opinion who will have Mathematical Figures to have no other Exiſtence in the Nature of Things than in the Mind alone. And it is wonderful to me that this Opinion ſhould be embraced by Perſons, who are otherwiſe moſt excellently ſkilled in the Mathematics: Among whom we may reckon (*l*) *Blancanus*, whoſe Words are theſe; *Though Mathematical Beings have no real Exiſtence, yet becauſe their Ideas do exiſt both in the Divine and Human Mind, as the moſt exact Types of Things, therefore the Mathematician treats of thoſe Ideas which of themſelves are primarily intended, and are true Beings.* And of the ſame Sentiment is (*m*) *Voſſius. There is not any Sphere* (ſays he) *in the Nature of Things that only touches in a Point*; *for it always with ſome Part of its Superfice touches the ſubjected Plane in a Line, as* (*n*) *Ariſtotle ſhews Protagoras to have objected againſt the Geometricians.* Which Sentiment notwithſtanding is abſolutely falſe, and eaſy to be refuted from the foregoing *Diſcurſus*, and what is moſt oppoſite to it ſeems, in my Opinion, to be moſt true; *viz.* That all imaginable Geometrical Figures are really inherent in every Particle of Matter, I ſay really inherent in Fact and to the utmoſt Perfection, though not apparent to the Senſe; juſt as the Effigies of *Cæſar* lies hid under the unhewn Marble, and is no new Thing made by the Statuary, but only is diſcovered and brought to Sight by his Work-

(*l*) Libro de Natura Mathem. p. 7. (*m*) Voſſius de Mathem. p. 4. (*n*) I. Metaph. cap. 2.

Workmanſhip, *i. e.* by removing the Parts of Matter which involve and overſhadow it. Which made *Michael Angelus*, the moſt famous Carver, ſay, *That Sculpture was nothing elſe but a Purgation from Things ſuperfluous. For take all that is ſuperfluous* (ſays he) *from the Wood or Stone, and the reſt will be the Figure you intend.* So if the Hand of an Angel (at leaſt the Power of God) ſhould think fit to poliſh any Particle of Matter without Vacuity, a Spherical Superfice would appear to the Eyes of a Figure exactly round; not as created anew, but as unveiled and laid open from the Diſguiſes and Covers of its circumjacent Matter. Nay I will go farther and affirm that whatſoever we perceive with any Senſe is really a Mathematical Figure, though for the moſt part irregular; for there is no Reaſon why irregular Figures ſhould exiſt every where, and regular ones can exiſt no where. Moreover if it be ſuppoſed (*viz.*) that Mathematical Things cannot exiſt, there will alſo be an End of thoſe Ideas or Types formed in the Mind, which will be no more than mere Dreams or the Idols of Things no where exiſting.

But having not Leiſure to handle this Queſtion more largely, let us again return from this Digreſſion to our Enquiry concerning the Manner of attaining the certain Knowledge of Mathematical Axioms; about which we ſhall note, in the *third* and laſt Place; That the Truth of certain Propoſitions do neither appear from the immediate Intuition of the Mind, nor the frequent Obſervation of Senſe nor yet from any ſuppoſed primary or original Notions, but is deduced by a certain implicit and as it were virtual *Diſcurſus*, of kin to an intuitive Notion, either from the declared Signification of the Terms themſelves, or from the ſuppoſed Generation of the Thing, which is manifeſtly poſſible and agreeable to the Suffrage of the Senſe: Which

Which ſeems to be the Caſe in moſt Mathematical Axioms.

Ex. gr. The Conſequence ſeems to be ſufficiently evident, *That a Whole is greater than its Part, or that a Part is leſſer than its Whole*, from the proper Signification which is underſtood of the Words *Whole* and *Part*, *Greater* and *Leſſer*. For by greater than another is denoted that which contains another, or has ſomething beſide what is equal to that other: by *leſſer than another* is meant that which itſelf, or its equal, is ſo contained in another that ſomething remains beſides. But a *Whole* more ſtrictly deſigns *that which contains another and ſomething more*; *a Part, that which is ſo contained in another, that if it be taken from that other ſomething will remain over and above.* Whence it appears that *Greater* in reſpect of *Whole*, and *Leſſer* in reſpect of *Part*, is, by the Signification of the Words, as the Genus to its Species, or as a more univerſal Term to one leſs univerſal, and conſequently it is rightly predicated according to the infallible Rules of Logic, *that a Whole is a greater Thing, and a Part a leſſer Thing.* (*o*) In the ſame Sort it will preſently appear from the Notion of Equality, *That Magnitudes which are equal to the ſame Third are equal to one another.* As if, with *Apollonius* and certain others (*p*) that be ſuppoſed to deſign a Thing equal to another, which being compared with another will entirely agree with it, *i. e.* will fill the ſame Space and occupy the ſame Place; from whence will follow the ſaid Axiom by a peculiar Quickneſs with the moſt ſpeedy Impulſe of Mind, and as it were inſtantaneous *Diſcurſus.* For ſuppoſing that any Magnitude A do fill the Place X, and moreover that the Magnitude B is equal to A, and becauſe of the ſuppoſed

(*o*) Apud Proclum, p. 54

(*p*) Hobb. in Philoſ.

Signification

Signification of Equality, does fill the ſame Place X; alſo that the Magnitude C is equal to A, and conſequently does in like Manner fill the Place X; then becauſe it is ſhewn that B and C do fill the ſame Place X, therefore B and C will be equal from the ſaid preſuppoſed Definition or Signification of Equality. The certain Knowledge indeed of that Axiom might depend upon ſuch a *Diſcurſus*, but the Mind diſcovers it with no Trouble, and as it were virtually rather than explicitely; which Diſcurſus *Proclus* blames that moſt famous Geometrician *Apollonius* for having invented, yet ſo that, were it worth the while, and Opportunity permitted, it ſeems no Difficulty to vindicate that great Man from Cenſure.

Whence it may be noted by the Way, that the Truth of moſt Axioms may be reſolved into the Definitions or Explications of the Terms or Words whereby they are expreſſed (being gathered as *Poriſmata* from them by a certain eaſy and tacit Ratiocination); which Definitions Geometricians are yet wont to neglect by Reaſon of their too great Evidence: *The Signification*, ſays (*q*) *Ariſtotle*, *of taking equal Things from equals is not explained, becauſe known.*

After the ſame Manner ſome Principles may be deduced by an implicit Diſcurſus, from the ſuppoſed Generation of the Subject. As ſuppoſe a Circle to ariſe from the drawing about of a Right Line, one of its Extremes remaining fixed which is ſtiled the Center; hence is immediately inferred that Axiom with ſcarce any Axiom at all of the Mind, *That all Right Lines drawn from the Center of a Circle to its Circumference are equal.* Alſo from the ſuppoſed Generation of a Right Line, we ſeem to gather (like Perſons ignorant of it before)

(*q*) I. Anal. Poſt. c. 8.

that

that all Right Lines do interſect or cut one another in only one Point. As when the Right Line A B is indefinitely produced till it cut the Line E F, it can only cut it in the Point Æ. (FIG. II.) There is no need of learning theſe Principles any otherwiſe, than from the Definitions or Explications of the Words. But we have ſaid enough in anſwer to the grand Argument by which our Adverſaries endeavour to overthrow the Certitude of Mathematical Demonſtrations; which Controverſy I cloſe up with the Words of *Lucullus* in *Cicero*. *As the Scale of a Balance is depreſſed by impoſing Weights into it, ſo muſt the Mind neceſſarily yield its Aſſent to Things clear in themſelves.*

But thoſe who ſtudy to detract not from the *Certitude* and *Evidence*, but from the *Dignity* and *Excellence* of the Mathematics do bring another Device. For they attempt to prove that Mathematical Ratiocinations are not *Scientific*, *Caſual* and *Perfect*, becauſe the Science of a Thing ſignifies to know it by its Cauſe; according to that Saying of *Ariſtotle*; *We are ſuppoſed to know by Science, when we know the Cauſe.* And to uſe the Words of *Pererius*, who was no mean Peripatetic, *A Mathematician neither conſiders the Eſſence of Quantity, nor treats of its Affections, as they flow from ſuch Eſſence, nor declares them by the proper Cauſes by which they are in Quantity, nor forms their Demonſtrations from proper and eſſential, but from common and accidental Predicates.* Thus they. To which I anſwer, that thoſe ſcientific Conditions, which *Ariſtotle* prefixes to Demonſtration, who was moſt obſervant of its Laws, do moſt fitly agree with Mathematical Ratiocinations. For *firſt* he requires that the Premiſſes be *Univerſally* and *Neceſſarily true*: And what Neceſſity can be thought ſtronger, than that which Mathematical Axioms pretend to, whoſe Truth is eternal and unchangeable?

able? *Secondly*, he wills them to be *Primary* and *Immediate*, *i. e.* that they be proved by no precedent Argument, by no previous Notion: And who does not ſee that this agrees with the ſame Principles, which do not prove but aſſume Things, as ſelf-convincing? *Thirdly*, he alſo directs them to be *More Known* and *More Evident* than the Concluſions inferred: But there is none who does not preſently yield his Aſſent to theſe, as ſoon as they are heard and underſtood by him; and they are alſo more known than the Concluſions deduced from them, becauſe, if we uſe a lawful *Diſcurſus* the Truth of theſe appears by them. *Laſtly*, he demands them to be the *Cauſes* of their Concluſions; which laſt Condition may be accepted two Ways: Either *firſt* only as they contain the Reaſon which neceſſarily cauſes the Concluſions to be believed as true, and produces a certain Aſſent, *i. e.* as the mean Term aſſumed obtains a neceſſary Connection with the Terms entring the Concluſion; whence ariſes that which is called a *Demonſtration* τȣ ὅτι *that a Thing is*: or *ſecondly* more ſtrictly, as this mean Term applied is more than a neceſſary Effect and certain Sign, *i. e.* as it is a proper Cauſe of the Attribute or Property, which is predicated of the Subject in the Concluſion; and hence is that called a *Cauſal Demonſtration*, or a *Demonſtration* τȣ διότι *why a Thing is*. But there is no Reaſon to doubt, but the laſt Condition underſtood in the former Senſe agrees with the Premiſſes of every Mathematical Syllogiſm, ſince there are no ſuch Syllogiſms, which do not moſt ſtrongly compel the Aſſent; nor does this follow becauſe the Premiſſes are neceſſarily true (for otherwiſe they are not admitted by Mathematicians), but this Neceſſity argues that there is an eſſential Connection and Cauſal Dependance of the Terms between themſelves in which it is founded, becauſe the Accidents

cidents may be ſeparated, and conſequently the accidental Predicates are only attributed to the Subject contingently. *(r) Things Eſſential* (ſays *Ariſtotle*) *are neceſſarily in every Genus, but Things Accidental are not neceſſary:* And every ſuch kind of Argumentation begetting a leſſer Degree of Science is reckoned a more *low* and *ignoble Demonſtration*, becauſe it ſhews a Thing to be ſo only from its *Effect* or *Sign*, not from its *Cauſe*; but yet this moſt clearly convinces the Mind, and moſt validly confirms the Truth. There is therefore no Mathematical *Diſcurſus* which proceeds not thus far. But that the foreſaid Condition taken in the latter Senſe does alſo agree with many Mathematical Ratiocinations, *i. e.* that the mean Term aſſumed in them has the Force of a Cauſe in Reſpect of the Property attributed to the Subject in the Concluſion, *Ariſtotle* is our firſt Author: He who, as has been juſt now ſaid, moſt accurately knew and treated largely of the Nature of Demonſtration, and conſequently whoſe Authority is of the greateſt Weight in this Affair; he, I ſay, fetches his moſt clear and ſtrong, and perhaps his only Examples of Cauſal Demonſtrations from Mathematical Diſciplines. *Ex. gr.* he brings that celebrated Theorem, wherein it is demonſtrated *that the Angle in a Semicircle is a Right one*, *(s)* for an Inſtance of a *Demonſtration* from the *Cauſe* both *material* and *formal*. *(t)* And comparing the *Mixed* or *Phyſico-Mathematical* Sciences, which he calls *Senſible*, with the *Pure*, he ſays thus, *To know that a Thing is, belongs indeed to ſuch as are converſant in the ſenſible Sciences, but to underſtand why a Thing is pertains to thoſe that are ſkilled in the Pure.* *(u)* And again, ſpeaking concerning Syl-

(r) I. Poſt. c. 6. *(s)* II. Poſt. c. 11. *(t)* I. Poſt. c. 10. *(u)* I. Poſt. c. 11.

logiſms of the firſt Figure. *The Mathematical Sciences* (ſays he) *conclude their Demonſtrations in this Figure, and in brief all Sciences that enquire why a Thing is.* Where he ſuppoſes the *Demonſtrations* of Mathematics to be eſpecially *Cauſal.*

But ſetting all Authority aſide to come to the Truth of the Matter, it ſeems plain that Mathematical *Demonſtrations* are eminently *Cauſal*, from whence, becauſe they only fetch their Concluſions from Axioms which exhibit the principal and moſt univerſal Affections of all Quantities, and from Definitions which declare the conſtitutive Generations and eſſential Paſſions of particular Magnitudes. From whence the Propoſitions that ariſe from ſuch Principles ſuppoſed, muſt needs flow from the intimate *Eſſences* and *Cauſes* of the Things. But I would become too prolix and troubleſome to your Patience, if I ſhould now go about to explain more diſtinctly how Cauſal Demonſtrations do ariſe from Mathematical Principles, and ſo finiſh the remaining Part of this Diſquiſition, I therefore reſerve it till hereafter.

LECTURE VI.

Of the Cauſality of Mathematical Demonſtration.

WE have treated in Part concerning the *Evidence* and *Certainty* of the Mathematics in the laſt Lecture; it now remains that we ſpeak of their Dignity, and ſhew more diſtinctly that they are really *Scientific* and *Cauſal*, and after what Manner; alſo, that we anſwer the principal Objections, that our Adverſaries bring againſt us.

As

As to what pertains to the Manner of *Causality* we may take notice with *(x) Aristotle* that there are three Things to be considered especially in every Demonstrative Science; *viz.* *1st*, The *Subject* whose necessary Affections or Properties it contemplates, investigates, or demonstrates. *2dly*, The *common Axioms* whereby it seeks and demonstrates the Affections concerning the *Subject*. *3dly*, The Affections themselves, which are to be demonstrated of the *Subject*. There is Nothing that occurs very observable concerning the *Subject* of Mathematical Demonstrations, unless, as we shall explain by and by, that it is always some Species of Magnitude which is specified, determined and differenced from others by some reciprocal Property; *Ex. gr.* a Right Line, an Angle, a Triangle, a Circle, a Cube, a Sphere, *&c.* are Subjects of Mathematical Demonstrations.

But concerning the Affections to be demonstrated I observe that they are of two Kinds, *viz. Common* and *Proper*. Those are *Common* which agree with their Subject *necessarily*, but not *solely*, as being also capable of being truly attributed to other Subjects. Thus, it is the *Common Affection* of an *Isosceles Triangle to have three Angles equal to two right ones*; of a *Square to have four right Angles*; of the *Circumference* of a *Circle to be cut by a Right Line only in two Points*; for it happens also to a *Scalene Triangle to have three Angles equal to two right ones*; and to an *oblong Parallelogram to have four right Angles*; and to innumerable *Curve Lines* besides the *Circumference* of a *Circle*, *that they only can be cut in two Points by a Right Line*; and hence it is apparent that such Affections do not flow from the particular Nature of their Subject, but from some more universal Reason; and that they agree not with it

(x) I. Post. c. 8.

immediately,

immediately, but as it is comprehended under ſome higher and more extenſive Genus of Magnitude: Moreover ſuch Affections being too extenſive cannot enter the Definition of a particular Subject, nor ſuffice to determine it, nor can it follow that the Subject is ſuppoſed, from ſuppoſing them. But *proper Affections* are ſuch as agree with their Subject both *neceſſarily* and *ſolely*, *i. e.* they do ſo reciprocate with their Subject, that if they be ſuppoſed, it is alſo ſuppoſed of Neceſſity. Thus it is the proper Affection of a *Circle* among all Figures *to have equal Radii*, and every Figure that emits *equal Radii* from the *Center* to the *Perimeter* or *Circumference* is a *Circle*. So alſo it agrees with the ſame Figure *that if any Point be aſſumed in the Diameter, and a Right Line be erected perpendicular to the ſaid Diameter meeting the Circumference, the Square of the intercepted Line is equal to the Rectangle (or Product) of the Segments of the Diameter*, or which is all one, *the intercepted Line is a Mean Proportional between the Segments of the Diameter*: This, I ſay, agrees with a *Circle*, and to whatſoever Figure this agrees, that is a *Circle*. In like manner, it agrees with a *Circle that every two Right Lines that can be drawn from the Extremities of the Diameter to any Point in its Circumference will make a Right Angle*; and reciprocally every Figure with which this Affection agrees will be a *Circle*. Thus again, it agrees interchangeably with *parallel Right Lines*, *that if they are indefinitely continued they can never meet*; *that other Right Lines interſecting them do make the alternate Angles equal*, *or the external Angles equal to the internal ones*, *or the internal Angles equal to two right Angles*; *that all intercepted Right Lines drawn at equal Angles are equal to one another*; and *that equal intercepted Right Lines do make equal Angles*. From whence it appears, that the Subject is determined

and

and limited by any of theſe Affections, and conſequently that any of theſe may be rightly ſuppoſed or aſſumed in defining the Subject, ſince they are connected together with ſuch an eſſential, cloſe and reciprocal Tie, that if any one be ſuppoſed, the reſt muſt neceſſarily follow. Theſe Things indeed are denied by *Ariſtotle*, who aſſirms, that there can be no more than one Definition of the ſame Thing; but notwithſtanding, according to his own frequent and never enough to be commended Saying, *It is a pious Thing always to adhere to the Truth.* It appears alſo hence that theſe Affections, on the Part of the Thing, are by Nature of equal Order and Degree, and have no Dependence one upon another. Which is clearly confirmed from hence, becauſe their Subject may be divers Ways generated in reſpect to them. *Ex. gr.* A *Circle* may not only be generated by the *Rotation of a Right Line*, but alſo by the *drawing of Perpendiculars*, by the *Affection of right Angles*, and as many other Ways, as it has ſuch reciprocal Affections or Properties. And the ſame Reaſon holds for all other particular Magnitudes. But if any one ſuch Affection be taken at pleaſure before others for the Definition of its Subject, it ſo far ſupplies the Place of a Cauſe, in reſpect of the reſt; becauſe by the Intervention of it, as a Mean, the reſt do neceſſarily follow and become known. As if a *Circle* be defined from the *Equality of its Radii*, it will thence be demonſtrated, that any *Perpendicular Line*, intercepted between the *Diameter* and *Circumference*, is equal to the *Rectangle* of the *Segments* of the *Diameter*; and that the *Angles* in the *Semicircle* are *Right ones*, and conſequently that *Equality of the Radii*, as to the Manner of our Diſcurſus, will be the Original of theſe Affections. But if a *Circle* ſhould be defined (as it may be) to be a *Figure endowed with ſuch a Property that if a certain Right Line be aſſumed*

in

in it; and any Perpendicular be erected from that to the Perimeter of the Figure, the Square of ſuch Perpendicular will equal the Rectangle of the Segments of that Right Line: Or if it be defined a Figure wherein, if a certain Right Line be taken, two Right Lines any how drawn from its Extremities to a Point in the Perimeter do make a right Angle; from either of the Definitions the foregoing Affection of the *Equality of the Radii* may be eaſily deduced and demonſtrated, and conſequently that Equality will be reſpectively, as the Effects of the ſaid Affections, and the Knowledge of that will depend upon the Suppoſition of theſe. And in like manner if *Parallel Right Lines* be defined from the Equality of the alternate Angles made by a Right Line interſecting them, the remaining Properties of *Parallel Right Lines*, related above, will ariſe from thence. I deny not but ſome of theſe reciprocal Affections do ſeem more ſimple and evident, more obvious and manifeſtly poſſible, than others; as the *Equality of the Radii*, already mentioned, ſeems more eaſy and plain, than the other Properties of a *Circle*, becauſe it is entirely deduced from a Generation by the Rotation of one of thoſe *Radii*: And that negative Property ſeemed to *Euclid*, as the moſt eaſy and clear of all Properties belonging to *Parallel Lines*, *that how far ſoever they be produced they can never meet*; though he was not ſo right in this, as is thought by ſome; among whom, for many Reaſons, I beg leave to ſubſcribe my own name. I alſo acknowledge the Expedience of beginning an Argumentation, or of defining a Subject, from ſuch Affections as are moſt eaſy and familiar, rather than from others; *ex. gr.* to define a *Circle* rather from the *Equality of its Radii*, than from that *Equality of a Square with a Rectangle*, which was juſt now mentioned. As to our Apprehenſion I allow the former the Preference, though

though it is all one, as to the Nature of the Thing, from which the Difcurfus takes its Rife, for which foever Link of the Chain you take hold of, the Whole will follow; but we ufually feize upon that which is moft obvious and ready. It is here as in the Progrefs of a *Circle*, from whatfoever Point of the Circumference you take your Beginning, you will meafure over the Whole. Such in Reality and no other is the mutual *Caufality* and Dependence of the Terms of a *Mathematical Demonftration*, *viz.* a moft clofe and intimate Connection of them one with another; which yet may be called a *formal Caufality*, becaufe the remaining Affections do refult from that one Property, which is firft affumed, as from a Form. Nor do I think there is any other *Caufality* in the Nature of Things, wherein a neceffary Confequence can be founded. Logicians do indeed boaft of I do not know what kind of Demonftrations, from *external Caufes* either *efficient* or *final*; but without being able to fhew one genuine Example of any fuch; nay I imagine it impoffible for them fo to do. For there can be no fuch Connection of an *external*, *ex. gr.* *efficient Caufe* with its *Effect*, (at leaft none fuch can be underftood by us) through which, ftrictly fpeaking, the *Effect* is neceffarily fuppofed by the Suppofition of the *efficient Caufe*; or any *determinate Caufe* by the Suppofition of the *Effect*. Nay there can be no efficient Caufe in the Nature of Things of a philofophical Confideration which is altogether neceffary. For every Action of an *efficient Caufe*, as well as its confequent *Effect*, depends upon the *Free-Will* and Power of *Almighty God*, who can hinder the Influx and Efficacy of any *Caufe* at his Pleafure; neither is there any *Effect* fo confined to one *Caufe*, but it may be produced by perhaps innumerable others. Hence it is poffible that there may be fuch a *Caufe* with-

out

out a *subsequent Effect*, or such an *Effect* and no peculiar *Cause* to afford any Thing to its Existence. There can therefore be no Argumentation from an efficient *Cause* to the *Effect*, or contrarily from an *Effect* to the *Cause*, which is lawfully necessary. *Ex. gr.* Because there is Fire it does not necessarily follow that there is Fewel for it to feed on, or Smoak sent from it; since History relates that, in Fact, it has happened otherwise. Neither, on the contrary, is the necessary Existence of Fire inferred from Ashes or Smoak. For who doubts but God can immediately create Ashes and Smoak, or produce it by other Means? Perhaps you will say, that Ashes and Smoak denote an intrinsecal Relation of Fire. I answer briefly, This supposes the Argumentation not to proceed from the *efficient Cause* or the *Effect*, but from the *formal Cause* or *Causate*; yet however a Thing of the same Nature and as some speak the same *Specifically*, as Ashes or Smoak, can exist without the Efficacy of Fire, and take its Rise from other Causes, which makes for our Purpose. Nor does the Astronomer, from the Height of the Sun, wholly demonstrate its Continuance above the Horizon, or the past Time of the Day: For we read of the Sun's having once been fixed in Heaven, and another Time of its going backwards. In like manner from that most celebrated and trite Example of a Demonstration from the *efficient Cause* (which is used by *Aristotle*, and other Writers of Logic) of the Earth's Interposition between the Sun and Moon, it does not follow that the Moon undergoes an Eclipse; for, if God please, the solar Rays may pass through the Body of the Earth, or reach the Moon by an indirect Passage without touching the Earth; or otherwise the Moon may be enlightened some other Way: Nay the Sun itself does not infer Light; for at the Death of our Lord, the

the Setting of the better Light of the World, the Sun as if ſtruck with Fear and confounded with Shame, drew in his Rays, and hid his Face, and even at Noon-day ſuffered an Eclipſe, without any Moon to intercept his Light, or any Cloud to darken his Brightneſs. A Defect of Light then cannot be concluded from the Interpoſition of an opaque Body, nor this from that. I own according to the Law and Cuſtom of Nature, that ſuch Effects do always proceed from ſuch Cauſes; and therefore we may pardon *Ariſtotle* for ſuppoſing Nature ſubject to an intrinſecal Neceſſity, and not obnoxious to an external ſuperiour Power: but in reality it is one thing to happen naturally, and another to exiſt of Neceſſity. For neceſſary Propoſitions have an univerſal, immutable and eternal Truth, ſubject to nothing, nor to be hindered by any Power. *Science* (ſays (*y*) *Ariſtotle*) *is comprehended of Neceſſity, whence it is that it is eternal: For all theſe Things that are ſimply neceſſary are eternal.* Again. (*z*) *The Concluſion of a Demonſtration muſt be eternal.* Becauſe therefore the *Efficacy* of Agents may be ſtopped, or changed, and every *Effect* may proceed from various *Cauſes*, there can be no Demonſtration from an *efficient Cauſe*, or from an Effect. And the ſame Reaſon holds of a *final Cauſe* and its correſpondent *Means*, *i. e.* no determinate *Means* will follow from the *End*, nor will the *End* neceſſarily follow from the *Means*. We have nothing then to wonder at, that there are no Demonſtrations in Geometry drawn from an *efficient* or *final Cauſe*, but do all proceed from the Form and inward Conſtitution of the Thing expreſſed by the Definition. They are therefore to be blamed, who require ſuch Demonſtrations

(*y*) VI. Eth. c. 3. (*z*) I. Anal. Poſt. c. 7.

from

from Mathematicians, as themſelves never ſaw or dreamed of.

From what has been ſaid it follows that the Syllogiſm in which one eſſential Affection is connected with, or inferred from another, is a *Cauſal Demonſtration*, *i. e.* one deduced from a *formal Cauſe:* And ſuch a Syllogiſm, *ex. gr.* is the following one. *In every Figure having equal Radii, the Square of a Perpendicular is equal to the Rectangle of the Segments of the Diameter: The Figure* Z *has equal Radii* (viz. *by Hypotheſis, or what already appears*)*: Therefore in the Figure* Z, *the Square of a Perpendicular is equal to the Rectangle of the Segments of the Diameter.* Here a certain Affection, *viz. the Equality of a Square with a Rectangle* is demonſtrated of the Figure ſubjected, by an *Equality of the Radii*; which, in reſpect of that, is a *formal Cauſe*, as was ſhewn above. Such alſo is this Syllogiſm. *Right Lines never meeting, if interſected by a Right Line, do make the alternate Angles equal: But the Right Lines* A, B, *(by Hypotheſis, or what has been demonſtrated) do never meet one another*; *therefore a Right Line interſecting the Light Lines* A *and* B, *makes the alternate Angles equal.* And this may ſuffice concerning the Affections to be demonſtrated.

As to *Axioms*, I obſerve, that they either agree univerſally to all Quantities, *viz.* all Lines, Superficies, Solids, and Angles, and by Reaſon of theſe to Numbers, Weights, Times, and all other ſecondary Quantities; or particularly to particular Quantities: Thoſe may be named *Univerſal*, theſe *Particular*. *Univerſal Axioms* declare certain eſſential Affections of all Quantities, ſo ſimple and clear that they can ſcarce by Hypotheſis be demonſtrated by others prior to them, at leaſt they need no Demonſtration. Thus it agrees abſolutely with all Quantities, and may be pronounced of them in general,

general, *That Quantity is divisible into homogeneous Quantities*, *i. e.* a Line into Lines, a Superfice into Superficies, a Body into Bodies : *That homogeneous Quantities may be compounded or added to one another : That a lesser Quantity may be subducted from a greater : That every Magnitude does fill a Space adequate to itself : And that every Magnitude is capable of a determinate Situation* ; *can rest* ; *can be moved with any Motion*, *direct or circular*, *uniform or ununiform*, *swift or slow*. Indeed such *absolute Axioms* are not mentioned by Geometricians, by Reason of their too great Evidence, but they ought to be understood, because of other *Axioms*, and for the sake of the Definitions of particular Magnitudes, and all kinds of Hypotheses. *Ex. gr.* When it is said *Magnitudes*, *which are congruous to one another*, or *which fill the same Space*, *are equal* ; it is supposed, as a thing possible, for Magnitudes to fill Space. When a *Right Angle* is defined from such a Position of one Right Line upon another ; it is supposed a thing possible, for a Right Line to obtain such a Position. When a *Circle* is defined from the *Rotation of a Right Line*, that Rotation or Motion is taken as possible to be done. And to Quantities compared together may be attributed such Affections as these, *viz.* the Equality of two Quantities following their Equalities to a third ; the Equality resulting from Congruence, or the Completion of the same Space ; the Equality arising from the Composition or Division, the Addition or Subtraction of Equals ; and such like. The same Way do Affections (which because of their Simplicity and Evidence either cannot, or need not, be demonstrated) express the *particular Axioms* belonging to particular Quantities. As *ex. gr.* It is the Property of a *Right Line*, *that it can only be intersected by another Right Line in one Point* ; *that it has no Part common*

with

with another Right Line; *that it cannot include Space, or constitute a Figure with another Right Line.* It also agrees with it, *that it can lie between any two assigned Points*; *that it may be infinitely, or indefinitely produced*; *that it may be the Radius of a Circle.* These are Things required by Geometricians, but may be boldly pronounced, being Affections of a *Right Line*, and easily deducible from its Definition, whatsoever it be. Which *Axioms* may perhaps be capable of Demonstration, as I have said above; but because their Truth is most easily perceived and granted, it is neither necessary, nor expedient to be done. Since therefore these *Axioms* do contain Affections essential either to all Quantities, or at least to some particular ones; and since they necessarily agree together (I mean some respectively with some) it is apparent that they are rightly applied to Demonstration, and that *causal Demonstrations* may be made from them. Take an Example in the following Syllogism; *Those Things which are congruous to one another, are equal to the same Thing: The Magnitudes* A *and* B *are congruous* (by Hypothesis, or what is proved before) *therefore the Magnitudes* A *and* B *are equal to the same.* Where the Equality of two Magnitudes in respect of the same, is deduced from its *formal Cause*, *viz.* from the Congruity of these Magnitudes. But at present I will add no more concerning *Axioms*, only I affirm, that since all *Mathematical Theorems* are derived from these, *i. e.* from the *general Affections* of all Magnitudes, and from the *reciprocal Properties* of particular Magnitudes, it sufficiently appears, that they are demonstrated from their Causes. It is therefore meet that I proceed to what remains of the Disputation I have undertaken against the Impugners of Mathematical Demonstration, and consider briefly the Instances they bring against it.

First,

First, They aim at the very Head of Geometry, and deny that the Proof of the very first Proposition of the Elements is deduced from proper Causes, and therefore is not demonstrated by the best Reason: For they say it is there inferred, that a Triangle will be Equilateral from hence, because it may be constructed between two equal Circles, which agrees not with an Equilateral Triangle essentially, but accidentally; because it will be Equilateral, though these Circles were not drawn at all, or were entirely wanting. To this Instance and such like it is differently answered by different Persons, though indeed appositely enough by all. I shall pass by the Answers of others, and shall give an Answer of my own, without borrowing any thing. And first I shall take notice, that the word *Demonstration* is taken many Ways. As 1*st*, For any particular scientific Syllogism, according to *Aristotle*'s Definition, *A Demonstration is a Syllogism producing Science*; this may be termed *Simple Demonstration*. 2*dly*, For a System of more such Syllogisms connected together in a certain Series, and conspiring together for the Proof of one Proposition; which Sort may not unfitly be named *Compound Demonstration*. 3*dly*, For the ultimate Syllogism, whereby the proposed Conclusion is immediately confirmed, to which the other Syllogisms do all aim and conduce: Which being supposed, I observe that if the particular Syllogisms of a *Compound Demonstration* be all *Causal*, especially the last, by which is given as it were the finishing Stroke; then the whole *Compound Demonstration* deservedly ought also to be reckoned *Causal* and *Scientific*. Moreover I take notice, that certain Things assumed or proved may, in the Course of the whole Demonstration, seem accidental in respect of some one (*ex. gr.* the Ultimate) Conclusion, which yet in Respect of others may be proper and essential;

essential; nor is there any need for all the Prædicates in the Series of a *Compound Demonstration* to agree essentially with the Subject of the finishing Conclusion; but it suffices for every Thing so to agree with the Subject of its proper Conclusion. From which Observations most or all the Instances brought against Mathematical Demonstrations may be overthrown. And consequently, if the particular Syllogisms (brought either for the Construction, or Demonstration of the abovesaid first Proposition of the Elements) be *Demonstrations* simply *scientific*, the Proposition ought to be reckoned as *scientifically demonstrated*. We will therefore examine them; but for brevity's sake, we will substitute *Enthymems* for Syllogisms, and insinuate the Necessity of the Consequence. A Proposition (which I imagine unknown to none of you) is as follows.

Upon any given Right Line A B *to make an Equilateral Triangle*; or which is all one, if we reduce this Proposition to the Form of a Theorem (since every possible Problem may be taken for a Theorem, as far as that Possibility is demonstrable) it will be as follows. *An Equilateral Triangle is possible to be made upon any given Right Line* A B. (FIG. III.)

CONSTRUCTION.

1. Enthymeme. *Any Right Line may be the Radius of a Circle. Therefore* A B *is the Radius of a Circle, whose Center is* A.

The Antecedent contains the essential Property of a Right Line, as is remarked above.

2. Enth. *By the same Reason, with the Center* B *and Interval* A, *a Circle may be described. Let therefore the Circles* B C D, A C E, *be supposed to be drawn, because it is shewn that it may be done.*

3. Enth.

3. Enth. *Two equal Circles deſcribed by a common Radius will mutually interſect each other : Therefore the Circles* B C D *and* A C E *will interſect each other : ſuppoſe in the Point* C.

The Antecedent is manifeſt from that moſt evident Property of a Circle, that it is on every Side incloſed and terminated.

4. Enth. *A Right Line may be drawn from one given Point to another. Therefore the Right Line* A C *may be drawn from* A *to* C.

The Antecedent is the Property of a Right Line, as we have ſaid before. *Let* A C *therefore be drawn, becauſe it may be done.*

5. Enth. *By a like Reaſon may be drawn the Right Line* B C. *Let it therefore be drawn.* Now it is plain, that a Triangle A C B is here conſtituted from the Definition and Nature of a Triangle : And the Conſtruction of the Problem is finiſhed. It next remains to be demonſtrated that the Triangle A C B is equilateral, and what follows may be converted into this Theorem.

A Triangle made of Right Lines drawn from the Centers of two equal Circles, deſcribed by a common Radius to the Interſection of theſe Circles, is equilateral.

The following Enthymemes do ſerve for the Demonſtration of this Theorem.

1. *Right Lines drawn from the Circumference of a Circle to its Center are equal to one another. Therefore the Right Lines* A C *and* A B *are equal.* The moſt noted Property of a Circle whereby it is defined is in the Antecedent.

2. *By the ſame Reaſon the Right Lines* B C *and* A B *are equal.*

3. *Thoſe Things which are equal to the ſame Third are equal to one another. Therefore the Right Lines* A C *and* B C *are equal to one another, becauſe they are proved to be equal to the ſame*

Line

Line A B. The Antecedent is the most evident and noble Property of Magnitudes compared, of which it was spoke above.

4. The ultimate and decretory Syllogism follows, which finishes the Whole. *Every Triangle which has three equal Sides is Equilateral. The Triangle* A B C, from what is just now demonstrated, *has three equal Sides. Therefore the Triangle* A B C *is Equilateral.* The major Proposition is the Definition of an Equilateral Triangle; and the *Cause* of the Conclusion is most evidently contained in the Premisses. For I cannot imagine what *Cause* can be supposed more near and intimate, why the Triangle A B C is Equilateral, than this, *that it has three equal Sides.*

We have seen then, that all the Syllogisms of this Proposition, which serve both for its Construction, and the Demonstration of that Construction, are so many true Demonstrations, as being deduced from the essential Attributes of the Things subjected; the last especially being in the highest Degree *Causal* and *Scientific.* I hope then enough has been done for this Instance.

But as I remember *Pererius*, and others, do produce another Instance, also blaming that celebrated Proposition which is the thirty-second of the first Element, as not scientifically demonstrated. For they say that here also, to demonstrate that all the Angles of a Triangle are equal to two right ones, one Side is produced, and a Parallel drawn to another; the Possibility of which Performance is entirely extrinsecal and accidental to the Thing proposed; nor has the Equality of the Angles in the Triangle, the Thing to be proved, any Dependence upon it. Therefore it does not follow from hence that this Demonstration is *Essential* or *Scientific.* These most subtle, or rather captious Disputants,

putants, if I mistake not the Matter, require Conclusions without any *mean* or middle Term found or assumed for their Deduction, or which is the same, demand an Argumentation without an Argument. *Aristotle* does indeed reject *Heterogeneous* Arguments, *i. e.* such as are drawn from Sciences of another Nature; but these Men seem to reject all Arguments, expecting a Thing should be proved of itself, without suffering any Thing to be granted. But to come to the Business. 1. *Aristotle* brings this very Proposition for an Example of those Things that are essentially inherent to their Subject, and causally demonstrated. (*a*) *We know* (says he) *essentially and not accidentally, when we understand something so to agree with another, as it does agree in Reality, and that by Principles proper to it. Thus we know the Property of having three Angles equal to two right ones, when we understand that to which it agrees by Reason of itself, and consequently we know by the Principles which properly belong to that Thing.* 2. I briefly reply, because a Triangle is constituted of Right Lines, the Properties of a Right Line do so far pertain to it. But it is the Property of a Right Line that it may be produced; therefore this Production is not altogether accidental or extrinsecal to a Triangle. In like manner it is also the Property of a Right Line, as was before demonstrated, that another Right Line may be drawn parallel to it through any Point without itself. Therefore this also agrees essentially with a Triangle, as far as Right Lines (*i. e.* its Sides) do enter its Constitution. Moreover, 3. I imagine our Adversaries do not deny the Truth of that Proposition, nor therefore that it may be demonstrated. Therefore some *Mean* ought to be assumed for demonstrating it. An external Angle

(*a*) I. Post. Anal. cap. 7.

is

is aſſumed and ſhewn to be diviſible into two Parts equal to the two internal and oppoſite Angles of a Triangle; whence it moſt evidently follows that all the internal Angles are equal to two right ones. And I do not ſee that any *Mean* can poſſibly be aſſumed more convenient, or more intimate than this. Again, 4. I here anſwer as in the former Inſtance: If the particular Syllogiſms are examined, from which the Demonſtration of this thirty-ſecond Propoſition is taken, it will be found that their whole Force depends either immediately or mediately upon Definitions or univerſal Axioms. From whence it will appear that theſe Demonſtrations are *Scientific*; and conſequently ſo is the whole Demonſtration made up of them, and the ultimate Syllogiſm whereby the Propoſition is immediately demonſtrated. After the ſame manner may eaſily be anſwered all the Inſtances that can be brought.

That I may at length finiſh this ſomewhat long, and I fear diſorderly Diſſertation, becauſe too haſtily compoſed and delivered; it ſeems to me that every certain and evident Diſcurſus, flowing according to the irrefragable Rules of Logic, from Principles univerſally and perpetually true, and conſequently wherein a neceſſary Connection of the Terms is found, is moſt properly, ſcientifically and perfectly a Demonſtration: And that all other *Cauſality*, which is here applicable, beſides this Connection already explained, is mere Fiction, ſupported by no Argument, nor confirmed by any Example: And that Demonſtrations, though ſome do outdo others in Brevity, Elegance, Proximity to their firſt Principles, and the like Excellencies, yet are all alike in Evidence, Certitude, Neceſſity, and the eſſential Connection and mutual Dependence of the Terms one with another. Laſtly, that Mathematical Ratiocinations are the moſt perfect Demonſtrations.

I had

I had indeed explained these Things somewhat more fully and largely, if some little Business intervening had not disturbed my Thoughts, and shortened my Time for Study; and if a Kind of Illness, not indeed very grievous, but yet troublesome, had not seized me for some Days. Therefore I beg to take my Leave of you for the present Season, wishing that Health to you which I cannot enjoy myself.

Here ended the first Year after the Institution of this Professorship, which happened to have only one Term. I have borrowed the two first Lectures of the following Year, to encrease the Number, and fill up the Paper that remains here.

LECTURE VII.

Of the Nature of First Principles.

IT is a Custom very agreeable with good Manners, and I believe no where more confirmed by frequent Practice than among yourselves, for Friends that meet together after a long Absence to embrace with a more ardent Affection, and address one another with a more liberal Conversation. In compliance with which Custom to Day, if Nature had bestowed, or Art procured for me but a moderate Faculty of speaking, I confess indeed very many Things might be pertinently urged. For I am pushed on with the truest Incentives of a most hearty Affection, and instructed with the most splendid as well as copious Argument of Speech, to return due Thanks for your singular Benevolence experienced upon myself, to set forth your diligent Study bestowed upon the liberal Sciences, and to applaud and

and congratulate your Patience ſuch as is becoming Philoſophers. But ſince both my own Diſpoſition is very unmeet and averſe to Oratory, as well as in ſome Meaſure the Reaſon of my Office; and ſince you yourſelves, I imagine, do not come hither to have your Ears tickled with rhetorical Compliments, but to compoſe your Minds to the Severity of Philoſophy; not ſo much deſiring to hear Speeches made to you, as to have the Science of Things explained to you: I will therefore reſtrain my Tongue from breaking out into pathetical Excurſions; and wholly omit every kind of Preface. Only give me leave, moſt courteous Auditors, officiouſly to embrace you with the Arms of Gratitude and Benevolence, heartily wiſhing you all Health, and praying that our meeting together again may be delightful and auſpicious. And ſo, without more ado, I apply myſelf to the Work of my Office, propoſing now to purſue what I left the laſt Term, and endeavour to finiſh what was then begun.

Be pleaſed then to recollect what I at that Time propoſed to treat of, and how far I proceeded. I undertook to erect an Entrance preparatory to the Diſciplines I was engaged to treat upon, *i. e.* to handle certain Things which are neceſſary to be premiſed concerning the Mathematics. And this I did by treating largely, 1*ſt*, concerning their *Name*, ſhewing why they obtained the Title of Diſciplines after a peculiar Manner to themſelves. 2*dly*, Concerning their *general Object*, how far it extends itſelf. And, 3*dly*, Concerning their *Diviſion*, as well according to my own, as the Sentiments of others. Next I began to treat concerning the *Manner* whereby they are converſant about their Object, *i. e.* the Invention and Aſſertion of the Properties agreeing with their Object, by a certain and evident Diſcurſus or Argumentation, which is wont

to

to be denoted by the Name of *Demonſtration:* Whoſe Nature I endeavoured to illuſtrate from the Difference between the Mathematical Way of arguing, and that which is uſed in moſt other Sciences, by a diligent Compariſon of both; aſſaying afterwards to vindicate the *Certitude* and *Excellence* of Mathematical Argumentations, as much as was requiſite from the Inferences and Tricks of Adverſaries.

Theſe Things being diſcuſſed according to my Ability, the next thing ſhould be (and my Mind inclines me ſo to do) to come to the Explanation of the *Species* or Kinds of *Mathematical Demonſtration*, and treat alſo of *Mathematical Invention*, a moſt noble Subject, if it did not ſeem neceſſary firſt, to conſider the integral Parts of a Mathematical Syllogiſm, *i. e.* to enquire concerning the Premiſſes of every *Mathematical Diſcurſus*, what Sort they are, and how divided.

As to what pertains to the Premiſſes of every *ſcientific Diſcurſus*, theſe are either *firſt Principles*, or *Concluſions* derived in a continued Series from *firſt Principles*, which after they are ſo derived, have themſelves the Force, and are in the Room of *Principles*, in reſpect of the *Concluſions* which may be inferred from them, or proved by their Help. For the whole Force of any *Demonſtrative Ratiocination* is reſolved into the *Certitude* and *Evidence* of the *firſt Principles:* All the Truth, the Validity, and Evidence of every Science adheres to theſe inſeparable Roots, and depends upon theſe unſhaken Foundations. Wherefore we will firſt of all treat of theſe, in a few Words more generally concerning the Nature of Principles; then concerning their Differences; and laſtly, concerning their different Species ſeparately.

As to what pertains to *Principles univerſally*, *Ariſtotle* in more than one Place rightly obſerves, that

that as there is no Progreſs in natural Motion from Infinity or to Infinity, but there muſt be a Beginning from ſome Term, to end at ſome Term, ſince Infinity cannot be paſſed over, (*i. e.* if a Progreſs be aſſumed from Infinity, it will never end here, nor will a Progreſs tending from hence to Infinity, ever end any where): So in the diſcurſive Operation of the Mind, which is like a Motion continually ſucceſſive, there ought to be ſome appointed Bound for the Diſcurſus to take its Beginning from, *i. e.* all Propoſitions are not to be proved by others in a continual Series, but ſome ought to be aſſumed by him that demonſtrates, and granted by him that hears; otherwiſe every Examination, Confirmation, or Declaration of the Truth, which is undertaken, will be endleſs and vain. As no Houſe can be built, ſo no Science can be erected but upon ſome Foundations. Such Propoſitions therefore are termed *Principles*, becauſe from theſe (which are aſſumed *gratis* and willingly granted, as it were by the mutual Conſent and Agreement of the Teacher and Learner) the Argumentation takes its Beginning, proceeding from thence to Things more remote. They are therefore defined by *Ariſtotle*, *Immediate Propoſitions*, becauſe they are ſupported by no *Mean* or Argument from ſomething elſe; or becauſe Aſſent is given to them immediately, and at once, without mediate Reaſoning. Which is not ſo to be taken as if *Principles* were required to be ſimply indemonſtrable, and can no way be demonſtrated or proved; for thus very few or no Axioms of any particular Science can be called or accounted Principles. For I doubt very much, or rather am inclined to believe, that, except that one only Foundation of all Reaſoning, *That contradictory Propoſitions cannot be both true or both falſe*, no other Axiom is ſimply demonſtrable. I ſay Axioms, for concerning Definitions and Hypotheſes

potheses the Case is somewhat different, as we shall see by and by, which yet may be proved or illustrated after their own Way. However the *Principles* of a particular Science not only may, but ought to be demonstrated by the Master, if the Scholar requires it. For the Teacher of a Science is bound by his Office, if he desire to discharge it faithfully and answer his Character, to take away all reasonable Scruple from the Student; therefore if the Principles which he assumes be obscure, they are to be illustrated with Examples; if doubtful, they are to be confirmed from other Principles more known and indubitable, by prolonging the Discursus, if need be, and the Student require it, even to the very first Principles of all. *Ex. gr.* If any one doubt that *Principle* in Optics, *That the Species of a visible Point is carried or irradiated directly to every Point of the circumjacent Medium*; it is hence confirmed, because we experience, that an objected Point may be beheld by every Situation of the Eye, except an opaque Body be somewhere interposed in a Right Line from the visible Point to the Eye. And indeed most Theorems of Geometry are *Principles* in respect of Optics, Mechanics, Astronomy and other Parts of Mathematics, *i. e.* they are supposed as Truths in them, without any Demonstration at all. But if the Truth of any Theorem be not apparent to the Student, it is incumbent upon the Optician (or Master of any other Science) to demonstrate it, or at least to shew where it may be found demonstrated. Nay if he hesitate at any Geometrical Axiom, the Teacher cannot in Reason avoid the Necessity of demonstrating it: For no Demonstration can be reckoned accurately perfect, and strictly scientific, which reaches not the original Fountains of Science, even to some thing simply indemonstrable, confirmed by its own Force, and evident from its own Light. *For then only* (says the

the Philosopher) *we are supposed to know a Thing, when we know its first Causes and Principles, even to the very first Elements.*

But some will ask, How can the Truth of Geometrical Axioms be demonstrated? I will answer, by other Axioms more simple, if any such there are, which are to be drawn from some higher and more universal Science, as *Metaphysics*; I say *Metaphysics* which is, or ought to be, the Treasure of the most general and simple Notions; and is therefore by *(b) Aristotle* named the *Mistress of all Sciences*; by *Proclus*, *The one shoeless Science from which others receive their Principles.* But if, by the Definition of the Terms of the Axiom proposed there appear no Axioms more Simple; as if any one should doubt whether the Whole be greater than its Part; if no Theorem or Axiom in Metaphysics can be found more certain, more evident, more simple than this, by which it may be demonstrated, we are to have Recourse to the Definitions of a *Whole* and a *Part*, *Greater* and *Lesser*; from the right Position of which, it will not be difficult to demonstrate that Axiom. And the same Reason holds in others. Whence also it appears, that it pertains not to the Nature of Principles, nor is required of them, that they appear necessarily true in themselves, or immediately evident to every Capacity; but only to him who comes ready and prepared for learning that particular Science, to which the said Principles are subservient, *i. e.* to the studious and teachable Mind. *Ex. gr.* The Theorems of Geometry which (as was just now said) do acquire the Place of *Principles* in Optics or Astronomy, are more manifest to one skilled in Geometry, and do most easily command his Assent; but are hard to be conceived and yielded to,

(b) Anal. Post. I. 9.

by

by one ignorant of that Science; yet they do not therefore ceaſe to be *Principles* belonging to thoſe Diſciplines: at leaſt it follows from thence, that he who is no Geometrician is an unfit Perſon to learn them. *Ariſtotle* therefore teaches wiſely and circumſpectly, that Demonſtration proceeds not abſolutely from Things manifeſt, but only in ſuch ſort, that the Things admitted do draw their Concluſion after them, overſpreading it with their Light, if any they have. The *Principles* therefore of no particular Science are neceſſarily and ſimply ſelf-evident or indemonſtrable, but only ought to be credible and ſufficiently manifeſt to a well prepared Hearer. (*c*) *Proclus* argues not ill to this Purpoſe. *No Science* (ſays he) *demonſtrates its own Principles, nor makes any Diſpute about them, but looks upon them as ſelf-evident; and afterwards they are more conſpicuous.* And *Ariſtotle* himſelf, *I call alſo them Principles in any particular Science, which cannot be demonſtrated, i. e.* cannot be demonſtrated in a particular Science, otherwiſe they would not be *Principles*; but perhaps ſome of them both can and ought to be demonſtrated without it. Again (*d*) *Ariſtotle* intimates that a Geometrician as ſuch, lays not down his Principles, nor converſes with that Science where it fails him; but has Regard to ſome other Science; and, where all others fail, has at laſt Recourſe to the Science which is common to all others, *viz. Metaphyſics.*

But according to *Ariſtotle* the primary Condition of Principles is, that they be univerſally and neceſſarily true, *i. e.* do ſuffer no Exception of Place, Time or Chance; and it is repugnant to the Nature of a Subject for the Predicate not to agree with it. Otherwiſe the Concluſions inferred would become falſe and uncertain, and not a certain and

(*c*) Lib. 2. p. 22. (*d*) Phyſ. I. 2.

firm

firm Science, ſuch as is expected from Demonſtration, but Error or a doubtful Suſpicion would be produced. For in every ſcientific Syllogiſm conſiſting of one or more immediate *Principles*, the *Principle* aſſumed is the Major Propoſition in the firſt Figure; and therefore unleſs it be univerſally true, there can be no Argumentation, as is well known in Logics. And if there be any Weakneſs or Imperfection of the *Principles* (ſuch eſpecially as *Particularity* and *Contingence*) it will be neceſſarily derived upon the Concluſions. Nevertheleſs it may be of Uſe about this *Verity* of *Principles*, to take heed that it be not of one Genus nor altogether Univocal. For the *Verity* of that *firſt Principle* concerning the impoſſible Coexiſtence of Contradictory Propoſitions as to Truth or Falſhood, does ſeem to differ, as it were, in Specie from the *Verity* of all other *Principles*. For with reſpect to its Origin, whatſoever it may be concerning others, this Notion at leaſt does ſeem to be immediately connate with our Minds, and implanted in us by God, together with the Faculty of Reaſoning to which it is intrinſecally annexed. For there can be no Reaſoning without the Admiſſion of this Principle, nay all Ratiocination tends to this, to this it is reduced; ſo that the Adverſary is compelled to contradict himſelf by admitting the greateſt of all Abſurdities that Contradictory Propoſitions may be both true. If this be not granted, all Reaſon, all Diſquiſition or Diſputation about Truth is entirely vain and inſignificant. This depends upon no other previous Notion, Suppoſition or Argumentation, but is included in all Reaſonings, as the Foundation upon which they are built, and the Inſtrument whereby we are rendered capable to reaſon about other Things. Therefore this Principle ſeems to be eminently true above others. *(e) Where-*

(e) Metaph. III. 3. & XI. 7.

fore

fore all Demonstrations (says *Aristotle*) *are reduced to this Notion. For this is by Nature the Principle of all other Axioms.*

Although in Strictness, because a valid Syllogism should walk upon two Legs, and it is not sufficient for only one of the Premisses to be undoubtedly true, it is perhaps necessary, that one or two Axioms ought to be required as preparatory to all Reasonings; *viz.* these, *That Sense in its own Way is an undoubted Criterion of Truth, or that the Appearance of a Thing is a certain Discovery of its Existence.* Also *that the Possibility of a Thing is argued from the Existence of its Like; or that from an entire Parity of Reason a Consequence may be drawn of a Possibility of Existence.* For all Science, all Argumentation seems to depend upon a tacit Supposition of these. Since no other Truth of other indemonstrable Principles does seem to be required besides a sufficiently manifest Possibility of the Conception which is formed in the Mind, concerning the Existence of some Property; *i. e.* that we conceive and suppose something to be done, which really may be done. As *ex. gr.* when we suppose that two Things may fill the same Space, be congruent with one another, or coextended: That a Right Line may be drawn between two Points: That a Right Line may be turned about with one of its Extremes at rest, till it come to its first Position: That the Earth may be interposed in the same Right Line between the Sun and Moon: Because there is Nothing impossible or inconsistent contained in these Positions or Conceptions; therefore these are called *Hypotheses*, and ought to be granted as true. And their Truth is nothing else but the possible Connection of a Subject with its Predicate, which we clearly perceive, but perhaps cannot otherwise prove, but by a similar Example or Experiment,

i. e. by

i. e. by Help of the *Principles*, which, we have juſt now ſaid, do ſeem to be ſubjunct to the firſt Principle concerning Contradictories: For perhaps we apprehend that and that only, as poſſible, of which we have in ſome ſort experienced the ſame in Specie, or ſomething very like it. In like manner the Falſhood of any *Hypotheſis* ſeems to be nothing but the Conception or Poſition of a Thing as effected or exiſting, which cannot be effected or exiſt. As if one ſuppoſe a rectilineal Triangle to be Quadrangular; a Body to be indiviſible; or a Man to be void of Senſe and Reaſon; if a Square be required to be made or ſuppoſed to exiſt with its Diameter commenſurate to its Sides; a Triangle two of whoſe Sides are equal to the third; or a Circle whoſe Circumference is four times its Diameter: Since it is repugnant for theſe Things to exiſt, at leaſt ſince never the like has at any Time occurred to the Mind, or the Experience, it follows that all ſuch Propoſitions ought to be repudiated, and not admitted into the Liſt of *Principles.*

From which Obſervations it ſeems to follow, that every *Demonſtration*, to make it effectually ſuch, does in ſome ſort ſuppoſe the Exiſtence of God; not only on the Part of the knowing Power or Faculty, but alſo on the Part of the knowable Object. *Carteſius* has very well obſerved, that to make us abſolutely certain of our having attained the Truth, it is required to be known whether our Faculties of apprehending and judging the Truth be true, which can only be had from the Power, Goodneſs, and Truth of our Creator. But becauſe alſo the Truth of indemonſtrable Principles depends, on the Part of the Object, upon the poſſible Exiſtence or Effection of the Things ſuppoſed; and all Poſſibility intrinſecally denotes a Reſpect to the Cauſe or Power by which the

Things

Things do exiſt, which are called or conceived to be poſſible; therefore a Demonſtration ſuppoſes the Power which effecteth all Things that are conceived or ſuppoſed under the Notion of Poſſibles, *i. e.* the infinite and incomprehenſible Power of God, which can produce whatſoever Effects we are able to conceive as poſſible, and innumerable other beyond our Comprehenſion. Every Demonſtration, I ſay, ſuppoſes true Hypotheſes; the Truth of an Hypotheſis intimates the poſſible Exiſtence of the Thing ſuppoſed; this Poſſibility denotes the efficient Cauſe of the Thing (ſince otherwiſe it would be impoſſible for it to exiſt); and the efficient Cauſe of all Things is God. But I will not purſue this Digreſſion any farther.

Hence alſo it follows, that Demonſtrations may be made of Things, which never had Exiſtence any where; becauſe it is ſufficient for a Demonſtration to aſſume true Hypotheſes, *i. e.* ſuch as imply no Inconſiſtence in themſelves. *Ex. gr. Galilæus* thinks that he invented a new Science concerning Motion, *by ſuppoſing that heavy Things are naturally carried towards the Center of the Earth with a Motion uniformly accelerated*, i. e. with ſuch a Motion, that as it recedes from Reſt, it continually ſuperadds to itſelf equal Moments of Celerity in equal Times. But if it be falſe (as I think it not always true concerning many Cauſes) that there is ſuch a Motion in the preſent Œconomy of Nature; yet becauſe ſuch a Motion may exiſt at the Pleaſure of God, as implying nothing in it contrary to Poſſibility, therefore the Concluſions, which reſult by a lawful Inference from ſuch a Suppoſition, ought to be accounted for lawful Demonſtrations. In like manner though what is ſuppoſed in Mechanics, *viz. that every Point of heavy Bodies do preſs, endeavour, or incline to Motion along Right Lines parallel to one another*

other and perpendicular to the Horizon, and consequently that equal Weights do equiponderate at equal Distances; I say, though this be really contrary to Nature, and in that respect false; yet because it may be clearly conceived, that all Bodies may have such Propensions, the Conclusion therefore, which is built upon such an Hypothesis, ought to have the Dignity and Title of a *Demonstrative Theorem*. And the same Way, though what *Ptolemy*, *Copernicus*, and all other Astronomers advance, *viz. That the Motion of the Stars is in perfect Circles* or *Ellipses*, and *that they are every Way regular and equable*; also *that they keep the same Periods of the Times, and the same Orbits, with a perpetual Constancy*, and other such Things of this variable and uncertain Nature; I say, though I imagine all these to be false, at least unknown in respect of those Stars; yet because nothing hinders, but God may create such a World, where the Stars will exactly agree with such Motions; therefore the Demonstrations depending upon such Hypotheses are most true, and their Astronomy true, not indeed of this World, but of the other, which is supposed capable of being created by God. For God has given us the Power of creating innumerable imaginary Worlds in our Thoughts, which himself, if he please, can cause to be real. Lastly, though no such Notions be ever found in the Nature of Things, as Geometricians suppose to be described by *Spiral Lines*, *Quadratrices*, *Conchoids*, *Cissoids*, &c. notwithstanding since nothing hinders, but there may be such, as well as many others not unlike, which we daily Experience, therefore the Conclusions, which follow from such Suppositions, are rightly demonstrated. For the Dominions of Reason do far exceed the Limits of Nature; the intelligible World is vastly farther extended and more diffusive than the sensible World,

World, and the Underſtanding contemplates many more Things than the Senſe.

Every particular Science of this Kind produces its own Hypotheſes, which require no other Proof, but to be explained and demonſtrated by ſome Example or Experiment more intelligible, and ſuitable to the Capacity of the Learner, and their Poſſibility made evident as far as it may be done; to which if he obſtinately refuſe to acquieſce, nothing remains but to give up all Thoughts of any farther proceeding, and the Way-ward Perſon be left to his own Liberty, as an unfit Learner of the Science propoſed. *Ex. gr.* If any one deny that the *plane Figure* (which is called a *Circle*) *may be produced by the Rotation of a Right Line*, and will not be convinced, that any ſuch Thing can be done or conceived (by the obvious Uſe of a Pair of Compaſſes, or the Revolution of a Wheel above its Center), he is to be admoniſhed to apply himſelf to ſome other Study, and no more concern himſelf with Geometry.

Moreover it will alſo appear hence, what and what Sort of Truth that Kind of *Principle* obtains, which is wont to be called a Definition; *viz. that it is a Propoſition ſhewing the Name of ſomething that reſults from ſome poſſible Suppoſition.* As for Example, (for I always ſtudy to illuſtrate Matters with the moſt eaſy and familiar Examples) if we ſuppoſe three Right Lines ſo to meet in ſome Plane, as to include Space, or conſtitute a certain Figure, I call that included Space or conſtituted Figure a *Triangle*; whence we have the following Definition of a Triangle, *A Triangle is a plane Figure comprehended by the Concurrence of three Right Lines.* If we ſuppoſe a Semicircle to be revolved about its Baſis or Diameter which is at reſt, till it be reſtored to its firſt Situation, I ſtile the Body produced by that Rotation a *Sphere*; whence the Definition

nition of a *Sphere* will be, *a Body generated from one compleat Revolution of a Semicircle about its Diameter.* Laſtly, If we ſuppoſe the Earth to be placed between the Sun and Moon, from which Poſition the Light of the Sun is intercepted, and the Obſcuration of the Moon, which is called an *Eclipſe*, reſults; hence the Definition of an *Eclipſe* is, *an Obſcuration or Privation of Light in the Moon by Reaſon of the Interpoſition of the Earth.* Hence we perceive that the Truth of a Definition is merely arbitrary as to its Subject. For that is no more than a mere Name impoſed contingently, and at pleaſure; being either feigned by the Teacher of the Science of his own Authority, or taken from common Uſe, or approved by the Conſent of the Learned; and no where ſignifies the Thing defined from its own Nature, but altogether from the Inſtitution of Men: Wherefore that Name can no otherwiſe be demonſtrated to agree with the Predicate, than by appealing to the Authority of Lexicons, to vulgar Uſe, to the Suffrages of the Learned, or at leaſt by arrogating to one's ſelf that Right, which belongs to any Teacher. But as to the Predicate, it appears that the Truth of any Definition depends upon the Poſſibility of the Hypotheſis which it includes, ſo that to make a Definition true, the Name aſſigned muſt belong to a Thing following ſome poſſible Suppoſition expreſſed in it. From whence moreover it appears, that Definitions of their own Nature are no otherwiſe demonſtrable, than the Hypotheſes themſelves are, from which they proceed; *i. e.* than by ſhewing that the Name is adapted to a Thing having a manifeſtly poſſible Condition in Nature, according to what is inculcated above. For properly ſpeaking, that which is impoſſible and inconſiſtent has neither Definition nor Affection. We may underſtand with *Ariſtotle*, what is ſignified by the Word

Hircocervus

Hircocervus, but it cannot be defined; becauſe ſuch a Thing cannot exiſt. As to the Truth of all other Axioms, it is derived, as was juſt now inſinuated, from the Preſuppoſition of the antecedent Definitions, by a lawful Argumentation. As *ex. gr.* theſe Axioms which occur in the Elements: *All Right Angles are equal. Right Lines include no Space: All Right Lines drawn from the Center of a Circle to its Circumference are equal*; theſe, I ſay, may eaſily be inferred from the juſt Definitions of a Right Angle, Equality, included Space, and a Circle; but ought to be inferred ſo, as to preſerve the Dignity of Axioms. And I doubt not but, after the ſame manner, Things, which ſeem moſt clear of themſelves, and do moſt readily command the Aſſent of every Hearer, may with the utmoſt Quickneſs be gathered from Definitions. And becauſe the Suppoſitions from whence theſe Definitions do reſult, as above, are of all Things the moſt evidently poſſible, as being daily agreeable to innumerable obvious Experiments, and moſt ſimple in their own Nature, ſo as not to eſcape the Obſervation, or exceed the Capacity of any one; but do moreover follow theſe Axioms, not after long Circumſtances but immediately; hence the Diſcurſus by which they are proved becomes imperceptible, or altogether none at all, as it uſually happens; thoſe Things which are moſt eaſily done, are not perceived how they are done. Juſt as it happens with an accompliſhed and ſkilful Muſician, who ſcarce ſeems to himſelf to touch the Inſtrument ſo much by Art, as Inſtinct, hardly perceiving the Motion of his own Reaſon, or the Exerciſe of his Memory. For becauſe we daily ſee various Magnitudes in part to agree with one another, as to all the Sorts of Dimenſions applied to them, *viz.* to fill the ſame Space, or be extended between the ſame Bounds; we therefore eaſily grant

grant ſuch to be ſuppoſed: And alſo ſince it is confirmed by Uſe, that the Habitude or Relation of Magnitudes one with another, which reſults from this Suppoſition, is called Equality; we thence eaſily either deduce of ourſelves, or grant to others affirming it (by Reaſon of our ſpeedy Apprehenſion of the Poſſibility of the Hypotheſis, and the Agreement of the Definition), that whatſoever Magnitudes are equal to the ſame Magnitude, are alſo equal to one another. Therefore even the moſt plain Axioms do ſcarce any otherwiſe differ from other Theorems, but as they approach nearer to the firſt and moſt ſimple Hypotheſes and Definitions, and conſequently are more briefly and eaſily demonſtrated.

From what has been ſaid, may be known the Original of all Natural Science, and the genuine Method of reaſoning even from the firſt Fountains of Knowledge; which is nearly thus. The Mind, from the Obſervation of the Things objected, takes Occaſion of framing like Ideas, which, as ſoon as it clearly perceives to agree with the Things that may exiſt, it affirms and ſuppoſes; then appropriating Words to them forms Definitions, and from the Conſideration and Compariſon of theſe together it draws Conſequences and makes Theorems, which being joined together into certain Syſtems do compoſe particular Sciences.

From whence again it ſeems to follow, that there is no need, at leaſt in Speculative Sciences, for ſuppoſing any *phyſical Anticipations*, *common Notions*, or *congenite Ideas*; ſince the Mind may be ſufficiently inſtructed without them, and by its Native Power acquire to itſelf the neceſſary Principles and Means of Science, as has been ſhewn. The Thing indeed is different with Regard to practical, by which I chiefly mean moral, Sciences: For the Principles of theſe do not ſo much

ſeem

ſeem to be gathered by Diſcourſe, as to flow from Appetite or natural Inſtinct. *Ex. gr.* Such Principles of moral Science as theſe; *Whatſoever is agreeable to Nature, pleaſant, and profitable, is to be loved, embraced and purſued: Every Thing hurtful to Nature, unpleaſant, and unprofitable, or which brings Loſs, Grief, or Deſtruction along with it, is to be abominated and avoided.* I ſay, ſuch Axioms do not ſeem to depend upon, or be derived from, any Argumentation, but to be known the ſame Way as we ſee, that bitter Taſtes, ſtinking Smells, frightful Spectacles, and other Things ungrateful to Senſe are avoided, even by Brutes themſelves, and the contrary Things embraced by them. Therefore we affirm nothing concerning ſuch Sciences, but confine ourſelves to ſpeculative Sciences. Nor do I very ſtiffly deny, that there are at all ſuch common Notions in theſe; but I am hence inclined to think, that they are not ſuppoſed neceſſarily, much leſs, that there is any need to invent, or deviſe any *Platonic Remembrances*, and I do not know what Reſuſcitations of the Mind as aſleep.

Moreover it ſeems no leſs to appear hence, that the Truth of Principles does not ſolely depend on *Induction*, or a perpetual Obſervation of Particulars, as *Ariſtotle* ſeems to have thought; ſince only one Experiment will ſuffice (provided it be ſufficiently clear and indubitable) to eſtabliſh a true Hypotheſis, to form a true Definition; and conſequently to conſtitute true Principles. I own the Perfection of Senſe is in ſome Meaſure required to eſtabliſh the Truth of Hypotheſes, but the Univerſality or Frequency of Obſervation is not ſo.

I might here adjoin many Things, but theſe may ſuffice to be ſpoken in general, concerning the Nature of Principles. And indeed I have prolonged my Diſcourſe upon theſe Things longer than

than I thought, and perhaps than I ought, or will be acceptable to you; the Meditation insensibly drawing me on. Yet I hope not altogether unprofitably, since it is in the highest Degree expedient for such as study the *Demonstrative Sciences* to have a thorough Knowledge of the Nature of Demonstration itself. Wherefore I hope you will pardon this Freedom, and take what I have said in good Part, as proceeding only from an attentive Consideration of the Thing, and examine it freely and diligently.

I now apply myself to distinguish the Species of *Principles*, *i. e.* to enquire how many different Sorts of *Principles* there are: Which Controversy though it may be easily decided from what has been already said, yet I think it worth the while to relate the Thoughts of others, that ye may be better able to judge what is most agreeable to Reason, after a due Consideration of the Opinions of all. But I am not willing to provoke your Patience farther at the first Onset, wherefore I will refer this Disquisition, with some other Things concerning *Principles*, perhaps not unworthy your Observation, unto the next Lecture.

LECTURE VIII.

Of the Division of First Principles.

I HAVE very lately made some general Observations concerning the *Nature*, *Condition*, *Origin* and *Truth* of *Principles*. It remains that we enquire what Authors deliver and what Reason dictates concerning the Number of their different Species.

Since

Since *Aristotle* seems a little obscure, and almost inconsistent with himself, in this Matter; we must not entirely follow his Opinion, yet we will endeavour to find it out by comparing different Places, and examine it when found. In the *Second Chapter* of the *first Book* of the latter Part of his *Analytics*, he makes three Kinds of *Syllogistical Principles*, viz. *Axioms*, *Hypotheses* and *Definitions*. For first he distinguishes them into *Axioms* and *Positions*; and then subdivides *Positions* into *Hypotheses* and *Definitions*. The Nature of an *Axiom* he thus explains, *that it is such a Syllogistical Principle, as cannot* (or as ought not to) *be demonstrated, and the Learner ought to have* (*i. e.* understand or admit) *it necessarily*. And an *Hypothesis* and *Definition*, as they are comprehended under the more general Name of *Position*, he defines conjunctly to be *such a Principle of Demonstration as likewise cannot* (or ought not to) *be demonstrated, and is not understood by the Learner of Necessity*. Then these, as they are distinguished from one another he defines thus. *An Hypothesis is a Position which takes Something to be or not be*; as that there is Magnitude, that Unity is granted. A *Definition* he pronounces to be *a Position which assumes that Something is*: as that Unity is an undivided Quotity (or Quantity). But in the tenth Chapter of the same Tract, he seems to assign three other Kinds of *Principles*, viz. *Common Axioms*, *Hypotheses* and *Postulates*. And he thus distinguishes *Hypotheses* from *Postulates*: *When* (says he) *he who demonstrates assumes without Proof whatsoever may be demonstrated, and if they are agreeable to the Learner, supposes them, neither is this simply an Hypothesis but in respect of him alone; but if the Learner have no, or even a contrary Opinion of these Things, then is such an assuming of them a Postulate. And an Hypothesis and Postulate differ in this. For a Postulate is that which is besides, or contrary to the Notion of the Learner; or which, when it is demonstrable, is received and applied without Demonstration.* So that from the Comparison of these Places, there seem to be *five* Sorts of *Principles*, according to *Aristotle*, *viz.* *Axioms*, *Indemonstrable Suppositions*, *Definitions*, *demonstrable Suppositions*, and *Postulates.* But those before are contrary in Specie to these deliver'd here. For there he seems to deliver *Principles* absolutely indemonstrable, a *Position* being defined that which is not to be demonstrated; but here he expresly declares the *Hypotheses* and *Postulates* assumed to be demonstrable. For reconciling which Things, it may be said, that in the former Place the Philosopher respects the *first Principles* of every Science simply, which certainly should not be demonstrated, since thus they would not be the first; but in the latter, he points at the particular Principles of the subjected Sciences, which nothing hinders but they may be demonstrated (as has been shewn above;) or at least, he means that no *Principles* may, or ought to require, or admit of Proof in that Science, where they are used as such, tho' in others they may.

But something I dislike in this *Aristotelian* Account of *Principles* and their Explication, which I speak with all due Regard to the Honour of that great Man, for whom, notwithstanding, I preserve the greatest Veneration and Esteem, by reason of his most profound Wisdom and extensive Learning, and would have all Men to do the same. His *Trichotomy* indeed into *Hypotheses*, *Definitions*, and *Axioms*, as to what belongs to the Members of the Division in general, and with Respect to every Science, seems to be most perfect; but as to the Explication otherwise. For he shews in his Examples, that he understands nothing else by an Hypothesis

Hypothesis than the *Position* or *Assertion* of the Existence of the Subject concerning which it is treated in any Science or Demonstration. As, (*f*) *That Unity may be given. That Magnitude may exist. It must be taken for granted*, (says he) *that both Unity and Magnitude do exist, but the Existence of the rest is demonstrated.* But such an *Hypothesis* seems to be altogether unfit for Science, since nothing can be inferred from it, nor is it wont to enter any Syllogism. For pray what Conclusion can follow or be derived from hence *that Magnitude may be, or may be given*; *that it may or can exist?* None indeed that I can find. But from hence *that it is such, that it is endowed with such a Property, that it may obtain such a Situation and such a Motion*, it may follow, from the admitting and comparing of some Properties, that it obtains others along with them. Therefore the aforesaid Supposition is not rightly taken for a *Principle* of Demonstration. For it belongs to such a *Principle* that it be fit to beget something, as a Conclusion from itself, and serve for the Proof of others. But from the bare Position of a Subject, *That it is*, nothing else can follow but *That it is*, viz. *It is, therefore it is.* I own indeed, that antecedently some Knowledge or Conception of a Subject is presupposed to the Science of all Things, as far as every Proposition is gathered from incomplex Terms, which can be no otherwise apprehended than as significative of Things having some Kind of Essence, *i. e.* by conceiving or supposing that they are; but incomplex Terms, implying Essence, are not therefore the Principles of Demonstrations, but rather the Matter or Integral Parts of them.

I do also very much disapprove of that Assersion of *Aristotle*, *that a Definition affirms nothing*,

(*f*) I. Post. 10. 8.

or receives neither Part of a Contradiction ; *i. e.* he takes a *Definition* not for an entire Propoſition, but only for its *Predicate* ; as *ex. gr. that he is a rational Animal* is the *Definition* of a Man, and for that Reaſon a *Principle* of *Demonſtration* ; but not this Propoſition, *A Man is a rational Animal.* But how agreeable is this with his own Definition of a Principle, *viz. that it is an immediate Propoſition* ; and how conformable to the Nature and Quality of a Principle, which requires that it be a *Truth*, and ſuch a *Truth* as may have other *Truths* deduced from it ? For ſince *Truth* is the Quality of a perfect Propoſition, and not of a ſimple Term, therefore nothing can be drawn from the Apprehenſion of the latter. Why, according to him, is a *Definition* named a certain *Poſition*, if nothing be put or affirmed ? How, laſtly, can it but be very abſurd, thus to take a *Definition* with *Axioms*, which are perfect Propoſitions, and with *Hypotheſes* which, according to himſelf, do affirm ſomething, are compared, conjoined, and agree together the ſame way as *Principles ?* The *Definition*, which is accounted a *Principle* of Demonſtration, is really a compleat Propoſition predicating concerning the propoſed Subject ſome Affection of itſelf, which is uſeful for inferring other Affections. I ſay it is a certain ſpecial Propoſition of a demonſtrative Syllogiſm, ſhewing the Cauſe of the Property demonſtrated, as far as it may be done. Indeed an incomplex Definition, or the Predicate of a complex one, may be, and moſt frequently is, the Mean, or Argument found and made choice of, for raiſing a Demonſtration ; but it is not therefore a Principle, no more than a *Whole* and a *Part* are therefore Principles of Demonſtration, becauſe that Axiom, *The Whole is greater than its Part*, is reckoned among Principles. I ſay nothing that *Ariſtotle*'s Affirmation is not

not always true, *that Axioms cannot be demonſtrated*, becauſe his Words, as was hinted above, do admit of ſome Excuſe, and an uſeful Propoſition. But of the other two kinds of Principles he ſubjoins *viz. Hypotheſes* and *Poſtulates*, which, tho' otherwiſe demonſtrable, are aſſumed by the Demonſtrator as granted, theſe I imagine differ nothing at all from *Axioms*. For whatſoever may be demonſtrated is a *Theorem*; but a *Theorem* which is not proved in any particular Science, but is taken from ſome ſuperior one, obtains the Place of an *Axiom* in that particular Science.

But I ſee very little Foundation for *Ariſtotle*'s Diſtinction between an *Hypotheſis* and *Poſtulate*, that a Learner ſhould willingly ſubſcribe to that, but diſſent from this. For howſoever it be concerning the preconceived Opinions of a Learner, which matter nothing, whether they agree or diſagree with the Mind of the Teacher; yet before the Learner comes to an efficacious Demonſtration, it is neceſſary for him to give his Aſſent to certain Principles propoſed, otherwiſe he will perceive no Science to have been inbred with him. It may happen, that the Learner may have Prejudices, but what is this to the Purpoſe of the Science? If he have any, he muſt throw them off, or lay them aſide; and be convinced by the Maſter's Arguments, or inſtructed by clear Examples of the Matter propoſed, before he can obtain a perfect, abſolute, and properly called Science. For pray what Energy will there be of a Demonſtration, what Effect, if the Learner can't aſſent, can't acquieſce, nay can't firmly adhere to the Premiſes? Nor will I ſay how juſtly that can be called a *Poſtulate*, which may be demonſtrated. For why is that taken precariouſly, which may be aſſumed of right, and wreſted by Violence? Or why does not the Learner oppoſe the idle Perſua-

ſions

ſions of the Maſter? So that I can't ſee what led the Philoſopher to this Diſtinction, nor does his Interpreters remove the Scruple.

As to what is ſaid by *Proclus* (for firſt of all I aim at him) while he profeſſes to follow *Ariſtotle*, he, in my opinion, renders all things worſe. For 1*ſt*. He attributes three kinds of Principles to *Euclid*, *viz.* *Axioms*, *Hypotheſes*, and *Poſtulates*, whoſe Differences he expounds according to the Sentiment of *Ariſtotle*: But as if *Definitions* were not *Principles*, nor did either *Euclid* or *Ariſtotle* ever account them for *Principles*, nor did the latter moſt expreſly diſtinguiſh them from *Hypotheſes*. Therefore the Blindneſs of *Proclus* ſeems wonderful, both in wholly omitting *Definitions* in his Enumeration of *Principles*, and in confounding them with the *Hypotheſes* of *Ariſtotle*; while he very incongruouſly attributes thoſe Things to the *Definitions* and *Poſtulates* of *Euclid*, which *Ariſtotle* aſcribes to his demonſtrable *Hypotheſes* and *Poſtulates*. For how are *Euclid*'s Definitions and Geometrical Poſtulates demonſtrable? How is it neceſſary for the Sentiment of a Learner to be oppoſite to the Poſtulates of *Euclid?* Or how can that be truly adapted to them, *that however a Learner refuſe his Aſſent, yet he is admitted a Hearer whether he will or no?* What is this elſe but to overturn the Foundation of Geometry, and deſtroy all Learning at once? Whereas the Poſtulates of *Euclid* do carry ſo clear a Poſſibility, and may be illuſtrated with ſo many familiar Examples, that no Genius capable of Science can any way impugn, or find Fault with them: Nay, otherwiſe a Teacher would become immodeſt, importunate and trifling, who ſhould require or ſuppoſe it; and in vain would go about to teach or demonſtrate, his Poſtulates being not admitted. But why do I oppoſe *Proclus*, when he oppoſes himſelf, and ſeems to remove

thoſe

those undigested Notions in the beginning of his third Book, which he had inserted from *Aristotle* in his second. *It is always necessary*, says he, *that the Principles of these be indemonstrable and self-evident*, at the same Time adjoining many other Things to the same Purpose clearly repugnant to what was before advanced, and to *Aristotle*'s Description of Postulates, which he seems to espouse.

But dismissing *Proclus*, let us see what *Ramus* says to these Things: He blames *Proclus*; but how? Why so, as entirely to take away all Difference of Principles, indeed with a singular Moroseness. But upon what Arguments? *Because*, says he, *Definitions*, *Divisions*, and all other *self-evident Propositions are admitted into Disciplines, not in the name of a Postulate, or an Axiom, but only of their own Clearness and Perspicuity.* Which contain almost as many Paralogisms as Words. For who ever believed *Definitions* to be admitted into any Discipline under the Title of a *Postulate*, or an *Axiom?* Who that treated accurately of any Science did not separate *Definitions* from *Axioms?* And tho' no Body had distinguished them, could they not therefore be distinguished? Whence then are there so many little Distinctions of them? But, says he, they are admitted only *in the Name of their Clearness*, *i. e.* I suppose, not as they are *Definitions* or *Axioms*, but because they are *clear:* Be it so, what follows? Therefore he concludes, they ought not to be distinguished: A fine Consequence indeed, and very like the following one. The Sun and a Candle are beheld not in the Name of the Sun and a Candle, but because they shine clearly; therefore the Sun and a Candle ought not to be distinguished; or therefore the Light of the Sun and of a Candle are the same. But he argues moreover, That this Difference of *Princi-*

ples

ples is only uſed by *Euclid* in his firſt Book, in the following Books it is contemned: Contemned is it, how does that appear? Certainly he elſewhere uſes other *Definitions* and other *Axioms* as occaſion requires; it is true he adds no more *Poſtulates*, becauſe there ſeems to be no need of more: But where does he confound thoſe Species of *Principles*, or declare his Contempt of any of them? Unleſs not unſeaſonably to name them be to contemn them.

But perhaps he will object the moſt weighty Authority of *Archimedes*, who promiſcuouſly calls the Principles laid down before his Iſorrhopics *Poſtulates*, or Things required. *We require it as a Poſtulate*, ſays he, *that equal Weights hanging by equal Lengths do weigh equally, or are in Æquilibrio.* And after the ſame manner does *Euclid* in his Optics call all the *Principles* he aſſumes *Hypotheſes*: *Geminus* with *Proclus*, and *Eutocius* did once make the ſame Obſervation concerning *Archimedes*: To which Inſtance I anſwer, that perhaps *Archimedes* ſtudying Brevity, and not willing to make too great an Apparatus to a ſmall Book, did on purpoſe neglect that extreme Exactneſs, which he obſerved in his *Books of the Sphere and Cylinder*, *of Spiral Lines*, and other more curious Pieces, where he ſeparates Definitions from Axioms. Nor is it any wonder for the ſame Words to be ſometimes more, and ſometimes leſs extenſive, according to the Deſign and Purpoſe of the Writer. Like as the *Stoics*, thoſe famous Reformers of Things, as well as Words, do give univerſal Propoſitions the Title of *Axioms*, as if they meant to make all Propoſitions equal in Dignity, as they have done of Virtues and Vices. Nor do I deny but the word Poſtulate, or Petition, from its vulgar Signification, may be fitly enough attributed to all kinds of Principles. For a Teacher muſt in Part *peti-*

tion

tion, becauſe he muſt by all means procure the Aſſent of the Learner. And this ſurely is more modeſt than to be ſaid *to command*, as the Maſters of Diſciplines do often call their Dictates *Precepts*, i. e. *Commands*.

Rivaldus argues not ill upon this Place of *Archimedes*, *We may petition* (ſays he) *that this or that be ſo named*; *then that this or that be taken as eſtabliſhed*, *which we know by the Light of Nature*; *laſtly*, *that this or that is poſſible to be done. But every thing that can be done*, *or ſo named*, *we cannot term an Axiom*, *nor will it be allowed that the Knowledge which is innate to our Minds is a Definition.* Which is appoſite enough. I adjoin *Proclus*: *Some now*, ſays he, *think it proper to call all Principles Petitions as they do all things ſought Problems. Archimedes* therefore who ſtudied Brevity, and was willing to comprehend his Principles together in one Body might not unfitly aſſign to them the name of Petitions, becauſe he could not equally adapt the Title of Definitions or Axioms to them all. And by the ſame Authority might *Euclid* and others call their Principles *Hypotheſes*. For that Word alſo is capable of a moſt extenſive Acceptation: Nor can any Thing, which is uſeful to go before a Demonſtration, be improperly called an *Hypotheſis*, i. e. a *Suppoſition*, or as it were, a Foundation laid, upon which the following Demonſtrations are to be ſuperſtructed. *Archimedes* is wont to ſpeak thus: *ex. gr.* Before his *Books of the Sphere and Cylinder* after his Definitions and Axioms; *Theſe things*, ſays he, *being laid as a Foundation*: Before the Definitions premiſed to his Book concerning *Conoids and Spheroids*: *Theſe are laid as a Foundation*: In his Book concerning *Spirals*; *The Things* (ſays he) *of Uſe for their Demonſtration are laid down before*; where the Words rendered *laid as a Foundation*,

and

and *laid down before*, are evidently of the ſame ſignification in the Original. *To ſuppoſe* then univerſally ſignifies *to premiſe*, or *to lay down as a Foundation*; in which Senſe it agrees with all *Principles.* So alſo *to aſſume*, or *take for granted*, tho' it be more properly accommodated to Axioms: As in his Books concerning the *Sphere* and *Cylinder*, where *Archimedes* being about to lay down *Axioms* after the *Definitions* he had delivered, ſays, *Theſe I aſſume.*

I muſt not paſs over that new Genus, or at leaſt new Name of Principles, which the juſt now mentioned *(g)* Commentator of *Archimedes* has hence coined for us, called a *Subſidy* or *Reſerve*. *Archimedes* had ſpoke of other Premiſes to his Demonſtrations, after his Definitions. *Therefore*, ſays he (*h*), *after we have writ of Theorems and the* Epitagmata *which are uſeful to their Demonſtrations, we will next proceed to write to you of Problems.* Hence *Rivaltus*, interpreting *Epitagmata* Subſidies or Reſerves, impoſes the Name of *Subſidies* to certain *Definitions*, which in my Opinion are miſplaced. But *Archimedes* by *Epitagmata* ſeems to underſtand nothing elſe but certain ſubſidiary Propoſitions or *Lemmata* made uſe of in the Courſe of the following Book, which were requiſite to the Demonſtration of its primary Theorems; therefore the *Epitagmata* which follow, or are inſerted in their Order, are to it like thoſe *Cohorts*, which the Writers of the *Roman* Hiſtory are wont to call *Epitagmata* or *ſubſidiary Cohorts.* Tho' I very much ſuſpect that *Archimedes* uſed no ſuch Words, but perhaps ἐπιτάγματα has crept in by the Heedleſneſs of the Tranſcribers for ἐπὶ ταῦτα; ſo that inſtead of the *Epitagmata which are uſeful to their Demonſtrations*, as above, it ſhould have

(g) Rivaltus.

(*h*) In libr. de Conoid. & Spheroid.

been,

been, *the other Things which are useful to their Demonstrations.* Tho' I deny not but the Name *Epitagma* or *Subsidy* is here apposite enough, and is somewhere to be found in *Pappus*; yet so that we can scarce know from the Context in what Sense it ought to be taken. But I am afraid these Fightings with Shadows, these Trifles, these worthless Distinctions give you little Delight: To me indeed it is grievous that while hunting after Accuracy I find myself fallen into Loquacity.

That therefore I may the more speedily rid my self of this Question, passing by the Opinions of others about the Matter, I thus briefly and consonantly apply to what has been said.

The Kinds of *Principles* simply so called, *i. e.* such as are indemonstrable, which cannot, or ought not to be demonstrated, are two, *viz, Hypotheses* or *Postulates*, and *Definitions*.

Hypotheses are Propositions assuming or affirming some evidently possible Mode, Action, or Motion of a Thing, *ex. gr. Suppose a Point to be carried with a direct Motion from the Place* A *to the Place* B: *or let it be granted that a Point may be so carried. Suppose a Right Line be carried about, with one of its Extremes fixed or immoveable, 'till it be turned to its first Situation :* Or *let it be taken for granted that a Right Line may be so turned. Suppose two Right Lines to meet, or intersect one another, so as to go different ways after their meeting.* Or *let it be granted that two Right Lines may so meet. Suppose a right-angled Triangle to be revolved compleatly about one Leg of the Right Angle. Suppose the Right Line* AB (Fig. IV.) *with the extream* A *to be turned about uniformly* (i. e. *so as as make equal Angles in equal Times) and the Point* A *in the same Time to be carried uniformly along the Right Line* AB, i. e. *so as to make equal Intervals in equal Times. Suppose a Point to go about in the Circumference*

cumference of a Circle or Ellipsis so as to make equal Angles in equal Times, in respect of a Point assigned, which let be the Center of the Circle, or Focus of the Ellipsis. Suppose a Right Line to be extended from some Point of a lucid or enlightened Body to the Eye. Suppose the Moon to be placed in a Right Line between the Sun and the Eye. Suppose a Ray to be derived from a visible Point through the Center of the Eye, or to the Center of the Tunica Retina. Of such Positions the Sense it self proves, and Experience clearly attests that they are not rashly assumed, but ought to be admitted, *i. e.* that they contain nothing repugnant to Possibility. From whence it appears by the Way, that as there is a very near Affinity between *Axioms* and *Theorems*, which was observed by the Ancients, so there is the same between *Hypotheses* and *Problems*. For as a *Problem* shews the Manner, and demonstrates the Possibility of some Structure; so an Hypothesis assumes some Construction which is manifestly possible. To which Purpose *Proclus* speaks well according to the Sentiment of *Geminus*. *In a Postulate or an Hypothesis*, says he, *as in a Problem, what is easy to be done is assumed; in an Axiom, as in a Theorem, what is easily known is granted.*

A *Definition* is a Proposition wherein a Name is imposed or ascribed from some possible Supposition of a Thing clearly resulting; which Supposition, being expressed in the Proposition, determines and circumscribes that Name. As, insisting on the above mentioned Hypothesis, *What results from the Meeting of two Right Lines intersecting on one another may be called a* rectilineal Angle: Or a rectilineal Angle *is that which is made from such a meeting. The plane Figure which is produced from the Rotation of a Right Line may be called* a Circle: Or a Circle *is a plane Figure which is produced by the Circumduction of a Right Line. The Solid which proceeds*

ceeds from the Revolution of a rectangular Triangle about one Leg of the Right Angle may be named a Right Cone: Or a Right Cone *is a Body generated by such a Revolution. The Curve Line which is made from two uniform Motions,* viz. *Right and Circular, may be called a* Spiral: Or a Spiral *is a Curve Line engendered by such a Composition of Motions. The Motion in the Periphery of a Circle or Ellipsis making equal Angles in respect of an assigned Point may be called* a Mean Motion: Or a Mean Motion *is that which is so affected. The Right Line extended from any Point of a lucid or enlightened Body towards the Eye may be named* a Ray. *The Privation of the apparent Light by the Interposition of the Moon may be called an Eclipse of the Sun. The Ray flowing from a visible Point thro' the Center of the Retina, may be called* the Optical Axis. From which Examples the Nature and Origin of a Definition abundantly appears; that in it the Name reciprocally agrees with the Thing, and the Thing with the Name: Or that the Signification of this is adequate to the possible Existence of that.

From these two emerges a third Kind of *Principle* by a Syllogistical Consequence, which is wont to be called an *Axiom*, *Dignity*, *Pronunciatum*, *Common Notion*, or *Anticipation*. But this is nothing but a certain Theorem in some *superior precedent Science*, which is clearly deduced and demonstrated from the proper *Definitions* and Hypotheses of that Science either immediately, or by other intermediate Theorems; and consequently is assumed without Proof in the subordinate Science, or at least emerges from some *Hypothesis* or *Definition* belonging to that Science by a most easy and evident Consequence, in the form of a *Consectary*. Which Species of *Axiom* is wont to be called *proper* to that peculiar Science, as the other

is

is called *common*, as being *common* to all the Sciences ſubjected to the ſaid *primary Science. Ex. gr. That thoſe Things which are equal to the ſame, are equal to another*, is accounted a *common Axiom*, becauſe it agrees with Numbers, Times, Motions and Weights, as well as Magnitudes; and is only demonſtrated in Metaphyſics, as having there the Reaſon of a Concluſion, or Theorem: But *That all Right Angles are equal*; or *That two Right Lines include no Space*, theſe are *proper Axioms*, obtaining the firſt Place in Geometry only, as being inferred and after a Sort demonſtrated from the Definitions of a Right Angle and a Right Line. But theſe Things we have already ſufficiently expounded in the Examples above.

Thus we have come at laſt exactly to *Ariſtotle*'s firſt Diviſion in the Second Chapter of the firſt Book of the former Part of his Analytics, *viz.* into *Hypotheſes*, *Definitions* and *Axioms*; though we diſapprove his unaccurate, at leaſt obſcure Explanation of them. We have alſo come up to our *Element-Compoſer*, who in like manner diſtributes *Principles* into three Claſſes, *viz. Definitions*, *Poſtulates*, and *Pronunciata*. For it is all one whether indemonſtrable Suppoſitions be called *Hypotheſes* or *Poſtulates*; only they are not thought to be therefore called *Poſtulates*, becauſe the Demonſtrator aſſumes them precariouſly, and as it were begs them: For they have an irrefragable Certitude and Evidence, in no wiſe inferior to the Clearneſs of *Axioms*; nay ſeem more clear than many *Axioms*, becauſe theſe depend and are derived from thoſe. They may alſo put on the Form of *Axioms*, as *Problems* do that of *Theorems*, neither do they at all differ from thoſe, except as to their Form, and becauſe they cannot be demonſtrated like thoſe.

The

The Modesty of the Name ought by no Means to detract from the Excellence of the Thing.

But we may take Notice of something that may be objected against what has been said, *viz.* that two Propositions are reckoned by *Euclid* for *Postulates*, to which the Explication here brought of a *Postulate* or *Hypothesis* does not agree, *viz.* these; *That all Right Angles are equal to one another*; *And if a Right Line insisting upon two other Right Lines do make the internal Angles at the same Parts of the insisting Line lesser than two Right Angles, that those two Right Lines produced towards these Parts do at length meet.* I answer, this is unaccurately done by *Euclid*, (if it be done by him, and these Propositions have not crept into a Place not belonging to them, by the Fault of others) and therefore they are more rightly reckoned *Axioms* by *Geminus*, *Proclus*, and most other Interpreters. For they are really Theorems consequent to the Definitions of a Right Angle and a Parallel Line.

After I had thought of these Things concerning *Principles* and their Division, by chance casting my Eyes upon that elegant and useful Book of *Alphonsus Borellus*, containing the Elements of Geometry digested in a New Method, which he calls by the Name of *Euclid restored*, I found he had there bestowed the greatest Care and Subtilty in illustrating the *Nature* and *Distinction* of *Principles*, and that both in the Proem of the Work, and especially in those that immediately go before the first Proposition of the *Elements*. Perhaps I should have observed something among some of his Dictates, if they had offered themselves before; but since they contain scarce any thing different from our own Thoughts, from what I myself have thoroughly handled heretofore; and since we have already discoursed more than enough

upon

upon this Matter, for the preſent, I will paſs them by untouched: yet afterward, when Opportunity permits, I will perhaps examine one or two Points, and eſpecially thoſe which the Opinion of *Clavius* concerning the Nature of Definitions ſeems to contradict. In the mean Time I betake myſelf to certain particular Things to be obſerved concerning *Poſtulates* or *Hypotheſes*, *Definitions* and *Axioms*.

As to *Hypotheſes*, both their Foundation and Reaſon, their Matter and Extenſion, may be obſerved in general. The Foundation and Reaſon of *Hypotheſes* (as we have often intimated, for we cannot, if we would, avoid oftentimes repeating the ſame Thing, which is not indeed altogether amiſs, but partly uſeful in ſuch Lectures as theſe; ſince the Senſe of the Words, and the Meaning of the Speaker, are by this Means more clearly perceived and deeply rooted), the Foundation, I ſay, of *Hypotheſes* is evident from Experience, or through ſome Senſe whereby we apprehend Things offered from without; or laſtly, through the ſecret Conſciouſneſs, whereby we perceive internal Motions, and the Actions remaining within us. For nothing ought to be ſuppoſed, whereof we can make no Experiment, nor can illuſtrate or confirm it by ſome appoſite Example: ſince the Poſſibility of an *Hypotheſis* can be ſhewn no otherwiſe; of which notwithſtanding the Student muſt have a certain Science. That *Hypotheſis ex. gr.* in Optics, *That a Ray or luminous Right Line may be extended from any (at leaſt a Phyſical) Point of a viſible Object to the Eye whereſoever placed in a homogeneous Medium*; this, I ſay, would by no means be admitted, if it could not be ſupported by this notorious Experiment, that an Object is every where ſeen, except there be by a Body placed ſomewhere in a Right Line between it and the Eye. Nay it would ſeem incredible and almoſt impoſſible (by

reaſon

reaſon of the Unintelligibleneſs of the Manner of its Performance, and the imperceptible Subtilty of its Nature), if Experience did not plainly confirm us in the Truth of it. So if any Thing leſs probable, or leſs examined, be delivered to a Student, in the Room of an Hypotheſis, the Maſter of the Science is bound to ſhew it by a plain Example or Experiment, (or as *(i) Ariſtotle* ſays, *by Senſe or the Finger*) ſo that before he proceed farther to Demonſtration, there muſt remain no Heſitation concerning the Poſſibility or Truth of the Thing ſuppoſed.

And every Action, Motion, or Mode of Being that falls under Obſervation, or may be apprehended by Experience, is the Subject of *Hypotheſes.* Eſpecially the Subject of *Mathematical Hypotheſes*, which we principally reſpect, is extended to all the Affections of Magnitude obvious to any Senſe. So that to comprehend the Subject of Mathematical Hypotheſis rightly, the general Affections, of which every Magnitude is capable, ought to be diligently weighed. Wherefore it will next be fit to treat of them.

Some are very ſolicitous to find ſome *primary Notion* and moſt *eſſential Property* of Magnitude, from whence all the reſt do flow: Perhaps a Labour fruitleſs and without foundation; ſince it may be there is none (as indeed in my Judgment, there is none) to which ſuch a *Prerogative of Nature*, ſuch a *Primacy of Order* does really in ſo peculiar a Manner belong; but Magnitude has many Properties, which do all agree to it equally in a like Connection, and are linked with it in the cloſeſt Chain, being involved and united both into it and into one another. Wherefore being not ſolicitous concerning their Order, I will ſtrictly

(i) Poſt. II. 7.

and

and largely endeavour to explain ſuch *primary Affections* of Magnitude, as are moſt obſervable, and which ſupply Matter for Mathematical Hypotheſes. But I perceive I have undertaken a Buſineſs worthy a larger Expoſition than to be finiſhed in a few Words, and which I had rather not begin at all than be obliged to leave abruptly; and ſince I remember I have ſo often had the Experience, how much eaſier a Pardon is obtained for a Fault in Brevity than in Prolixity, and how much better it is to abridge myſelf, than nauſeate my Hearers, I will reſerve theſe Things to the following Lectures.

Μόνῳ τῷ σοφῷ Θεῷ δόξα. Ἀμήν.

FINIS.

MATHE-

MATHEMATICAL
LECTURES

Read in the

Univerſity of *Cambridge*,

An. Dom. MDCLXV.

MATHEMATICAL LECTURES.

LECTURE IX.

Of the Termination, Extenſion, Compoſition, and Diviſibility of Magnitudes.

I Am very ſenſible how nice and difficult a Buſineſs I undertake, in attempting to treat of the *common Affections* and *Properties of Magnitude*, which occur to Experience, and conſequently afford matter for *Mathematical Hypotheſis*, and therefore I cannot but ſpeak ſomething by Way of Preface and Premonition. For theſe are Things, which it is very difficult not to render more perplexed by explaining, not to obſcure by illuſtrating; Things for the moſt Part of ſo ſubtle and abſtract a Nature, that the Imagination ſcarce can comprehend them, ſcarce can aſſign to each their juſt Bounds, or ſeparate one from another, and conſequently do elude the moſt piercing Sagacity, and fly away and eſcape him who endeavours diſtinctly to catch at their vaniſhing Ideas: So that what St. *Auguſtine* is reported to have ſaid of Time, may not undeſervedly be applied to moſt of them. *If none ſeek of me what Time is, I know; If any ask me I don't know.* For what *ex. gr.* is *Extenſion?* What *Space?* What *Motion?*

tion? Every one, that ſpeaks of theſe, imagines himſelf to be clearly underſtood, even by the moſt Vulgar; but if you examine their Breaſts, you will find moſt of them linked in inextricable Snares, heſitating in their Thoughts, and entangled in their Speech. Nay, the moſt ſubtle Philoſophers, after the moſt diligent Contemplation with the exacteſt Care imaginable, when they come to diſcourſe of theſe Things can hardly ſpeak conſiſtently, either one with another, or the ſame with themſelves: and ſeldom do any handle them ſo, but monſtrous Paradoxes, and moſt grievous Difficulties, ſeem to follow.

Carteſius, ex. gr. from his Conception of Space infers the *infinite* or (to ſoften the Expreſſion) *indefinite Extenſion* of Mundane Matter, with the *Impoſſibility of Vacuum*; and the *Immediate Contiguity of Bodies* which were at a Diſtance from one another before, by annihilating or removing all the intermediate Bodies; and ſuch like Things as theſe: Which his Adverſary *Hobbs* condemns and explodes (how juſtly I will not diſpute), as contrary to common Senſe. But does himſelf afford any Thing more clear and certain, or leſs incoherent and more blameleſs? Let us conſider him a little: He terms *Space* the *Idea* or *Phantaſm of Body*; *Place the Coincidence of Space with the Magnitude of a Body*; *Motion the leaving of one Place and acquiring another.* Now who does not ſee how repugnant theſe Things are with one another, and how very obnoxious to moſt ridiculous Conſequences; to ſuch *ex. gr.* as theſe: Therefore the Place of a Body, (*viz.* of this School) will be nothing elſe, but the *Coincidence* of my, your, or any ones *Phantaſm* with the *Magnitude* of the School. As if the *Pope* of *Rome* did not reſide in the *Vatican* Palace, nor live at *Rome*, but was placed every where in the Fancies of all

Men

Men that think of him: By which means he may easily be conceived an universal Pontiff. Therefore the Motion of a Stone or Arrow will be the leaving of one Coincidence of a *Phantasm* with a *Magnitude*, and acquiring with *Coincidence*: And while the *Turk* is marching an Army into *Hungary*, he is only wandering in your Fancy and encamping in your Brain. But pray does the *Magnitude* of a Body coincide or coexist with a *Phantasm* or *Idea* of the Mind? How can the Coincidence of a Body with a Phantasm be lost or acquired? How does a Phantasm separate and come between distant Bodies? How can a Phantasm be occupied, be filled, divided, measured and subjected to so many other Attributes, which himself is not afraid to assign to Space, after he has delivered this imaginary Definition of it? What if no Man, no Fancier should exist in the Universe, would there therefore be no other Thing? Or would all Things necessarily be at Rest, but they could not be at Rest, since the Phantasm of Space does also belong to the Definition of Rest? Could there, I say, be therefore no Space, no Place, no Motion in Being? How mysterious, nay how absurd and contradictory are these Things? These few Instances out of many I have produced by the by, to shew how hard, how difficult these *common Properties* of Magnitude are to be conceived and explained, since the most ingenious Men entangle themselves in Labyrinths, Difficulties and Inconveniences, while they are endeavouring to handle them with the greatest Accuracy. For which Reason I am the more pardonable, if I shall handle these Things, recite and explain them, perhaps after a meaner and poorer manner, more accommodate to common Sense than to metaphysical Conceptions; and so far only as I judge useful to my Purpose, *i. e.* as they are subservient to *Mathematical Hypotheses*. But to come to the Purpose.

I. *Of*

I. *Of the Termination of Magnitude.*

Of the principal and more common Affections of Magnitude the *first* that offers itself to us (for I confine myself to no Order, since as I took notice in the last Lecture, there is no Foundation of Order on the Part of the Thing between the *reciprocal* and *essential Properties* of the same Thing) I say, the *first* that occurs, while we are contemplating Magnitude, and presents itself to our Sense and Thought, is its *Termination.* Indeed we can approach nothing with Sense, but as it is terminated; we cannot penetrate the inward Parts of any Body, but only view its outward Film with the Eye, and touch it with the Hand. Neither can we conceive any Magnitude in Thought, at least distinctly, but only as it is contained and comprehended within some Limits. We may indeed have a confused Imagination of some Magnitude in Power, suppose a Right Line, as *Aristotle* said, infinite; *i. e.* produced or encreased at pleasure, or to a greater Distance than any Distance assigned, which consequently we denominate infinite. Nor is the Philosopher's Definition of Infinite improper, though very subtle; (*i*) *That is infinite, from which if one take any Quantity, something still may be assumed beyond.* But this is nothing else but to consider many Lines successively, according to a certain arbitrary and indeterminate Power, and not one real indeterminate Line distinctly; which according to the Philosopher again we cannot comprehend in the Mind. (*k*) *An infinite*, says he, *as such cannot be conceived or known.* The same is of an *infinite Subduction* or *Subdivision*, by which nothing else is understood, but that a Subtraction or Division may be continued at pleasure, without being brought to an Impossibility of proceed-

(*i*) Phys. III. 9. (*k*) Phys. I. 5.—II. 10.

ing

ing farther. Again, (*l*) *Aristotle* ſpeaking of Mathematicians ſays, *Mathematicians do neither want nor uſe infinite Magnitude, but take as much as they pleaſe, when they are minded to terminate it.*

When we conceive a *Line*, we form an Idea of ſomething like a very fine Thread extended between two Extreams; or at leaſt returning to itſelf with one Extreme, as is done in Curve Lines which include a Figure. When we think of a *Superfice*, we imagine ſomething like an exceeding thin Cuticle or Plate encompaſſed with a very narrow Margin. When we Paint the Effigy of a *Body* with the Pencil of the Fancy, we for the moſt Part repreſent to ourſelves a certain opaque Lump on every Side covered with an exquiſitely fine and thin Veil. When we imagine an *Angle*, we conceive ſome intermediate Space included between two or more Lines or Superficies, or ſome ſuch Thing. Nor is it otherwiſe concerning *Analogical Quantities*, *viz.* When we think of a *Weight*, we think of ſome Power capable of elevating ſome terminated Magnitude, *ex. gr.* one or more Pounds: When we meditate upon *Motion*, we imagine a ſucceſſive Tranſition of ſome Body from this Term to that: When we reflect upon *Number* we imagine the Repetition of an Unit, beginning ſomewhere and ending ſomewhere, or of a Multitude bounded between two extreme Units taken incluſively. I ſpeak almoſt according to the vulgar Notion; for in reality Units are not the Terms of Numbers, though themſelves have their Terms, *viz.* the ſame with the Magnitudes they repreſent.

Therefore every Quantity is conceivable by us a different Way, being terminated in ſome manner, and as ſuch, conduces not a little to Mathematical Hypotheſes. For from hence eſpecially we deduce the various particular Species or

(*l*) Phyſ. III. 11.

Dimenſions of Magnitude; and in ſome ſort demonſtrate. that they are not feigned at random, but have a real Exiſtence after their own Manner. For we may argue thus: A *Body* or *ſolid Magnitude* (which no Perſon denies, as being palpable, and whatſoever can be preſuppoſed farther) on no Part runs out to Infinity, but is terminated on every Side: Which *Term* or Boundary is not diviſible inwardly, or *as to its Thickneſs*; for if it ſhould be ſo diviſible, not the Whole, but only ſomething of it without would be the Term, contrary to the Hypotheſis. Hence there is given ſome *Term* of a *ſolid Magnitude* indiviſible *as to Thickneſs*, which is called a *Superfice:* And ſo we have one Mathematical Hypotheſis, and the Definition reſulting from it. Moreover the ſaid *Superfice* is not any where unlimited, but is included within ſome Ambit or Extreme, and that Extreme, by a like Diſcurſus with the foregoing, is indiviſible towards the inward Parts or *as to its Breadth:* Let the *Term* then of a *Superfice* be ſuppoſed indiviſible *as to its Breadth*, which call a *Line:* So another Hypotheſis and its connate Definition is had. In like manner this *Line* is not infinite, but inwardly, *i. e.* on either Hand it is included by a *Term as to its Length*, and by a like Reaſon are theſe *Terms* perfectly indiviſible: let the Term then of a *Line* be ſuppoſed indiviſible *as to its Length*, and call this a *Point*; which is every Way indiviſible, as partaking of the Indiviſibility of a *Superfice* as to *Depth*, a *Line* as to *Breadth*; and is immediately indiviſible in reſpect of *Length* as being the Term of a *Line*. Hence a third Hypotheſis with its conjunct Definition of a *Point*.

Whence it appears that *Points*, *Lines*, and *Superficies* are not deviſed by Mathematicians without Foundation. For though as *Terms* they ſeem ſcarce any thing elſe but Negations of farther

ther Extenſion; yet as we have ſeen, they are Negations founded in the Thing, and well perceived by the Underſtanding, *viz.* like *Shadows* and *Darkneſs* in *Phyſics*, or *Improbity* and *Ignorance* in *Ethics*; but if conſidered in another reſpect, they ſeem to be Attributes very real and poſitive. *Ex. gr.* It agrees, and is attributed to a Superfice, to be two Ways diviſible, to be encreaſed, diminiſhed, meaſured, be congruent, made equal, exceed, be deficient, alſo to be every Way moveable, and to reſt. Nay, as I have intimated, *Superficies* only are immediately objected to the Senſes, do ſubject the Rays of Light to Colours, refract and beat back the Undulations of Sound; theſe do receive the firſt Impetus of Motions; by theſe alone do Bodies mutually touch one another, ſeeing they cannot pervade or penetrate any Part of one another. Almoſt the ſame or the like Attributes belong to Lines; by theſe are reckoned the Diſtances of Things; according to theſe are directed the Rays of Light, the Deſcent of heavy Bodies, and all ſorts of Motion; by theſe are diſtinguiſhed the Confines of Light and Shadow; about theſe at reſt are Bodies revolved; and laſtly, theſe are capable of being produced, contracted, divided, meaſured, and every way compared. Nor do Points themſelves ſeem to want ſome kind of Reality, as having a ſomewhat obſcure, and very ſubtle Entity. For theſe alſo do obtain Motion and Reſt; Motion indeed together with the Bodies in which they are, but Reſt is often peculiar to them; as *ex. gr.* to the Center of a Wheel, the Poles of the Earth or Heavens: for ſuch Gyrations are performed about ſomething at Reſt, and do preſerve ſome Place of themſelves immutable. Alſo the Moments of Bodies do conſiſt about a Point, *viz.* the Center of Gravity; in it they gather and unite their Powers; are in ſome Sort ſupported

and

and ſuſtained by it; according to it their Motions obtain their Direction. Laſtly, towards one middle Point in the Earth do all Things of their own accord, as with conſpiring Wiſhes either incline and fall, or by a direct Paſſage fly back and recede from it. But let us hear *Proclus*'s Elogium concerning a Point. (*m*) *The Centers*, ſays he, *in reſpect of Energy do ſuſtain the Compoſition of the Spheres to which they belong, bounding their Diſtances, comprehending their Powers, and uniting them together into themſelves: And the Axes, while themſelves remain ſtably fixed, do turn, revolve, and carry them about them. And the Poles of Spheres, as determining the Axes, and of themſelves comprehending all other Circumgyrations, do plainly denote that thoſe Powers are not made up and compounded, but that themſelves are the ſole Commanders of the Union of thoſe diſtant Things, and of the Ceſſation of the Motion. Whence* Plato *affirms them to be made of Adamant, a thing fixed, laſting and ſtable, and ſhewing their Subſtances to be thus durable, he ſays that the whole Circumgyration is unitedly performed about theſe.* Thus *Proclus*, whoſe Words in my Opinion are more ſpecious and popular, than true and accurate. For notwithſtanding I am not of his Sentiment concerning theſe Indiviſibles, I do not think that *Superficies*, *Lines*, or *Points* poſſeſs any ſeparate Exiſtence or proper Efficacy from themſelves; or are otherwiſe diſtinguiſhed from a ſolid Magnitude, than in Thought; but I rather imagine, that in Reality there is only one Species of Magnitude, which may be ſundry Ways extended, differently divided, and undergo the various Conſiderations of *Thickneſs*, *Breadth* and *Length*, and affords to our Reaſon a fit Cauſe or Occaſion of deviſing that Diſtinction of Magni-

(*m*) Τά τε γὰρ κέντρα κατ' ἐνέργειαν, &c.

tude,

tude, as it were into three Species, so very useful and accommodate to this Science. But these Things may suffice to be spoken concerning the Termination of Magnitude. For a more opportune Place will offer itself for treating about its particular *Figuration.*

II. *Of the Extension of Magnitude.*

This is succeeded by *Extension*, whereby is signified that the *Terms* of Magnitude are not immediately conjoined or do coexist, but have something interposed between them. For the Reason of a *Term* or Extreme requires, that something be supposed to be comprehended within the *Terms.* (n) *Extremes* (says the Philosopher) *cannot consist together*; *for that which has no Parts can have no Extreme*, *for an Extreme is different from that to which it is the Extreme*; *and elsewhere*, *a Term is one Thing and that to which it is the Term another.* We cannot indeed conceive any Magnitude, but as *extended*, and having Bounds distant by some Interval: We cannot conceive a *Line* but as a Path drawn between two Places as Extremes, not a *Superfice* but as a Floor lying within its Limits, nor a *Body*, but as a Vessel, or Chamber, containing something within its Walls. For Experience will suggest to us such Representations and Ideas of Magnitudes. In like Manner some Sort of *Extension* agrees with analogical Quantities after their Way. For between that *Force* which is capable to lift up one Pound, and that which can raise Ten Pounds, there lies a mean Power capable of elevating two, three, *&c.* Pounds; from whence a Pound is *extended* after its own Manner. And a certain *Duration* intercedes between the first

(n) Phys. VI. 1.

and

and laſt Inſtants of a Year, a Month, a Day, or an Hour; according to which is the *Extenſion* of *Time*. Alſo there lies ſome Mean between the Beginning and End of *Motion* correſpondent to the Space moved over. Laſtly, the *Extenſion* of *Number* is the ſame with the Magnitude which it denominates and repreſents, *viz.* The Two, whereby a Line of two Palms is expreſſed is *extended* to the Length of two Palms; the Two whereby a Field of two Acres is denoted is ſtretched to the Breadth of two Acres. Since therefore it ſufficiently appears by our Conceptions taken from Experience that all Magnitude and Quantity is ſome how *extended*, it will be lawful for Mathematicians to ſuppoſe this, and draw what Conſequences they can from ſuch Suppoſitions: and ſuch Hypotheſes as theſe following ones will be of Force. *Ex. gr. A mean or middle Line may be aſſumed between two aſſigned Points: A mean Superfice may lye between two expounded Lines: Some interjected Body may be conceived between two extreme Superficies: Some mean Time may be underſtood between two Inſtants: Some intercepted Weight may be placed between two Moments: Some intercurrent Motion may be directed between two Terms.* And every Suppoſition thus aſſumed is lawful. And ſo much for *Extenſion.*

III. *Of the Compoſition of Magnitude.*

The next Affection of Magnitude, which follows its *Extenſion*, is its *Compoſition*, *i. e.* that Magnitude contains within it or conſiſts of different Things. For becauſe it is extended, and its Extremes are diſtant from one another, therefore the *Whole* is not in the ſame indiviſible Place; whence different Things may be aſſigned in it; and conſequently it is compounded of different

different Things, *i. e.* of *Parts :* For a Magnitude is called a *Whole*, as it is compounded of different Things contained in it, and thoſe different Things are called *Parts.* And by equal Reaſon, ſince the ſaid *Parts* taken ſingly are not the *Whole* taken conjunctly, (for if they could be the whole Magnitude taken conjunctly, they would coincide with the Extreme of the *Whole*, or with the Extreme of the *Part* adjacent to it, and conſequently there would be no other Mean nor *Part*) therefore in like manner different Things may be aſſigned in it, and conſequently it is compounded of other *Parts*, and theſe again of others, and ſo on *ad infinitum*, *i. e.* as long as we can imagine it to be compoſed of *Parts* ſtill more minute. Whence it follows, that every Magnitude conſiſts or is conſtituted of Magnitudes homogeneous to itſelf, a Line of Lines, a Superfice of Superficies, and a Body of Bodies ; but not a Line of Points, or a Superfice of Lines, or a Body of Superficies. For Points *ex. gr.* in reſpect of a Line, except in the Caſes mentioned above, are nothing elſe but Negations of further Extenſion, and do ſcarce obtain any Thing poſitive ; and moreover as Terms they denote ſomething interpoſed, as not being able to cohere immediately of themſelves ; and the Whole of a Line, whatſoever it be, is imagined between them. They are alſo indiviſible, and therefore, if two be ſuppoſed to lie one upon another, they will mutually touch each other through the *Whole*, *i. e.* they will coincide and coexiſt, and conſequently do conſtitute nothing which has Extremes or is extended. So reaſons the (*o*) Philoſopher, ſpeaking of Atoms ; *For ſince they touch one another in one Magnitude, and the Magnitude is one and continued, and they are taken together, they do make*

(*o*) De Gen. & Corrupt. l. 1. c. 2.

the

the Whole no greater, becauſe, though the Whole be divided into two or more Parts, it becomes no leſs than before: So that if they be all joined together they will make no Magnitude. And as theſe are in reſpect of a Body, the ſame is a Line in reſpect of a Superfice. The ſame Way does a Time conſiſt of Times, not Inſtants; a Motion of Motions not indiviſible Tendencies: a Velocity of Velocities, and a Weight of Weights neither of Degrees nor Impetus's abſolutely the leaſt: a Number of Units, and Units of Fractions, not Cyphers. Hence alſo it is apparent, that a Point may be any where at pleaſure aſſumed in a Line, a Line and a Point in a Superfice, and a Superfice a Line and a Point in a Body. For becauſe ſome of the infinite, or rather indefinite (*i. e.* more than any Determinate Number of) Parts of a Body begins or ends every where, therefore its *Term* every where is accounted a Superfice, a Line terminating any Part of that Superfice, and a Point any Part of that Line. Nor is this contrary to common Senſe, ſince we often appeal to that, as being the Teſt and Index of Experience, which, as has been often inculcated, is the Foundation of Hypotheſes. For we can have no poſſible Conception of any Magnitude, but as compounded of *Parts*, nor of theſe *Parts* but as ſome how extended and conſequently made up alſo of *Parts*. A Thing perfectly incompounded obtaining a poſitive Place in Matter as it is beyond all Senſe, ſo does it exceed all Imagination. It is therefore lawful for Mathematicians to ſuppoſe this *Compoſition*, and whatſoever immediately follows it. Such Suppoſitions, not to uſe Repetitions, as I ſhall ſubjoin in treating of the following Property, which has the cloſeſt Connection with this.

Of

Of the Divisibility of Magnitude.

Divisibility is the inseparable Companion of *Composition.* For since, as was just now shewn, Magnitude is compounded of Parts really distinct; these may exist asunder, at least be considered separately, *i. e.* they may be really or mentally divided or resolved into Parts. Wherefore the Philosopher raises from hence the Definition of Quantity; *To be that which may be divided into those Things which are in it, each Part of which (supposing the Parts to be only two) or every one of which (if more) is capable to exist and that determinately* (*p*). Consequently *Divisibility* being essential to Quantity, therefore that may be conveniently defined from it. And this aptly agrees with the common Conceptions of Men. For some assert an indivisible Quantity in Words, but none I believe can paint its Image in the Mind: Extension vanishes with Divisibility, and the whole with its Parts. The Philosopher deservedly enquires (*q*) *What that is which cannot be divided?* Why Nothing at all. This prevails in all Magnitude; and by a like Reason in all its Parts also: As All do consist of Parts, so may All be resolved into one kind of Parts or another. There is no Part in any kind of Magnitude, which is absolutely the least. Whatsoever is divided into Parts, is divided into Parts which are again divisible. *I say,* says (*r*) *Aristotle, whatsoever is continued is always divisible into Parts again divisible.*

I am not ignorant, for few can be ignorant, how difficultly this Doctrine is admitted by some, and entirely rejected by others; and with what

(*p*) Met. IV. 13. (*q*) De Gen. & Corrupt. l. 2.
(*r*) Phys. VI. 1.

Stiffness

Stiffneſs the Controverſy about the perpetual *Diviſibility* of Quantity, and *Compoſition* of Magnitude is every where treated, *viz. Whether it do conſiſt of Parts indiviſible, or homogeneous*; which I am ſenſible is involved in many Difficulties, and obnoxious to many contradictory Querks, eſpecially by Reaſon of the intervening Conception of Infinity, which is not perfectly comprehenſible to us. But I have no Mind at preſent to turn over ſo many Trifles, to untie ſo many Knots, and to enter upon a trite Queſtion ſo vexatious, prolix, and perplexed; the accurate handling of which would fill a whole Volume, and require more Care and longer Delay, than would at this Time be worth the while to lay out upon it. It may ſuffice that the perpetual *Diviſibility* and *Compoſition* of Quantity out of common homogeneous Parts, as we have intimated, does anſwer well to the Ideas of Men; and that moſt of the excellenteſt Philoſophers have ſuppoſed and defended it. Among whom in the firſt Place we may reckon *Plato*, if *Ariſtotle* be to be credited. *For alſo Plato*, ſays (*m*) he, *does therefore make two kinds of Infinites, becauſe he thinks there is an infinite Procedure both in Augmentation and Diminution.* Next, *Ariſtotle* himſelf not only aſſerts but ſtrongly proves it in many Places. *vide Phyſ. Auſc.* VI. I. *De Gen.* & *Corrupt. L.* 2. and in a particular very learned Book concerning indiviſible Lines. Again the whole School of the *Stoics*, and among them the moſt acute *Chryſippus* is ſaid to have given their Suffrages to this. Alſo among the modern Philoſophers the moſt ſubtle *Carteſius* gives his voice, and not only well nigh demonſtrates that Matter is infinitely diviſible, but that it actually is divided; which he does by an Argument in

(*s*) Phyſ. IV. 6.

Phyſics

Physics fetched from the continued Motions performed along the unequal Interstices of excentric Circles.

Add to these the necessary Consent of all Mathematicians ; for though they scarce do any where openly suppose this, yet they often assume it covertly ; and except it be true, most of their Demonstrations must fall to the Ground : They assume it covertly, I say, as in the Definition of a Right Line, whether it be said to lie evenly between its Points, or be defined to be the shortest of all Lines that can be drawn from one Point to another. For how can a Line consisting only of two Points lie at all between its Points. And if, in Condescension to our Adversaries, the Semidiameter of a Circle be supposed to consist only of three Points, it will be equal to the side of an Hexagon inscribed within that Circle ; but the sixth Part of the Circle's Circumference will not reach to four Points, for then the whole Circumference would consist of twenty and four Points, and consequently would be four times its Diameter, contrary to the manifest Demonstrations of *Archimedes*, and even to common Sense itself, whereby the Circumference of a Circle is known to be lesser than the Perimeter of its circumscribed Square : And if the sixth Part of the Circle's Circumference do not reach to four Points, then according to the Hypothesis of the Advocates for Indivisibles, it can by no means exceed three ; and therefore it will not be greater than its Subtense, nor consequently will a Right Line be the shortest of all Lines which can be described between the same Points. And the like Difficulty will follow, if the Semidiameter of a Circle be supposed to consist of five Points ; for the Circumference of sixty Degrees will not reach six Points, because then the whole Circumference

would

would contain thirty and ſix Points, *i. e.* it would exceed three and a half of the Diameter, which is again contrary to common Senſe, as may be eaſily demonſtrated. Which Conſideration alone may ſuffice to overthrow the contrary Opinion, at leaſt it plainly declares its Repugnance with Mathematical Principles. Alſo ſince a Right Line is ſuppoſed to be drawn from a Point to a Point, how can that conſiſt with Indiſtance, or the immediate Coherence of Points? Moreover when it is aſſumed that two Right Lines after Concourſe do immediately ſeparate, or depart, from one another, and cut not one another any where ,but in one Point, nor have any common Part beyond the Point of Interſection, and the like; theſe things are manifeſtly deſtroyed by the Suppoſition of Indiviſibles. For if the Circumference of a Circle be ſuppoſed to conſiſt of any Number of Points to every one of which *Radii* are drawn from the Center, it is very evident, that the Circumferences of more concentric Circles will conſiſt of the ſame number of Points with the former, and conſequently are equal to it, which is moſt abſurd: Or otherwiſe theſe *Radii* do touch, meet, or interſect one another in ſome Place elſe than the Center. And as to Geometrical Concluſions, How can a Right Line be biſſected conſiſting of unlike Points? How can any Line be divided into the ſame Number of equal Parts which are ſuppoſed in any other? How, if the Legs of a Triangle be any way unequal, can Parallels be drawn to the Baſis through any Points of the greater, which paſſing through the leſſer Leg do not coincide, interſect, or touch one another, contrary to the Nature and Definition of Parallels? And if the Legs be much greater than the Baſis, how can Parallels grow uniformly or keep the ſame Proportion with the Parts intercepted to the Vertex of the Legs, ſo as not by much

much to exceed the Bafes, which yet are fenfibly leffer? How, in the fame Right Line indefinitely produced to any Number of Centers (fuppofe ten Millions, or as many as you pleafe) can Circles defcribed through the End of the faid Right Line touch one another only in one Point: According to that moft manifeft Precept of Geometry, whence it plainly follows, that a Right Line, how fmall foever and near the Point of Contact, if it cut the Circumference of thefe Circles, it cuts it in an indefinite Number of Points, and confequently in an Infinity of Points in Power? How, according to our Adverfaries, can a mean Proportional be found between two Right Lines, one *ex. gr.* confifting of feven and the other nine Points; or how can a third Proportional be exhibited to the fame feven and nine? For if, for finding the Mean, a Semicircle be made upon thofe Lines joined together as a Diameter, and a Perpendicular be erected from the common *Term* of the Segments, that Perpendicular will not be the Mean Proportional required between the faid Right Lines, becaufe there can be no fuch, according to the contrary Suppofition. How does not this entirely deftroy every Incongruity of Magnitudes, which is fhewn by Geometricians in fo many Examples, and fupported with fo many Demonftrations? Since a Point is the common Meafure of all Magnitudes, and every one Magnitude is to another as a Number of Points to a Number of Points, if Lines confift of Points, Superficies of Lines, and Bodies of Superficies. How is not the whole Doctrine of Afymptotical Lines thus effectually overthrown; a Doctrine indeed wonderful, but no lefs certain and evident than any other Part of Geometry, which either invincibly confirms the infinite Divifibility of Magnitude, or coincides together with it; fince it is clearly demonftrated by it, that the

fmalleft

ſmalleſt Line is not exhauſted by a continued Decreaſe *ad infinitum*, nor made equal to a given Line but very little greater, by a continued Increaſe *ad infinitum?* How laſtly is not all the Difference alſo of Motions, as to Velocity, taken away by this means. *Ex. gr.* If a moveable Point run through five Points in one Time, how can another perform the ſubduple, ſubtriple, or ſubquadruple of that Space in the ſame Time, when the Whole is not capable of being divided into theſe Parts? Nay, I could deviſe and produce even an Infinity of ſuch Inſtances, whereby it may be proved from this Aſſertion of Compoſition out of Indiviſibles, that the whole of Geometry is altogether ſubverted and deſtroyed, having nothing left in it ſound and ſolid: And thereby a huge and deplorable Ruin, Confuſion, and Inconſiſtency is brought upon this moſt Divine Science; whoſe Principles *(t)* notwithſtanding, beſides their Evidence and the Rigour of its Reaſonings, are ſo firmly eſtabliſhed, as well by their wonderful Conſonance one with another which could not happen if they were falſe, as by their perpetual and exquiſite Agreement with Experience; ſo that the Poles of the *(u)* World will be ſooner removed out of their Places, and the Fabrick of Nature deſtroyed, than the Foundations of Geometry fail or its Concluſions be convinced of Falſity.

But we muſt leave this Queſtion, and I ſhall briefly obſerve to you, that all the principal Arguments, which are brought againſt the perpetual Diviſibility of Quantity, are either mere begging the Queſtion, or depend upon falſe Suppoſitions, or laſtly have no Relation at all to the Matter. *Epicurus* objects for the Patronage of his Atoms, that if the Parts of Magnitude be infinite, it is unintelligible how a finite Magnitude can conſiſt of

(*t*) Ariſt. de Cœlo I. 5.

(*u*) Ariſt. Eth. I. 8.

ſuch Parts. And what is this, but to beg the Queſtion, or conclude a Thing from itſelf? For it is ſought, whether a finite Magnitude (we ſpeak not of an infinite one) can have an Infinity of Parts. Our Adverſary ſays it cannot be, the Thing is unintelligible. But he had more appoſitely required an Explication of the Manner how it may be done, than to have concluded that it cannot be done. To which Queſtion I might anſwer, that it is indeed contrary to Reaſon for a finite Magnitude to have any determinate Denomination of Parts (*ex. gr.* its Hundredth or Thouſandth Parts) infinite, nay it is a Contradiction for it to have more than a Hundred or a Thouſand of ſuch Parts; but I do not ſee any Contradiction in its having more than ten Millions of Parts, or more than can be expreſſed by any Number, nay, rather I conceive it to be very agreeable to Reaſon. It is certain that as whole Numbers may be infinitely encreaſed by Addition, ſo on the contrary may Fractions be infinitely decreaſed by Diviſion, *viz.* as a Number may be conceived greater than a Thouſand, ſo may a Part the ſame way be conceived below a thouſandth Part; it is the Sign of Magnitude, to which they correſpond, to encline equally on either Side to Infinity. Nay it is plainly taught and demonſtrated by Arithmeticians, that an infinite Series of Fractions, decreaſing in a certain Proportion, is equal to a certain Number, or to Unity, or to a Part of an Unite; *ex. gr.* that ſuch a Series of Fractions decreaſing in a *ſubſeſquialter Proportion* is equal to *Two*, in a *ſubduple Proportion* to *Unity*, in a *ſubtriple* to *one half*; from whence it is not inconſiſtent for ſomething finite to contain in it an Infinity of Parts: eſpecially ſince nothing agrees with Number, which does not with more right agree with Magnitude, which Number repreſents and denominates. And indeed if we do but conſider, that

that as the Multitude of Parts encreases so does their Magnitude reciprocally decrease, it will be no Difficulty to imagine what way a finite Thing may consist of infinite Parts. So that if it have three Parts each of these is no more than one third Part of the Whole, if four, one fourth, *&c.* their Smallness compensating the Multitude. But *Epicurus*, or *Lucretius* in his Name urges:

> Præterea nisi erit minimum, parvissima quæque
> Corpora constabunt ex partibus infinitis.
> Ergo rerum inter se summam minimamque
> quid esset?

> *Besides if we in Matter don't admit*
> *Some Particle, than which none can be less,*
> *Then the minutest Bodies will contain*
> *Parts without Number;* ———
> Right so far, but what's the Consequence.
> ——— ———*and of Consequence*
> *No Diff'rence will be found 'twixt Great and*
> *Small.*

He imagines that, if our Hypothesis be admitted, the least Quantity will equal the greatest, a Grain of Poppy will be as much as the whole Universe, and a Fly no less than an Elephant; because those, as well as these, do contain infinite Parts. But this way of arguing proves nothing: For what hinders a small Thing from having as many lesser Parts as another greater Thing has greater; and that a Shilling may be distributed into as many Pence as a Pound into Ounces; or that a Foot may contain as many Octants as a Mile itself does Furlongs. And why may not the same Proportion which is between the Globe of the Earth and a Grain of Sand, be between that Grain of Sand and some other minute Particle of Matter, *i.e.*

as

as often as the firſt contains the ſecond, ſo often does the ſecond comprehend the third? Since GOD is able to create a World in all Reſpects like this, which may be no greater than the minuteſt Piece of Duſt or Sand. Therefore both what is greater and what is leſſer may conſiſt of infinite Parts, only the Parts of that will be greater, and of this leſſer; *viz.* ſo much leſſer in Proportion, as this Whole is leſs than that Whole.

But again they inſiſt that at leaſt, according to our Aſſertion, it muſt follow that Infinits may be unequal; becauſe the Number of Parts in a Line of two Feet will be twice as much, as an infinite Number of Parts in a Line of one Foot, ſince whatſoever the former Number be, it is moſt evident, it muſt contain this twice; but (ſay they) it ſeems abſurd for an infinite to be exceeded, contained, or multiplied. I anſwer, that the Queſtion is again begged in this principal Argument of our Adverſaries: *i. e.* they conclude the ſame thing from itſelf expreſſed in other Words. For an infinite Number denotes nothing elſe, but that the Thing to which it is attributed may be divided or conceived to be divided *ad infinitum*; which we aſſert to agree as well with the Line of one Foot, as that of two; notwithſtanding one is double the other: This on their Part they deny in other Words, but bring no new Argument to ſupport their Opinion. Number indeed (as has been often inculcated) whether finite or infinite has neither Equality nor Inequality of itſelf, in reſpect of another Number, unleſs ſo far as each Number deſigns and repreſents a Magnitude of the ſame Kind; wherefore, to ſay that this infinite Number is greater than that infinite Number, and to pronounce this abſurd, is all one as to ſay that this Magnitude which is conceived to be divided *ad*

infinitum

infinitum is greater than that which is alſo conceived to be divided *ad infinitum*, and hence to conclude the Thing abſurd, *i. e.* to deny our Poſition, but not to oppoſe it with any new Device. Beſides I affirm, that it ſeems no way abſurd for an Infinite to be contained within an Infinite, *i. e.* for an infinite Magnitude to be contained within an infinite Magnitude, or an infinite Number within an infinite Number; for if a Right Line be ſuppoſed to be extended infinitely in Space, which is imagined by the moſt Part to be immenſe, it will doubtleſs contain an infinite Number of Feet, an infinite Number of Paces, and an infinite Number of Furlongs: Alſo an infinite Right Line will be oftner contained in an infinite Superfice; and this Superfice again innumerable Times more in an infinite ſolid Body. And the ſame way may infinite Years, more infinite Days, and yet more infinite Hours, and laſtly moſt of all infinite Moments, be eaſily conceived in an eternal Duration. You will ſay theſe Poſitions are impoſſible and abſurd. I anſwer, ſince the Adverſary builds his Arguments upon the Nature of Infinite, it may ſurely be lawful for us to ſuppoſe it, and though the Poſition of the Thing itſelf may perhaps be impoſſible, yet the Conſequence is manifeſt and perceptible; *viz.* that it is no where repugnant (as they would have it) with the Nature of an Infinite to be contained in another Infinite: as it is ſufficiently evident that to have Feet or Horns is not repugnant to the Notion of an *Hircocervus* (i. e. a Creature half Goat half Buck) though it be naturally impoſſible for ſuch a Creature to exiſt. And the *Epicurean* Advocates of Atoms do own as much themſelves: What elſe means their *Vacuum* infinite in Magnitude, and their *Atoms* infinite in Multitude, which *Plutarch* relates to have been taught by *Epicurus* himſelf? And the ſame is atteſted by *Lucretius*,

patet

————————patet ingens copia rebus
Finibus exemptis in cunctas undique partes.

A Multitude immense extends itself
To every Part of the unbounded Space;
There being no Limits to be set to Things.

Which being supposed it plainly appears that an infinite Number is in Fact comprehended within an infinite Number, and an infinite Space within an infinite Space. For in an infinite Number of Atoms are contained an infinite Number of Octonaries, a more infinite Number of Quaternaries, and again a more infinite Number of Pairs, and an infinitely more infinite Number of Unites. And the same of Spaces.

Lastly *Zeno* objects against our Opinion, that a Space consisting of infinite Parts cannot be passed over successively, and consequently he thus takes away Motion from the Nature of Things. I reply in a few Words, that this will follow rightly, if the moveable Body be supposed infinitely slow, but if it have any Velocity, that will answer to some determinate Part of Space, which will consequently be measured by the moveable Body in a Time assigned.

I observe that they who would have Magnitude constituted of a finite Number of Indivisibles (which Opinion is still more repugnant to the Laws of Geometry) do yet agree in most Things said against the Composition from Indivisibles. With whom perhaps may be reconciled (since it differs no otherwise than in the Manner of Speaking) the Opinion of *Galilæus* and others following him, who think it to be compounded of an infinite Number of Atoms. But I pass by this Opinion, for if I should minutely examine all Things that occur

cur to my Thoughts, my Discourse would grow to an immense Bulk. I therefore leave many Things to be corrected by your more mature Judgment, and supplied with greater Care.

But not to prolong this tumultuary Discourse *ad infinitum*, I deny not but it is difficult to be understood, how every single Part can be divided so as all not to be actually reduced by the Division to Indivisibles, or to Nothing or what is next to Nothing: Nor yet do I think, by reason of the Imperfection of the Mind of Man and the Smallness of our Capacities, that therefore the Truth is to be deserted, when proved by so many evident Tokens, and supported by so many strong Arguments. *It is indeed*, says *Aristotle*, *contrary to Reason to submit to, or sink down under our Infirmity, because we cannot repel all Instances; and cast ourselves into greater Errors, because we are not able to free ourselves from lesser Difficulties.* To whom *Cartesius* (*x*) agrees in a like Prudence. Though we are not able to comprehend how this indefinite Division can be performed, yet we ought not therefore to doubt, but it may be performed; because we clearly perceive it to follow of necessity from the Nature of Matter, a Thing most manifestly known to us, and we do also perceive it to be of that kind of Things, which cannot be comprehended by our Minds, as being finite.

It follows therefore that every Quantity is compounded of Parts that are compounded, and may be divided into Parts that are again divisible, and consequently that Mathematicians may build Hypotheses upon these Foundations. Such *viz.* as these and the like: *From any greater Magnitude may be subtracted one equal to any lesser: Between two homogeneous unequal Magnitudes may be assumed a*

(*x*) Princip. II. 34.

Mean

Mean Magnitude of the ſame Kind: A Point may be aſſumed any where in a Line; a Point and a Line in a Superfice; and a Point, Line, and Superfice in a Body: Every Magnitude has its homogeneous Parts capable of being denominated by any Number, ex. gr. *its Tenth, Hundredth, Thouſandth,* &c. *Parts; nor is it contrary to Reaſon, if, for Speculation's ſake, they be ſuppoſed to be any how divided*, &c. But it is *not* my Deſign to enumerate all Hypotheſes, but only to open their Fountains. Other Attributes of Magnitude remain, which Time will not permit me to purſue farther at preſent.

LECTURE X.

Of Space, and Impenetrability.

SINCE the Thread of my Diſcourſe has led me, for the ſake of Mathematical Hypotheſes, to treat of the more common Affections of Magnitude; and ſince I have already ſpoke ſomething (little indeed conſidering the Dignity of the Subject, but enough for our Deſign) concerning ſome Things which firſt offer themſelves, *viz.* the *Termination, Extenſion, Compoſition, and Diviſibility* of Magnitude; it now follows, that I ſhould touch upon what remains, *viz.* its *Occupation of Space, Determinate Poſition, Mobility, Menſurability, Proportion*, and whatſoever elſe occurs from whence Mathematicians do, or lawfully may, draw Hypotheſes ſuited to their Ratiocinations.

In the firſt Place, it is wont to be attributed to Magnitude, that it *occupies*, or *fills Space.* But it is difficult to explain what this *Space* is. For if we either attend to vulgar Conceptions, or examine

the

the more ſubtle Sentiments of Philoſophers, it is not eaſy to determine whether there really is any *Space* diſtinct from Magnitude or not; the Opinions on each ſide ſeeming both to depend upon very ſpecious Arguments, and be preſſed with weighty Difficulties.

On the one Hand, theſe Arguments ſeem to make it ſufficiently plain, that there is really no ſuch Thing as *Space* exiſting ſeparate from the Quantities of Things. And that firſt, becauſe, if it be unproduced and independent, it muſt conſequently be alſo eternal and immenſe (for were it not (ſay they) that ſuch a Thing is for the moſt Part conceived and ſuppoſed by the Aſſertors of real *Space*; if ſuch a Thing be not, then every Reaſon will fail upon which it is ſuppoſed, as will appear to any one who weighs the Cauſes of framing it;) but for any Thing to partake of the ſingular Attributes of the Divine Nature, ſuch as not to be created nor dependent upon God, ſeems contrary, as well to right Reaſon, as Religion. Again if we examine the Idea of *Space* whatſoever it be, we ſeem to apprehend nothing by it but a certain Extenſion and indefinite Capacity; which, ſince they are Properties of Magnitude itſelf, do argue no Difference of Space from Magnitude; for why ſhould that differ in the Thing, which agrees in the Properties? And this is not only the Argument of *Carteſius*, but of *Ariſtotle* himſelf. *If* (ſays the Philoſopher) *the Magnitude of Things have nothing in itſelf different from Space, then wherefore is the Bulk of a Thing diſtinguiſhed from its Space?* Moreover if *Space* be any Thing different from Magnitude, we may enquire to what Claſſis of Things it is to be referred: For every Thing either ſubſiſts of itſelf, or is an Accident to another Thing; but neither of theſe ſeems to agree with *Space*. The Patrons of *Space* do not exalt it to the

Dignity

Dignity of a Subſtance, nor will the Thing itſelf bear it. Neither is it an Accident, becauſe it is extrinſecal to all Subſtance; ſince it is not carried about with it, but remains, though that be taken away, and depends upon no other Thing. I paſs by the Device of *Zeno:* That every Thing is ſomewhere, therefore if *Space* be any Thing diſtinct from other Things it muſt exiſt ſomewhere; whence there will be a *Space* of a *Space*, and another *Space* of this ſecond *Space*, and ſo on infinitely (as (*y*) *Ariſtotle* obſerves) which is ridiculous. By ſuch Arguments as theſe is the real Diverſity of Space from Magnitude oppoſed: but it is defended from Arguments which are equally ſtrong in Appearance.

For *firſt*, if we appeal to the common Conceptions of Men, the Notion of a Space diſtinct from Things does ſeem to be either innate or acquired. *All Men* (ſays (*z*) *Ariſtotle*) *do in Thought ſeparate the* Ubi *of Things from their* Eſſe. The Vulgar are accuſtomed to imagine that there is ſome common *Subſtratum* to all Things, which is infinitely extended, and circumſcribed within no Limits; which is perfectly penetrable, and eaſily admits every Thing within itſelf, not reſiſting the Entrance of any Thing; which receives the Succeſſions of moveable Bodies, determines the Velocities of Motions, and meaſures the diſtances of Things; which is immoveably fixed, has none of its Parts tied to any Thing, nor can poſſibly be any where tranſferred from where it is; which laſtly is a Receptacle of immenſe Capacity, or as the (*a*) Philoſopher ſpeaks *an immoveable Veſſel*, containing within it all the Things that either are, or can exiſt. Such is the Notion of *Space*, which is engraven in the Imaginations of all Mortals. And very many

(*y*) Phyſ. IV. 3. (*z*) Ibid. IV. 1. (*a*) Ibid. IV. 6.

Things beside seem to argue the real Existence of such a Thing, as well as this Consent of the Imagination: To make the Force of which apparent and effective, certain Positions or Assertions are to be laid down, whereby the Arguments brought for the Reality of *Space* are supported.

First then Matter is not infinitely extended; at least, which is enough for our Purpose, it is not so of Necessity. For from whence can it have this Necessity? Is it from itself? This is impious, since the sacred Writings do often expresly ascribe the Origin of all Things to God: *All Things* (says *(d)* St. *Paul*) *were created by him and for him.* And thus sung the four and twenty Elders, *(e) For thou hast created all Things, and for thy Pleasure they are, and were created.* Again, as the Evangelist *(f)* St. *John* expresses it, *All Things were made by him, and without him was not any Thing made that was made. For all those Things*, says the Prophet *(g) Isaiah, hath mine Hand made, i. e.* all Things whatsoever without any Exception: And innumerable such other Expressions occur every where in Scripture. Nor is there any Reason why we should believe Matter to have an infinite Substance necessarily of itself. Is it then from God? Who imposed this Necessity upon him who is a perfectly free and independent Agent, that he should attribute Infinity to Matter? How does it appear to have been attributed to it? I do not dispute whether or no he is able to do so, for who can assign Limits to the Divine Power? But it seems far more credible that, as he has limited the Powers of other Things, so he has appointed certain Bounds to Matter. The *holy Scriptures* do seem plainly to attest as much. *(h) Behold* (says

(d) Eph. iii. 9. *(e)* Rev. iv. 11. *(f)* Joh. i. 3.
(g) Isa. lxvi. 1. *(h)* 2 Chron. ii. 6. & vi. 18.

the

the most wise King, more than once) *the Heaven and the Heaven of Heavens cannot contain thee, i. e.* the whole Universe is too narrow to exist with God; he transcends the utmost Bounds of Things, and consequently Matter is not in fact extended *ad infinitum*, much less is it so of Necessity.

To this it is replied by (*i*) *Cartesius*; *It is necessary for Matter to be infinitely extended, for this Reason, because we conceive its Bounds every where; we do not only imagine certain Spaces to be extended indefinitely beyond ourselves, but they are moreover truly imaginable; i. e. we perceive that they are real, and consequently that a bodily Substance indefinitely extended is contained in them; since the Idea of that Extension, which we conceive to be in all Space, is altogether the same with the Idea of a bodily Substance.* But this Argument seems to contain in it more of Subtilty than Solidity. For *first*, no Body either does or can conceive Matter to be actually infinite; but to conceive it to be indefinitely extended, is the same as to imagine it to have no Terms or certain Bounds; as the vulgar Part of Mankind do think the Surface of the Earth to be infinitely extended; or as one standing upon the Shore thinks the Sea to be encompassed with an uncertain Bound; or as we conceive the Grains of the Sand of the Sea to be indefinitely many. Moreover because we can imagine certain Spaces beyond any determinate Bounds; it by no means follows that Matter does actually exist beyond. However it may be probably gathered that it therefore may exist, because whatsoever we conceive as evidently possible, that may be effected by the Divine Power. But who in his right Mind will deny, that we may imagine innumerable Things, which neither are nor ever will be? Nothing is repugnant, and

(*i*) Princ. II. 21.

we may easily imagine with the vulgar, that the Earth reaches to the utmost Bounds of Heaven and the farthest Limits of the Universe: we may suppose in our Minds the Sun to be a thousand Times greater, the Moon many Parasangs nigher; the Stars vastly more numerous, and innumerable other Things, which are by no Means impossible, nor altogether absurd; but are these Things therefore true in fact? No certainly, they are no more than so many Dreams or Deliriums of sick Men. Imaginability then does at most only prove the Possibility of a real Thing, but no where its actual Existence. The World is not proved to be actually infinite from the Imagination, but only to be greater in Power than any finite, (*i. e.* determinately finite) Thing.

But to be satisfied how very much *Cartesius*'s great Subtilty has failed him in this Case, let us search and weigh a little the Origin of this our Imagination of *Spaces* beyond the World, and we will certainly find it like most other Things, to be derived no otherwise than from the Senses. For since we scarce attain any Thing by any Sense, but we still experience something equally sensible by proceeding beyond it; especially when lifting up our Eyes to Heaven we behold the vast Chasm on every Side contained within no perceptible Limit, but running forth into Regions unknown to us; hence an Occasion is offered of describing in our Fancy a certain immense or indeterminate Gulph of heavenly *Space*, in which the Clouds are suspended, the Winds blow here and there, and the Stars seem to swim like so many Fishes: from which Sensation notwithstanding, or Imagination, it seems very absurd to infer any Thing concerning the true Extent of the Universe, whether it is finite or infinite. For every Sensation is of Things particular, and from the

the Exiſtence of a particular Thing, we may conclude that ſomething like it may exiſt, but not that it actually does exiſt, as has been ſometimes taken notice of before.

I ſay nothing as to the Parity of Reaſon in attributing *Eternity* and *Independence* to Matter, as well as a *neceſſary Infinity of Extenſion*; for as there is ſome Space beyond any Limits of the Univerſe, ſo has it been before any Beginning. We are wont to have the ſame clear Imagination of ſome Time after the End of any Time, and conſequently by this way of arguing, Matter may be demonſtrated to be neceſſarily eternal, whence it follows that it is alſo independent: which Properties notwithſtanding of the Divine Perfection, it is moſt dangerous to attribute to any other than the great God himſelf; and is in the higheſt Degree to be ſhunned by a Chriſtian Philoſopher. It may be therefore taken for granted, that Matter or Body is not altogether unbounded; at leaſt it is not ſo neceſſarily. Let this be firſt ſuppoſed.

Let it be alſo aſſumed, *ſecondly*, that it is in the Power of God to augment or diminiſh the Matter that now exiſts, according to his Pleaſure, *i. e.* to create, or reduce to Nothing, what Portion of it he pleaſes. Faith commands, and Piety compels us to admit this; nor does Reaſon oppoſe, but rather defend and confirm it. For ſince we can conceive Matter to be larger than any Thing determined, therefore nothing hinders, nay it evidently follows from thence, that God can cauſe it to be ſo. But if it may be enlarged, by the ſame Power it may be diminiſhed; and the Web which he hath newly wove, he can with the ſame Eaſe unravel. And becauſe we can imagine Matter more contract, nay ſuppoſe it Nothing at all, it is therefore in the Divine Power to perform it.

Moreover,

Moreover, *thirdly*, it is most easy to conceive, and ought by no Means to be denied, that God can preserve every Thing in its present State and Situation, so as not to be intrinsecally changed by any extrinsecal Accidents, much less to have its Nature entirely destroyed; *viz.* that a Right Line, a plain Superfice, the Circumference of a Circle, the Roundness of a Sphere, and such like Things may remain, whatsoever happens without them, *i. e.* though all circumjacent Matter be any how changed, taken away, or annihilated. Which Things being lawfully supposed and laid down, the Reality of *Space* distinct from Magnitude does seem to be many Ways established.

As *first*, since Matter may be finite, and God is infinite in Essence, he must subsist beyond the Bounds of Matter, otherwise, he would be enclosed within its Limits or some Way bounded, and therefore could not be infinite. Therefore something is beyond, *i. e.* some sort of *Space.* And if God do not exist beyond the Bounds of Matter, our Imagination would be capable to conceive a Place where he is not; and consequently would in some Sort transcend the Manner of the Divine Existence; whence it would follow, that we could not apprehend or conceive God to be immense.

Next, God can create other Worlds beyond this, as also we can imagine them to be created, not no where, but some where; there will therefore be given some Space wherein they may be placed and exist. And God will also be present in these new produced Worlds, yet without being the least affected with Motion himself (for all kind of Immobility and Immutability is an undoubted Attribute of the Divine Perfection) which can no otherwise be understood, than by conceiving him to have before been present in the *Space*, where they

they are now reposited. Therefore the Conceptions which we have, or ought to have, concerning the Divine Infinity, Power, and Immutability do involve some distinct *Reality* of *Space.*

Moreover the material World, from the Hypothesis which we have asserted, will be limited and endowed with some Figure, and consequently may be supposed of any Figure. Let it therefore be Spherical; and because it may also be lawfully done, let some other spherical World, or Body, be in like Manner supposed to be contiguous to it, which will touch the former in only one Point; therefore there will lie some Mean, *i. e.* some *Space* between the other Points of the Spheres. For let any two Points be assumed in the Superfice of the contiguous Spheres without the Contact, I say some Space will lie between these; If you deny it, then these two Points will meet one another, contrary to a most clear Demonstration in Geometry.

Also let the two Centers of the Spheres be connected by a Right Line passing through the Contact as Geometry also teaches and proves; and let two Radii be understood to proceed from the Centers to the said Points without the Contact; then because, according to the Opinion of our Adversaries, the said Points are contiguous, they will constitute a Triangle of three Right Lines, two of whose Sides will be equal to the third, in like manner contrary to a most clear and certain Theorem of Geometry. Again let the Matter, which goes to constitute two concentric Spheres, be supposed in any Place, and let the interjacent Matter between their Superficies be annihilated, or removed out of the Way, (which as has been supposed may be done by the Power of God) then these Superficies, if no *Space* come between, will meet one another, though the one were a thousand times greater than the other: For we may suppose from

from what has been ſaid that both the ſpherical Superficies do retain their Magnitude, the Evacuation of the middle Body, which happens extrinſecally and changes nothing within them no ways hindering it; the Divine Power ſome how preſerving their Magnitude and Poſition. In the ſame manner if what is between the Vertex and Baſis of a Pyramid be taken away, ſince there is no Space left, therefore the Point of the Vertex will lie next to all the Points of the Baſis, and conſequently will be congruous and equal to the whole. Theſe and innumerable ſuch other Things do ſeem to follow, from the Denial of *real Space*, which are no leſs repugnant to the common Conceptions of Men, than the Principles of Geometry.

Beſides it ſeems ſomewhat harſh to ſuppoſe the Matter of the Univerſe entirely immoveable, as to the whole of it, or to imagine that nothing exiſts any where, except one ſolid Sphere; becauſe ſuch a Sphere could not indeed be transferred by God, nor (to uſe the Words of *Plato) admit a Peripheron* or Rotation about its Axis, which the taking away of Space does manifeſtly infer. For ſince in every ſuch Motion, the Parts retain the ſame Situation to, and the ſame Diſtance from one another, howſoever the Whole be carried; it can be no otherwiſe conceived to be moved, but from a ſucceſſive Change of *Space*, *viz.* ſo as one Part may enter the Space left by the foregoing one; from whence by the Denial of Space, we take away the Mobility of Matter. *Ariſtotle* in a certain Place obſerves ſomething like this, where he ſays, *That Motion alone gives Occaſion of Diſquiſition concerning Place or Space (as ſcarce being capable of Conception without the Poſition of Space) and the Heaven above all Things ſeems eſpecially to be in Place, becauſe it is moſt of all moved:* nor yet is this any how varied (in reſpect of the firſt or principal diurnal Mo-

tion,

tion, which the Philoſopher ſeems to reſpect) according to the Situation and Diſtance of the Parts, but as the Whole is carried about. It is therefore ſo far moved, or not at all moved, as its Parts do change their *Spaces*; and thoſe Parts which are now at the Riſing of the Sun, do anon, reach the height of the Meridian, and as ſoon as they have paſſed that do immediately decline to the Weſtward. Nor will it here ſuffice *Carteſius* to diſtinguiſh Action from Motion, ſince no Effect of this Action can be imagined without a change of Space.

I will yet add one ſmall Argument to theſe: I aſk what it is that makes the Way between two diſtant Bodies eaſy, the Paſſage ready and quick? Is it becauſe the intermediate *Space* is prepared for receiving them within it? Why then does the contrary happen, that we can hardly thruſt any middle Body between two contiguous ones, nay we cannot do it at all, without impreſſing a Motion upon it ſufficiently ſtrong for ſeparating and removing them from one another? Is it not becauſe there is wanting an Interſtice capable of a middle Body? Suppoſe *ex. gr.* the Body C to reſide between the two Bodies A and B, and let the Body C be underſtood to be removed, ſo as no other can be permitted to ſucceed it (the Propenſion of the neighbouring Bodies to Motion being taken away, or the Effect a little while reſtrained by a ſuperiour Power); then according to our Adverſaries, there will immediately reſult the moſt cloſe Contiguity of the Bodies A and B, without the Application of any Force, or Intervention of any Action; they will embrace one another of their own Accord, and preſently no Diſtance will be left between them; and conſequently it will be rendered very difficult for the Body C by a contrary Impetus to reſtore itſelf into its former Place,

or

or come again between the Bodies A and B, except these Bodies be separated with a strong Force. But it can scarce be understood, why so much Force is required for so small a Separation of Things contiguous, more than for moving together Things separated at any Distance; why they should meet together of their own accord, and be put asunder difficultly. What should be the Cause why they lost their former State with no Labour, with no Motion, and are scarce restored to the same with a vehement Force and much Motion? Since, as the Way is the same from *Thebes* to *Athens*, and from *Athens* back again to *Thebes*, so the Force is the same, and the Motion equal, for conjoining Things that are distant, and disjoining Things that are together. Moreover, it is somewhat obscure why, according to the contrary Sentiment, in the same Instant wherein the middle Body slides away, the adjacent Matter should not immediately touch one another, and the Intervention not be shut up to the succeeding Matter; because scarce a Motion that is infinitely swift, much less a slow and Snail-like Motion (such as are often to be found in Nature) does seem to suffice for preventing that Congress; since it requires no Action here, and instantly emerges by the mere Rebounding. But if the terminating Bodies do easier or sooner close together than Part of the intervening Matter can overtake the preceding, then every Flux must be obstructed, and Motion stopped and taken away; the Disagreement of which with continual Experience is unknown to none. But are not these Things more simply and evidently dispatched by saying that a Passage is more difficult to be broke through the Joinings of adjacent Bodies, because an Interval is wanting for the Reception of the intervening Body; but the Transit is easy between the Bounds

of

of Bodies ſomewhat diſtant, becauſe a middle Field lies open, which is penetrable and capable of the Entrance of ſo great a Body; and conſequently if a Veſſel be emptied the Sides will not fall together, nor break in Pieces if filled again (ſince the former ſeems impoſſible, and the latter not neceſſary) but they will invariably retain the ſame Poſition, the ſame Diſtance, and the ſame Capacity.

I paſs by the Reaſons and phyſical Experiments which are brought for an empty Space (whether entirely filled or interſperſed with Bodies), both becauſe I have already ſpent too much Time upon theſe Things, whoſe Examination would ſtill require much Labour, and becauſe moſt of them may be ſolved, or at leaſt eluded by thoſe neatly contrived Hypotheſes of *ſubtle Matter, circular Motion, and indefinite Diviſibility.*

Thus for the moſt part is the Matter diſputed on both Sides; what then ſhall we finally determine? How ſhall we reconcile theſe contrary Probabilities, and decline the Difficulties that on every Side beſet us? I on my own Part will advance nothing for true in a Caſe ſo nice and dubious, nor aſſert any thing confidently; but if I ſhould be neceſſitated to give my Opinion, and compelled to declare what to me ſeems moſt to reſemble the Truth, I would not be too averſe to the common Conceptions of Men, nor oppoſe the ſacred Laws of Geometry. I would ſay *firſt*, that *Space* is a thing really diſtinct from Magnitude; *i. e.* that ſomething is deſigned by that Name, that a Conception anſwers it, that it is founded in the Nature of Things, that it is different from the Conception of Magnitude, and though Magnitude had no Exiſtence at all, yet there would be Space. I would ſay, *ſecondly*, that Space is not

any

any thing actually existent, and actually different from Quantity, much less that it has any Dimensions proper to itself, and actually separate from the Dimensions of Magnitude. You will perhaps say, What will it be then ? What means this Riddle ? I do not very much promise myself, nor dare hope that I shall satisfy you with mine Answer, but because Form requires it, I reply, that *Space* is nothing else but the *mere Power*, *Capacity*, *Ponibility*, or (begging pardon for the Expressions) *Interponibility of Magnitude*. I thus explain my Meaning : Before the Creation of the World, there was no Body any where (as is reasonable and pious to believe) but yet it was possible for the greatest Body whatsoever then to exist, and obtain a determinate Position by the Will and Power of God, *i. e. there is Space*. There lies no Body, there is found no actual Dimension beyond the Mass of the Universe ; but it is possible for a Body to be constituted and a real Dimension to be extended beyond that itself, *i. e. there is an Ultramundane Space*. If all the Matter be excluded by the divine Power from between these Walls, there will actually be no Body between them, but there will remain a Capacity of putting some Body between them, *i. e. there is an intermediate Space*. Lastly, no Magnitude can be interposed between two adjacent or contiguous Magnitudes ; *i. e. no Space or Interval is between them*. A Rope of ten Feet may be extended between those Towers, *i. e.* the Space or Distance of ten Feet is between them.

Here it may be observed by the Way, that the Nature of every particular *Space* is in some sort *determinate*, and in some sort *indefinite* ; *Determinate* as to the Mathematical Species and Quantity of its Figure ; for it is not every Capacity whatsoever, but only the Capacity of a similar and equal Magnitude ; *Indefinite* as to its other Qualities and physical

physical Species, also as to the Individuities of the Magnitudes, if I may so speak, for it is the Capacity of every Magnitude equally great and endowed with a similar Figure; *ex. gr.* the Space of a Cubical Vessel between the Sides is computed by receiving any Cube equally great, whether it be of Water or Air, but it cannot be adequately filled with a pyramidal or spherical Body, nor will admit a greater Cube. Hence every positive Interval endowed with actual Dimension and really extended of itself, divisible, terminated, pertransible, or congruous to Bodies, is not denoted by the Word *Space*; but it only signifies that a Body may be so extended, may be so figured, is adaptable to such a Measure, and may exist either together in the same Instant or successively by Motion. I say it has no actual but only potential Figures, Dimensions and Parts consentaneous to its Nature; by which Means the Capacity of admitting a Body includes the Capacity of admitting Lines and Superficies, respectively; the Power of interposing a Line of four Feet contains the Powers of interposing a Line of one, two, and three Feet, and all others denominated by a lesser Number. The Power of interserting a potential Circle implies perfect Rotundity. Neither can the Quantity or Quality of *Space* be determined immediately or of itself, but by the Measure or Determination of some real Magnitude occupying it; as, *ex. gr.* the Quantity of the *Space* between two Cities can be no otherwise known, than by measuring the Length of a Line stretched upon the Earth or passing through the Air.

This Name therefore of Space is not of a mere Nothing or Thing feigned at pleasure, as of an *Hircocervus* or *Chimera*, but is deservedly to be placed in the same Order of Beings with *Creability*, *Sensiblitiy*, *Mobility*, and such Possibilities; and there are scarce any but who adjudge some

sort

ſort of Reality to theſe. Nor do I ſee why this *Space* may not be a Being as well as *Contiguity*, to which it ſeems to be directly oppoſed. For *Contiguity* is the Mode of Magnitudes which ſignifies that no Magnitude can come between them but by moving them out of their Places: And on the contrary *Space* is that Mode of the ſame which intimates that ſome other Magnitude may be interpoſed without moving them out of their Place.

And this Notion of *Space* being ſuppoſed and granted, we may untie the Knots and remove the Difficulties of both the aforeſaid Opinions. For firſt nothing can be gathered hence derogatory to the Prerogatives of the Divine Perfection, by ſuppoſing a Being really eternal and infinite, unproduced and independent upon God; but rather his unlimited Power of producing and diſpoſing Bodies at his Pleaſure is aſſerted. Neither does the Idea of ſuch a *Space* coincide with the Idea of Magnitude; but differs as far from it, as Power does from Act. Nor does it bring any other new real Beings into the Account beſides Subſtance and Accident, but only denotes ſome Mode or Poſſibility of both. Nor will this *Space* require another Place; becauſe it exiſts no where in an actual Manner, but will however be every where after its own Manner; becauſe God can place Magnitudes any where. Nor is this contrary to the common Senſe and Speech of Mankind, who, when they think or pronounce Space to intercede, do underſtand nothing but that ſome Body may be interpoſed between aſſigned Limits. Nor can any Infinity of Matter be deduced hence, but ſuch Extenſion will follow as God ſhall pleaſe to aſſign it. Neither does this at all derogate from the Divine *Ubiquity*, which only ſignifies that God is preſent to all *Space*, or that ſomething may exiſt every where. It alſo conſpires and agrees with Geo-

metry

metry most precisely: for neither does this require that some actually real *Mean* shall always intercede between two *Points*, or any two *Terms*; but that sometimes, and in some Cases, a *Line*, *Superfice* or *Body* may intercede. It in like manner satisfies the Experiments and Phænomena of Natural Philosophers, affording them as much *Vacuum* as suffices for receiving Bodies, and performing their Motions; nor yet mingling any fictitious *Vacuum* endowed with real actual Dimensions such as *Epicurus* with his Followers dreamed to be one half of the Universe, and the first Principle of Bodies. Again it appears hence that *Space* is immoveable and cannot be carried about with Bodies; because when one Body loses its other Confines or Interstices, yet this Possibility remains, and nothing hinders, but other Bodies equally near and intermediate may be substituted and succeed.

I observe by the Way that this Notion of *Space* seems to be almost direct contrary to the Definition of it which is delivered by (*k*) Mr. *Hobbes*. He defines *Space* to be the *Phantasm of a Thing existing, as existing*. But if *Space* be a *Phantasm* (as indeed it is not, but the Object of a *Phantasm*, something imaginable, and not the Effect of Imagination) it will rather be the *Phantasm* of a Thing as possible, than as existing. For when we conceive *Space* we conceive that some Magnitude may exist, though not always that it actually does exist; as before the Creation of the World, or without the present World, according to what was said above. Which does also more agree with his own foregoing Reasonings, than the proper Definition of it which he gathers from thence. For if all Things were conceived to be destroyed, he affirms the *Phantasm* of *Space* would remain in the Mind; but to feign all Things taken

(*i*) Cap. VII. de Corp.

out

out of the Way, and at the ſame Time to imagine the ſame Things as exiſting are direct Contradictions. It follows then that *Space* is rather the Idea of Things as poſſible. But, he ſays, *No Body affirms that there is Space, for that Reaſon becauſe it is occupied, but becauſe it can be occupied:* Where he differs not from the Truth, but from himſelf: For *Space* by Occupation ceaſes in ſome ſort to be *Space*, as far as Power is extinguiſhed by Act, and a Thing ceaſes to be farther poſſible which already exiſts: Nor is it improperly ſpoke by the Vulgar, *that Nothing can be poured into a full Veſſel, but the Want of Space.*

But I know not what bewitching *Siren* has drawn me upon her Rocks, and held me entangled in her Nets, while I am doing what in me lies to avoid them. This out of the way Philoſophy has put a ſtop to my Courſe, while I am ſailing with all my Speed to the principal Port of the Mathematics. That I may therefore finiſh this Digreſſion concerning *Space* (indeed too prolix and ſpacious), and circumſcribe it as a Figure within Bounds, I will only remark one Thing more conducing to my Purpoſe; *viz.* that whatſoever natural Philoſophers do determine, this Method of conceiving *Space*, which I have been deſcribing, is moſt agreeable, and abundantly ſufficient for Geometricians: If any Thing more can be diſcovered in it, or attributed to it, it will no where make againſt them; but they require no more than to have ſuch an Interval granted, whereby the Figures of Magnitudes and their Properties may continue ſafe, that they may not be confounded or perverted by a poſſible Annihilation or Remotion. *Ex. gr.* If two Circles or two Spheres do touch one another, and any two Points without the Contact be taken, as above, in the Circumference of a Circle, or the Superfice of a Sphere, then

Geometry

Geometry requires not that any real or actual Right Line ſhould lie between theſe two Points, but only a certain potential one; *i. e.* it requires that a Right Line is poſſible to be drawn or interpoſed, or that theſe Points touch not one another; ſince if ſuch Interſtice be taken away, or if theſe Points be ſuppoſed to touch, then the Nature of Circles and Spheres with their Properties is entirely deſtroyed. Such a *Space* therefore ought to be indulged Geometricians for the Foundation of their Hypotheſes, and the more, becauſe the *Congruity*, *Commenſuration*, *Determinate Poſition*, *Motion*, and the very *Proportion* itſelf of Magnitudes agrees with it, and may be explained by it. For *Congruence* is fitly deſcribed by a Poſſeſſion of the ſame *Space*, *Menſuration* by a congruous Application or Succeſſion; a *Determinate Situation* and *Motion* by the Identity and Alteration of *Space*; and how *Proportion* depends upon, adheres to, and is illuſtrated by theſe, will perhaps hereafter appear.

To accommodate theſe Things to our Purpoſe, a Mathematician may frame ſuch Hypotheſes as theſe from what has been advanced. *That this or that Space may be filled*, i. e. *that Lines, Superficies or Bodies may be interpoſed between any aſſigned Points, Superficies or Bodies reſpectively, which, by Reaſon of ſome Property of their Nature, or precedaneous Suppoſition, do not touch one another.* And on the contrary, *That every Magnitude fills Space*, i. e. *that a Magnitude cannot be placed between two Magnitudes, but the adjacent Magnitudes on either Side are ſeparate and at a Diſtance, according to the Manner of the Magnitude ſuppoſed. That no Space is tied to any particular Magnitude but may be ſucceſſively filled, as the Thing will ſuffer, by innumerable others, according to its Meaſure and the Exigence of the adjacent Magnitudes*; for, as before was explained, *Space* is not a particular, but a kind

kind of general and indefinite Capacity: And reciprocally. *That no Magnitude is tied to any particular Space.* And which may be looked upon as a consequent Axiom from the foregoing Hypotheses, *That more Magnitudes than one taken together cannot adequately fill the same Space:* For more Acts than one do also argue more Powers than one, or one Act does perfectly fill up and exhaust only one Power; therefore more Magnitudes than one require more Spaces than one, or one Magnitude takes up the whole constitutive Capacity of only one Space: As the Existence of *Peter* fills and as it were satiates the whole Possibility of *Peter*, and causes that no other *Peter* can exist the same in Number. And by what Reason any Plurality of Magnitudes do occupy one *Space*, by the same Reason may as many other Magnitudes as you please occupy that same Space; from whence the whole Infinity of possible Magnitude may be contained in the Space of one Grain of Barley; which seems to be inconsistent and contradictory to sound Reason. Also because Magnitudes may obtain the same Space, they will also possess the same Termination and Extension and other conjunct Affections of Magnitude, and consequently will become entirely the same; for we scarce do, or, I believe, can conceive any Thing which constitutes or distinguishes Magnitude except these Affections.

What this last Supposition or (as some chuse to call it) Axiom pronounces or signifies, is wont to be expressed by the Word *Impenetrability*, which many make the primary of all the Attributes of Magnitude, but how deservedly let them see themselves; for I am for no *Preference of Affections*, but do esteem all reciprocal and equal, as to *Degree*. Only it will be of use to us to take Notice, that this Position is very necessary to Mathematicians,

cians, and, as we have ſeen, is drawn from ſound Reaſon, and is agreeable to perpetual Experience. For whatſoever in Mechanics is deduced from the *Pulſation*, or *pulſive Force*, of Bodies depends upon this ; Alſo whatſoever in Geometry ariſes from the *Dependence of Motions* (of which kind is that moſt elegant Deſcription of Curve Lines invented by *Carteſius* in his Geometry, which is performed by the Impulſe or Truſion of Rules in a certain ordinate Reaſon) ; becauſe if a Plurality of Magnitudes taken together can fill the ſame Space, or which is all one, can one penetrate another, then one would not neceſſarily give way to another, from whence the Suppoſition of Pulſation would be in vain, and no Effect would reſult, at leaſt from a ſcientific Neceſſity. Therefore the *Impenetrability* of Magnitude is neceſſarily ſuppoſed by Mathematicians, and conſequently it was not foreign to the Purpoſe to ſhew its Agreement with Reaſon, and that it is not ſuppoſed unlawfully.

By equal Right it may on the contrary be ſuppoſed, that no particular Magnitude can occupy more Spaces than one taken together. For one Act cannot ſatisfy a Plurality of Powers ; nor can the Poſſibility that *Peter* and *Socrates* may exiſt, be filled with the Exiſtence of *Peter alone.* And by what Reaſon one particular Magnitude can poſſeſs more *Spaces* than one, by the ſame Reaſon may it ſuffice to poſſeſs as many *Spaces* as you pleaſe : and a Grain of Poppy, or the Magnitude of the minuteſt Grain of Sand, may be capable to fill all Space and be coextended with the whole Infinity of poſſible Magnitude, which no Body in his right Mind can be eaſily led to think.

I muſt not omit taking Notice, that the ſame Magnitude by occupying a Plurality of *Spaces* will obtain a Plurality of Extenſions, Terminations, and all other Affections of Magnitude; from whence it will not continue one Magnitude, but become many. Neither is this Supposition unprofitable, but very necessary to Mathematicians: and whatsoever is supposed or demonstrated by them concerning Determinate Position depends on this. For how *ex. gr.* is a Point not in vain supposed or shewn to exist within or without a Circle, if it can exist both within and without at the same Time? How can that Line be said to make such or so great an Angle with this, if it can constitute any other Angle at the same Time while it obtains a different Position? How can a Right Line be demonstrated to touch a Curve from hence, because the Whole falls without the Curve saving the Point of Contact, when it is repugnant for it at the same Time to lie altogether within it? How lastly can a Point be proved not to be the Center of a proposed Circle from hence, because it does not bisect the Diameter, if, by reason of the various possible Situations, the same Point can bisect the Diameter and not bisect it at the same Time? Whatsoever then may be said of the Popish Divinity, except the Hypothesis be true, that it is not possible for the same Magnitude to fill more Spaces than one at the same Time, there is an entire End of all Geometry. But we cannot now add every thing worthy of Observation concerning *Determinate Position*; no more than concerning the other remaining Affections of Magnitudes which are to be reserved for the following Lectures.

I will only add this one Observation more, that there is a great Affinity and Analogy between *Space* and *Time*. For as *Space* is to *Magnitude*, so does *Time* seem to be to *Motion*; so that *Time* is in some sort the *Space* of *Motion*. For when *Time* is called a *Year*, a *Month*, or a *Day*, nothing

seems

seems to be signified but that such or so great a *Motion* is performed, or intercedes, or may be interposed in the mean while; *ex. gr.* one Period of the *Sun* in the *Ecliptic*; one Return of the *Moon* to the *Sun*; or one *Revolution* of the *Heavens* (or the *Earth*) about its *Axis*. But this by the by, for *Time* itself now forbids us to treat more fully concerning *Time*.

LECTURE XI.

Of the Congruity and Equality of Magnitudes.

IN the foregoing Lecture we have spoke sufficiently concerning the Nature of *Space* and certain Mathematical Hypotheses which are drawn from thence. The next Affection of Magnitude, which offers its self, is *Congruity*; the Supposition of which is as it were the chief Pillar and principal Bulwark of all the Mathematics. For from hence, in my Opinion, is taken the formal Reason of *Equality*, which is all in all in the Mathematics; and, as (*k*) *Proclus* says, *the most original Affection in Quantity*: at least it is in fact the most principal Criterion, and affords the leading Argument of the same; as it will be perhaps worth while to shew.

The *fourth Proposition* of the *first Book* of the *Elements* (which by *Proclus* is not undeservedly called the most simple and evident in Speculation) demonstrates the *Equality* in all respects, of two Triangles having two Legs equal and the Angles contained between those two Legs also equal, from

(*i*) Ad. 4. I.

the

the *Congruity* of the Sides and Angles ; only assuming the Axiom, *That two Right Lines comprehend not Space*, or which comes to the same, *That two Right Lines having the same Terms are congruous.* From this is demonstrated the *Equality* of *Triangles* and *Parallelograms* constituted upon the same Basis, and between the same Parallels, only applying the Axiom, which is also demonstrable by *Congruity*, (as shall be hereafter shewn) *If equal Quantities be added to Equals, the Wholes ; or if equal Quantities be subtracted from equals, the Remainders shall be equal to one another.* From thence by the Axiom ; *that Things equal to the same third are equal to one another* (which Axiom may in like manner be demonstrated by *Congruity*) the same is demonstrated concerning *Parallelograms* and *Triangles* constituted upon equal Bases. From these, applying also the Definition of *Proportionals*, is deduced the *Proportionality* of *Parallelograms* and *Triangles* of equal Heights, with their Bases, or of equal Bases, with their Heights. Hence the *Similitude* of *equiangular Triangles* ; then, in equal *Triangles* and *Parallelograms* having one Angle equal, the reciprocal Proportion of the Sides about the like Angles ; and interchangeably the Equality of the Sides of the Figures are derived from the reciprocal Proportion of their Sides ; and all the other principal Affections of plane Figures, which are especially contained in the *sixth Book* of the *Elements.*

Also otherwise, without applying the *fourth Proposition* of the *first Book* of the *Elements*, these abovementioned *Equalities* and *Proportionalities* of Triangles and Parallelograms are deduced by that excellent *Method of Indivisibles*, the most fruitful Mother of new Inventions in Geometry, which was not long ago published and applied to common Use by *Cavallerius.* The Foundation of which most elegant and useful Method (as its

Author

Author does not obſcurely intimate) is from *Congruity*, and is demonſtrated by *Congruity*, as will appear to any one who does but attentively conſider the firſt Propoſitions of his ſecond Book concerning the Geometry of *Indiviſibles*, or ſome few of the firſt Propoſitions of the ſame Author's firſt Exercitation.

In like manner the *eighth Propoſition* of the *firſt Book* of the *Elements* about the *Equality* of Angles ſubtended by equal Sides, in Triangles, whoſe Legs are equal (which is another plentiful Fountain of Geometrical Theorems, eſpecially abounding with ſuch as reſpect the Affections of Circles) is there demonſtrated, and can be no otherwiſe demonſtrated, than by this *Congruity*, either immediately, or mediately.

I paſs by many other particular Demonſtrations depending upon the Suppoſition of this, which are extant in *Archimedes*, *Pappus*, and many other famous Geometricians. From whence the moſt ſagacious *Willebrord Snellius* calls *Congruity*, the moſt elegant Utenſil that belongs to the Furniture of Geometry. They therefore who deſpiſe and reject it in mathematical Demonſtrations, as ſavouring too much of mechanical Bungling, do endeavour to overthrow the very Baſis of Geometry; but without either Wiſdom or Succeſs. For Geometricians do not perform their *Congruity* by the Hand but the Thought, not by the Senſe of the Eye but the Judgment of the Mind. They ſuppoſe an accurate and perfect *Congruence*, which no Hand can perform, nor any Senſe diſcern, and from that Suppoſition draw juſt and logical Conſequences. Here is no need of Rule or Compaſſes, no Labour of the Hands, but the Whole is the Work, the Artifice, and Device of the

(*l*) Snell. Præf. ad Cyclometr.

Reaſon;

Reaſon; nothing is required which ſavours of Mechaniſm, but only as far as every Magnitude is involved in ſome Sort of Matter, is expoſed to the Senſes, or is viſible and palpable; ſo that what the Mind demands to be underſtood, the Hand can execute in Part, and the Praxis can in ſome meaſure emulate the Theory. Which Imitation notwithſtanding, is ſo far from weakening or depreſſing the Strength and Dignity of *Geometrical Demonſtration*, that it affords it a much more ſtrong Confirmation and an higher Advancement, by ſenſibly proving the Reality and Poſſibility of the aſſumed Suppoſition, which indeed (as we have often inſinuated) is the genuine Foundation of all Science; and thus eſtabliſhing the Authority of Reaſon by the Suffrage of Experience. Conſequently they, who aſperſe the Knowledge of Mechanics in thoſe Demonſtrations where *Congruity* is applied, do rather accuſe them of the greateſt Perfection, than of any Defect or Blemiſh, and in Reality do the ſame as to reproach them for their excellent Familiarity and Facility, for their too great Evidence and Nobleneſs. Nor indeed has *Ramus* himſelf any Thing here to find Fault with, though one that has no great Favour or Good-Will towards the Ancients, but willingly gives his Vote, and very much approves, commends, and uſes the Method of Reaſoning, which is drawn from *Congruity*. *This Kind* (ſays (*m*) he) *of Euclidean Demonſtration, ſo expedite and facile I do very willingly embrace.*

But why do I go about to defend the Method of Demonſtration, which is commonly received and uſed by the very Princes and Ringleaders of Geometry (viz. *Euclid*, *Archimedes*, *Apollonius*, *Pappus*, and others) againſt ſuch pitiful

(*m*) Schol. Matt. Lib. VIII. 170.

Smatterers?

Smatterers? Rather let us conſider the Nature and Quality of this Mathematical Congruity a little nearer. *Congruity* is wont to be deſcribed by the *Occupation*, *Poſſeſſion*, or *Repletion* of the ſame *Place* or *Space:* which may be conceived to be done three ways, *viz.* by *Application*, *Succeſſion*, or *Mental Penetration.* (1) By *Application*, when one Magnitude is conceived to be ſo laid upon, or applied to another, as immediately to touch that other with all its Parts, and no where recede, or be ſeparated from it: As when a Meaſure is applied to, and coextended with the Thing meaſured (as a Yard-Wand to the Selvage of a Web; or aſſigned Right Lines to the Surface of the Earth) in which *Application* all the Parts of one Longitude do exactly anſwer to and immediately touch the Parts of the other, and conſequently theſe are congruous to one another after this manner. (2) By *Succeſſion*, when one Magnitude is conceived to enter the Place of another Magnitude removed; as when Water is poured out of a Veſſel and Wine poured in, theſe Magnitudes are ſaid to be congruous by reaſon of the *Identity of Space* which they ſucceſſively occupy. (3) By *Mental Penetration*, when we conceive the Magnitudes of two Bodies to grow together, coincide, and as it were unite into one by the Poſſeſſion of the ſame Place in the ſame Time: By which *Congruity* nearly the Writers of Perſpective do ſuppoſe a Table interpoſed between the Eye and a radiant Object, every where perſpicuous, and as it were penetrated with the lucid Cone or Pyramid ſo as no where to hinder the Rays from paſſing through, but to receive them all upon it, and retain their *Veſtigia* as impreſſed upon or united into it.

Of theſe Ways of *Congruity*, that which is performed by real *Application* agrees with *Lines* and *Superfices*

Superficies only, which by reaſon of their Indiviſibility may touch the Whole of one another immediately, and by this Contact, as it were penetrate one another and coincide in one. Whence Geometricians do account ſuch congruous *Lines* and *Superficies* as one: Which ſeems to have been meant by *Euclid*, when he denies *Space* to be comprehended between two Right Lines, as alſo a ſolid Space between two Planes. The Points which terminate a Plurality of contiguous Lines, they always account for one common Point; as alſo the extreme Lines which determine a Plurality of conjunct Superficies they take for one Line; and laſtly the Superficies which terminate Bodies they ſuppoſe to coaleſce into one Superfice. And this is reckoned as a Poſtulate by *Vitellius*, viz. *that when two plane Superficies do touch one another, they become one Superfice.* And by the ſame Reaſon, the concave Circumference of a Circle coincides with the convex Circumference of another included concentric Circle, which is perfectly contiguous to the former: Alſo the concave Superfice of a Sphere coincides with the convex Superfice of another included concentric Sphere, which is perfectly contiguous, as before.

But Bodies by reaſon of their internal Thickneſs have only their external Superficies contiguous, and conſequently no Part of them can be congruous by *Application.* Wherefore ſome of the Moderns do utterly deny them to have any *Congruity* at all. But at leaſt the *Congruity* performed by *Succeſſion* (*viz.* by Means of a common Space) pertains, and is extended to all Magnitudes univerſally: Since no Magnitude is peculiarly tied to any one *Space*, nor, on the contrary, any *Space* to one Magnitude, but the Place left by one may be occupied by any other equal and ſimilar Magnitude.

Laſtly,

Laſtly, The *Mental Congruity* of Magnitudes is not abſurdly ſuppoſed to be alſo of Solids, whatſoever the above named Philoſopher may think. For *firſt*, no *actual* or *real Penetration* is aſſerted by it, but only it is abſtracted in the Mind; neither does the *excluſive Force* of Bodies, which hinders *real Penetration*, come into Conſideration; but the general and indefinite Capacity of admitting an equal Body is only conſidered ſeparately by itſelf, which is the principal Property of Space. Which Manner of Conception the Philoſopher does often abſolve from Falſity. *Neither*, ſays (*h*) he, *when they abſtract, does it become falſe*. *Secondly*, This *mental Penetration* is no otherwiſe ſuppoſed by Mathematicians, than as *real Penetrability* is deſtroyed by it, and demonſtrated to be abſurd. For becauſe it is ſuppoſed that two Bodies fill the ſame Place, they demonſtrate from thence, that the Magnitude of both is the ſame, and therefore that by *penetrating* one another they ceaſe to be two; and conſequently that two Bodies (*i. e.* formally two Bodies) cannot *penetrate* one another. It is lawful to ſuppoſe any Thing however falſe and abſurd, that ſuch Falſhood and Abſurdity may be the better underſtood. Nor can ſcarce any negative Propoſition be convinced of Falſhood, any other Way than by detecting the Falſities that follow from the Suppoſition of its Truth. Thus therefore do Mathematicians apply this *Penetration*, which is ſuppoſed in the Mind, as thoſe apply it, who endeavour to demonſtrate the *Impenetrability* of Magnitude itſelf from the Suppoſition of *Penetration*. For Mathematicians only uſe it for diſcovering or proving the *Equality* or *Inequality* of Magnitudes, by which Means I affirm that two Spheres

(*n*) Phyſ. II. 2.

deſcribed

deſcribed with equal Diameters are equal; for the Center of the one may be conceived to be congruous with the Center of the other; whence, by reaſon of the *Equality* of all the *Radii*, the external Superfice of the one will not exceed the external Superfice of the other, therefore the Whole of the two Spheres will be congruous, therefore they will have the ſame Magnitude, *i. e.* they will be equal. But if the Diameter of the one be ſuppoſed greater than the Diameter of the other, if the Centers be conceived congruous, the ambient Superfice of one will exceed that of the other, becauſe, by reaſon of the ſuppoſed unequal *Radii*, it is farther diſtant from the common Center; therefore the Magnitude of both will not be the ſame, *i. e.* they will therefore be unequal.

But if any one do neverthelеſs oppoſe this *fictitious Penetration*, as not ſufficiently ſatisfactory; I add, that this mental Congruity may be conceived by Succeſſion, *viz.* by conceiving the one to vaniſh, and the other to be ſubſtituted in its Place, *i. e.* to be interpoſed within the ſame Term, or contained within the ſame Ambit; by which Means there will be no Difficulty, but this *Penetration* may be conceived almoſt the ſame Way, whereby a Sphere revolved about its Axis does penetrate itſelf; as one Part does perpetually ſucceed in the Place of another. Whence it appears that *Congruity* is nothing elſe but *the Occupation or Completion of the ſame Space or Place*, whether in the ſame Time or ſucceſſively, from which there reſults a ſort of Identity of Magnitudes, or Coalition into one. For indiviſible Magnitudes becauſe applied to one another, (according to their Indiviſibility) do fill the ſame Space in the ſame Time, and as it were coincide together; but ſolid Magnitudes every Way really diviſible are conceived

ceived to be in the ſame Space, either at different Times by *Succeſſion*, or at the ſame Time by *mental Penetration*, and are united and identified between themſelves by the Intervention of that Space, as far as their Quantity is united and identified with it. But that this Affection may be yet more apparent, I obſerve moreover that *Congruity* (eſpecially that which is conceived by *Appoſition*) may be underſtood to be handled various Ways, and as it were by certain Degrees.

Firſt, So, that the whole Magnitudes taken together do poſſeſs the ſame Space in the ſame Time, the Situation of the Parts being no where varied. By this may be congruent all Right Lines, plane Superficies, Peripheries of equal Circles, Superficies of equal Spheres, ſimilar Spirals in equal Circles, Cylinders, or Spheres; and all other Magnitudes whatſoever, which are ſimilar and equal. This is the higheſt Degree of moſt *perfect Congruity*.

Secondly, So, that they coincide with the ſame Space ſucceſſively by Parts, the Situation of the Parts again being no where changed. By this Way may be adapted the Perimeter of every Right lined Figure to a Right Line extended at Length, and the Surface of a Priſm to a Plane Superfice ſtretched upon a Level. Which is the next Degree of *poſſible Congruence*.

Thirdly, So, that all the Indiviſibles of each Magnitude may ſucceed in the ſame Place, and neither of the two vary the Poſition of their Parts. By this Method while a Wheel or a Circle runs forwards upon a Right Line always contiguous to it, and in the ſame Time is turned about its Center, its Periphery is congruous to the ſaid Right Line; becauſe all the Points of the circular Periphery are continually applied in a ſucceſſive Order to all the Points of the Right Line. Therefore,

fore, to obſerve this by the by, it is manifeſtly perceived from *Congruity*, that a Right Line may be made equal to the Periphery of a Circle, and conſequently the Quadrature of a Circle is not a Thing altogether impoſſible in its Nature, which is thus expreſſed by the above-mentioned moſt acute (*i*) Geometrician in his *Cyclometria: Such is the Mechanical Revolution of every Circle till it return to the ſame Point of the Periphery, where the Circumduction was begun; which indeed argues, and as it were lays before the Eyes, that a Right Line may be really exhibited equal to the Perimeter of a Circle.* And by like Reaſon a Cylinder turned about its Axis proceeds upon a plane Superfice, and its curved Superfice is exactly equal to the ſaid plane Superfice: Becauſe all the parallel Right Lines, which lie diſpoſed one after another in the Superfice of the Cylinder, are applied, by a continued uninterrupted Series, to all the parallel Right Lines in the plane Superfice.

Fourthly, So, that all the Indiviſibles of both Magnitudes do occupy the ſame Place in the ſame Time, the Situation of the Parts of one being in ſome meaſure unvaried, but yet their Order preſerved, and the former Contiguity of the particular Parts retained. By this Way the Periphery of a Circle, or any other Curve, may be ſo ſtretched or extended as to paſs into a Right Line, and conſequently be congruent with a Right Line; and on the contrary a Right Line may be ſo incurvated, as to degenerate into the Periphery of a Circle, or any other Curve Line. And the ſame Way may any curve Superfice be extended into a plane one, and reciprocally any plane Superfice into a curve one. And indeed (to explain the Matter a little farther) it may be often plainly

(*i*) *Snellius.*

enough diſcerned how curve Lines may be made out of, and reſolved into Right Lines, alſo from what plane Superficies may ariſe curve ones; which may be ſtiled the *Involution* or *Evolution* of *curve Lines* and *curve Superficies. Ex. gr.* as to curve Superficies, the curve Superfice of a Cylinder is nothing but a Right angled Parallelogram, having its Baſis equal to the Periphery of a Circle, which is the Baſis of the Cylinder, and of the ſame Height with the Cylinder, all whoſe Right Lines parallel to the Baſis are bent or incurvated into the Peripheries of Circles; from whence the cylindrical Superfice is congruous with this Parallelogram, if any ſide of the Cylinder (*i. e.* any Right Line drawn from Baſis to Baſis upon its Superfice) be applied to the Side of the Parallelogram, and thence the whole Superfice expanded into a Plane; or if by the Application of the Side of the Parallelogram to any Side of the Cylinder, its Plane be rolled about the Cylinder, and as it were do clothe and cover it on every Side. In like manner a conical Superfice is only the plane Sector of a Circle having its Radius equal to the Side of the Cone, and its Arch equal to the Periphery of a Circle which is the Baſis of the Cone, and whoſe concentric Arches are incurvated into as many perfect circular Peripheries: Or rather otherwiſe, a Conical Superfice is only a Right, angled Triangle, whoſe Altitude, or Perpendicular, is equal to the Side of the Cone, its Baſis to the Periphery of a Circle which is the Baſis of the Cone, and all whoſe Right Lines parallel to the Baſis are bent into ſo many circular Peripheries. So alſo the curve Superfice of a Sphere (with every Superfice of a plane Figure which is generated by a like Rotation) may be eaſily reduced to a trilineal Plane comprehended within two Right Lines conſtituting a Right Angle, and a curve a curve lined ſubtenſe. But how that is done, it does not belong to this Place to explain. But as to Curve Lines, beſides the Circumference of a Circle (which is nothing but a Right Line every where ſimilarly and uniformly bended through all its Parts) I ſay, beſides this, the cylindrical Spiral (which is the moſt ſimple, uniform and ſimilar, as to its Parts, of all other Curves) is nothing but a Right Line equal to the Diagonal of the aforeſaid Parallelogram (to which the cylindrical Superfice is reduced) it being circumvolved about the cylindrical Superfice. Concerning the Reduction of other Curves to Right Lines, or to other kind of Curves, I am at this Time ſilent, leſt I ſhould be both too prolix, and at the ſame time too obſcure in a Thing only handled by the by. To this Mode alſo belongs, or is very near of kin to it, that *Congruity* of which equal Figures included within the ſame parallel Lines or Planes are capable; of which all the Lines or Planes intercepted between the ſame Parallels are equal. As two Triangles or Parallelograms not equiangular to one another, or two Pyramids, Priſms, Cones, Cylinders unequally inclined, conſtituted between the ſame parallel Right Lines or the ſame parallel Planes, and upon equal Baſes. For as one of theſe is congruous to another, the Situation of the Parts of one ought to be accommodated to the Poſition of the Parts of the other, yet without diſturbing their Order, or loſing their former Contiguity.

The *fifth* Way is, when the *Congruity* may be ſo performed, that the Poſition and Order of certain Parts is changed. This Way of Congruity of all the moſt imperfect and difficult to be underſtood, agrees with homogeneous Figures altogether unlike to one another. *Ex. gr.* A Triangle is no otherwiſe congruent with a Circle, a Cone with

with a Sphere, than by tranſpoſing the Parts of either, by applying a Part of one to a Part of the other, and a part of the Reſidue in one to a part of the Remnant in the other; and ſo perpetually, till the Buſineſs be finiſhed, and all the Parts of the one be at length applied to all the Parts of the other; which Thing whoever deſires to have diſtinctly explained I adviſe him to go to the above mentioned Places of *Cavellerius.*

From theſe Things it will appear to him who more attentively conſiders that all Magnitudes of the ſame Kind may be ſome way made congruent to one another, *i. e.* Lines to Lines, Superficies to Superficies, and Solids to Solids, either the Wholes at the ſame Time, or by their Parts (or Indiviſibles) ſucceſſively, the Situation of the Parts being retained, or taken ſomething at large, or at leaſt tranſpoſing them: I ſay all Magnitudes may be congruous by taking *Congruity* at large, for any Coincidence though inadequate; by which means a leſſer Right Line laid upon a greater Right Line will be congruous to it, *i. e.* will coincide with it wholly, though not with the Whole of it.

But *Congruity* more ſtrictly taken, is only attributed to equal Magnitudes, which neither any where exceeding, nor falling ſhort of, its Bounds, do preciſely occupy the ſame Place, *i. e.* do juſtly fill it, and are contained by it. And indeed ſome do place the *formal Reaſon* of *Equality* itſelf, in the *Aptitude* or *Power* of ſuch *Congruity* with which Magnitudes are oftentimes endowed, and from thence define it, in my Opinion, not badly. Of the Ancients the great *Apollonius* was of the ſame Mind, as appears from his Demonſtration of that celebrated Axiom of *the Equality of Things equal to the ſame third*, which *Proclus* produces and impugns. Which Demonſtration depends upon this Definition of *Equality. Thoſe Things are equal to one another*

whic

which possess the same Place. And lately our Countryman Mr. *Hobbs* has also defined *equal Bodies* to be *such as can occupy the same Place. But a Body* (says he) *may occupy the same Place, which another Body occupies, though it be not of the same Figure, if it can only be understood to be reduced into the same Figure by the Flexion and Transposition of its Parts.* Which Assertions of *Hobbs*, his great Adversary does largely canvass and very acutely endeavour to refute; but according to my Judgment, not to dissemble the Truth, not with the utmost Efficacy. For I am notwithstanding more of the Opinion of *Apollonius*, and think that *Equality* is appositely enough defined from a *possible Congruity.* I will give some Reasons for my thinking so, and examine this Matter a little more curiously (proceeding gradually), because it seems worth the while, and makes something for our Purpose.

And *first*, though it may be somewhat questioned, whether it be expedient to assign any Definition of *Equality*, for *(p) Aristotle* seems to think it not at all necessary; because the Notion of *Equality* is perspicuous of itself, and its Signification abundantly plain to every one. *To subduct Equals from Equals*, says he, *assumes not (i. e.* explains not) *what Affections do signify, nor does it assume* (or explain) *what the common Terms (*i. e. of Principles or Axioms) *signify, because it is manifest.* Though I say it may be thus doubted whether *Equality* ought to be defined at all, nevertheless I think it for the Benefit of the Mathematics, to have what is understood by it distinctly defined, and explained. For since *Equality* is an Affection of that Kind that it does not immediately occur to the Sense or Experience, but results from an instituted Comparison of Things, (at least without Comparison

(p) Post. I. 10.

riſon it is not apprehended by us) and ſince Things may be differently compared with one another, therefore it ſeems to be required of us to determine from what and what Sort of Compariſon, when and after what manner we conceive *Equality* to reſult, by ſome certain Argument, undoubted Criterion, or annexed Sign evident, reciprocal, and expreſſed by a Definition; that we may have a diſtinct Notion of it, and that no Cauſe of Doubt or Difference may poſſibly ariſe. It is indeed needleſs for thoſe Things which are more immediately and frequently expoſed to the Senſes, (of which the firſt indemonſtrable Hypotheſes do conſiſt) to be explained in other Words beſides their vulgarly received Names, becauſe they impreſs the ſame diſtinct Ideas of themſelves upon all Men. For I take no Notice of their Opinion, who think the Species of *Equality*, *Similitude*, and ſuch Relations, to be implanted in us by Nature; ſince that Device (as we have ſeen above) is unneceſſary and unſuitable for the Sciences; nor does it depend upon any ſolid Reaſon, that I can perceive, except certain Metaphyſical Perplexities and Niceties of Words. But to cut off all Occaſions of Diſpute, it ſeems to be of Uſe to the Sciences, moſt accurately to determine all the other ſecondary Conceptions, which do any how reſult from the Compariſons of theſe firſt Hypotheſes one with another, by confining theſe firſt Hypotheſes from whence they ariſe. For, ſtrictly ſpeaking, in raiſing any Science from its firſt Foundations, it is ſcarce lawful to apply any Word, which is not before defined, or at leaſt to which we cannot moſt evidently demonſtrate ſomething anſwering in Nature. Which ought to obtain ſo much the more in this Affection of Magnitudes, which we are now treating of, becauſe it bears the principal Part, and almoſt always occurs in every mathematical

thematical Subject and Discourse, and consequently it rightly behoves all Students of those Sciences to have one agreeable and common Idea of it, clear, distinct, and consentaneous to Reason; and that they do not apprehend it confusedly or disagreeably. And indeed, since we ourselves do seek and dispute what this *Equality* is, wherein consists its *formal Reason*, and how it ought to be defined, it may be an Argument that it ought to be defined. To this I add, that the Definition of *Equality* ought to be known and ready, at least because it is incumbent upon me to defend this, *that all Axioms are to be accounted for Theorems*, and may and ought to be demonstrated, (if the Thing require it) and that especially from the Definition of the Terms of which they consist: from whence the Truth of these Axioms may appear concerning the *Equality* of Things equal to the same third, of the Sums or Differences of equal Quantities added or subtracted from Equals, and the like. I add also that through a want of this Definition there would happen, nay perhaps in Fact has happened (to the Disparagement and Detriment of this Science) an Occasion of Quarrels, Animosities and Broils in the calm and peaceable Province of Geometry. For one or two convenient Definitions would perhaps have easily quieted, decided, and taken utterly away the Strifes between *Clavius* and *Peletarius*, and other skilful Geometricians, concerning the *Angle* of *Contact*, (which were encreased by angry Minds and contumelious Words) if the Definitions of *Equality* and *Angle* had but been rightly constituted, and the Ambiguity of these Words taken away. It is therefore expedient to lay down some Definition of *Equality*; let this be holden in the first Place.

Moreover *secondly*, because as I have said often heretofore, and am fully persuaded, that every Definition

Definition ought to be ſought from ſome poſſible Suppoſition depending upon manifeſt Experience; and ſince if we attentively weigh and examine whatſoever is of kin to this Buſineſs, I believe no Hypotheſis will offer itſelf more accommodate for founding the Definition of *Equality* on, than this of the poſſible *Congruence* of Magnitudes: therefore this ought by all means to be embraced and acknowledged. That no one more accommodate does offer itſelf, will evidently appear to any attentive Perſon by manifeſt Tokens. For no Hypotheſis is more frequently obſerved, expoſed to the Senſes, beheld with the Eyes, and touched with the Hands; none is underſtood more clearly, or ſuppoſed more poſſible. And when the Queſtion is about the *Equality* or *Inequality* of Things, the Contention is always determined by appealing to *Congruity*. Which is a ſufficient Sign that this Notion of *Equality* moſt aptly agrees with the common Conceptions of Men; and that when Men ſay two Magnitudes are equal, nothing is underſtood but that by their Application to one another they are congruous between themſelves, or at leaſt do fill up the Capacity of the ſame Space.

And I will yet confirm this by an Experiment very familiar to me. I have often been aſked by ſuch as were unaccuſtomed with Geometry, What that famous Problem meant or did ſignify about the *Quadrature of the Circle?* The Anſwer was ready, that it was to find a rectilineal quadrilateral Plane rectangular and equilateral, whoſe Area or Space included within the linear Perimeter may be moſt accurately equal to the propoſed Circle, *i. e.* to the Plane Area which is circumſcribed by the circular Periphery. But they then were wont to inſiſt upon what is meant by this *Equality*. For how, ſay they, can a round circular Space be equal

equal to an angular Space, when they cannot be congruous and adequate to one another? This Doubt (which sufficiently intimates that most Men do understand nothing by *Equality* but the *Congruity* of Magnitudes itself) will be easily removed, if we suppose the said quadrilateral Figure (as if it consist of Wax, or of any other Matter, soft and perfectly flexible) by the Inflection, Transposition or Compression of certain Parts to be some how transformed into a circular Figure, and then being applied to the Circle is exactly congruous to it; in which Case, I say, these Figures do become equal, and the *Quadrature* is performed which we sought with so much Study. To this Answer, which is purposely adapted to Men's preconceived Notions, they immediately acquiesce; from whence it is sufficiently apparent that by *Equality* is understood nothing else but a *possible Congruity.*

To this *thirdly* may be added that which seems to me the most conclusive Argument of all, which is as follows: *Equality* is most appositely defined from that Property, upon which all the Theorems about the *Equality* of Magnitudes do depend, from which they are deduced, and to which they are ultimately referred; from whence consequently the remaining Affections of equal Magnitudes, as such, are derived: But all the Things demonstrated about the *Equality* of Magnitudes do depend upon *Congruity*, are either mediately or immediately deduced from it, and demonstrated by it, and lastly are ultimately resolved into it. Therefore *Equality* is most appositely defined by it. The Truth of the major Proposition of this Syllogism is sufficiently clear from the Nature of a Definition, whose Office it is to exhibit some primary Affection, from whence, as from a formal Cause, the remaining Properties of the Thing defined are inferred by a lawful Discursus. Therefore if equal

Magnitudes

Magnitudes be defined to be ſuch as are capable of being preciſely congruous to one another, and their Affections of being demonſtrated from this expreſſed Affection of equal Magnitudes as ſuch; it will be ſufficiently apparent, that the Definition from thence is lawful. But things are thus, and the Minor is equally true. For in fact whatſoever is demonſtrated about the *Equality* of Things in the Elements, and conſequently every where elſe in the Mathematics, depends upon this Axiom, *That the Things which are congruous are equal*, as was ſhewn in the Beginning of this Lecture, and will perhaps be hereafter ſhewn more clearly. Conſequently they, who receive this Axiom as put for the Definition of *Equality*, ſeem to do very rightly; to whom (beſides the abovementioned *Apollonius* and *Hobbs*, I may add the learned *Borellus*; *For*, ſays (*q*) he, *if no Name were yet impoſed for Equality, it might be ſaid that thoſe Things which are mutually congruous may be called Equals, and this would be a Definition, not an Axiom*; therefore he thinks this Axiom to differ no otherwiſe from the *Definition* of *Equality*, than in the manner of expreſſing it, and grants that it may be eaſily changed into a Definition. But I do not entirely agree with this moſt learned Man's Inſinuation, that it becomes rather an Axiom than a Definition, becauſe of the Name of *Equality* being firſt impoſed and vulgarly received. For though the Names of ſome Kind of Things, *viz.* of a Triangle, or a Circle, be received and commonly uſed, yet, it is requiſite for thoſe Names to be defined, to prevent confuſed Notions concerning thoſe Things and Words. For the Vulgar diſtinguiſh not, but frequently keep the Ideas anſwering to the accuſtomed Names very confuſed

(*q*) Eucl. Reſtit. p. 16.

and

and inadequate; whereas the Genus and Reason of Sciences require very distinct and adequate Conceptions; and consequently Teachers of Sciences ought to define the most received Names of Things, and clear the Signification of Words from vulgar Confusion; especially of such Things as are not obvious to the Senses and leave not clear Ideas of themselves upon the Mind. Though the Name of *Equality* is no otherwise received than as it designs what is expressed in the said Axiom, *viz. That Magnitudes, which are said to be equal, are congruous* to one another. Therefore that Axiom contains a Definition of *Equality* most agreeable to the Ideas of the Vulgar.

To these Things it may be adjoined *fourthly*, that our Adversaries are able to devise no Notions of *Equality* more fit, nor, by excluding this Notion, can aptly interpret what they mean or distinctly understand by *Equality*. The Antagonist of *Hobbs* reminds him of his two other Descriptions which he thinks to be more apposite than that taken from *Congruity*. He demands of *Hobbs*, Why he could not at the same time, and in the same Words have said, *That is equal to another, which is just as much as itself*; *or those Things are equal whose Quantity is the same*; *or if neither of these please, to have invented another Definition?* To which Words it may be answered in the first Place: It is probable, that most acute Man was not able to invent a Definition more accurate than these two which he brings; for if others had occurred it is likely he had not omitted them. But these two do either seem to signify nothing at all, or to result into *Congruity*. I do not indeed dislike, but willingly embrace, that Definition, which seems to be borrowed from *(r) Aristotle*, *that those*

(r) Met. IV. 16.

Things

Things are equal, whose Quantity is the ſame, if by it is denoted not an actual, but a poſſible Identity of Quantity, as it ought to be underſtood, leſt the Propoſition be convinced of manifeſt Falſity by attributing the ſame Quantity to equal Things, *i. e.* to Things actually different: I ſay, I find no Fault with this Definition ſo underſtood; but I aſk how the Quantities of two Things can become the ſame otherwiſe than by *Congruity*; *i. e.* except they coincide or are as it were co-united together ſome of the above expounded Ways, *viz.* by *Application*, *Mental Penetration*, or the *Intervention of ſome mean Space?* For indeed I can hardly ſee or conceive how the Quantities of two Things which are really diſtinct from one another can poſſibly be the ſame. But as to the other Definition, *viz. that is equal to another which is juſt as much as itſelf*; firſt I oppoſe to it that logical Law preſcribed by *(s) Ariſtotle* with the higheſt Reaſon. *Since a Definition is delivered for the ſake of declaring a Thing, and we do not declare from Things taken unadviſedly, but from ſuch as are prior and more manifeſt; from hence it appears, that he who defines not from ſuch Things, defines not at all.* I ſay, I object this moſt juſt Law againſt the above-cited Definition; for who does not, with as equal Eaſe conceive what is *equal to another*, as what is *as much as itſelf?* But perhaps to one who more thoroughly conſiders it, the Word *as much* will be found to ſignify nothing elſe but *as much the ſame*, or, *whoſe Quantity is the ſame*; and conſequently this Deſcription, if rightly underſtood and explained, will differ nothing from the foregoing one, but will the ſame Way fall in with our Hypotheſis of *Congruity*. Conſequently our Adverſaries are unwarily forced

(s) Top. VI. 4.

to

to establish our Opinion while they are studying to overthrow it; and do sufficiently betray themselves, that in reality they hardly differ at all from us, as they most gladly would.

Lastly, I omit, that *Euclid* is expressly said to have defined *equal Magnitudes* to be *those which fill the same Place* in a Book, which I never saw concerning *Gravity* and *Levity*. My Author is *Ramus*. But a greater Light will accrue to this (*t*) Cause (greater, I say, to the Nature of both *Congruity* and *Equality*) from a Discussion of those Arguments, which I deny not to be in Appearance sufficiently valid, that are produced on the contrary Part by *Proclus*, and the above-mentioned most learned Man; which I abstain from, for the present, lest I should be too prolix.

LECTURE XII.

An Examination of the Objections brought by Proclus, *&c.*

OF the more common Affections and Properties of Magnitudes, which occur to Observation and introduce Mathematical Hypotheses, the last that offered itself was *Congruity*; from the Supposition of which, we have in Part declared in the preceding Lecture, that the *Equality* of Magnitudes results and is aptly defined by it. Which Doctrine notwithstanding *Proclus* and *Hobbs*'s celebrated Antagonist in his Confutation of the *Hobbian* Geometry do strenuously oppose, as they think, with invincible Arguments. It now re-

(*t*) Schol. Math. VII. p. 163.

mains and is incumbent upon us to weigh the Efficacy of the Things objected in the Balance of Reaſon, and ſee whether the War be ended, and they have obtained a Victory as compleat as they imagine. Which we undertake to examine the more readily, becauſe there will ariſe no ſmall Light to theſe Things from theſe Conflicts of contrary Sentiments and Reaſonings. Certain Sparks of Truth, by no means to be ſlighted, ſeem capable of being ſtruck forth; and yet I will not trouble myſelf very much with removing every little Cavil, but will more diligently examine the Arguments which by a candid Acceptation do ſeem to approach nearer the Buſineſs, and to contain in them ſomething of more weighty Moment, being mindful of *Ariſtotle*'s Divine Precept, (*u*) *That Things will be more credited if the Arguments on both Sides be firſt heard. For it does not become us to give Sentence without hearing the Cauſe, or condemn any Side unheard. They who are willing to judge well of the Truth ought not to be Adverſaries, but Arbitrators.* I will therefore, as far as I am able, propoſe ſuch Arguments from them as are moſt nervous.

They pretend then *firſt*, that the ſame univocal common Reaſon, and general Notion of *Equality* ought to be aſſigned for all thoſe Things to which *Equality* is truly attributed and juſtly agrees. But *Equality* is with the ſame Reaſon and like Propriety of Speech wont to be attributed and truly to agree, not only with Magnitudes (*viz.* which have this peculiar *Congruity* we are contending for) but alſo with all homogeneous Quantities, which are fit to be compared together, (*viz.* Motions, Times, Velocities, Weights, Numbers, *&c.*) though *Congruity* do by no means ſquare with

(*u*) De Cœlo I. 10.

them.

them. *Equality*, says *Proclus*, *agrees with all Quantities in common Continued and Discrete:* And the other Adversary, *Is not the Notion of Equality the same in all these, ay and in all other Things as many as are capable of Equality or Inequality?* (v) Whereby he makes, that, about whatsoever Equality they are conversant, the Axioms laid down in the Elements of Geometry both are and lawfully may be accommodated to all Quantities indifferently; from whence they are stiled *common Axioms*. *Each of these*, says *Proclus* again, *is not only truly spoke of Magnitudes but of Numbers, Motions, and Times.* And *Aristotle* himself speaks to the same Purpose, *It is* (says (x) he, bringing an Example of a common Principle) *common to all Quantities that where equal Things are taken away, the Remainders are equal.* Therefore, say they, the Reason of *Equality* is unadvisedly taken from *Congruity*, because it is proper to Magnitudes alone, and agrees not with other Quantities, and consequently is no where coextended with *Equality*, but confined within much stricter Bounds. For from the justest Prescript of Logic, *the Thing defined ought to be exactly coequal and convertible with the Attribute by which it is defined.*

To this primary Exception, that it may be sufficiently apparent to some who urge us pressingly, I answer briefly, in the *first Place*, that the *Equality* of Magnitudes only is here properly and principally defined. *Secondly*, that it may be lawfully and rationally defined alone by itself. *Thirdly*, that this Definition (I mean the Definition fetched from *Congruity*) may be fully adapted to all Quantities its own Way. *Fourthly* and *Lastly*, that it is necessary, at least lawful, for the sake of greater Perspicuity and Security, that the

(v) Elench. p. 10. (x) Met. XI. 4.

Equalities

Equalities of other Quantities be defined ſeparately. By the more diſtinct Explanation of which Particulars, and the different Approbation of equal Judges of the Buſineſs, I imagine the Objection brought will be compleatly anſwered.

As to the *firſt* Point, there is no Controverſy about it; for our Adverſaries deny not that Magnitudes only are eſpecially capable of *Congruity*, but they rather place the Force of the Argument in it; and it is apparent enough of itſelf, ſince to fill Place, to occupy Space, to touch, be applied, or in ſome Sort penetrate one another is an Attribute proper and peculiar to Magnitudes. Therefore this Definition, if it be a Definition, does properly agree and ſquare with theſe only.

But *ſecondly*, I ſay the *Equality* of Magnitudes is properly defined by itſelf alone. For ſince Quantity, and the conſequent or concomitant Affections of Quantity, (*viz. Extenſion*, *Termination*, *Compoſition*, *Diviſion*, *Menſuration*, &c.) do primarily and properly agree with Magnitudes; why may not *Equality* primarily agree with them too, and conſequently be properly defined in reſpect to them? The Philoſopher teaches that the Definition of a *Genus* does primarily and properly agree with the principal *Species* of thoſe which are unequally attributed to it, and with the reſt ſecondarily, conſecutively and by ſimilitude. *The Reaſon*, ſays (*y*) he, *of a Thing agrees with all its inferiour Species, though not the ſame Way, but to theſe primarily, to theſe conſecutively.* A Definition, taken ſimply, agrees properly with its firſt *Genus*, therefore a Definition ought to be made in reſpect of that. But are not the Values and Eſtimations of all other Quantities not only known but alſo named and denominated with Reſpect to Magnitudes?

(*y*) Met. VII. 4.

tudes? Do not the very Words themſelves of *Greater* and *Leſſer*, *Whole* and *Part*, *Finite* and *Infinite*, *Continued* and *Diſcrete*, *Extended* and *Contracted*, *Proportion* and *Diſproportion*, and ſuch others, which are ſo often aſcribed to other Quantities, draw their Origin no where elſe than from Magnitudes, and are ſecondarily transferred from theſe to other Quantities? And that not contingently and undeſervedly, but neceſſarily and with the higheſt Reaſon. For certainly other Things accidentally ſubject to a mathematical Conſideration have their Degrees, their Intenſions and Remiſſions, but can no way be comprehended or expreſſed, but by making a Compariſon of the Magnitudes, (in which they are, upon which they act, which they produce, or about which they are ſome Way converſant) and by applying Words borrowed from the Attributes of Magnitudes. *Ex. gr.* How can the *Weight* or *Momentum* of a gravitating Thing be conceived, or why is it called *ſo much*, *ſo great*, or *ſo little*, but as it is in ſo great a Body, or is capable to lift ſo great a Body, or ſuſtain ſo great a Magnitude? How can it be underſtood to be *Diviſible* or a *Whole*, but as the Body to which it inheres, or which it reſpects, has its particular Parts endowed with ſuch a Virtue, or anſwering to ſuch a Power? From whence is the Title of *finite* obtained, but either from the Terms of the Magnitude to which it belongs, or at leaſt from the Bounds of the Body extended which it can raiſe or ſuſtain? In like manner it may be predicated *Commenſurable* and *Incommenſurable*, becauſe either its Subject or Object is found to be affected with *Proportion* or *Diſproportion* to other Magnitudes in like manner endowed with Weight, with which it is compared. So alſo *Motion* is accounted *ſo much*, (*long*, *ſhort*, *great*, *little*, either abſolutely or comparatively) from the Magnitude of

Space

Space gone through, *ſo terminated* from the Limits of the Space ſo far as it is extended, *Menſurable* from its Dimenſions, a *Whole* from its Compoſitions, and *Diviſible* from its Diviſibility. And the ſame Way (for I ſometimes do purpoſely heap up more Examples than are requiſite for illuſtrating the Thing propoſed, having a View to the Uſefulneſs of Things leſs common, that I may thereby gradually inſtil ſome (z) *Guſt* preparatory to the Mathematics in general, and inſinuate Notions which may be hereafter profitable for ſomething) I ſay, the ſame way is *Time* conceived and denominated from the Magnitude of the Space run through by ſome Body determinately moveable, as the Sun or Moon, and it alſo borrows from them its *Terms*, *Extenſion*, *Proportion* and *other Affections*, with reſpect to the Magnitude of the ſame which it obtains. Alſo *Velocity* is computed from the Magnitude of the Space run through (not indeed abſolutely, but comparatively, from the Magnitude of the Space paſſed over by another Body determinately moveable, *viz.* the Sun or Moon; *i. e.* from the Magnitude of Space gone through in ſo much Time) and is *limited*, *compounded*, *divided*, *meaſured*, and every way compared by a like Relation to the Magnitude of the Space; nor can it be ſcarce any other Way eſtimated. As to *Numbers*, it has been abundantly ſhewn, that they are no otherwiſe Partakers of Quantity and Proportion than as they are Symbols deſigning Magnitudes. Nor am I entirely by myſelf, and deſtitute of all Authority, when I affirm thoſe Things (though oftentimes the Queſtion and Subject I undertake are diſtinctly explained by none that I know of, having ſcarce any Guide or Companion to take off the Troubleſomeneſs of my Paſſage through thoſe rugged Paths; ſo that I am the

(z) Γεῦμα.

more

more pardonable if I ſeem ſometimes to ſtumble or proceed with Difficulty) however I ſeem to have the chief of the Philoſophers agreeing with me in this Buſineſs, whoſe Words are ſufficiently for our Purpoſe. *Since*, ſays (*a*) he, *whatſoever is moved from one Term goes forward to ſome other Term, and every Magnitude is continuous, therefore Motion is ſo far the Conſequent of Magnitude. For Motion is continuous by reaſon of the Continuity of Magnitude, and becauſe of Motion Time is alſo continuous. For how much ſoever a Motion is, ſo much Time does alſo ſeem to have paſſed : But Priority and Poſteriority are originally in Space from the different Poſition of its Parts*; *and ſince an Order of Parts is in Magnitude, the ſame will be alſo of Neceſſity in the Motion which analogically anſwers it*; *moreover a Priority and Poſteriority is alſo found in time, becauſe one of theſe is always conſequent to the other* (*viz.* as to the Affections and Attributes of this Sort). Thus he clearly aſſerts the Continuity of Motion and Time, as well as the Quantity of Magnitude to be Conſequents of the ſame Claſſis. Again, elſewhere, *Motion*, ſays (*b*) he, *follows Magnitude, and Time Motion as theſe are Quantities and continued and diviſible. For becauſe Magnitude is ſuch, therefore Motion is ſo affected, and by reaſon of Motion, Time.* Thus the Philoſopher in his Phyſics, ſo that he could have ſcarce pronounced any thing more appoſitely, plainly, or fully to our Purpoſe; except perhaps what he delivers in his *Metaphyſics* be more expreſs than theſe, and may tend more to ſtrengthen and illuſtrate our Opinion. For thus he ſpeaks concerning Motion and Time. (*c*) *Motion and Time are ſome Way ſaid to be Quantities and Continuities, becauſe the Things whoſe Affections they are (or to which they belong) are capable of Diviſion. I mean not the*

(*a*) Phyſ. IV. 86. (*b*) Ib. IV. 18. (*c*) Met. IV. 13.

Thing

Thing itself which is moved, but that along which it is moved (i. e. *the Space gone through*). *For because that is a Quantity, Motion is also a Quantity, and Time because of this.* Thus does *Aristotle* give us his Suffrage and Authority. It is therefore just since other Quantities refer their Quantity, and Affections connected with Quantity, to Magnitude (at least its Knowledge and Comprehension) that also the *Equality* of the same *(i. e.* the Identity and Coalition of their Quantity) be taken from the *Equality* of Magnitude; and as they are Quantities by *Analogy* and *Secondarily*, so in like manner to obtain an *analogical* and *borrowed Equality*. Which will yet more manifestly appear not to be different to the Truth, to him that examines the Thing more closely and intimately, and consults the common Sense and Consent of Mankind. For *ex. gr.* if it be enquired of any Mortal (whether Philosopher or one of the Vulgar) what he means by saying *Two Times are equal*, I imagine he will return presently, and without Hesitation, that he means two equal Spaces run through by the same Body uniformly moved (as two equal Parts of the Sun's diurnal or annual Revolution) or by different Bodies carried by an equal Velocity. If what he signifies by the *Equality* of two *Weights*; he will say that the extreme Force of this is capable to elevate or sustain a Magnitude equal to another Magnitude of the same Species, which the extreme Force of another is capable to elevate or sustain: nor will they determine otherwise who are consulted about the *Equality* of *Motions*, *Velocities*, and all other Quantities whatsoever, always alledging the *Equality* of certain Magnitudes in respect of which the said Quantities are constituted and denominated *equal*. So that we can scarce distinguish or totally abstract the *Equality* of other Things from the *Equality* of *Magnitude* even in Thought, scarce by excluding

it

it can apprehend that they are equal, think or exprefs how they are equal, or diftinctly conceive what *Equality* itfelf is. Since therefore every other *Equality* does inwardly include and fignify that, as by Nature prior and principal to itfelf, conftitutive and definitive of itfelf, therefore other Quantities are only equal fecondarily and lefs principally, dependently and confecutively, derivatively and by participation, by habitude or analogy. Whence that the Apprehenfion may be more clear, the Judgment more certain concerning other *Equalities*, it is firft neceffary to know and diftinctly apprehend what the *Equality* of Magnitudes fignifies and wherein it confifts, and confequently that of right it ought to be firft defined by itfelf. Which was the fecond Thing we undertook to explain and prove.

But, moreover, *thirdly*; Our *Congruity* does alfo agree with all Quantities whatfoever, as they are any Way *terminated*, *extended*, *compounded*, *divided*, *meafured*, or admit other Affections of Magnitudes (as has already been fufficiently fhewn), and efpecially by means of the *Congruity* of the Magnitudes in which they are, and which they refpect. *Ex. gr.* It may be conceived that two moveable Points (or two any other moveable Things equal and fimilar) are carried with an equal Velocity along two Right Lines, or two Peripheries of equal Circles: it may be alfo underftood that thofe Lines or Peripheries, as capable of *Congruity*, are applied to one another, fo that the faid Points or moveable Things are put upon one another, and confequently are congruous, as well in the Beginning as in the Progrefs of their Motion, by reafon of their fuppofed equal Celerity or Velocity; therefore from the perpetual *Congruity* of the moveable Things and Coincidence of their Orbits, it is no way difficult to conceive that the Motions themfelves are congruous, united, and coalefce;

and consequently that they have the same Quantity, or are equal to one another. In like manner, in the Course of any Body (suppose of the Sun or the Earth), the Quantity of whose Time is determined by an equable Motion, if two Points or Terms be conceived to be assumed by which the Beginnings of the Motions run through, and consequently of Times, may be computed; and these Terms are conceived to be applied one upon another, as was just now shewn, so that thence the two Motions beginning from them may be congruous, then the Times themselves will be confluent, and pass on together. And if the Beginnings of two Years be conceived as conjoined, it will be easy to imagine them to exist together as proceeding with an equal Tenour, and as it were penetrate one another, and pass into one. Which is all one as if you should say, if two equal Things begin together, they will end together. Whence it will be lawful also to judge, what Way one Time can be really congruous with another Time: since Time is best measured and determined by the equable circular Motion, often repeated, of the same most noble and constantly moveable Thing, as (d) *Aristotle* observes; *An uniform circular Motion is the best Measure, because its Number is most known.* For a Circle being measured so often by the periodical Revolution of the same moveable Thing does always continue one and the same: Hence by means of it *Motion* and *Time* (their Parts still beginning and ending in the same Point of the Periphery) are as it were united together and identified, and consequently are most perfectly congruous. Wherefore the Year comes back upon itself, Months and Days return, Ages are renewed, the Places and Periods of Seasons are restored; and to use that

(d) Phys. IV. 14.

trite Saying of the Vulgar, *Time itſelf ſeems to be a Circle*, by reaſon of the circular and often repeated Motion which determines it. *As one and the ſame Motion* (ſays the (*e*) Philoſopher) *may be performed again and again, ſo may one and the ſame Time, as a Year, the Spring, or Autumn.* But we have not Leiſure to ſpend any more Words concerning Time. And the ſame Reaſon holds with Velocities, which in like manner by means of the *Congruities* of the Spaces paſſed over by them, are themſelves congruous, and conſequently may be demonſtrated equal. Moreover if two heavy Bodies of the ſame Species, *ex. gr.* two equal Spheres of Water or Air, be ſuppoſed congruous by the *Mental Penetration* already explained; at the ſame time their Gravities or Weights will coincide, or become congruous, and by the ſame Reaſon be apprehended equal. In like manner *Congruity* may be ſome Way attributed to equal *Reaſons* or *Proportions* themſelves, as they all coincide and become the ſame with ſome one thing expounded by *Numbers, Lines*, or ſome *other Quantities*, which *expounded Reaſon* has a certain Reſemblance of Space, in reſpect of the infinite Reaſons it may repreſent and expreſs, as it were receiving them all into and uniting them with itſelf. So alſo *Numbers* may be *congruous*, as far as they are equal, *viz.* by the *Congruence* of the equal Quantities which they repreſent and denominate. Conſequently Quantities of every Kind, as they receive the other Properties of Magnitudes, ſo do they Congruity after their own Way, *i. e.* analogically, conſecutively, and by Participation from the *Congruity* of the Magnitudes by which their Quantity is determined: and conſequently the Definition of *Equality* reſulting from the Suppoſition of *Con-*

(*e*) Phyſ. IV. 12.

gruity

gruity is not at all diſagreeable to them; nay is ſo much the more agreeable, as *Equality* itſelf is agreeably and reaſonably aſſigned.

But I proceed to the *fourth* Head of my Anſwer, *viz.* That it is neceſſary, or at leaſt lawful, to define or explain ſeparately the *Equalities* of other Quantities, *viz.* from the reſpective *Equality* of the Magnitudes in which they are, and about which they are any way converſant. For (as was before inſinuated) the common Reaſon of ſuch things as are unequally attributed (or predicated) does ſeem to require that the Things which are primary in their Genus, and conſequently are as Meaſures of the reſt be defined in the firſt Place by themſelves, ſince the reſt are declared of Conſequence from a peculiar Relation to thoſe that are prior to them. Thus again the Philoſopher, who was moſt ſenſible of thoſe Things: *Wherefore* (*t*) *it is firſt of all to be diſtinguiſhed how many ways the Particulars are predicated of thoſe Things that are unequally attributed (or predicated) and then to be explained how they are referred to that which is firſt in the ſaid Genus (or Predicament;) for it is the Property of ſome Things to have, of ſome to affect, and of ſome to be other ſuch ways attributed.* Thus, ſince *Equality* agrees with more Things than one, to Magnitude indeed originally and principally, and to other Quantities (*viz.* Motions, Times, Velocities, moving Powers) *ſecondarily* and leſs *principally*; therefore the Reaſon of that *Equality*, which agrees with Magnitudes, is firſt to be conſtituted; then it is to be explained how the *Equalities* of other Quantities are referred to it, and conſequently they become ſeparately defined. *Ex. gr.* equal Velocities, according to *Ariſtotle*, may be defined to be thoſe whereby the ſame or equal Spaces are

(*t*) Met. III. 2.

paſſed

paſſed over in the ſame Time. *That,* (*u*) ſays he, *is of an equal Celerity which is moved through an equal Space in an equal Time.* And again, *Thoſe Things which paſs over an equal Magnitude in an equal Time are of an equal Celerity.* Lo here Magnitude enters the Definition of Things of equal Celerity. So that it ſeems *Ariſtotle* himſelf thought it not amiſs, by it to define the Equality of Velocity. And the ſame Way may equal Times be defined to be thoſe, in which ſome noted Body carried with an equable Motion (*viz.* the *Sun* or *Moon* by determining the Time) performs *equal* Parts of its Courſe, which are coexiſtent with their *equal* Spaces. In like manner *equal Weights* (I ſpeak abſolutely without regard to mechanical Applications varying the *Momenta* of the ſame heavy Bodies) may, in reſpect of the Subject, be defined to be *thoſe which are in Magnitudes the ſame in Specie and equal in Quantity*; in reſpect of the Object, *the moving Powers of equal Magnitudes the ſame way ſituated, as to all the Conditions of the Parts*; or *which can elevate the ſame, or equal Magnitudes of the ſame Species*; and *which are endowed with equal Forces and Powers.* Certain ancient Philoſophers with *Ariſtotle* (*x*) did define equal Weights from their ſubjacent Matter, to be *thoſe that conſiſt of equal Principles, or of equal Particles of Matter.* Laſtly, *Equal Numbers* may be defined *ſuch as repreſent Magnitudes the ſame Way divided.*

By theſe and the like Means may the *Equalities* of all kinds of Quantities be defined, and perhaps this will be of great Uſe to their diſtinct Comprehenſion. There are not wanting Examples of the moſt excellent Authors, who not only pretend ſeparately to define the *Equalities* of the ſaid Quantities *equivocally, i. e.* by the ſame Word ſignify-

(*u*) Phyſ. VII. 4. (*x*) De Cœlo IV. 2.

ing different Things; but alſo for the ſake of greater Perſpicuity *ſynonymouſly*, *i. e.* by different Words ſignifying the ſame Thing. For *Euclid* in the *eleventh Book* of his *Elements*, has defined *Equal ſolid Figures* to be *ſuch as are contained within ſimilar Planes equal in Multitude, and Magnitude.* And the great *Apollonius* (in the Beginning of the *ſixth Book* of his *Conics*, which was lately tranſlated from *Arabick* into *Latin*, and publiſhed by the excellent *Borellus*) has defined *equal Conic Sections* to be *ſuch as being laid upon one another are congruous.* To paſs by what I have already taken Notice of, that *Euclid* in his *Book* of *Gravity* and *Levity* has defined *thoſe Things* to be *equal in Magnitude which fill the ſame Place:* And I am apt to think there may be ſome *Definition* of *equal Weights*, to which this concerning *equal Magnitudes* is preparatory. But what is near to our Purpoſe *Euclid* has delivered a different Definition of a *Part* concerning *Magnitudes* and *Numbers*. And the ſame Perſon, in the *fifth* of his *Elements*, has thought it of Uſe to define the *Analogy* of *Magnitudes* apart, and in the *ſeventh*, to give a different Definition of the *Proportionality* of *Numbers*; from whence he ſeems to lay himſelf under a Neceſſity, whenſoever he was to ſpeak of other Quantities, to define alſo particularly their *Proportionality*, or at leaſt to accommodate to them that which is delivered concerning the *Proportionality* of Magnitudes. Wherefore if it be amiſs (which our Adverſaries pretend) to define the ſame Word differently, as it is attributed to Things different in *Genus* or *Species*, we alledge that thoſe famous Authors are guilty of admitting it, with whom we are not very much aſhamed to err.

But at length (to finiſh our Examination of this Objection) I deny not, but the Reaſon brought would for the moſt part be of force, if any other more

more general and convenient Notion of *Equality* could be aſſigned. But no other is to be found, at leaſt none better than this, which depends upon any *Hypotheſis* more evident to the Obſervation of the Senſe, and Capacity of the Mind. Indeed (as we have noted in the preceding Lecture) the celebrated Man there mentioned has attempted two Notions, nor I imagine was he able to deviſe any better, which yet, as we have ſhewn, when examined do entirely fall in with this of ours, and the ſame Quantities, or the ſame *as Muches* of different *Things*, can be conceived no otherwiſe, than by ſome Sort of *Congruity* either *proper* or *analogical.* For that I may add this one Thing, to be ſome Sort of Illuſtration or Confirmation of what was then ſaid; the ſpecifical Identity of Quantity is not ſufficient to conſtitute *Equality* (for then all Circles, all Spheres, and every ſimilar Figure would be equal) but a certain *Numerical Identity* is required for this, not indeed *actual*, but however *poſſible*, ſuch as is beſt exhibited by that Coincidence and Coalition of Quantities, which emerges from *Congruence.* This Notion therefore does peculiarly ſquare with Magnitudes (which are properly and primarily Quantities) and with other Quantities after ſome manner; and ſince other Quantities may and ought to be defined by the *Equality* of Magnitude, than which no other can be deviſed more convenient; theſe Things, I ſay, conſidered, it ſeems as if this ought to be willingly admitted and approved of againſt every oppoſite Argument. This principal Argument therefore being overthrown, which ſeemed to carry with it the greateſt Appearance of Probability, we will now attack its ſecond, which, as our Adverſaries truſt, is no leſs ſtrong and invincible, but in my Opinion is much more weak and inconcluſive.

The

The Poſſeſſion or *Repletion* (ſay they) *of the ſame Place* is extraneous and accidental to *Equality*; nor are *Magnitudes* leſs *equal*, though they *poſſeſs not the ſame Place*, than if they do *entirely poſſeſs* it. And diſſimilar Figures cannot occupy the ſame Place, except the Situation of their Parts be changed. *But what* (urge they) *do Motion and Place and Tranſmutation relate to Equality? For a Pyramid even while it remains a Pyramid is no leſs equal (howſoever diſſimilar) than when it is tranſformed; and while it remains elſewhere it is equal (however not in the ſame Place) no leſs than when it is moved in the ſame Place. Therefore Equality ought no more to be defined in reſpect to Place* (when there is need of aſſuming a Tranſpoſition of Parts) *than a Man becauſe he may be Prince of* Tranſylvania. Thus do they ſeaſon their Argument as with Salt, leſt it ſhould perchance putrify or be of leſs Taſte.

But I anſwer, that a Reſpect to the Space occupiable by itſelf is not accidental or extrinſecal to any Magnitude, but is neceſſarily and intimately connected with it; to every act agrees an Habit, intrinſecal and connate with itſelf, to the Power which it anſwers, and which it fills. I ſay it agrees not more eſſentially to the Nature of Magnitude, that it is capable of being terminated, extended, compounded or divided, or be the Subject of any other Attribute, than that it can fill ſo much, and ſuch alike Capacity of itſelf, *i. e.* ſo much, and ſuch alike, or an equal and ſimilar Space. And from the Fountain of this Suppoſition do flow many neceſſary Mathematical Hypotheſes; as may ſufficiently appear from what has been already ſhewn. Moreover, though it does not happen neceſſarily to Magnitudes, as ſuch, to poſſeſs this or that definite Place or Situation; yet it neceſſarily agrees with them, as equal, to be ſome way capable of having the ſame Quantity, and conſequently of filling the ſame Place; as well becauſe it will plainly follow, that they in fact do occupy the ſame Space, ſince they actually have the ſame Quantity, as becauſe this poſſible Identity can be no other Way conceived. Again, it is hence moſt clearly apparent that this *Capacity of poſſeſſing the ſame Space* does not happen contingently to equal Magnitudes, ſince to him that ſeriouſly weighs the Thing, Geometricians demonſtrate nothing elſe concerning any Magnitudes compared together, as to *Equality* or any *Proportion*, but as they are capable of being congruous, or to occupy the ſame Place. When, *ex. gr. Euclid* ſhews *the triple of a Cone* to be *equal to its circumſcribed Cylinder*; when *Archimedes* demonſtrates *the Superfice of a Sphere to be equal to four times the greateſt Circle of the ſame Sphere*; and when the ſame Perſon teaches *that a Circle is equal to its* Radii *drawn into its Semiperiphery*, it comes to the ſame, and their Arguments prove nothing elſe (to any who examines them from their firſt Principles) but that ſuch Magnitudes are capable of being congruous to one another. For their Demonſtrations depend particularly upon the *fourth* and *eighth Propoſitions* of the *firſt Book* of the *Elements*, where the *Equality* of *Triangles* is demonſtrated from their *Poſſibility* of *Congruence*. Therefore, if a Capacity of filling the ſame Place be a Thing accidental to thoſe Magnitudes, then it follows that the principal Geometricians have demonſtrated nothing neceſſary to them, which ſounds ſomething harſh to Mathematical Ears.

Moreover, an *Occupation of Place* is not more extrinſecally, nor leſs intrinſecally conjoined with Magnitude, than *Motion*, or *Mutation of Place*; and as Magnitudes whereſoever placed are conceived equal, ſo Figures howſoever quieſcent and unknown do obtain

obtain and preserve the same Nature. Nevertheless no Geometrician refuses to define Figures by any Motion by which they can be generated with Ease. Thus *Euclid* thought fit to define a *Sphere* from the Revolution of a Semicircle about its Diameter, a *Cylinder* from the turning of a Parallelogram about its Side, and a *Cone* from the Rotation of a Triangle about its Leg; *Apollonius* a *conical Superfice* universally from the Transit of a Right Line encompassing a circular Periphery; *Archimedes* a Conoid and Spheroid from plane Portions of conical Sections turned round their Diameter: And some Geometricians do the same way define at their Pleasure any Magnitudes (*Lines*, *Superficies*, and *Solids*) from Motions circular, direct, parallel, or mixed. Which Definitions are not only the most lawful, but the best: For they not only explain the Nature of the Magnitude defined, but, at the same time, shew its possible Existence, and evidently discover the Method of its Construction: They not only describe what it is, but prove by Experiment, that it is capable of being such; and do put it beyond doubt how it becomes such. And the Reason is the same, the Virtue equal of this our Definition derived from *Congruity*; for it not only explains what the *Equality* of Magnitudes is, but that they are capable of being equal: It plainly discovers by what Means *equal Magnitudes* are effected, known, and explored, teaching it by a Method, which is most frequently in Use, and every where wont to be applied for the discerning and judging *Equality*. Therefore this Definition ought to displease none, who knows the Nature of Definitions, and observes how they always result from some possible Supposition.

Many Things do yet remain, which I thought to touch, but they are of light Moment, and their Solution may be easily perceived and deduced from what

what has been already ſaid and inſinuated; ſo that what remains concerning *Congruity* and *Equality* may be eaſily ſupplied by your ſelves. For it is both troubleſome to you and myſelf to continue thus long in a tedious Diſputation about a Matter ſmall and trifling. Nor would it be right to detain you from Arguments ſo much more ſublime, which yet are to come. Therefore, moſt worthy Auditors, adieu for the preſent. In the ſucceeding Lecture I purpoſe to betake myſelf to another Province, in applying thoſe Affections of *Proportion* and *Analogy*.

LECTURE XIII.

Of the erroneous Comment of Proclus, *and others upon the eighth Axiom of the firſt Element*, &c.

THE laſt I handled of the Attributes and Properties of Magnitudes, which are ſubſervient for Mathematical Hypotheſes was *Congruity*, and have treated at large, that the Notion of *Equality* is moſt rightly fetched thence. The Subject now ſeems to require me to paſs elſewhere, but ſuch is my Infelicity, I can't diſmiſs this Buſineſs before I adjoin one or two little Remarks, by way of Conſectary, relating to the farther Declaration and Uſe of my Purpoſe.

Firſt then I obſerve, that, from what has been delivered, may be diſcovered a remarkable Error of *Proclus*, and moſt Interpreters, who have commented after him, upon the *eighth Axiom* of the *firſt* of the *Elements*. The *Axiom* is thus expreſſed, *Things which are congruous to one another are alſo equal.*

equal. This *Proclus* denies to hold convertible universally. *It does not* (says he) *truly agree with all Magnitudes, but only with those of the same Species, or such as are most perfectly similar.* And with him agrees *Borellus*; *But convertibly* (says he) *that those Things which are equal are congruous to one another, is not true in all Magnitudes; but in those of the same Species, as Right Lines between themselves, and the Circumferences of equal Circles, as* Proclus *observes.* But this Exception more diligently looked into, is not only unnecessary, but (which seems wonderful to have escaped such sagacious Persons) will be found utterly false. For by *Congruity* they there understand either an *actual* or *potential Congruity.* But whether Way soever it be taken their Assertions differ from Truth. If they be taken concerning *actual Congruity*; they are most evidently convinced of Falsity, because neither all equal Right Lines, nor the Circumferences of equal Circles, nor Magnitudes howsoever equal or similar, are actually congruous, but are often most distant as to Place; as much *ex. gr.* as the *Antarctic Circle* is distant from the *Arctic* and contrary to it in Situation, though alike in Species, and altogether equal in Magnitude: If concerning *potential*, it appears from what is already demonstrated, and not what is to be demonstrated, that it is also falsely affirmed *that some equal Magnitudes are not congruous.* For on the contrary it is most true that all equal Magnitudes howsoever different in Specie, or unlike to one another, are capable of *Congruity.* It is indeed true, that Magnitudes of the same Species, and most perfectly similar to one another (*viz.* as Right Lines, Circles described with equal *Radii*, and equal rectilineal Angles) do admit an *actual Congruity* after a certain peculiar Manner, *viz.* the Order of the Parts being retained, and the Situation no where varied; also

their

their *poſſible Congruity* is eaſily apprehended, and perhaps immediately inferred from their Definition. But this does not leſs truly agree with all other equal Magnitudes which are capable of being rendered moſt accurately congruous by the Tranſlation of certain of their Parts, and the Mutation in Part of their Figure; *i. e.* the Parts of one (which differ nothing from its Whole) will exactly poſſeſs the Space of the other. But the Retention or Alteration of Figure neither adds any Thing to, nor derogates from the *Equality* or *Congruity* of Magnitudes; nor is it of any Conſideration here, whether the Comprehenſion of poſſible *Congruity* be eaſy or difficult. For it is as true which is lawfully demonſtrated by a thouſand Chains of Arguments, as that which is perceived at firſt View, or immediately inferred by one only Syllogiſm. *Euclid* indeed has demonſtrated the *Congruity* of any even rectilineal Figure with a determinate Square, and (as far as poſſible has attempted the ſame) of any ſolid Figure contained within plane Superficies, *i. e.* he has taught or inveſtigated the Method of meaſuring them. *Archimedes*, proceeding farther has compared Circles, and circular Sectors, alſo curved, conical, cylindrical, and ſpherical Superficies, and demonſtrated them to be congruous with one another by the moſt evident Conſequences. When *ex. gr.* *Archimedes* demonſtrated that a Circle is equal to a rectangular Triangle, whoſe Baſis is equal to the Radius of the Circle, and Cathetus to the Periphery (or which comes to the ſame, to the Square whoſe Side is a mean Proportional between the Radius and Semi-periphery of the Circle) he did nothing elſe (we will find) but demonſtrate that the Area of a Circle or regular Polygon having an indefinite Number of Sides may be divided into ſo many minute Triangles which are equal to juſt ſo many little Trigons of the ſaid

Triangle;

Triangle; and the *Equality* of thoſe Triangles is demonſtrated in the Elements from *Congruity* alone. From whence conſequently *Archimedes* has demonſtrated the *Congruity* of a Circle with a Triangle howſoever diſſimilar they be to one another. Alſo when the Superfice of a Cone is by the ſame Perſon demonſtrated to be equal to the Area of a Circle, whoſe Radius is a mean Proportional between the Side of the Cone and the Semidiameter of the Baſis; he demonſtrates nothing elſe (as is plain by having Recourſe to the firſt Origin of Demonſtration) but that this Superfice does as it were conſiſt of an Infinity of little Triangles, every one of which are congruous to as many particular Triangles compoſing the ſaid Circle. Thus the *Diſſimilitude* of Figures is no Hindrance to *Congruity*; but whether they be *ſimilar* or *diſſimilar*, ſo they be *equal*, they either always are, or ought to be, capable of *Congruity*. Therefore the ſaid *eighth Axiom* can either be no Way, or elſe every Way, convertible; no Way, if what is there accounted *Congruity* deſign *actual Congruity*; every Way if it be only taken for *potential*, i. e. *Thoſe Things which are capable of Congruity are equal and convertible:* After which manner Reaſon does rather require it to be underſtood. For it is better thus to explain that moſt uſeful Axiom, to hold every Way convertibly, than to be no Way capable to be converted; and to contain an eſſential Affection of Magnitude, than only to reſpect an accidental Property. For to be actually congruous has no Affinity to the *Nature of Magnitude* or *Equality*, but happens to them contingently, and (ſince an Act always argues a previous Power) is applied for no other Cauſe, but as a *Potential Congruity* may be known by it, which only does intimately agree with *Equality*, and is perpetually reciprocal with it. For as it is reckoned connate and moſt cloſely connected

with

with Magnitude *not to be actually divided, but to be divisible*, and this *Divisibility* is distinguished and known separately from actual *Division*, however fortuitous or arbitrary; so it accidentally happens to *equal Quantities* as such, that they are actually congruous, but it agrees inseparably and perpetually that they are capable of being so; but that Act is subservient, and therefore is wont to be applied for shewing this Power. Therefore *Proclus* and most others treading in his Footsteps do wrongly explain this *Axiom*, not taking sufficient Notice of the Difference between *actual* and *possible Congruity*, only respecting actual *Congruity*, which is not here to be attended to.

The excellent *Clavius* is one who has kept himself free from this Contagion; whom therefore his most learned Countryman *Tacquet* has wrongfully blamed. *Clavius*, says he, *has not converted this Axiom rightly, for it is false that those Things which are universally equal to one another are mutually congruous; for dissimilar Magnitudes may be equal. yet they will not be congruous; but if they be similar and equal, it will hold convertibly.*

But I rather admire the singular either Knowledge or good Fortune of *Clavius*, who has happily avoided the common Error, and wholly omitted this Exception which depends upon so false a Foundation, and has truly explained that Axiom, though not fully and sufficiently clear. But in this I have been too prolix, though I am silent as to some Things.

Secondly, I observe that the Axioms which relate to *Equality* may be demonstrated from this Definition of *Equality* laid down: which argues its Convenience and Excellence. For Axioms as certain Theorems (which has been often admonished) ought to be capable of being demonstrated from the lawful Definitions of the Terms of which they consist.

consist. Therefore *Apollonius* has illustrated that which *Ramus* calls the *most bright Sun in the Mathematics*, *That those Things, which are equal to the same, are equal to one another*, by a Demonstration fetched from hence. Let the two Magnitudes A and C be each singularly supposed equal to a third Magnitude B. I say the Magnitudes A and C are equal. For since by the Hypotheses the Magnitudes A and B are equal, the same (by the foregoing Definition of *Equality*) are capable of being congruous; therefore let them fill the Place Z. Also since the Magnitudes C and B are equal by the Hypothesis, if C be put upon B occupying the Place Z; also C (from the Definition of *Equality*) will be capable of occupying the Place Z. Therefore both A and C are capable of filling the Place Z. From whence reciprocally (from the Definition of *Equality*) A and C will be equal. Q.E.D.

But *Proclus* objects against this Definition, that it depends upon the Assumption of those two Axioms, *Those Things which possess the same Place are equal*; and *those Things which occupy the same Place with another, do occupy the same Place between themselves:* Both of which he affirms to be far more obscure, and difficult to be granted, than the Conclusion proposed to be demonstrated. But in Defence of that great Geometrician I briefly answer. *First*, it is apparently false, that the Consideration of Place or Space is more obscure and unknown to us than that of *Equality*. Since, from what is before proved, *Equality* can only be illustrated from it. Also *Congruity*, or a Possession of the same Place, may be supposed, because it may be discerned to be possible by Sense; but *Equality* does not immediately occur to the Sense, but results from some supposed Comparison; therefore the Notion of *Congruity* is clearer than that of *Equality*. And since, *those Things which occupy the*

same

ſame Place are equal is the moſt commodious Definition of *Equality* (as methinks we have ſufficiently proved) it will therefore be more ſimple and evident than any other Propoſition including *Equality:* As the Definition of a Triangle is more ſimple and clear than any Theorem about a Triangle. *Secondly*, as to the other Axiom, *Thoſe Things which occupy the ſame Place with another, do occupy the ſame Place between themſelves*; I deny that any Thing can be clearer, much leſs that this is more obſcure than the propoſed Concluſion. For, if tryed to the bottom, it will be found a Propoſition plainly identical, and differs no more from it, than *that Peter is Peter*; for it is reduced to this Propoſition without changing its Senſe, but only for the ſake of Perſpicuity giving Names to the Magnitudes; as Z the Place common to B and A is the ſame with Z the Place common to B and C. Or this Categorical Propoſition, *Thoſe Things which occupy the ſame Place with another do occupy the ſame Place between themſelves*, may be reduced to this equivalent Hypothetical Enunciation, *If the Magnitude* A *occupy the Place* Z *belonging to the Magnitude* B, *and the Magnitude* C *occupy the Place* Z *belonging alſo to the Magnitude* B, *then the Magnitudes* A *and* C *do occupy the ſame Place* Z. Where that which is ſuppoſed in the Antecedent is repeated in the Conſequent. And what Propoſition, I beg can be more manifeſtly true than this? Certainly not this, *Thoſe Things, which are equal to the ſame, are equal to one another*, becauſe it muſt firſt be known what *Equality* is, and what is ſignified by it, before the Truth of this Propoſition can be comprehended. But yet *thirdly*, I deny that the ſaid trifling and ſilly Axiom is preſuppoſed, or applied in a Demonſtration. We only infer, becauſe a Magnitude is ſuppoſed to occupy the Place Z, that

C which

C which is equal to that Magnitude is alſo capable to occupy the ſame Place Z; which immediately follows from the foregoing Definition of *Equality.* Nor do we uſe any different Principle. Let any one take Notice: To be ſure *Proclus* uſes all his Strength to oppoſe the Demonſtration of *Apollonius:* And he gravely concludes: *All Axioms ought to be delivered as immediate, and clear by their own Light, manifeſt and meriting Aſſent from themſelves. For he who uſes Demonſtration in the moſt evident Things does not eſtabliſh their Truth but weaken the Evidence, which we have without Learning in our preconceived Notions.* To which Opinion, as to vulgar Uſe, I willingly ſubſcribe, nor is there any need to confeſs that it is too ſcrupulous to examine Things commanding ſo eaſy an Aſſent. But I think it is not unuſeful, to ſhew by ſome Experiments for the further Declaration of the Genius of Demonſtration, the Nature of Science, and Diverſity of Principles, that the utmoſt Rigour does even require the Demonſtration of Axioms, that they in reality are capable of being demonſtrated, and that Definitions well conſtituted are ſerviceable for demonſtrating them. Nor do I think him worthy of being impeached of *Madneſs* or *Pride,* who attempts ſuch a Thing, either for theſe Cauſes, or the Exerciſe of his Genius, of which Things notwithſtanding a very ſevere *Ariſtarchus* among the Moderns (I wiſh not guilty of the ſame Vices himſelf) lets not to accuſe ſuch an one, and conſequently *Apollonius* himſelf a Man of the greateſt Sagacity and moſt conſummate Learning in the Mathematics. However relying upon the Example of ſo great a Man, I will not be afraid myſelf to demonſtrate, entirely from what has been ſaid, the two next Axioms to the ſaid firſt. The *ſecond* Axiom is this; *If equal Quantities be added to equal Quantities.*

tities the Sums (or *Wholes*) *will be equal:* Which I thus demonſtrate. Let A and B be two equal Magnitudes, which conſequently (from the Definition of *Equality*) are capable of *Congruence*, and of filling the ſame Place. Let them therefore occupy the Place X, and let the Magnitude C be added to A, whoſe Place let be Y. Therefore X+Y is the Place of the Sum A+C. Alſo let the Magnitude D equal to C be added to B, from whence in like manner (from the Definition of *Equality*), D will be capable of filling the Place X: and conſequently B+D will be capable of occupying the compounded Place X+Y; *viz.* the ſame which A+C is capable of occupying. Therefore (from the Definition of *Equality*) B+D will be equal to A+C. Q. E. D. By a like Diſcurſus will be demonſtrated the next ſubſequent Axiom; *If equal Quantities be taken from equal Quantities the Remainders will be equal.* For again, let there be two equal Magnitudes A and B, of which conſequently there may be a common capable Place X. Let the equal Magnitudes C and D be taken from thoſe, whoſe common Place alſo let be Y. Therefore the remaining Place X—Y will be a common capable Place to both the remaining Magnitudes A—C and B—D. Therefore the Remainders A—C and B—D are equal. Q. E. D. And by the ſame Method may any Theorem (or Axiom) pertaining to abſtract *Equality* be demonſtrated, by help of the ſaid Definition, which ſhews its Excellence and Convenience. But diſmiſſing this Obſervation, I remark,

Thirdly, That, from what has been ſaid, it may be eaſily perceived what is *Equal to*, what *Greater*, and what *Leſſer than* another: For ſcarce any of theſe can be any way explained but from a Reference to an oppoſite *Equal*, or more immediately from a Relation to *Space*. 1. With Reſpect to *Space*,

Space, that will be called *Unequal*, which is always and neceſſarily *Incongruous* with another, *i. e.* which being any how applied to another (either at the ſame time, or ſucceſſively, or by mental Penetration, or retaining the Situation of the Parts, or changing their Order any of theſe Ways as explained above) will no way exactly coincide with it, but either exceed or fall ſhort of it. Conſequently of two *unequal Species*, that will be *Greater*, which being thus applied to, or put upon the other, will exceed it, *i. e.* will occupy the whole Space of the other, and ſome farther Space beſides; or a Part of which will be congruous with the Whole of the other, or fill the whole Space of the other: that *Leſſer*, which being applied to the other will fall ſhort of it, or coincide with a Part of the other, or will occupy a Part of the Space which is poſſeſſed by the other. 2. But with reſpect to an *Equal* that will be called Unequal, which contains in it another (or what is equal to another) and ſomething beſides; or is ſo contained in another (or in ſomething which is equal to another) that ſomething remains over and above. That, *viz.* is *Greater* which contains another (or which is equal to another) and ſomething beſides: That *Leſſer* which is ſo contained in another (or in that which is equal to another) that ſomething is ſtill remaining. Or with Mr. *Hobbs*, *a Magnitude* may be not unelegantly defined *Greater than a Magnitude* (he ſays a Body than a Body, but it is better to ſpeak more univerſally) *when a Part of that is equal to the Whole of this: Leſſer*, *when the Whole of that is equal to a Part of this*; though perhaps ſomething is wanting in thoſe Definitions. For it may be objected that they anſwer not thoſe unequal Magnitudes, of which one comprehends the other. Which yet may be eaſily excuſed or pardoned, becauſe every Magnitude is reckoned *Equal* to itſelf in the moſt perfect Manner, and *Identity* does eminently contain *Equality*, which is every where ſuppoſed in the Demonſtrations of Geometry. Or theſe Definitions may be corrected and ſupplied by expreſſing them thus; *A Magnitude is Greater than a Magnitude, when a Part of that is equal, or the ſame, with the Whole of this : Leſſer, when the Whole of that is equal, or the ſame, with a Part of this.* Which Definitions of *Inequality*, *Greater* or *Leſſer*, will alſo agree *analogically* with other *Quantities*, each its own Way, (*viz.* with *Motions*, *Times*, *Velocities*, *Weights*, *Numbers*,) as has been largely explained concerning *Equality*.

I will only advertiſe one Thing concerning the ſaid *Inequality* thus to be taken, that the *Exceſs* and *Defect*, or that which abounds or ſupplies, is here always meant of Things *homogeneous*. For Quantities of a different Kind are not capable of being compared together in reſpect to *Equality* or *Inequality*. Which will be afterwards more diſtinctly explained, when we come to treat of *Proportion*.

But ſhall I never extricate myſelf from theſe Quirks and Trifles ? Shall I always ſpend my time in examining what is of no Value ? In ſo plentiful an Harveſt, ſo rich a Vintage, ſo great a Store of moſt important Diſquiſitions, why do I only glean the ſcattered Ears, ſearch the neglected Boughs, and gather the fallen Grapes ? When a Chace after the important and difficult Things in the Mathematics is offered, a Chace ſo full of Variety, ſo pleaſant, and ſo certain; wherefore do I dwell ſo long upon thoſe little Queſtions, like one hunting after Flies ? I ſhun things of Conſequence, ſport in ſerious, am gravely ridiculous, ſtudiouſly ſeeking after, and nicely repeating and inculcating every the ſlighteſt Matter. Shall I thus inceſſantly follow ſo many diſtant By-ways, ſo many uncouth Turnings, and ſhall I never return again into the beaten

Paths

Paths of the King's high Road? Shall I grow old in theſe outer Courts of *general Matters?* Shall I perpetually tarry in the Entrance of the Sciences? Shall I always ſtick in the Threſhold? Shall I only knock at the Doors of the Mathematics, and never enter within the Walls of the Houſe, nor penetrate its more ſacred Receſſes? Shall I ever be upon the Parley, ever ſkirmiſh at a Diſtance, and never engage Hand to Hand, or come to a deciſive Battle? What do I but raiſe Miſts and Doubts, ſow Strifes and Contentions, raiſe Storms and Tumults in that Science, which promiſes, which boaſts of nothing but what is clear and evident, certain and tried, calm and ſerene? And by diſputing more freely, and bringing many Things to the Scrutiny, I ſeem to detract and derogate from the Certitude and Evidence of the Mathematics, which is ſo contrary to Jarring and Contentions? Thus am I wont to upbraid myſelf, and perhaps alſo others do the ſame; at leaſt not without ſome ſeeming Cauſe, or Appearance of Juſtice.

Notwithſtanding I am able to alledge ſomething in my own Excuſe to wipe away thoſe Reproaches; and ſince ſo much of the Time deſtined for this Lecture is now paſſed over, contrary to Expectation, ſo that I am unable, though not unwilling to enter upon another new Subject: I humbly beg of you to pardon this, and indulge me with a little of your Patience while I am in ſome ſort defending theſe Trifles, and explaining the Reaſon of the Deſign, I have hitherto gone upon. As to theſe little Niceties I anſwer, that thoſe Things are not always ſmall which ſeem ſo; ſince the Stars appear very ſmall, and the Sun not great; we are therefore to have a thorough Knowledge from whence the Appearance of a Thing beheld comes, and whither it tends, before its Magnitude

nitude can be judged of. Thoſe Things which are ſmall in Bulk, are ſometimes endued with vaſt Strength, and thoſe which contain nothing in them notable, do often draw after them very great Conſequences. The Origins of the greateſt Things are almoſt conſtantly ſmall; the largeſt Stocks grow from ſmall Seeds, immenſe Rivers ſwell from ſmall Fountains, and the Nature of *Truth* and *Error* is moſt remarkably fruitful; a vaſt Light is on every Side diffuſed from ſmall Sparks of Truth, and a huge Crop of Errors ſprings from the leaſt Root of Falſhood: In the Sciences eſpecially, from ſlender Threads are ſuſpended the greateſt Weights, nor are the leaſt Things contemned without the greateſt Damage. As a whole Machine periſhes and becomes unfit for Uſe, by the miſplacing of one Wheel, and a huge Elephant often periſhes by the Breach of a little Vein; ſo ſometimes one only Notion, which may ſeem ſmall and barren, if ill placed and badly underſtood, will from a fruitful Offspring of Conſequences derive upon any Science a vaſt Confuſion, a groſs Darkneſs, and a manifold Cauſe of Error. *Ariſtotle* (who alſo maintains his own Accuracy and ſtrict Diligence in ſome more minute Things) has wiſely obſerved in the Words moſt worthy of Notice which are extant in the *fifth* Chapter of his firſt Book *de Cœlo*: *Any little Wandering is preſently encreaſed and multiplied to ten thouſand times greater, by ſuch as recede from the Truth. As if one ſhould affirm that ſome leaſt Magnitude may be given; ſuch an one introducing a Minimum, will overturn the greateſt of Mathematical Things. And thence it happens that every Principle is more prevalent by its Power, than by its abſolute Magnitude. From whence what in the Beginning ſeems little, in the End will become very great.* So dangerous is it in the Judgment of the Philoſopher to lay aſide all

all Care of the leaſt Things, which have not only their Account, but alſo oftentimes an Advantage by no means to be ſlighted; eſpecially in thoſe Sciences, which climb e're we are aware from low and almoſt ridiculous Beginnings to an incredible Bigneſs and Height. I am not therefore to be very much blamed, if I ſometimes ſeem to be more curious and prolix than there is occaſion for, in things ſeemingly of not much Weight, ſince Reaſon requires, that I ſhould add ſome Light to thoſe Things, that I know to be of very great Moment.

But as to thoſe Controverſies which I frequently move, none, I ſuppoſe, can ſuſpect that any of them detracts from the Certainty of the Mathematical Sciences; ſince they are converſant about Things very remote from the Foundation of the Mathematics. Theſe Queſtions do ſcarce touch the outmoſt Skin of Geometry, much leſs reach its inward Bowels. Theſe Rams do not ſhake its Principles, nor overthrow, or at all diſturb, its Reaſonings. While Contentions and Strifes, Clamours and Janglings do ariſe, and make a Noiſe, in its Confines and Suburbs, a deep Peace and profound Silence dwells within the Walls, and in the Citadel itſelf; nothing is there heard of Controverſy or Oppoſition.

Albeit we take Examples as well elſewhere, as from the moſt modern Controverſies we have handled; it has been diſputed what was the genuine Notion of *Equality*, from whence it is moſt conveniently defined, whether it may be demonſtrated, what Axioms are aſſumed about it; but no Body doubts whether thoſe Axioms be true; and conſequently no Body will diſſent from the Concluſions inferred by their Help. It is enquired concerning the Nature and Number of Principles, and concerning the Method of obtaining the Knowledge

Knowledge of them, whether they are innate or comparate, whether they depend upon general Induction, or particular Observation only; but yet their Truth remains safe and sound, and is placed beyond all Doubt. It is doubted and controverted whether *Euclid* gives a good Definition of *Parallelism* from a Negation of the Meeting of Right Lines infinitely produced; but I believe no Body has denied, but there may be Right Lines, which by this Means can never meet together, and which are not unaptly stiled *Parallel*. It is denied by some whether the same *Euclid* has justly assumed it for a Principle, that two Right Lines will meet one another from that Part, on which the said Lines do make the internal Angles with an insisting Right Line lesser than two Right Angles; yet so that the Truth of the Proposition itself is called in Question by none. Also Geometricians contend, and the Matter is still undecided, whether *Euclid* has made a right Choice in that Affection of Proportionals by which he defines them; yet the Truth of that Proposition is preserved under the Form of that Theorem laid down, to which no wise Man refuses his Assent. I could produce many more Examples, by which it may appear, that the Differences among Mathematicians are no Prejudice to the Certainty or Evidence of the Mathematics, but do rather argue their invincible Truth and pure Brightness, which no Tumults of Disputations can overthrow, no Clouds of Discord overshadow. Nor is this to be wondered at, since it is not here contended about the Truth of *Principles*, but about the *Order* of some Propositions; not about the *Certitude* but the *Method* of Science, rather only about the Exteriors of Philosophy than of the Mathematics; the Knowledge of which is indeed of no little Weight, as conducing to a full, distinct and accurate Comprehension of the

the Things handled in the Mathematics, but when compared with the Principles of Geometry (theſe Principles, while the Truth of which continues ſafe, no very great Inconvenience can befal the Mathematics, no geometrical Concluſion can be rendered invalid); I ſay, when compared with theſe, the Things about which we are contending can be thought little or nothing at all: So true is that Saying alſo here,

——Minimas rerum diſcordia vexat,
Pacem ſumma tenent——

Diſcord (we ſee) *does vex the leaſt of Things,*
The greateſt are at Peace——

Neither therefore do I think this Contentiouſneſs or Inclination to diſpute about the Things belonging to this Science, to be of any ill Conſequence, ſince it affects not their Stability, but is uſeful to their Accuracy. Eſpecially ſince my Endeavours are for no other End but that by diſputing I may utterly eradicate and remove all Cauſes of Diſputation, weighing as far as I am able the Reaſon of Things in the Ballance of Experience; and reducing all Things from metaphyſical Niceties to common Senſe. Nor do I invent many Queſtions of myſelf, but find them ſomewhere (though for the moſt Part lightly touched), interpoſing my Opinion ſupported with ſome Arguments, and committing the ultimate Deciſion to your own Arbitration. I have alſo religiouſly kept and obſerved that moſt equitable Rule of (*d*) *Ariſtotle*, which, if I remember well, was quoted before, but is worthy of being often repeated. *Things ſaid will be more credited if the Reaſons be firſt heard on both*

(*d*) De Cœlo I. 10.

Sides

Sides of the Question. For it does not become us to give Sentence without hearing the Cause, or condemn any Side unheard. They who are willing to judge well of the Truth ought not to be Adversaries (on either Hand) *but Arbitrators.* Than which Sentiment nothing is more juſt, more ſacred, or more prudent.

Moreover I may be excuſed for dwelling longer than ordinary upon theſe general Things by way of Proem and Prelude: *Firſt*, Becauſe among them many Things are found not unworthy of Obſervation, nor every where obvious and vulgarly uſed, but either for the moſt Part do not occur, or elſe are more ſparingly explained; and alſo becauſe of certain Paradoxes, uſeful for whetting the Genius, and exerciſing the Judgment. Again, a diſtinct Conception generally ſeems to contribute very much to the eaſy Underſtanding and perfect Knowledge of what follows. For ſo many famous Problems being publiſhed by Mathematicians, ſo many excellent Theorems demonſtrated about various Principles, *viz.* about *Magnitude*, *Number*, *Space*, *Motion*, *Time*, *Velocity*, *Weight*, about *Compoſition* and *Diviſion*, *Termination* and *Figuration*, *Equality* and *Inequality*, *Symmetry* and *Aſſymetry*, *Proportion* and *Proportionality*, *Similitude* and *Diſſimilitude*, *Determination* and *Indetermination*, and other ſuch like Things; is it not of great Uſe to have the previous Notions of theſe *genuine* and *adequate?* Such as though I do not perfectly teach, at leaſt I give an Occaſion of acquiring, to you who more maturely examine the Reaſons propoſed. However it is of no ſmall Concern to the Students of thoſe Sciences to be familiarly acquainted with their common *Genius* and *Nature.* And indeed I have often conſidered that the moſt learned Men do ſometimes ſpeak crudely and improperly about Mathematical Things, and ſometimes reaſon falſly falſely from a leſs attentive Conſideration of theſe *Generals*, having imprinted depraved or confuſed Notions upon their Minds. Beſides, I willingly ſubmit to ſuch of you, I conſult your honeſt Pleaſure, who, being leſs fit for the more abſtruſe Myſteries of the Mathematics, do differ; and yet are both deſirous and capable to receive ſome Taſte of thoſe moſt pleaſant Sciences, to behold ſomething of their Pleaſure and Profit, as it were at a Diſtance; whom I would by no means ſend away deprived of their Hope, diſappointed of their Labour, and troubled at the too great Difficulty or apparent Obſcurity of Things: Nor do I deny but I have for the moſt part ſuited both the Matter of my Diſcourſe, and the Manner of expreſſing it to your Capacity, and many Things are ſaid, which I would otherwiſe have been ſilent of, many Things paſſed by, which I would otherwiſe have ſaid.

But I am afraid the dry Subtilty of the particular Demonſtrations, which the inward Parts of the Mathematics abound with, their extreme Rigour requiring the cloſeſt Attention, and their Way of arguing, will ſomewhat offend and deter the moſt. Thoſe Subjects (not to diſſemble) are in my Opinion not ſo convenient for publick Lectures of this Kind, therefore I willingly make ſome Delay in theſe which are not ſo barren and unpleaſant; yet ſtudying to interſperſe certain Things belonging to the more inward Part of the Mathematics, and henceforward I ſhall continue ſo to do.

Moreover while we are proſecuting thoſe *Generals*, I imagine ſome Time is to be granted them, who give their Attendance to theſe Lectures, and who, being not content juſt to taſte of thoſe Sciences, are deſirous to immerſe themſelves deeper, and wholly waſh in the Sea of Mathematical Learning, and be throughly inſtructed in the *Elements*

of

of *Geometry* ; to which I earneſtly intreat ſuch not to be negligent in applying their Studies ; otherwiſe I believe it will be impoſſible from theſe more abſtruſe Inſtructions, nay or ſcarce from the more clear of any Mathematical Diſcipline, to draw any Thing intelligible to the Hearers ; but like an enigmatical *Sphinx*, or ſome obſcure *Heraclitus*, I ſhall ſeem to utter mere Riddles, and be involved in thick Darkneſs. But if I knew that the moſt of you were initiated in the Elements of Geometry, I could I hope with ſome Fruit and Pleaſure to yourſelves, either lay open the loweſt Foundations of ſingular Diſciplines, and exhibit the principal Rules eſtabliſhed by their Demonſtrations ; or, what is very delightful to be known, and eſpecially becomes the Students of an Univerſity (on which ſort of *Perſons* it is incumbent above others to imbibe the Study of the ancient *Wiſdom* and Diſciplines from their Fountains) could ſearch out the Method of the old Mathematicians in inventing and demonſtrating their Theorems ; or (which is the principal Scope and higheſt Apex of the whole Mathematics) could exhibit certain general Methods, demonſtrated and illuſtrated by Examples, for the more eaſy Reſolution of all Sorts of Problems, the Invention of Theorems, and the Conſtruction and Demonſtration of theſe as well as thoſe ; many of which Sort of Methods moſt uſeful and elegant, unknown to the Ancients, at leaſt not committed to Memory, has the Induſtry of the Moderns invented and brought to Light. Of which Sort, by the Way (beſides the new Method of *Analyſis*, chiefly cultivated by *Vieta* and *Carteſius*, almoſt equal to every ſoluble Queſtion) is *Cavellarius*'s Method of *Indiviſibles*, which already has been, but never ſufficiently can be, praiſed ; the Method *Circa Maxima & Minima*, alſo very uſeful for the moſt expeditious Solution of very

many

many Problems; the various general Rules of investigating the *Tangents* of *Curves*; the Ways of producing *Curve Lines*, and investigating their Properties from the *Dependance* and *Composition* of *Motions*; the Ways of comparing different *Series* of *Magnitudes*, *increasing* or *decreasing* in a certain Order, and from thence determining the *Measures* of innumerable *Planes* and *Solids*; the general Rules for readily finding the *Centers* of *Gravity* in all Kinds of Magnitudes, also of easily deducing the Dimensions of the Magnitudes themselves from the Centers of Gravity found; with some few other Things of lesser Note. Any of which, if I should now undertake to handle, I am afraid the most Part would not perfectly understand my Meaning from the vanishing Words of an Oration; at least (to deal familiarly with you) if I may be permitted to make an Estimate of other People's Capacities from my own, I confess my self so dull and unapt that I can much easier understand that which is plainly laid before my Eyes, than that which is insinuated through the treacherous Caverns of my Ears.

Lastly, To put an End once to this excessive Loquacity, as for my own Part, it would be much easier for me (but I must not do it) to draw certain particular Subjects out of the wealthy Store of the Mathematics, or demonstrate some singular Conclusions, (of which a vast Plenty are common at every one's Hand) than to float on this Ocean of *Philosophico-Mathematical* Disquisitions. I do not therefore, in the Prosecution of these *Generals*, sacrifice any Thing to my own Leisure, but rather to your Profit; I do not gratify my own Desire, but, as far as I can guess, for the most Part yours: I act at your Pleasure, being always ready and most intent, as far as I am able, to satisfy and obey your ingenuous Requests, or more justly, your

your Commands. Thus I have pleaded my Cauſe without being cited; I have framed an Apology without being accuſed or challenged by any I know of; but how can I clear myſelf of Breach of Faith, and from the Non-performance of the Promiſe, by which I obliged myſelf in this Lecture to treat of *Proportion?* So it happens in many Things we oblige ourſelves, and promiſe others what we can hardly perform; we more eaſily engage our Faith than diſcharge it. Indeed to one who runs over this Subject in his Thoughts, ſo many Difficulties offer themſelves to be explained, ſo many Queſtions to be diſcuſſed, and ſo many different Sentiments to be conſidered, that I can ſcarce ſuſtain the entring ſo great a Sea for want of Time, the Term being ſo near an End. Nevertheleſs, by this Prelude I may perhaps gain ſomething, and pave the Way for expounding a moſt ſubtle Matter. And ſince I have ſaid nothing to the Purpoſe in this, I will endeavour to compenſate the Defect in the two remaining Lectures.

LECTURE XIV.

Of the different Acceptations of the Word Meaſure.

THE laſt Attributes of Magnitudes we conſidered were their *Equality* and *Inequality*, whoſe genuine Notions we have aſſerted as far as we are able. *Reaſon* or *Proportion* now follows in Order, becauſe this is almoſt nothing elſe but a certain Determination of *Equality* or *Inequality* reſulting from the Compariſon of Quantities. For ſince

ſince generally ſpeaking Quantities, which are comparable with one another, may receive infinite Modes of *Inequality*, by receiving from *Equality* (which is ſimple, and as I may ſay of one Mode), therefore the *Determination* expreſſed in Numbers, or other fit Terms, of ſome of theſe particular Modes appropriated to the Things compared, is wont to be called their *Proportion*, whereby is ſignified, whether they are *equal*, or upon what certain peculiar Account they are *unequal*. Yet this principal Property of Magnitudes, that we may the more diſtinctly and clearly explain it, ſeems to require both, that we firſt expound *Menſurability* that noble Affection of Magnitudes, becauſe of the *Symmetry* and *Aſſymetry* which neceſſarily intervenes with the Doctrine of *Proportion*, and that we conſider a little the *Aptitude* and *Ineptitude* of Quantities for *Compariſon*, which Things being well underſtood it will be eaſy to judge of the Nature of *Proportion*.

As to *Menſurability*, this, as to its Name, deſerves to be more curiouſly weighed, becauſe from hence a Name is impoſed upon that *Mother* and *Miſtreſs* of the reſt of the Mathematical Sciences, which is employed about Magnitudes, and which is wont to be called *Geometry* (a Word taken from ancient Uſe, becauſe it was firſt applied only to *meaſuring the Earth* and fixing the Limits of Poſſeſſions) though the Name ſeemed very ridiculous to *Plato*, who ſubſtitutes in its Place that more extenſive Name of *Metrics* or *Menſuration*; and others after him give it the Title of *Pantometry*, becauſe it teaches the Method of meaſuring all Kinds of Magnitudes. Though neither do theſe attribute a Name proper or adequate to it, ſince this Science does not only contemplate that Affections of Magnitude, but alſo ſome *others* with which nothing is interſperſed belonging to

Meaſure.

Measure. For it does not only respect the *Quantities* of Magnitudes, but investigates and demonstrates their *Qualities* also (*i. e.* with what *Disposition* of Parts, with what *Figure* they are endowed, whether *right* or *curved*, *plane* or *gibbous*, *direct* or *inflex*, *round* or *angular*) in like manner how they are *situated*, *i. e.* what *determinate Position* they obtain. I say it equally considers the *Species* and *Similitudes* of Magnitudes, as well as their *Measures* and *Proportions*. Moreover, as to Practice itself, it not only teaches to *compare* Magnitudes together by *measuring* them, but also to *constitute*, *describe*, and *transform them*, and to find their *Centers*, *Diameters*, and *Tangents* without any regard to Quantity.

From whence, by the Way, it appears that *Geometry* is not badly defined by most, *The Art or Science of Measuring*; or *the Science of Magnitude, as it is mensurable.* These Descriptions which are delivered by Mr. *Hobbes*'s Censurer, Mr. *Hobbes* does somewhere carp at, and pretend to correct, but produces no better Definition, nay one more elaborately unfit and evidently guilty of the same Fault. *Geometry* (says he) *is the Science of determining the Magnitude of any Thing not measured, by its Comparison with another measured Magnitude or Magnitudes.* But I ask those Definers of our Science; when the Geometrician *bisects a Right Line, or a Rectilineal Angle*; when he *erects* or *lets fall a right-lined Perpendicular* from a *given Point*; when he *draws* a *Parallel* to a *given Right Line* through a *given Point*; or when he *draws* a *right-lined Tangent* to a *given Curve*; when he *constitutes* an *equilateral Triangle*, or *Square*, upon a *given Right Line*; when he *describes* a *Circle* through *three given Points*, or *circumscribes* a *Circle* about a *given Triangle*; when he *investigates* the *Center* of a given *Circumference*, or the *Focus* of a given

Conic

Conic Section: I ſay, when he does many ſuch Things, and *reſolves Problems* reſpecting only the *Poſition* of *Magnitudes*; whether does he perform the Office of a Geometrician as he ought, and when he compares Magnitudes together this Way, as to their Quantity, what Relation have they to any *Meaſure?* Why, none at all; he only determines the *Situation* of *Lines*, and enquires after the *Poſition* of *certain Points*. I paſs by that the Geometrician equally conſiders the Motions by which Figures are generated, &c. Theſe Definitions therefore are inadequate and incongruous, and founded upon falſe Prejudices. He therefore aſſigned this Science a more appoſite Compellation, whoever he was, that thought it ought to be called μεγεθικὴν, i. e. *the Science converſant about Magnitudes, and which ſpeculates*, i. e. *enquires*, *invents*, and *demonſtrates* all its Affections. Conſequently it is not ill deſcribed by *Proclus*; *The Knowledge of Magnitudes and Figures, and their Limitations; Alſo of their Reaſons, Affections, Poſitions, and Motions of every Kind.* Yet it is not to be denied, but a great Part of this Science, and its chief Uſe, conſiſts in this, that the Quantities of Magnitudes are known and computed by *Compariſon*; *i. e.* that they are capable of *Meaſure*. Wherefore we will ſpend ſome Labour in explaining this Affection of Magnitude.

Firſt then we will endeavour to unfold the Ambiguities, and various Significations of the Word *Meaſure*, with its conſequent *Menſurable* from *menſurare* to meaſure, and other ſuch paronymous Terms; and that, as well becauſe a thorough Knowledge of this is both pleaſant and uſeful of itſelf, as leſt we fall into Error by being deluded and diſtracted by the various Significations of ſo dubious a Word, which ſometimes happens; and laſtly that we may have a more diſtinct Knowledge,

ledge, what is the principal Notion of this Property. And indeed if we regard the popular Uſe of the Word *Meaſure*, there ſcarce occurs any Word wreſted to more Significations, or that more frequently obtains, or more aptly admits of Metaphorical Senſes. For inſtance, to a *Good Man right Reaſon*, and the *Preſcripts of Virtue* are called the *Meaſure* of the Life and Manners; to an *Epicurean earthly Pleaſure*; to the *Covetous Man Gain*; and to the *Ambitious Temporal Power* and *Glory*; becauſe moſtly the Deſigns, Endeavours and Actions are by thoſe Men directed and adapted to ſuch Things: The *Cuſtom* or *Opinion* of the *People* is called the *Meaſure* of *Decency*, as to the external Circumſtances of Things: *Common Uſe* the *Meaſure* or *Rule* of *Speech*, and the *Signification* of *Words*. With (*a*) *Ariſtotle*, *Law* is deſcribed the *Meaſure* of *Juſtice*, becauſe a Thing is declared *juſt*, according to its Agreement with it. Alſo with the ſame, *Science* is termed the *Meaſure* of *Things*, becauſe the juſt Limits of (*b*) *Things* are determined by it, and it ſhews how they are related to one another, and to what they tend. With *Cicero*, it is put metonymically for the Judgment itſelf, or the *Faculty* whereby the *Quantity of Things* is diſcerned or eſtimated, when he ſays, *Whatſoever falls under the* Meaſure *of the Ears is called Number*; *i. e.* whoſe Quantity may be judged by the Ear. Alſo *Meaſure* is uſed for the definite Quantity of any Thing, as in thoſe golden Verſes of *Juvenal*,

——————Menſura tamen quæ
Sufficiat censûs, ſiquis me conſulat edam:
In quantum ſitis atque fames & frigora poſcunt;
Quantum, Epicure, tibi parvis ſuffecit in hortis.

(*a*) Top. VI. 2. (*b*) Met. X. 1.

Quantum Socratici ceperunt ante penates.
Nunquam aliud natura, aliud ſapientia dicit.

Which may be thus rendered,

Yet if I'm aſk'd what Meaſure *may ſuffice*
Of Store; I anſwer, juſt as much as will,
O Epicurus, *keep thee from th' Aſſaults*
Of Hunger, Thirſt, and Cold; what grows within
Thy little Gardens will afford enough,
Or what the Houſes heretofore contain'd
Of the ſage Followers of Socrates.
Nature and Wiſdom always ſpeak the ſame.

And elſewhere the ſame *Juvenal*,

———Sed quæ præclara & proſpera tanti
Ut rebus lætis par ſit *Menſura* malorum?
————————*But what Conditions are*
So fortunate and happy as t'obtain
A Meaſure, *juſt the ſame of good and ill.*

To which I add *Lucan*,

————————Fuit hæc *Menſura* Timoris
Velle putant quodcunque poteſt———
This was the Meaſure *of their Fear; whate'er*
Is in his Power, they think is in his Will.

i. e. the *Romans* feared all that from *Cæſar*, which they ſaw in his Power; and becauſe he was able to do all Things againſt them, they feared all Things from him. And no otherwiſe is that Sentence of *Heſiod* to be taken, where he commands Benefits to be returned in the ſame *Meaſure*, *i. e.* the *ſame Quantity* wherein they are received; or even with Intereſt ἀυτῷ τῷ μέτρῳ, καὶ λώιον: Alſo in the ſacred Writings the Word μέτρον *Meaſure* has ſometimes the ſame Senſe; as in *Rom.* xii. 3. *According as God hath dealt to every Man the* Meaſure *of* Faith, *i. e.* according to the *certain* and *definite Quantity* of Faith, which he hath diſpenſed to every one.

But

But it would be endless to rehearse all the trite, common and improper Acceptations of this Word. Yet one or two of the more noted of these deserves to be lightly touched, as coming nigher the Notion of *Mathematical Measure*, and in part *serviceable* to it. Such in the first Place is that, whereby *Measure* every where designs the Quantity of a Thing justly, duly, and conformably to Nature or Reason, which, if it either exceed or fall short of, is accounted for deformed, vitious, or monstrous; and consequently in respect of which, every Virtue in Morality, every Beauty in Nature, and every Utility in Art is estimated. In Morality, I say, every Virtue is reckoned as well from a certain *Moderamen* of the Affections as *Mediocrity* of the Actions, *i. e.* from their just and due Quantities discovered by the Prescript of Prudence, or right practical Reason. And in like manner Vice seems to consist in the Excess or Defect of this Quantity, and to be nothing but an *Exorbitance* or *Irregularity* of the Affections and Actions, from the *stated Measure* of the Manners. None of you can be ignorant that *Aristotle* constitutes the Form of Virtue and Vice in these. And *Plato* (contrary to what some suppose) most expresly gives his Assent the same Way in these Words, (*a*) *That which exceeds or falls short of the Nature of due* Measure *or* Mediocrity, *either in Words or Deeds*; *shall we not say that it constitutes the real Difference of good Men from ill?* To which Words *Socrates* puts his φαίνεται (*it is manifest*). And to this may be referred that of *Hesiod*,

Μέτρον πᾶσιν ἄριστον, ὑπερβασίη δ' ἀλεγεινὴ

Measure is best in all Things, and whate'er
Exceeds the Bounds of that, is counted bad.

(*a*) See the Dialogue inscribed Πολιτικὸς.

Whatsoever

Whatſoever agrees with or comes up to this *Meaſure* is ſaid to be a *Mean* or to preſerve a *Medium*, and is eſteemed Praiſe-worthy; and whatſoever recedes or falls from it is termed irregular, and is wont to be taken for a Vice. From whence every where they who moderate and govern their Affections well, eſpecially their Ambition and Animoſity, are ſaid to be *Temperate*; nor is any Policy to be accounted more worthy of Praiſe. But I unwittingly fall into *Ethics*, I will retreat; only give me leave to ſubjoin *Plato*'s Saying concerning *Pleaſure* in Compariſon with *Knowledge* and *Reaſon*. *Nothing*, ſays he, *can be more difficultly reduced to a juſt* Meaſure *than Pleaſure, and nothing is more eaſily contained within due Bounds than Knowledge and Underſtanding*.

Alſo in natural Things, *Shape* or *Beauty* is rated according to this *Meaſure*, *i. e.* according to a certain juſt Magnitude. Thus he is eſteemed monſtrous, or deformed, that exceeds a certain determinate Stature of Body by a Giant-like Tallneſs or Thickneſs, or is diſagreeably ſlender or ſhort, or has ſome Parts immoderately jutting out or ſinking inwards, or has any Thing deficient or redundant in Number or Bigneſs.

In like manner in artificial Things it is judged from ſuch a Meaſure what is comely and convenient. For almoſt all Arts aim at nothing elſe, but to give the Things, about which they are converſant, a certain juſt Quantity, accommodated to certain deſigned Uſes or Appearances. Whence *Plato* makes all Arts to be *Portions* of the *Art of Meaſure*, teaching to direct their Endeavours to a Medium, that Practitioners may render their Works uſeful and comely. *The Art of Meaſuring*, ſays he, *is ſo divided into two, that one of its Parts contains all the Arts, that compare together Numbers, Lengths, Depths, Breadths, and Velocities;*

and

and the other the remaining Arts respect what is moderate, decent, and *opportune, and whatsoever Things aim at a Mean, avoiding the Extreams.*

But we have exceeded our Bounds concerning this popular Acceptation; yet we will just glance at another of kin to it, according to which, *Measure* designs some *stated Pattern*, commonly known and proved, exposed to the Senses, or comprehended by the Understanding, by which the Quantities or Values of other Things ought, or are wont, to be examined. This Sort of *Measure* is twofold, *viz. Natural* and *Arbitrary*. The *Arbitrary* is such as is propounded by public Authority (as *Vessels, Weights, Rules*) for the Sake of Conformity or Agreement; from which other Measures do borrow their Right, Name, and Reason of *Measure*, and are no otherwise *Measures*, than as they agree with these Originals. But the *Measure* of every natural Thing is that which is the first and most perfect in that Genus: As the *Divine Nature* is the *Measure* of *Goodness* and *Wisdom*, because God alone is originally of himself *good* and *wise*, and other Things are only so far Partakers of *Goodness* and *Wisdom*, as they have any Agreement with, or Resemblance of the *Divine Goodness*. Every Thing, according to *Plato*, has such a *Measure*, the *eternal* and *indefectible Idea of itself*, *viz.* some most exact Pattern, from its Similitude or Correspondence with which it is accounted *true*, *comely*, and *perfect*, and if it disagree the least from it, it is so far *vicious*, *deformed*, and *imperfect*. And in the end of his *Philebus* he disposes *Measure* in the first Place among the prime and eternal Things. *Thou shalt tell all,* O Protarchus, *both sending Messengers elsewhere, and thyself speaking to them that are present, that Pleasure is a Thing to be put neither in the first nor second Rank; but it is first to be spoke concerning*

concerning Meaſure, what is agreeable and opportune to Meaſure, and all ſuch Things as are by Nature eternal. Where by *Meaſure* he ſeems to underſtand the *original Idea* of every Thing: but I ſpend Time in theſe Things.

Let us now leave theſe popular Things, and come to the Significations of *Meaſure*, which are uſed among Mathematicians. And the Definition or Deſcription of *Meaſure*, which (*u*) *Ariſtotle* delivers, agrees in Part with all theſe. *Meaſures is that by which the Quantity of a Thing is known.* But becauſe this Knowledge of Quantity may be differently apprehended according to various Degrees and Reſpects, conſequently the Name of *Meaſure* is taken more or leſs extenſively.

And *firſt*, *Meaſure* is often put for any Thing, which any way ſhews or notifies the Quantity of another, and denotes nothing elſe but a certain Argument, or Sign, or undoubted Criterion of ſome determinate Quantity. Thus the Arch of a Circle deſcribed from the angular Point as a Center, and intercepted between the Legs of a rectilineal Angle; And in *Spherics*, the Arch of a Circle deſcribed from the angular Point as a Pole, and intercepted between the Sides of the ſpherical Angle, is the *Meaſure* of both the ſaid rectilineal and ſpherical Angle; becauſe if the Quantity of that Arch (*i. e.* what Part it is, or what Reaſon it has to the whole Circumference of the Circle, or its Quadrant) may be known by an Inſtrumental *Menſuration*, or any other way, the Quantity of the ſaid Angle will be conſequently known from thence, *i. e.* what Part or what *Proportion* it has to four Right Angles, or to one Right one. Nor on the other hand may any Angle having its Vertex in the Center or Pole of a Circle be leſs

(*n*) Met. X. 1.

properly

properly said to be the *Measure* of the circular Arch; because, as far as by Hypothesis or Discursus it has a known *Proportion* to four Right Angles, it will shew the Reason of the intercepted Arch to the whole Circumference. For some do wrongly say that an intercepted Arch is the proper Quantity of its Angle; when the Arch is no more the Quantity of the Angle, than the Angle of the Arch; nay this is no more a *Measure* than that, either on the Part of the Thing, or from common Use; since their Quantities are carried on proportionally, connected necessarily, and shew one another reciprocally: And by the same Reason circular Sectors are named the *Measures* of Angles, and these of those. Moreover by this Means not only Magnitude is termed the *Measure* of Space, Space of Motion and Time, but interchangeably also, Motion and Time are called the *Measures* of Space, and Space of Magnitude; for as the Quantity of the Magnitude occupying the Space is known by a prior Knowledge of the Space; so far will the Quantity of the predeterminate Space run over be discovered by Motion or Time. So that if it can be known how much Time is passed since the Rising of the Sun, thence we may gather how much of its Periphery the Sun has run through in the mean Time. Which Permutation of Space, Time and Motion in respect of *Measure (x) Aristotle* has plainly taken notice of. *We don't only*, says he, *measure Motion by Time, but also Time by Motion, for this Reason, because they are interchangeably defined by one another. And we measure also Magnitude by Motion, and Motion by Magnitude; for if a Walk be great, we are said to have gone a great Way, and on the contrary, if the Way be great, to have*

(x) Phys. IV. 12.

had

had a great Walk; *in like manner we ſay the Time is great if the Motion be ſo*, *and the Motion great if the Time be ſo.* Farther to abound with Examples, the throwing of a Dart or Stone is this Way a *Meaſure* of Space, though more imperfectly; for as far as the Strength of the Thrower is known by a former Experiment, it may be thence known, how much Space is between his Station, and the Fall of the Thing thrown. Nay, ſince every Thing, every natural Agent, has a determinate Sphere of its Activity, it may as ſuch ſome Way diſcharge the Office of a *Meaſure*, *viz.* Since Fire exerts a Power of Heating to a certain Diſtance and is perceived to effect nothing beyond that; ſince a Flower, or any odoriferous Body, diſperſes its Vapours of Smell to a certain Place; ſince a viſible Object is beheld to a certain Diſtance, and diſappears farther off; ſince the Sound of the Voice is perceived by the Ears placed within a definite Bound, beyond which it is inſenſible; if it firſt be known by a particular Experience how great the Radius of every ſuch Sphere of Activity is, ſome Judgment may be made from thence concerning thoſe Interſtices, *i. e.* the Quantities of thoſe Powers being found will become a Kind of *Meaſures* of the Spaces. Thus, it is commonly ſaid by Hiſtorians, that the Diſtances of Places were computed from an Eſtimation of the Space, which a quick-footed Man was able to go over in ſome aſſigned Time: And alſo that Mariners judged the Tracts of the Sea, and Diſtances of Ports, from the Time of Sailing performed by a conſtant equable Wind. So Aſtronomers do very accurately meaſure Time by numbering the returning Synchroniſms of a ſuſpended Plumb-line. Alſo Shadow (though one of the moſt obſcure and ſubtle Things, and almoſt nothing at all) is a *Meaſure* of this Kind in many reſpects; its Motion upon

Dials

Dials ſhews the Quantity of Time; its Magnitude received upon a Wall diſcovers the apparent Magnitude of the Sun; and laſtly, it is ſubſervient for meaſuring the true Magnitude of the Sun in Eclipſes. Thus there is ſcarce any Thing but either is or imitates ſuch a *Meaſure*; and (what is eſpecially to be noted) Things the moſt different in Genus or Kind may be the *Meaſures* of each other, according to the Latitude of this Acceptation.

But *ſecondly*, ſomething more ſtrictly, that is called a *Meaſure* from the Quantity of which the Knowledge of Quantity does neceſſarily depend, as it is meaſurable; conſequently the Quantity of this is no otherwiſe known, than it can be known from a former Knowledge of that. Which Sort of *Meaſure* in reſpect to the foregoing already explained, may be ſaid to be *natural*, and *a priori*; becauſe it is not aſſumed ſo arbitrarily, but is required neceſſarily, and ſuggeſted by Nature itſelf for inveſtigating the Quantity of the Thing meaſured. Thus Magnitude is the *Meaſure* of Space, becauſe the Quantity of Space can be no otherwiſe comprehended, than by meaſuring, or ſome Way ſufficiently computing ſome real Magnitude occupying it. And Space is ſuch a *Meaſure* of Motion and Time. The Space, I ſay, run over equably with a certain Velocity by ſome noted moveable Body is the *Meaſure* of Time (at leaſt *mediately* by the Intervention of Motion) for it cannot be known how much Time is paſſed, but by eſtimating the Quantity of ſuch a Space. *Ex. gr.* an Arch of the equinoctial Circle intercepted between two Meridians paſſing through the Point of the Sun's Riſing in the Horizon and the Center of the Sun, is the natural and genuine *Meaſure* of the Time elapſed from the Riſing of the Sun to the given Inſtant. And according to *Ptolemy*'s Doctrine, an Arch in the Sun's Eccentric, is ſuch a *Meaſure* of the

the Time of the Year, which is taken in, while the Sun is paſſing that Arch. In like manner the *Meaſure* of the Velocity, wherewith any moveable Thing is carried uniformly, is the Space gone through in an aſſigned Time; for hence we make a certain Conjecture how much Space that moveable Thing will paſs over in any other determinate Time; and by the ſame Means we will be able to diſcover the Quantity of the Velocity.

But *thirdly*, in a yet ſtricter Manner, that is ſaid to be a *Meaſure*, which, by reaſon of a certain extraordinary Determination, Simplicity, Knowableneſs, or moſt eaſy Comprehenſion, may be moſt aptly applied for determining the Modes of Things, or comparing Quantities together. Thus when *infinite Curve-Lines*, or *indirect linear Orbits*, are extended between two aſſigned Points or Places; though the Diſtances of theſe are computed from themſelves, yet a *Right Line* by reaſon of its Unity and Simplicity is ſaid to meaſure that Interval. And though innumerable unequal Right Lines may be drawn from a *given Point to a Right Line given in Poſition*; yet a *right lined Perpendicular*, becauſe it is ſimple, and one, is ſaid to meaſure the Diſtance of the *Right Line* from thence. For the ſame Cauſe the Diſtance of a *Right Line ſubtended in a Circle*, or of a *leſſer Circle in a Sphere*, from the Center of the Circle or Sphere, is eſtimated by a *Perpendicular* let fall from the Center to the *Subtenſe* or *Plane* of the ſaid *leſſer Circle*. By like Reaſon the Diſtance of *Right Lines parallel* to one another is meaſured by any *right lined Perpendicular* intercepted between them; and the Diſtance of *concentric Peripheries* is computed from an *intercepted Portion* of any *Radius* drawn from the *common Center*, becauſe this is always of the ſame Quantity. So alſo *Apollonius* (or the *Arabian* that interpreted his Works) in the

fifth

fifth Book of his *Conics*, names the Right Line intercepted between the Vertex and Point in the Diameter aſſigned, a *Meaſure* ; becauſe there occurs none ſimpler, or greater, for determining the Quantity of the other Branches. The ſame Way, becauſe among Superficies a plane one is moſt ſimple and uniform, and among right lined Figures the Square is the ſimpleſt and eaſieſt known ; therefore a Square is uſually called and accounted the *Meaſure* of ſuperficial Figures, and their Quantities are referred to this, as far as it may be done. And the ſame Reaſon holds of a Cube in Solids, to which the Quantities of other Solids are reduced, becauſe of its manifeſt Determination, and the eaſily conceivable Property of its Nature. A right Angle alſo obtains the Place of a received *Meaſure* in rectilineal Angles, becauſe it is in ſome Degree more known than others, obtains a peculiar Name, and ſeems to include a more ſimple Relation of the inſiſting Line to that upon which it ſtands. So laſtly Geometricians endeavour to reduce all curved and compound Lines to a Right Line, which is the ſimpleſt of all Lines, and determine their Quantities from ſome Relation which they obtain to this. And the ſame Method is obſerved in other Quantities: For becauſe the diurnal Revolution of the Heavens, or (according to the more received Hypotheſis in our Times) of the Earth is the moſt conſtant, uniform, and known of all Motions ; therefore it is aſſumed and uſed for the *Meaſure* of other Motions, Times, and Velocities. And the Quantities of other Weights are by the Maſters of Statics reduced to the Quantity of Gold as the heavieſt Body, or of Oyl as the lighteſt. And in every other kind of Quantity, for Convenience ſake, ſuch an one is always required for a *Meaſure*, as is remarkable for its Simplicity or Mobility.

But

But *fourthly* to come nigher our Purpoſe, that is wont to be called a *Meaſure* which is aſſumed to render ſomething more known and determinate to to us than it was before, and is expounded with this Deſign, that other Quantities coming into Conſideration may, as to Quantity, be compared with it, or with one another by means of it; *viz.* that it may be inveſtigated how often this contains, or is contained in thoſe, or what Proportion thoſe obtain to theſe; and conſequently how they are related one to another, ſo that their Quantities may be ſome Way known and determined, which were before unknown and indeterminate. Thus a *Foot*, a *Palm*, a *Yard*, a *Cubit*, a *Pace*, a *Gill*, a *Quart*, a *Buſhel*, and the other Meaſures, whoſe Names among the Vulgar do ſignify a certain Length or Capacity, are therefore *meaſuring Magnitudes*, becauſe their Quantity is commonly ſuppoſed known and determined by Compact; from whence the definite Quantity of other unknown and indeterminate Magnitudes may be judged by a Compariſon with theſe, from Congruity, or a proper Diſcurſus. Thus alſo, when the Quantity is required of Chord-Lines ſubtending the Periphery of a Circle, or of regular Figures inſcribed within a Circle, the *Radius* of the Circle is wont to be aſſumed for a *Meaſure*, as the moſt known, and perfectly determined of all the Lines in a Circle; and is ſuppoſed to be divided into as many equal Parts, as are needful for Uſe, or as many as are needful ought to be allowed to every particular Chord or Side by the Application of Geometrical Theorems, or by whatſoever other lawful Method it is examined and computed: Or ſome Equation is ſought by an apt Ratiocination, by which the Relation of the ſaid Subtenſes or Sides to the Radius of the Circle may be notified or expreſſed: Or if it may be done, the very Chord

or

or Side which is ſought, is actually drawn and delineated, that its Proportion to the Radius may be eſtimated from a ſenſible Compariſon, or known by an organical or inſtrumental Menſuration: Or at leaſt two other Lines are applied, whoſe Proportion is the ſame with the Proportion of the ſaid Line to the Radius; and conſequently whoſe Reaſon being found, will diſcover the Reaſon required. For the Meaſuring or Dimenſion of Quantities may be performed, and the Reaſon of the Quantity propoſed to that known or determined by Nature expreſſed and eſtimated theſe different Ways, *viz.* by Numbers, or by ſome Equation, or by a ſenſible Computation from the ſame Terms immediately, or from other analogical ones expoſed to the Senſe; whoſe Dimenſion alſo found by ſuitable Inſtruments will exhibit the numerical Proportion. But theſe Things are to be explained more fully and diſtinctly elſewhere. To return to more Examples: By a like Means the Square of the Radius or Diameter is applied for finding the Quantities of the Areas of the reſt of the ſaid Figures, as the *Meaſure* with which they may be compared. Alſo after the ſame Manner, in eſtimating and comparing together the Sides, Superficies, and Solidities of the *regular Bodies*, the Radius of the Sphere is taken, in which they are included or inſcribed, and theſe are compared with it, its Square, or its Cube, that their mutual Proportion may be found and laid by for Uſe. Thus alſo is the Semidiameter of the Earth commonly applied by Aſtronomers in their Search after the true Diſtances of the Stars from one another, and their true Magnitudes, as a certain *common Meaſure*, to which their Quantities may be reduced. As when the Moon is ſaid to be diſtant ſo many Semi-diameters from the Center of the Earth, its Diameter is ſaid to be equal to ſo many Parts of the ſame Semi-diameter.

And

And the ſame of others. Nor (to obſerve by the Way) in this Acceptation of *Meaſure* is it of any Conſequence at all, whether the Magnitude ſuſtaining the Place of a *Meaſure*, be greater or leſſer than that which is meaſured : as in the Examples above the *Radius* is leſſer than a *Chord* of 120 *Degrees*, or the Side of a regular Triangle inſcribed within the Circle, but greater than a *Chord* of 36 *Degrees*, or the Side of a Decagon inſcribed within the ſame Circle. And the Semi-diameter of the Earth is greater than the Semi-diameter of the Moon, but far leſs than the Diſtance of the Moon. Alſo if there be aſſumed a Geometrical Pace, by a juſt Compariſon of it may be known the Length of a Foot, as well as that equal to a Furlong or a Mile. Here is no Regard how the Quantities ſo compared are affected with the Meaſure expounded, ſo that their Proportion can but be expreſſed by Numbers : For this Way all Magnitudes are commenſurable to one another, though the Proportion of ſome be inexpreſſible in Numbers; *i. e.* one of them may be aſſigned to which the Quantities of the reſt may be referred, and meaſured by it. Though the Reaſon of the *Radius* to a *Chord* of 90 *Degrees*, or the Side of a Square inſcribed within the Circle, can be preciſely explained by no Numbers, yet the Quantity of this may be compared with the Quantity of that, and ſo far they are commenſurate. Theſe Things, I ſay, I obſerve by the Way, becauſe of the following Acceptation, which is peculiar to the Mathematics, and of moſt frequent Uſe; according to which,

Fifthly, a *Meaſure* is more ſtrictly taken for *a Magnitude, which ſome Number of Times taken does conſtitute and compoſe another Magnitude, or which being ſome Number of Times taken from another Magnitude leaves no Remainder, but entirely exhauſts it.* By ſome Number of Times is here to be be underſtood once, or oftener, according to Unity or ſome determinate Number: From whence it appears that a *Meaſure* thus taken will never exceed the Thing meaſured, but either is equal to it, or ſome aliquot Part of it, *i. e.* which being ſome Times repeated according to any Number compoſes the Whole; or ſome Number of which does conſtitute and make up the Whole; or ſome Number of which being taken from the Whole leaves no Remainder. Thus *a Foot* is the *Meaſure* of a *Geometrical Pace*, that of a *Furlong*, and a *Furlong* of a *Mile* and a *League*; becauſe a *Foot* taken *five Times* makes a *Geometrical Pace*, and ſubducted away *five Times* deſtroys it: a *Pace* taken a *hundred and twenty five Times* makes a *Furlong*, and a *Furlong* repeated *eight Times* compleats a *Mile*. So alſo a *Minute* meaſures an *Hour*, an *Hour* a *Day*, a *Day* a *civil Month*, and a *civil Month* a *civil Year*. But a *Day* does not thus meaſure a *natural Month* or *Year*, nor a *Month* a *natural Year*. Becauſe 365 *Days* are ſhort of a *natural Year*, and 366 *Days* exceed it, and ſo for others.

And thus are *Meaſures*, and the Words paronymous to it always underſtood in the *Elements* of *Geometry* (though no Definition of *Meaſure* is to be found there, which ſeems a Wonder to ſome) as when an *Aliquot Part* is defined in the beginning of the *fifth Book* to be a *Magnitude of a Magnitude, a leſs of a greater, ſince it may meaſure the greater, i. e.* Since, if it be ſome Number of Times taken, it does ſo exhauſt the Whole, that nothing remains. For the Word καταμετρεῖν does there in the Original ſignify to *meaſure perfectly*. As alſo the ſimple Verb μετρεῖν does ordinarily denote the ſame; and moſt evidently in the Beginning of the *tenth Book*, where *Commenſurable Magnitudes* are defined to be *thoſe that are meaſured* (μετρούμενα) *by one and the ſame Meaſure*, i. e. *each of which the*

ſame

ſame Magnitude taken ſome Number of Times does conſtitute, and taken away ſome Number of Times does deſtroy. And a perfect Diviſion (or Subtraction, ſimple, or multiple, which leaves no Remainder) is always ſignified by μέτρησιν. Thus alſo the Philoſopher ſeems to uſe this Word, when he (y) ſays, *The Whole which is meaſured* (μετρούμενον) *ſeems to be nothing but a Meaſure taken ſome Number of Times.* Yet (z) *Ariſtotle* in his *Metaphyſics* affords one moſt ſtrict Acceptation, according to which *Meaſure* deſigns that which, being the firſt and leaſt in every Kind, is wont to be applied to a Thing indiviſible to Senſe (or the leaſt Thing uſually divided) for diſcovering the Quantity of others, *viz.* as an *Unit* in *Numbers*, a *Grain* in *Weights*, a *Farthing* in *Money*, a *Dieſis* in the *Intervals of Sound*, an *Inch* in Lines, are Meaſures, by Way of Eminence. *Ariſtotle* teſtifies that among the *Greeks* their *ſmalleſt Meaſure* in Length was a *Foot.*

But I have not Time to purſue theſe Things. Nor is it now lawful to adjoin which of theſe is the principal or moſt proper Notion or Acceptation, according to which *Menſurability*, the Affection of Magnitude now in Hand, ought to be underſtood. And many other Things are now to be paſſed by. For the Time reminds us to draw to a Cloſe, and I am afraid leſt ſome Wit ſmite me with an obvious Pun, and ſay, While I am talking about *Meaſure*, I take the leaſt Heed to the *Meaſure* of my Diſcourſe.

(y) Phyſ. IV. 14. (z) Met. X. 1.

LECTURE XV.

Of the Acceptation of the Words paronymous to Meaſure, *viz.* Menſurability, Menſuration, Commenſurability *and* Incommenſurability.

IN the laſt Lecture we were not negligent in our Endeavours to expound the different common Acceptations of the Word *Meaſure*. From whence it will eaſily appear how many Ways the paronymous Terms, *To meaſure*, *menſurable*, &c. may by accepted; *viz.* as many Ways reſpectively, as the Word *Meaſure* may be taken. It remains that we conſider according to which of theſe Ways eſpecially *Menſurability*, the Affection of Magnitude we are treating of, ought to be underſtood, and what is its primary Notion. Two of theſe Ways which are familiar to Mathematicians are eſpecially to be conſidered and carefully diſtinguiſhed, to which all others may be referred.

The *firſt* is more extenſive, but moſt proper, from which, as we ſhall ſhew, *Geometry* has taken his Name, and which according to its Office it principally reſpects; in which reſpect it denotes *to meaſure*, *notify*, *or determine the Quantity of ſome Magnitude with Regard to ſome other homogeneous Magnitude howſoever more known to us*, *or more determinate*, *by declaring*, *exhibiting*, *and repreſenting its Proportion to this in Numbers*, *or ſome other comprehenſible Way*: *i. e.* by ſignifying how great a Part that is of this, or this of that, how they are unequal, how much that exceeds or falls ſhort of this,

this, or by any other like Way. *Ex. gr.* Suppoſing any Longitude hitherto unknown to us, if we can by any Means agreeable to Reaſon (*viz.* either by an *inſtrumental Operation*, or *mental Ratiocination* depending upon lawful Hypotheſes, or Concluſions already demonſtrated) find what Relation it has in Quantity to any expounded Longitude well known by us; how often it contains, or is contained in that; how often it may be taken to exceed or fall ſhort of that; whether it is to it as one Number to another, or as one Right Line I am able to make, to another Right Line I am able to make, or as the Radix of ſome Equation ſubject to an Analytical Enquiry, and reſoluble by Art, then we are ſaid to *meaſure* that Longitude: Which Sort of Dimenſion of direct Longitudes is named *Mecometry* and *Euthumetry*, or by thoſe mongrel Words *Longimetry* and *Altimetry*. In like manner ſuppoſing any plane Figure; when we infer what Proportion it has to another plane Figure exhibited (*viz.* a *Square Foot*) and repreſent it by Numbers or ſome other Way, we are ſaid to *meaſure* it: Which Kind of Dimenſion of Planes may be termed *Empedometry*, and is vulgarly and barbarouſly ſtiled *Planimetry*. By a like Reaſon when we compare ſome Solid with a *cubical* Foot, or with an equal and ſimilar Cylinder, or ſome other known Body, and find its Reaſon to that; this is called *Stereometry*. Alſo ſuch a Compariſon of the Sides and Angles of a Triangle, by which, from certain Sides and Angles known in the ſaid Triangle, the Reaſon of the other Angles may be found to a right one, or the Proportion of the other Sides, to the one aſſigned and known, this is called *Trigonometry*. And when we endeavour as exactly as we are able to determine the Proportion between the Periphery and Diameter of a Circle, or between a Circle's Area, and the Square of its Diameter; that is termed *Cyclometry*. From which Examples,

Examples, brought deſignedly, it appears, as I ſaid, that this Notion of *Menſuration* is the moſt genuine and primary, ſince the principal Parts of the Mathematics are eſpecially converſant about it, and do conſequently receive their Denomination from it.

With reſpect therefore to this ought the Affection of Magnitude to be taken, which we are now treating about, called *Menſurability*, (in Greek μέτρησιν, *Meaſuring*, a Word more ambiguous, confounding the Power with the Act), which denotes nothing but that a Magnitude is capable of being compared with other Magnitudes of the ſame Kind, ſo that its Quantity however otherwiſe unknown and indeterminate is capable of being ſome Way known and determined from the Relation which it obtains to them. For this is connate and eſſential to every Kind of Magnitude, as far as every Magnitude is to any other homogeneous Magnitude, (*viz.* a Line to a Line, a Superfice to a Superfice, a Solid to a Solid) neceſſarily either equal or unequal after a certain Manner, which is knowable on the Part of the Thing, and determinable of itſelf; though the Knowledge of it is very often difficult to be acquired, and ſometimes can be no Way accurately comprehended.

Neither does this Affection agree with Magnitude only, but alſo (as we have particularly ſhewn in other Affections) to all other Quantities whatſoever (*Motions*, *Times*, *Velocities*, *Weights*) analogically and their own Way, as far as their Proportion to one another can be determined, exhibited, or expreſſed, and conſequently the Quantity of one diſcovered from its Relation to the known Quantity of the other. *Ex. gr.* We *meaſure* Time, when we ſhew it to be equal to ſo many Days, Hours, or Minutes; or be ſo to another known Time, as that Right Line, or that Periphery of

a Circle

a Circle is to this, whoſe Proportion to one another we know. We *meaſure* Velocity, when in a Time having ſuch Proportion to another known Time, we ſhew that the Space paſſed over is ſo much with Reſpect to a Space known; *i. e.* when we ſhew that Velocity to have a known Proportion to a known Velocity. Laſtly, we *meaſure* Weight, when we find, how great a Magnitude of a known Gravity it can elevate or ſuſtain, or what Proportion it has to another known Weight. And the ſame Reaſon holds in all other Quantities. But that this Property may be yet more clearly known, we will ſubjoin ſomewhat concerning certain Properties of *Meaſure*, and the *Way of meaſuring Magnitudes.*

The *firſt Property* of the Kind of *Meaſure* we are now upon, is, that it be *homogeneous* to the *Thing meaſured*; *i. e.* that it be capable of being compared with it according to Congruity and Incongruity, Equality and Inequality, Exceſs and Defect, Addition and Subtraction, and laſtly according to Reaſon and Proportion, *viz.* that a Line be capable of being the *Meaſure* of a Line, a Superfice of a Superfice, a Solid of a Solid, a Time of a Time, a Velocity of a Velocity, and a Weight of a Weight. But a Line cannot be the Meaſure of a Superfice, a Superfice of a Body, a Magnitude of a Time, or a Time of a Weight, according to this more accurate Acceptation of *Meaſure.* Indeed that more looſe and unauthorized Notion of *Meaſure* declared above, according to which every Thing that any Way argues, indicates, or notifies the Quantity of another is ſaid to meaſure it, I ſay, that may happen even to *heterogeneous* Quantities, and is not ſeldom attributed and applied to them by Mathematicians; which Way a Line may and is wont to be named the *Meaſure* of Time, a Superfice of Velocity, a Body of Weight;

Weight; and reciprocally Time the *Measure* of a Line, Velocity of a Superfice, and Weight of a Body.

But yet those Acceptations are to be distinguished with great Care, lest we unwittingly fall with Mr. *Hobbes* into many Labyrinths of Difficulties and Errors, by not observing that Distinction, nor taking Notice of the Ambiguity of this Word. Such Mistakes as these; That a Line has Proportion to a Time, and by like Reason a Superfice to a Velocity, a Solid to a Weight; because a Line does in some Sort measure Time, a Superfice Velocity, and a Solid Weight. That the Quantities of all Things are the same or homogeneous to one another; because all Things are subject to the same Measures, *viz.* Lines and Numbers. Lastly, that one Quantum may be the Quantity of any other, *viz.* that a Line may be a Quantity of Time, Velocity and Weight, nay of a Superfice and a Body, because it determines the Quantity of these as a *Measure.* Which monstrous Absurdities seem to have proceeded from no other Fountain than a Disregard of this Distinction: as we will shew very briefly. When Mr. *Hobbes* had laid this Definition as a Foundation to himself, *A Measure is a Magnitude of a Magnitude, one of another, when it is either Multiple of another, or by Application coincides with it*; and had noted farther that a Line passed over by a Motion, is often called a *Measure* of Time; hence it was easy for him to infer, that a Line sometimes coinciding with Time is therefore equal or unequal to Time; and consequently that a Line and Time obtain a Proportion to one another, the same Way as a Line is proportional to a Line. But if it had come into his Mind, that when a Line is said to be a *Measure* of Time, *Measure* is not strictly taken for the Quantum with which Time is compared according to Quan-

tity

tity (much leſs for an Aliquot Part, according to its proper Definition), but more looſely for any Notification or Argument of the Quantity agreeing with Time; I ſay, had he reflected ever ſo little upon this, he had not ſo inconſiderately mingled and confounded Things which are as widely diſtant as the Eaſt is from the Weſt. But thoſe Things are to be more throughly diſcuſſed elſewhere, when we come to treat, according to our Deſign, concerning *Homogeneous* and *Heterogeneous Quantities*.

In the mean while I will only add one Thing worthy of Animadverſion belonging to our Purpoſe; that *heterogeneous Quantities* are ſometimes as the *Meaſures* of others, becauſe they adminiſter a Kind of Knowledge of *homogeneous Meaſures*. *Ex. gr.* A propoſed Arch of the Equator intercepted between the Horizon and Center of the Sun in the Equator is therefore called the *Meaſure* of the elapſed Time of the Day, becauſe the Knowledge of its Proportion to the entire Circumference of the Equator argues the Proportion of that Time to the entire Day; *i. e.* is ſerviceable for its Compariſon to the proper *homogeneous Meaſure*. So alſo a Line moved over is ſo far a *Meaſure* of Velocity, as it denotes the Reaſon of this Velocity to another before known. Nor is the Caſe different in other *Meaſures* improperly ſo called: from whence that appears ſufficiently plain, which was juſt now inſinuated, and which is worth the while to conſider, that all the other Acceptations of *Meaſure* already explained do reſpect this, or are taken from it.

Moreover *ſecondly*, *Another Property* of this Kind of *Meaſure* is, that it has one only certain determinate Quantity, always conſtant and invariable, *i. e.* it is one and *indiviſible* (as *Ariſtotle* notes

notes in his (*c*) *Metaphysics*), admitting no Difference or Latitude, but having its Quantity immoveable, and as it were constituted in a Point. Otherwise the just Quantity of the Thing measured cannot be estimated by a Comparison with it; but it will still remain uncertain, indeterminate and unknown. Therefore whatsoever is doubtful in its Signification, or variable in its Nature, is so far unfit for a Measure. *Ex. gr.* A *Foot* for the size of a *human Foot*, a *human Palm* or *Cubit*; also a *Mile* taken at large (without putting *German*, *Italian*, or *English* to it) and all such like are not properly speaking *Measures*; because there is a vast deal of difference between the *Palm*, *Cubit* and *Foot* of a *Hercules* with his Club, and the *Pygmy* which had a Reed for his Spear. Nor consequently does he, who mentions the Length of two *Feet*, speak any Thing certain, unless he shew more plainly what *Foot* he means. And he, who says that two Cities are a Mile asunder, does not express the Quantity of that Distance, unless he respect some of the foregoing Miles, or speak more expresly, and sufficiently restrain the Sense of the indeterminate Word. Also if one say that a certain Longitude is equal to the Distance of the Sun from the Center of the Earth, he says nothing to the Purpose, unless he shew farther what Distance he means, whether the greatest, least, mean, or any fixed and determinate Distance in the Circumference of the solar Orbit. Lastly, if one affirm that a Right Line is equal to a Right Line drawn from the Center to the Ambit of a certain Ellipsis; the Dimension of that Right Line cannot be computed from hence, because an infinite Number of such Right Lines may be so drawn from the Center of

(*c*) Met. X. 1.

that

that Ellipsis all different and unequal to one another; and none can know which of these he designs, but by some farther *Determination.* Farther, it is to be noted, that this *Determination* of *Quantity* is not of one Way only, but admits of some Difference, and therefore the consequent Proportion of the *Measure* will also be something different. For one *Determination* is *natural* and *universal*, and another *particular* and altogether *arbitrary.* That is *naturally* and universally determined, which has a determinate Nature, and always respects those Quantities the same Way with which it is compared, or for the measuring of which it is subservient; from whence it is, that it is immediately apt for determining their Proportions in general: and consequently may be also now supposed known itself for notifying their particular Quantities. By which means the Radius of a Circle, and the Side of a Square are determined naturally; the Radius, I say, of a Circle is so determined, because the Subtenses of similar Arches, and all Right Lines placed any how similarly in a Circle, have the same Proportion to Radius, and are so determined in Quantity from a Relation to Radius, that it being particularly determined, their Quantity is always particularly determined at the same Time. As in every Circle (it is no Matter whether it be greater or lesser) the Side of the Hexagon is equal to the Radius, the Right Line of 30 *Degrees* is equal to the half of Radius, and the Chord of 90 *Degrees* is double the Radius in Power: whence if the Quantity of a particular Radius be determined and known (*i. e.* if it be subjected to the Estimation of Sense, or denominated by the Number of some particular known *Measure*) the Quantity of the said Lines may be thence known immediately. In like manner from a known Side of a Square, the Excess of the Diameter

meter above the Side, and the Quantity of other Lines determinately placed within the Square may be eaſily and certainly known. But it belongs to ſpeculative Geometry to apply this Kind of Determinations, and be converſant about ſuch Dimenſions, *viz.* to that Part which does not ſo immediately inveſtigate the Quantities of particular Magnitudes, as the Reaſons of univerſal ones; from which notwithſtanding the Dimenſions of Particulars do flow, or are founded in them.

But thoſe Meaſures are determined arbitrarily, which are applied for the meaſuring particular Quantities; which, ſince of themſelves they have no Aptitude peculiar to it, are choſen at Pleaſure from among infinite others of the ſame Kind; and are deputed by Compact or Inſtitution for this Office of *Meaſuring*. Which ſort of Determination is obtained by a *Pace*, a *Rod*, a *Furlong*, a *Mile*, and others employed in common Uſe, which the practical Geometrician aſſumes for the Dimenſion of particular Magnitudes. But we muſt dwell no longer upon Things ſo evident in themſelves.

A *third Property* of *Meaſure* is, that its Quantity is foreknown. For ſince (according to *Ariſtotle*'s Definition, *Meaſure is that whoſe Quantity is known)* the Reaſon of *Meaſure* eſpecially requires it to declare an unknown Quantity, itſelf muſt firſt of all be known. For nothing can be known by that which is unknown, nor illuſtrated by that which is obſcure. But the Knowledge of Quantities is of different Kinds: concerning which,

In the *firſt* Place, one Kind of *Knowledge* is *radical*, *abſolute* and *primary*, whereby the Quantity of a Thing is expoſed to the Senſes, and immediately diſcerned and eſtimated by them, being as it were ſeen by a Kind of Intuition without further Compariſon with other Quantities. By this whatſoever we are able to effect or exhibit in Geometry is is accounted known, and that unknown of whoſe Conſtruction we are ignorant. As if a Circle be propoſed to Geometricians, the Side is known of the inſcribed regular Trigon, Tetragon, Pentagon, Hexagon, Decagon, Pentecaidecagon, and all that proceed from theſe in a double Number (or even a Triple, becauſe any aſſigned Arch or Angle may be biſected by plain common Geometry, and triſected by the Conic Sections) but the Sides of moſt other regular Figures are more unknown, and ſcarce can be any Way exhibited ſcientifically. Moreover the Periphery of a Particular expounded Circle may this Way be ſaid to be known, becauſe its Quantity can be apprehended by Senſe, though it cannot be juſtly compared with a Right Line; and perhaps its exact Proportion to this can never be diſcovered by us. Notwithſtanding, as a Right Line repreſented to the Sight impreſſes its Species, and begets a certain Judgment concerning itſelf, by which it is ſaid to be known: ſo the Circumference of a Circle leaves the Idea of its Quantity upon the Imagination, according to which it is looked upon as known. Neither perhaps is a Right Line more proper and ſuitable for meaſuring the Lines of its own Kind, than the Periphery of a Circle for meaſuring circular Peripheries, and other Lines which may be referred to them. Again, thus, and no otherwiſe, are known all the primitive *Meaſures*, to which *Meaſures* of the ſame Kind are referred, whoſe Quantity can be ſcarce any Way explained but by pointing the Finger at them and anſwering him that enquires about their Quantity. *It is as much as you ſee or perceive by your Senſe.* Whence it follows that it is principally required for a Quantity to be eſtimable by ſome Senſe to make it this way known, and taken for an original Meaſure; and conſequently that it be both ſubject to Senſe, and have a mean Quantity ſo conſiſting within due Limits, that the Senſe may not be eaſily deceived in its Eſtimation, *i. e.* that if any thing conſiderable be added to it or taken from it, it cannot eſcape the Senſe. Wherefore (*d*) *Ariſtotle* well obſerves, that the leaſt ſenſible Magnitudes are moſt convenient for *Meaſures. Where nothing can be added or taken away but the Difference may be eaſily perceived and known by Senſe, that will be the moſt accurate Meaſure.* But leſſer Quantities are eſpecially ſuch, becauſe the Increments or Decrements of greater Quantities lie more hid from the Judgment of the Senſe. *That which is taken from, or added to, a Furlong, Talent, or univerſally any greater Meaſure may be more hid, than that which is taken from, or added to, a Foot, an Obolus, or leſſer Meaſure.* From whence the Philoſopher concludes, *That all Men make that eſpecially a Meaſure, from which nothing can be deducted, as to the Judgment of Senſe, and think they know a Quantity then, when they know it by ſuch a Meaſure.* Therefore are all great Magnitudes quite excluded from ſuch an *original Meaſure*, as unfit for it; becauſe their Differences can either not at all, or not exactly enough be judged of by the Senſe. For as *Opticians* obſerve, *the Diſtances exceeding two hundred Foot cannot be judged by Sight*, the Senſe which reaches beyond all others, but they all ſeem equal to one another; thus the Sun, Moon, and fixed Stars, though ſome be really removed from us ſo many Myriads of Miles farther than others, yet they all ſeem to have the ſame Diſtance, and be placed in the Perimeter of a Sphere having its Center as it were, in the Eye of every one: And even the Differences of thoſe Longitudes, which come nigher the ſaid Intervals are hardly computed by

(*d*) Met. X. 1.

the

the Senſe: From whence it alſo comes to paſs that (by Reaſon of the true Differences, not rightly attended to, of the viſual Rays proceeding farther) an objected Plane either of Land or Sea, ſeems to ariſe or ſwell into a gibbous Surface. But of this ſenſible Knowledge too much.

Secondly, Quantity is known from a Compariſon with any *Meaſure* judged by Senſe in a Way expounded; *viz.* when it is known what Relation in Quantity it has to that *Meaſure*, how often it contains, or is contained in it, how much it exceeds or falls ſhort of it. This Way known Quantities are ſaid to be *mediate* or *ſecondary Meaſures.* Magnitudes, I ſay, no where objected to the Senſes, nor any Way eſtimable by them, may ſuſtain the Reaſon of a *Meaſure*, if their Proportion to other Magnitudes already eſtimated by Senſe ſhall be found by an *Organical Menſuration*, or any lawful Ratiocination. *Ex. gr.* The Semidiameter of the Earth although ſeen to no Body, and beyond the Eſtimation of Senſe, may yet be the *Meaſure* of the Magnitudes and Diſtances of the heavenly Bodies; if it be known by proper Hypotheſes, and a juſt Diſcurſus how many *Furlongs*, *Paces*, or *Feet* it contains, or is equal to; or if it be ſo to ſome of thoſe *Primitive Meaſures* before known, as ſuch an expounded Right Line is to another Right Line exhibited.

But *thirdly*, that is ſaid to be known by a peculiar Reaſon, which is expreſſed in Numbers denoting its Relation to ſome expounded Quantity before eſtimated (whether it be eſpecially known to us by familiar Uſe, or be aſſumed *gratis* and at Pleaſure); if that before known Quantity be conceived, either as undivided (*i. e.* deſigned by Unity, or diſtributed into equal Parts, and denominated according to that Diviſion by a certain determinate Number, and then it be found what

Number

Number of thoſe equal Parts, or how many of thoſe Units, or what Part of that Unit agrees with the Quantity propoſed; that Quantity will be ſaid from thence to be perfectly known, *i. e.* known in the Parts of the given *Meaſure.* Moreover oftentimes a Quantity otherwiſe expounded to the Senſes and eſtimable by them (*i. e.* whoſe Reaſon to an expounded Meaſure may be eſtimated by ſenſible Limits) is nevertheleſs reckoned unknown, till its Proportion is reduced into Numbers, or explained by Numbers according to ſome ſtated *Meaſure. Ex. gr.* Although the Right Sine of 30 *Degrees* among others be drawn in a Circle and offered to the Eye, yet its Quantity will be reckoned partly unknown, till by Conſideration or Argument it be diſcovered equal to half the Radius; and then its Quantity will be eſteemed perfectly known. That Things are accounted unknown, whoſe *Reaſon* in Numbers to ſome *cuſtomary* and *uſual Meaſure* is unknown, ſeems to proceed from many Cauſes: As *firſt*, becauſe the Judgment of Senſe is more ſlippery, and uncertain, and leſs ſagacious and exact than an Eſtimation of Quantity founded in the certain Proportion of Numbers. *Secondly*, Becauſe Quantities, or the Reaſons of Quantities, are more eaſily and conveniently exhibited by the Symbols of Numbers repreſented in the Mind than really by the Senſes. *Thirdly*, Becauſe the ſenſible Species of an Object is more vaniſhing, unconſtant, and mutable, than Number, which is eaſily retained in the Memory, and committed to Writing, and is obnoxious to almoſt no Changes by Increaſe or Decreaſe. And *fourthly*, becauſe the Quantities of all Things are reduced by the Intervention of Numbers to a few very *familiar Meaſures*, which are eſtabliſhed by common Conſent. Which Cauſes (and whatſoever more there may be) of this Thing, (*viz.* why

that

that is accounted as eſpecially known, and perfectly diſcovered, whoſe Reaſon is expreſſed in Numbers to ſomething before known), though not unworthy our Conſideration, I now paſs by in order to haſten to ſomething elſe. So far I have touched upon the particular Knowledge of Quantities: But

Fourthly, Every Quantity is ſaid to be after a Sort known and determined (as we have ſaid above) whoſe general Nature we comprehend, though we are ignorant of its particular Quantity, or do not conſider it. Thus we know how a Radius is affected in a Circle, or a Side in a Square, though we are ignorant, or neglect the Quantity of this or that particular Radius of a Circle, or Side of a Square. Eſpecially thoſe Quantities are known which are laid down for the Generation of others, and conſequently determine every Thing following that Generation, and from thence naturally challenge the Place of a Meaſure. As if a Circle be ſuppoſed to be generated from the Revolution of its Radius, a Square from the drawing of its Side into itſelf, or from its direct parallel Motion; then becauſe the Quantity and Poſition of all other Lines in a Circle or a Square depend upon the Quantity of the Radius of the one or Side of the other with ſuch a Motion; conſequently thoſe are not undeſervedly reckoned as primarily known: and are general primitive Meaſures, from a Compariſon with which, the Things which obtain a ſimilar Situation perpetually determinate in reſpect of them, are conſequently known by a *General Method*; *i. e.* the conſtant Proportion may be known of theſe to thoſe, and therefore the particular Quantity of theſe may be alſo known, from a Suppoſition that the particular Quantity of thoſe is known. For, if the Proportion of two Quantities be found, the

one

one will be known from the Knowledge of the other.

Hitherto concerning the Properties of *Meaſure*; it now follows, according to our propoſed Method, that we add a few Things concerning the *Ways* of *Meaſuring*. Thoſe are various, but we will juſt glance at ſome of the moſt principal that offer themſelves to our Thoughts. *Homogeneous Quantities* then however unknown and indeterminate are compared together (or meaſured) with ſuch as are known and determinate.

Firſt, By ſeeking their Proportion by pure Reaſoning. Thus from a given Radius the Geometrician gathers the Quantity of the Side of an inſcribed regular Trigon, by demonſtrating from its own Principles that it is triple the Radius in Power. So alſo from the Foreknowledge of the apparent Diameter and true Diſtance of the Moon from the Eye, by help of the Canon of Sines conſtructed from geometrical Reaſonings, may be ſhewn the Quantity of its true Diameter. This Method is altogether theoretical, whereby the general Dimenſion of Quantities is performed, which Reaſon only can attain; and conſequently is ſtrictly perfect and exact.

Secondly, By organical Dimenſion alone, which ſerves for applying the Quantities of unknown Things to the Numbers of a determinate Meaſure; eſpecially thoſe Quantities which cannot be eſtimated by Senſe, at leaſt not commodiouſly and accurately. Thus we meaſure Arches and Angles by circular Quadrants diſtributed into Degrees and Minutes, and Longitudes by Rules and Scales divided into equal Particles. This Method is only employed about particular Quantities, and is purely mechanical, and therefore never ſtrictly preciſe and accurate.

The

The *third Method* is by Reaſoning and organical Dimenſion conjunctly, by the Labour of the Mind and Mechaniſm of the Hand. Which indeed is practical and converſant about Particulars, yet ſo as to need the help of general Theorems, whence it is lame on one Leg, but walks direct and certain with the other; which, as it applies the Rules of Geometry, has a certain Divinity and Participation of eternal and indefectible Truth, but as it requires mechanical Labour is fallible, mutable, and obnoxious to Miſtakes and Errors. By this Method we not only meaſure all Things that are placed within the Reach of our Sight or Feeling, but alſo innumerable Things inacceſſible to our Senſes, and hardly to be comprehended by the Mind; ſuch as the Profundity and Circumference of the Earth, the Magnitudes and Interſtices of the Stars, and whatſoever has any Proportion ſenſibly finite with Quantities ſubject to an organical Dimenſion or inſtrumental Menſuration. For from the Proportion of the Things mechanically meaſured to others exceeding that Dimenſion, we may alſo infallibly diſcover the Quantity of theſe by help of Geometry.

Fourthly, To theſe I ſubjoin the Method by which we anſwer ſuch as enquire after the Quantity of a Magnitude by really exhibiting it to the Senſes to be eſtimated or to be reduced to the Numbers of any known *Meaſure* by the ſaid mechanical Dimenſion. As if one aſk the Quantity of a Right Line touching a propoſed Circle from a given Point. The Queſtion will be ſatisfied in part by drawing that Right Line geometrically, and ſhewing it to the Eyes of the Querent. For thus he will either diſcern its Quantity by looking upon it, or find to how many Particles of a known Meaſure it is preciſely or nearly equal, by examining it according to ſome Scale.

The

The *fifth* Method is that whereby an unknown Quantity may be declared by ſome Equation, which expreſſes its Relation to other known Quantities, and conſequently offers it to the Mind to be comprehended; the artificial Reſolution of which Equation according to certain Rules accommodated for that purpoſe, and preſcribed in the Doctrine of *Analytics*, will entirely perform this Dimenſion, and diſcover the Quantity ſought either Geometrically or Arithmetically. Thus if there be given the Radius of a Circle, and Tangent of an aſſigned Arch, and the Quantity of the Tangent of the double Arch be ſought, putting r for Radius, a for the given Tangent, and x for the Tangent ſought, the Quantity ſought will be repreſented by this Equation: $xrr - xaa = 2rra$; or $rr - aa : 2rr :: a : x$. *i. e.* The Tangent of the double Arch ſought, being drawn into the Difference between the Squares of the Radius and the known Tangent of the ſingle Arch, is equal to twice the Square of the Radius drawn into the Tangent of the ſingle Arch. Or which comes to the ſame, by this Analogy: The Difference between the Square of the Radius and the Square of the given Tangent will be in proportion to twice the Square of the Radius, as the given Tangent is to the Tangent ſought. By which Theorem the moſt excellent *D. Pell* refuted the Quadrature of *Longomontanus*. Alſo if the Subtenſe of any Arch be given in Numbers, and Unity put for the Radius of the Circle, and the Quantity be ſought of the Subtenſe of the triple Arch: putting z for the given Subtenſe, and q for the Subtenſe ſought, the ſought Quantity will be declared by this Equation: $q = 3z - z^3$; or $qr^2 = 3zr^2 - z^3$. *i. e.* The required Subtenſe of the triple Arch will equal thrice the Subtenſe of the given ſubtriple Arch leſs the Cube of the ſaid Arch. Which Theorem may be uſeful for the

the ſame Purpoſe. But we will not dwell upon explicating thoſe Things any farther.

Yet I beg your Patience a little, while I am lightly touching upon the other principal Notion of *Meaſure*, that I may not trouble you again during the little Remainder of this Term: But if I ſeem more prolix than is fitting or cuſtomary, I would have you to interpret it, as proceeding from my exceeding Unwillingneſs to be torn from your Preſence and Society, and ſo ſoon to bid you Farewell. The other principal Acceptation of Meaſure according to which it always deſigns in the Elements that which being ſome Number of Times taken exactly compoſes and conſtitutes or ſome Number of Times taken away deſtroys and quite exhauſts the homogeneous Thing meaſured, has already been abundantly deſcribed in the preceding Lecture. As to which, the *Menſurability* here meant does alſo agree with all Quantities whatſoever; for every Quantity (Magnitude originally and ſimply, but all the reſt ſecondarily, and conſequentially) is its proper Way *menſurable* according to this Notion, *i. e.* is diviſible into any Number of equal Parts or Degrees; or is denominable, repreſentable, or explicable by any Number: as the *Radius* of a Circle however ſmall is ſuppoſed by Trigonometricians to be divided into a hundred thouſand, or a thouſand thouſand, or as many more as you pleaſe of equal Particles; and any Time however ſhort may be divided into any Number of minute Parts according to the Will of the Computant; alſo as many Degrees of any Velocity or Weight may be ſuppoſed as any one ſhall think convenient: For every Number is a fit Symbol of every Quantity, and capable to ſignify it: and as every mathematical Number, conſiſting of equal Units, is compoſed of Unity ſo often taken, and exhauſted by Unity ſo often taken away, *i. e.* is exquiſitely divided

and

and meaſured by it; ſo correſpondently the Quantity expreſſed by any Number (*i. e.* according to the Exigence of that Number diſtributed into ſo many Particles, anſwering to Unity) is meaſured by any Particle which is deſigned by Unity.

Here ſeems to be nothing of Difficulty or Obſcurity: and the Quantities compared with reſpect to ſuch a *Meaſure* are by Geometricians wont to be called *Symmetrous* or *Aſſymmetrous*, i. e. *Commenſurable* or *Incommenſurable*, and ſcarce any Thing in the Mathematics is more wonderful or more uſeful than the Contemplation of thoſe Properties, though nothing more remote from a vulgar Capacity and Conception. *Ariſtotle* obſerves, in an Inſtance taken hence, how much the Admiration of the unſkilful Multitude does differ and oppoſe the Opinion of learned and knowing Men; for the *Aſſymmetry* or *Incommenſurability* of the Diameter of a Square with its Side is reckoned among thoſe Things, which the Vulgar do eſpecially wonder at. *It (a) ſeems wonderful to all that a great Thing cannot be exhauſted by any very ſmall meaſure of another homogeneous Quantity*; *but on the contrary, a Geometrician would wonder at nothing more than if this did not happen.* *Plato* pathetically laments the common Ignorance of this Property, which he alſo calls a *ridiculous and ſhameful Ignorance reſting in the Minds of moſt Men:* And he ſeems to ſay that the Want of this Perception is not ſo much human as brutiſh. *I have wondered*, ſays (*b*) he, *at our Affection about theſe Things, and to me it ſeems not to be human, but rather an Affection of brute Beaſts.* Therefore he profeſſes himſelf aſhamed for the Sake of all his Countrymen, becauſe moſt of them were ignorant of ſo obvious a Property of Quantities; and being rather carried away with

(*a*) Met. I. 2. (*b*) Plato VII. de Leg. versùs Finem.

a contrary

a contrary Errour thought all Magnitudes of the ſame Kind to be *commenſurable. I am aſhamed*, ſays he, *not for my ſelf only, but alſo for all Grecians*, &c. Let us then take up a little Time in contemplating this wonderful Property.

As to *Symmetry* or *Commenſurability*, with the vulgar and foreign Writers it ſometimes denotes a due Quantity of any Thing conſtituted within determinate Bounds, agreeable to its Nature. Thus *Ariſtotle* (*c*) in his *Ethics. An over plentiful* (ſays he) *as well as over ſparing Quantity of Drinkables and Eatables do equally injure and deſtroy the Health, but a* commenſurable *Share does help, increaſe and preſerve it.* Where *Commenſurable* does ſignify moderate, convenient, neither exceeding nor falling ſhort of its due Quantity. Alſo *Plato* in his *Politics* ſays, *ſecondly, concerning what is commenſurate and beautiful and perfect and convenient.* Where *Commenſurate* is of kin to *Beautiful, Perfect*, and *Convenient*, which ſhew how it is taken. But the *Symmetry* of a Thing compoſed of various Parts does more often deſign a *decorous* and *apt Agreement* or *Conformity* in the Parts to one another, in which the *Beauty* and *Elegance* of Things does principally conſiſt: wherefore ſuch a *Symmetry* is chiefly conſidered in *Architecture*, and is thus defined by *Vitruvius* (*d*), *Symmetry is a convenient Conſent from the Members of the Work itſelf, and from the Parts ſeparated to the Appearance of the whole Figure, anſwerable to a Part ſuppoſed.* According to which Acceptations, it plainly appears on the contrary what is *Aſſymmetry* or *Incommenſurability*, viz. an *enormous, diſproportionate, diſagreeable, exceſſive*, or *defective Quantity of a Thing*. But paſſing by thoſe vulgar Acceptations;

(*c*) Eth. II. 2. (*d*) Vitruv. I. 2.

Secondly,

Secondly, *Symmetry* or *Commensurability* does sometimes denote any *Comparability together*, *as to Quantity*, of Magnitudes, or other Quantities; so that according to the other more extensive Acceptation of the Word *Measure* this signifies *to compare the Quantities of Things together*, *or to investigate the Proportion of an unknown Quantity to a known one.* In which sense *Symmetrous* is all one with *Homogeneous*; and *Assymmetrous* with *Heterogeneous*; as far as all Quantities of the same Kind are proportional to one another, and consequently are this Way *commensurable*; but Quantities of a different Kind have no Proportion to one another, and consequently can be no Way *commensurate.* Thus all Lines are *symmetrous* to one another, but a Line in respect of a Superfice, a Body, Time, Velocity, or Weight is *assymmetrous.*

But commonly among Geometricians those Quantities are more strictly called *commensurable*, which may be measured by the same homogeneous Quantity, *i. e.* perfectly divided so as to have no Remainder, and are quite exhausted by a continued Subtraction of it: or the same Quantity of which is an aliquot Part of both: or which is as one Number to another of that Kind, ascribing Unity to Numbers. Thus an *Inch*, a *Foot*, and a *Pace*, are *commensurate* Lines, because an *Inch* taken once makes itself, taken twelve Times makes a *Foot*, and sixty Times a *Pace*: or because those Longitudes are to one another as the Numbers 1, 12, 60. So also in Money a *Mark* and a *Pound* are *commensurate* because a *Groat* (or the third Part of a *Shilling*) measures both, *viz.* taken forty Times it makes a *Mark*, and sixty Times a *Pound*, or because they are to one another as 2 and 3. In Times, the *Cycle* of the *Sun* is *commensurate* with the *Cycle* of the *Moon*, because the former is to the latter

latter as 28 to 19, and one Year meaſures both. But theſe Things are plain enough.

Thoſe Quantities are *Incommenſurate* of which no common *Meaſure*, though ever ſo ſmall, can at all be found; there being none ſuch in the Nature of Things, which can compleatly divide both without a Remainder, or which may have any Proportion explicable by Numbers integer or fracted: conſequently if one of them be expreſſed by any Number, the other will be entirely inexplicable. A moſt famous and notorious Example of which Affection is that of the Side and Diameter of a Square, which are ſo affected together that no Line, though ever ſo ſmall, can meaſure both. But if the thouſand thouſandth Part of one, *ex. gr.* the Side be applied to the Diameter, or taken from it, as often as it can, there will always ſomething remain, and the Congruity or Diviſion can never be compleat. And this is that wonderful Property which almoſt exceeds human Capacity, and ſo puzzles ſuch as are unaccuſtomed with theſe Things; which perhaps will yet ſeem more wonderful, if we conſider the Obſervations we ſhall ſubjoin.

Firſt, That, if two *incommenſurable* Quantities A and B be propoſed, a Quantity may be found commenſurable, *ex. gr.* to A in any Proximity to B, or whoſe Difference from B is leſs than any aſſignable Quantity; which may eaſily be demonſtrated and inferred (if I remember well) from a Lemma demonſtrated in the third Book of *Theodoſius's Spherics:* From whence it appears that that, whatſoever it be, from which this (*e*) *Incommenſurability* ariſes, and by which an *Incommenſurable* Quantity exceeds or falls ſhort of another *Commenſurable* one by a Quantity expounded will be

(*e*) Vide Cavall. Exerc. p. 526.

infinitely

infinitely little, *i. e.* leſs than any Quantity aſſignable or comprehenſible to the Mind: Which is alſo equally manifeſt from the Extraction of the Roots of ſuch Numbers as are called *Irrational:* For there an Approach is always made nearer and nearer the true Value of the Root ſought, and yet the juſt Value can never be obtained.

Secondly, and eſpecially, That Quantities are not only ſimply *incommenſurable* but alſo ſeem to admit many (perhaps infinite) Degrees of *Incommenſurability*; ſo that one Quantity in reſpect of any Quantity expounded may be farther removed from *Commenſurability* than another, and another than this, and ſo on, till we come to ſome extreme, which is infinitely diſtant from the firſt. *Euclid* has obſerved that certain Lines are incommenſurable to any Line expounded not only in Length, but, which is more, even in Power: and alſo that the Biquadrates of ſome Lines are incommenſurable to the Biquadrate of a Line expounded, and reſpectively all the Superior Powers of theſe to the coordinate Powers of that. Therefore if a Power denominated by a Number at an infinite Diſtance from Unity be *incommenſurable* to an expounded Power reſpectively coordinate, the former ſeems to have infinite Degrees of *Incommenſurability* with reſpect to the latter. And thus the Circumference of a Circle ſeems to be with Reſpect to the Radius. For the Side of the inſcribed Square is *incommenſurable* to the Radius in Length, and conſequently the Ambit of the Square is *incommenſurable* to the Radius. Alſo the *Square* of the inſcribed *Octagon* is *incommenſurable* to the *Square* of the *Radius*, and conſequently the *Square* of the *Octogonal Perimeter* is *incommenſurable* to the *Square* of *Radius*. And thus the Ambits of all *regular Polygons* inſcribed in a Circle have their ſuperior Powers *incommenſurate* with the coordinate Powers of *Radius*; from whence the

the laſt of theſe *Polygons*, *i. e.* the Circle itſelf does ſeem to have its Perimeter infinitely *incommenſurable* with the *Radius*. Which if true, will put a final End to the *Quadrature* of the Circle, ſince the *Proportion* of the *Circumference* to the *Radius* is thence altogether *inexplicable* from the Nature of the Thing, and conſequently that Problem, requiring the Explication of ſuch a Proportion, is impoſſible to be ſolved; or rather it requires that for its Solution, which is impoſſible to be apprehended. For a Problem is reſolved in two Points, *viz.* either by ſhewing what it is, and how that may be done, which is required; or by diſcovering that it cannot be done. But this great Myſtery cannot be explained in a few Words; if Time and Opportunity had permitted, I would have endeavoured to produce many Things for the Explication and Confirmation of this Conjecture.

Laſtly, not to be any longer tedious, I would only admoniſh you farther, that the principal Reaſon of *Incommenſurability* ſeems to be founded in this, that ſince a *Mean Proportional Number* may always be found between two plane ſimilar Numbers (*i. e.* between ſuch as are generated from the Multiplication of *proportional Numbers*) becauſe the Product made by the Multiplication of plane ſimilar Numbers is always a Square Number, whoſe Root is that *Mean Proportional*; alſo between two ſimilar ſolid Numbers there always lie two *Mean Proportionals*: And by a like Reaſon between two ſimilar Plano-plane Numbers are three *Mean Proportionals*, and ſo on continually as to all other imaginary Dimenſions beyond; ſince I ſay, Things are thus in ſimilar Numbers, and it is demonſtrated in the *Elements*, that it happens quite otherwiſe in all diſſimilar Numbers; (for on the Part of the Thing there is no *Mean Proportional* Number between two diſſimilar plane Numbers, nor

between

between two diſſimilar ſolid Numbers, nor between two diſſimilar Plano-plane Numbers, and ſo on, which is alſo there ſhewn;) hence, if two Quantities are ſuppoſed to be to one another in the Reaſon of two plane diſſimilar Numbers, and a *Mean Proportional* be found between thoſe Quantities, which may perpetually be done, becauſe of the indefinite Diviſibility of every Quantity, there will be no Number in univerſal Nature which can repreſent or anſwer to this Quantity, and conſequently, thoſe being ſuppoſed and expreſſed by Numbers, this will be *incommenſurable.* By the ſame Argument, if two *Mean Proportional* Quantities be found between two Quantities expreſſed by diſſimilar ſolid Numbers (which the Nature of the Thing will permit to be done) the whole Series of Numbers, how great ſoever it be, will afford no Number capable of repreſenting them; and conſequently theſe, in reſpect of the Quantities expounded, will be altogether *ineffable* and *incommenſurable.*

From whence it appears by the Way, how much more infinitely narrow, and as it were poor, the *Nature* of *Numbers* is, than of all other Quantities; for comparatively ſpeaking, *rational* or *common Numbers* do ſuffice for expreſſing but very few Quantities: and both the Sides and Areas of moſt regular Figures are no otherwiſe to be exhibited and explicated than by *Surds* and *irrational Numbers.* But we can only now hint at theſe Things curſorily and in Haſte, which require a larger Explication.

Nothing now remains, but that I return my due Acknowledgments of Gratitude to you, my moſt judicious and courteous Auditors, for your great Patience and kind Indulgence of theſe Things of leſs Conſequence during the whole Courſe of this long Term. I wiſh what is to come may be more worthy your ſo benign and candid Attention, and more acceptable to your Deſires ; that it may more delight your ingenious Curioſity, and ſet a greater Edge upon our own poor Induſtry. In the mean Time I bid, I heartily wiſh you farewel, and ſo recommend you to the good God.

The Lectures hitherto are writ as they were read publickly, the Order being no where interrupted ; I now break the Series. For ſince I am neither obliged, nor able to exhibit all in fewer than ten Lectures at leaſt, by Reaſon of the Greatneſs of the Labour and Want of Time ; I have purpoſed to annex the three laſt to ſome few yet remaining.

FINIS.

MATHEMATICAL

LECTURES

Read in the

University of *Cambridge*,

An. Dom. MDCLXVI.

MATHEMATICAL LECTURES.

LECTURE XVI.

Of the Homogeneity and Heterogeneity of Quantities.

MOST learned Auditors, I am glad to find you in Health, and wiſh you a long Continuance of it, and without further Preface apply to my Taſk, proceeding in my former Method. I ſuppoſe you remember we propoſed to treat of the *General Affections* of Magnitudes, and of other Quantities from thence. A few of which having already diligently enquired into, as well as I am able, I have now reached nigh the very Soul of the Mathematics, *viz.* to *Proportionality*, on which almoſt every Thing depends in the Mathematics which is wonderful and abſtruſe. But ſince *Proportionality* conſiſts in the Compariſon of Proportions, and Proportion in the Compariſon of Quantities, it ſeems expedient by way of Preparation to conſider the *Comparability* of Quantities, eſpecially that which is requiſite to *Proportion*. For all Quantities cannot be ſo compared together, as to be ſaid to have a *mutual Proportion*, but only theſe that more nearly touch one another in a peculiar

liar Respect, for which Cause they are wont to be called *Homogeneous*.

We come now therefore to treat of the *Homogeneity* and *Heterogeneity* of Quantities. And it is here first to be noted, that besides the common Attributes, which agree with all Quantities distinguishing them from what is void of Quantity (*viz.* all Kinds of *Extension*, *Divisibility*, *Mensurability*, and the *like Affections*,) there are other Differences which distinguish Quantities from one another, and distribute them into subordinate *Genera* or Kinds; so that all those Quantities which are contained under one of those Kinds are called *Homogeneous*, and those under different Kinds *Heterogeneous*. Which subordinate Kinds of Quantities disposed as so many Classes and Predicaments of Quantity, almost the same way under Quantity as the common Predicaments under Entity; are very different from one another, having nothing common or similar beside the general Affections of Quantity: But the Agreement and general Reason of the Diversity of these is the Aptitude or Ineptitude, Capacity or Incapacity of Quantities to a Composition or Coalition into some Whole, or to a Subtraction or Constitution of a new Remainder: or, if I may so speak, it is the Addibility or Inaddibility of one Quantity to another, the Subducibility or Non-subducibility of one from another: or it is the comprehensibly certain Excess of one above the other, or Defect of one below the other; or it is the Incapacity of such an Excess or Defect, and hence of the Equality or Inequality of one with Respect to the other: In these Things, I say, with their Concomitants or Consequents is founded the Reason of *Homogeneity* and *Heterogeneity* respectively. For of the Things which are so affected, that they may be Parts of one Quantity conceiveable by itself, that they may be gathered into one Sum, aug-

ment

ment one another by Addition, or diminiſh by Subſtraction, differ from one another by a certain Exceſs or Defect, and may be properly and fitly ſaid one to be equal to, greater, or leſſer, than another, theſe are *Homogeneous* pertaining to the ſame Claſſes of Quantities comparable to one another: And what are otherwiſe are *Heterogeneous*, and to be referred to different and unlike Tribes. But if we purſue farther into the Original of this Diverſity, and examine whence ſuch an *Incomparability* of Quantities does ariſe; we will find it to proceed nearly from theſe Cauſes.

Firſt, from the very different Nature of certain Quantities, by which it happens that they cannot be ſubject to one *common Meaſure*, that may equally agree with both; nay, the Mind itſelf can no way connect or conceive them as one determinate uniform Compound; nor any way compare them together according to Equality or Inequality, Exceſs or Defect. Thus *ex. gr.* Magnitude, Weight, Velocity, Time, Reſiſtance, and Force are *Heterogeneous* and not to be compared together, becauſe they are ſo different in Nature that they meaſure nothing in common, nor can any of them be connected together, be congruous, or enter any Compound not very deformed and chimerical; they cannot be adequate, exceed or fall ſhort of one another, or any way be conceived to affect one another in Reſpect of their Quantity. For who can underſtand what is the Sum of two Years added to three Miles; or how much three Ounces of Weight exceeds two Minutes of Time; or what remains after the Deduction of four Degrees of Velocity from three Cylinders? No more can any Number of Muſical Tones be equal to ſo many Rays of Light, or the ſame Number of Smells to ſo many Colours. Their huge Diſſimilitude and Diſtance of Nature hinders them from being any intelligible

Way

Way referred to one another according to Quantity. The Quantity of Magnitude is continued, ſimultaneous, abſolute, and obvious to the Senſes: The Quantity of Time, vaniſhing, ſucceſſive, imaginable only in the Mind, conſequent and ſignificative of Motion: The Quantity of Velocity depends upon the conjunct Reaſons of Time and Space: Weight, Force, and Reſiſtance imply certain Actions and are eſtimated from certain Affections: ſo diſſonant are theſe to one another that they cannot poſſibly be conjoined into one. This is the firſt and principal Cauſe of *Heterogeneity.*

A *ſecond Reaſon* of this Difference is fetched from the various Degrees of Perfection as to Quantity; as ſome Quantities are extended and may be divided more ways than others, ſo that theſe are ſcarce Quantities in Reſpect of thoſe, and conſequently cannot be compared with them according to Quantity. Thus a Superfice is more ways diviſible than a Line, and a Body than a Superfice, nor is a Line any otherwiſe to a Superfice, and a Superfice to a Body, than a Point to a Line, *i. e.* than an Indiviſible to a Diviſible, or a Non-Quantity to a Quantity: For a Line is Nothing in Reſpect of a Superfice but as it were a long Point; and a Superfice is nothing in Reſpect of a Body but a broad Line, or a long broad Point. Therefore a Line, a Superfice, and a Body are not to be referred to one another, and conſequently are *Heterogeneous.* For thence it comes to paſs, that theſe cannot be compared together according to Equality or Inequality, nor ſo compounded as to make any Sum, nor one ſubtracted from another ſo as to have any Difference reſulting, *i. e.* being added they can beget no Encreaſe, nor deducted Decreaſe. The ſame Reaſon holds of Inſtants in reſpect of Time; of the Degrees of an encreaſing Velocity which are acquired in particular Inſtants in in Reſpect of the whole Velocity ; and of Momentary Conatus's in reſpect of Motion, Weight, and Power.

A third Origin yet of this Diverſity is an indefinite and incomprehenſible Reſpect of one Quantity to another, ſuch as between Things finite and infinite, or Things otherwiſe cognate in Name and Nature. From whence a finite Right Line and an infinite one are accounted of different Kinds, though in an infinite Right Line may be found every finite one, and that may be eſteemed as conſtituted of this infinitely repeated. Hence that celebrated Principle of (*a*) *Ariſtotle*, that there is no *Proportion of a finite to an infinite :* The Truth of which Sentence or Axiom the Sagacity of modern Geometricians ſeem in part to have broken ; while they demonſtrate a juſt Proportion and even Equality it ſelf of innumerable Planes and Solids produced *ad infinitum* with other finite Planes and Solids : which Prodigy that famous Geometrician *Torricellius* did firſt of all exhibit. From whence it appears that infinite Magnitudes are ſometimes *Homogeneous* with finite ones, ſince they are ſometimes equal to theſe, and ſometimes fall ſhort of them. Or from hence rather it may be inferred, that every Thing without Limits is not infinite in Quantity ; or yet more plainly, that the Infinity of a Superfice or Body does not always follow from an Infinity of one Dimenſion. The Reaſon of which ſeems not very difficult ; for it happens becauſe the infinite Diminution of one Dimenſion recompenſes the infinite Augmentation of the other. It is not therefore ſo much beyond Belief for a finite Magnitude however ſmall to be extended in Length *ad infinitum*. Therefore that it may hold univerſally, the before noted Axiom ought to be thus explained :

(*a*) De Cœlo I. 6.

There

There is no Proportion of a Thing finite in Magnitude or Quantity to a Thing infinite in Magnitude or Quantity of the ſame Genus. But we are not to underſtand in general, that there is no Reaſon between a limited Figure and an unlimited Magnitude. From theſe Roots ſprings the *Heterogeneity* of Quantities, and thoſe Things which on the contrary agree together, which by Nature are not ſo diſſimilar, nor conſtituted in a different Degree of Quantity, nor infinitely ſevered from one another, thoſe, I ſay, are *Homogeneous.*

But *Euclid* in the Definitions of his fifth Book defines *Homogeneous* Quantities to be theſe, one of which (*viz.* the leſſer) being ſome Number of Times taken or multiplied may exceed the other. The third Definition of that Book is ſuch: *Reaſon is a certain Habitude of two Magnitudes Homogeneous to each other*, *according to Quantity.* And, leſt any one ſhould doubt what he underſtands by *Homogeneous* Magnitudes, he ſubjoins; *Magnitudes are ſaid to have a Reaſon to one another when one being multiplied is capable to exceed the other.* Where our *Element Compiler* (as a moſt learned and famous Man in my Opinion rightly obſerves, in his Diſputation againſt *Meibomius*) delivers not theſe (as others beſide *Meibomius* expound, and, which I wonder at, the ſagacious *Clavius* ſeems to encline to, though elſewhere he ſpeaks differently) to ſhew what *Homogeneous* Magnitudes have a Reaſon to one another, as if ſome had none; but rather, what Magnitudes are *Homogeneous*, leſt any ſhould be deceived or held in Suſpenſe with the Obſcurity of that Word in the foregoing Definition. For when he there defines *Proportion to be the Relation or Habitude of Homogeneous Magnitudes*, indefinitely ſpeaking, he ſufficiently intimates, that he underſtands *Homogeneous Magnitudes* univerſally, and not only *certain particular Magnitudes*; otherwiſe,

if

if he had not thought that all *Homogeneous* Quantities are *mutually proportional*, it would have been out of the Way for him to insert them in his Definition as the Subject of *Proportion*; and it would have been more right for him to have excluded those, and put some adequate Subject in their Place. He will therefore have all *Homogeneous Quantities* to be affected with *Proportion* to one another; therefore two Lines, one finite and the other infinite, (though Lines do in general agree,) are not *Homogeneous* in *Euclid*'s Opinion; because a finite Line, how often soever taken, will never exceed an infinite One; and the same happens in every finite Respect of every other Thing infinite in Quantity (I say in Quantity not local Extension, as was before insinuated;) and in like manner it plainly appears that Points, Lines, Superficies and Bodies are *Homogeneous*; seeing that innumerable Myriads of Points cannot exceed one of the smallest Lines, nor a Million Million Superficies transcend one of the most minute Corpuscles. So also *plane cornicular Angles or Angles of Contact*, if they be Angles, or any kind of Quantity (each of which Assertions is doubted and denied by famous Mathematicians, concerning which I determine nothing at present) I say, if these *cornicular Divergences* which are made by the meeting of Right Lines with Curves, be truly Angles, and endowed with Quantity, at least they will not be *Homogeneous* with rectilineal Angles, because every the least and the most acute rectilineal Angle infinitely exceeds an innumerable Number of these Cornicular ones: As *Euclid* has demonstrated concerning the *Angle of Contact* made by a Tangent with the Periphery of a Circle; *Apollonius*, concerning those made between Tangents and the Conic Sections; and (*b*) *Archi-*

(*b*) *At least it follows from his Demonstrations.*

medes,

medes, concerning thoſe made between a ſpiral with its Tangent; and our ſelves may do the ſame, by one only univerſal Demonſtration fetched from a Compoſition of Motions, concerning all Curve Lines bended towards the ſame Parts; ſo that thoſe Angles of Contact are no otherwiſe to rectilineal Angles, than a Point to a Line, or a Line to a Superfice.

But all *finite Lines* however diſſimilar are *homogeneous* to one another, not only Right Lines to Right Lines, but Curve Lines to Right Lines, and all Curve Lines to one another; though as far as it does not appear concerning the determinate Proportions of moſt Curve Lines to Right Lines as of the Circumference of a Circle or Elipſis to ſome Diameter, it may be doubtful what is the Proportion between them; becauſe *ex. gr.* the Diameter of a Circle taken four times exceeds the Circumference. Moreover the preſent Age has this to glory in, that the *Proportion* of certain Curve Lines to Right Lines is now diſcovered with admirable Subtilty, and plainly demonſtrated; which was thought by former Geometricians impoſſible to be inveſtigated. In like manner all *finite Superficies* are Homogeneous, even Planes with Curve Superficies, becauſe the Proportion of theſe to thoſe is not only poſſible but eaſy to be demonſtrated; as it is ſhewn by *Archimedes* to what circular plane Area the curve Superfice of a right Cone, a right Cylinder, a Sphere or any Portion of a Sphere is equal. And the ſame Way are all *finite Solids homogeneous.* Nay, if Angles are at all Quantities and participate of Equality or Proportion (which as we have ſaid is doubtful) even rectilineal Angles will be *homogeneous* to ſome curvilineal ones, in this Senſe, becauſe ſome of theſe are demonſtrated equal to ſome of thoſe, *viz.* by *Proclus* in his *third Book* at the *twelfth Axiom.* However all rectilineal Angles are

homogeneous

homogeneous to one another. Theſe Things ſeemed ſo manifeſt to *Archimedes*, that he doubted not to aſſume this for a Truth that *Every determinate Magnitude may be as many Ways added to itſelf, or multiplied, as to exceed any other Magnitude of the ſame Claſſis.* To which *Clavius* premiſes a like Poſtulate in the *tenth Element. Let it be required that every Magnitude may be ſo often multiplied, till it may exceed any Magnitude of the ſame Kind.* Nor is it leſs manifeſt that all *finite Times* are *homogeneous*, becauſe the ſhorteſt Space of Duration being often repeated will exceed the longeſt Interval leſs than Eternity. Alſo all *Velocities* are homogeneous, for the ſloweſt Degree of *Velocity*, being often enough repeated, will tranſcend the moſt rapid *Velocity* of the *Primum Mobile.* But an *infinite Velocity* ſeems inconſiſtent; for a moveable Body endowed with ſuch a Velocity would meaſure any Diſtance in one Inſtant, and conſequently would poſſeſs more Places than one at the ſame Time, *i. e.* would be congruous to a Space exceeding itſelf, how great ſoever it be, which ſeems impoſſible. Again all *Numbers* are *homogeneous* to one another, as they are all fit to repreſent Magnitudes of the ſame Kind; even ſuch as may be accounted *heterogeneous*, as they are applied for expreſſing Quantities of a different Kind; nay every Number however *heterogeneous* it be to itſelf, as the ſame does repreſent *heterogeneous* Quantities; for there is no Number which may not be Linear, Plane, Solid, Plano-plane, Plano-ſolid, Solido-ſolid, or be conceived under all Dimenſions whatſoever, whether natural or fictitious, at the Pleaſure of the Computant. Laſtly all *Weights*, are *homogeneous*, aſſigning Gravity to ſolid Bodies only, as in reality it only is in Phyſics; For if Gravity be attributed like Magnitude to Lines and Superficies, as Geometricians ſuppoſe, when they inveſtigate the Centers of

Gravity

Gravity to a Triangle, Parallelogram, plane Parabola, and other plane Figures; alſo to the Superfice of a Sphere, Cone, Cylinder, and other curve Superficies; and to all Lines whether curved or compounded Right Lines; this, I ſay, being ſuppoſed, all *Weights* are not *homogeneous*, but only theſe that are of Magnitudes of the ſame Kinds. Whence (*c*) *Ariſtotle* ſeems to reprehend *Plato* not undeſervedly, becauſe, in his *Timæus*, he imputes the Differences or Exceſſes of Bodies in Gravity to a Multitude of Superficies. For how many ſoever the Gravities may be of Superficies, they cannot conſtitute or be encreaſed to the Gravity of an aggregate Body, ſince they are of a different Kind, and therefore are unſuitable. Nor indeed have all theſe Things any other Tendency but to inſtruct us what Quantums may be compared together as to Quantity; for there is no Fault greater in Geometry than to ſeek or aſſert the Proportion of *Heterogeneous* Quantities to one another. As if one enquire how many Right Lines are equal to ſuch a Square, how many circular Peripheries do make ſuch a Circle, how many Squares ſuch a Cube, or how many Times ſuch a Space or Weight. From whence *Vieta* that great Maſter of *Analytics* preſcribed this Law to be firſt obſerved in all analytical Diſquiſitions. (*d*) *Let that be the firſt and perpetual Law of Equalities or Proportions, which becauſe it is conceived of Homogeneals, is called the Law of Homogeneals, and is this, that Homogeneals are compared with Homogeneals* (i. e. excluſively with them only.) (*e*) *For* (as he goes on) *thoſe Things which are heterogeneous, it cannot be conceived how they can be affected one with another, as ſaid Adraſtus.*

It is true that ſuch Expreſſions do often occur with thoſe that apply the excellent Method of Indi-

(*c*) De Cœlo III. 1. (*d*) Iſag. cap. III. (*e*) Cap. xix.

viſibles

visibles to the Solution of Problems or Demonstration of Theorems: All those parallel Lines are equal to such a Plane, the Sum of those parallel Planes constitutes such a Solid; but they explain their Meaning, and say that they understand nothing by Lines, but Parallelograms of a very small, and (pardon the Expression) inconsiderable Altitude, and by Planes nothing but Prisms or Cylinders of an Altitude not to be computed: Or at least, by a Sum of Lines and Planes, they denote no finite and determinate, but an infinite or indefinite Sum equal in Number to the Points of some Right Line. From which sort of infinite Sum of inferior *Homogeneals* if any one assert a superior *Homogeneal* to be composed (*viz.* from an Infinity of Right Lines a plane Superfice, of concentric Peripheries a plane Circle, of plane or curve Superficies a solid Body,) which the great *Gallilæus* doubted not to assert, he will easily be convinced of Error, or contradicted. But however, passing by this Controversy, that Use can be no Offence to our Doctrine; for this Precept is of irrefragable Force in the Opinion even of those who embrace that Method with both Arms, *viz. That Things heterogeneous cannot be compared together by a definite Quantity or Number.*

Which Thing though it be so apparently true and in the highest Sense agreeable to Reason, yet our Countryman Mr. *Hobbs* (as I have already shewn in Part) has lately controverted it, and as much as he was able covered a Thing so clear in a thick Mist. He feared not to compare *Lines* and *Times* together, as *homogeneous Quantities* obtaining a *mutual Proportion*, though Things of the most distant Nature. For because Longitudes run through by Motions of equal Celerity are to one another as the *Times*: *By Permutation*, says (*f*) he, *it will be*,

(*f*) De Corp. cap. 16.

as

as a Time is to a Longitude, ſo is a Time to a Longitude. As if he ſhould ſay, Becauſe a Furlong is to a Thouſand Paces, as one Hour to eight Hours; Therefore permutably, as a Furlong is to an Hour, ſo is a Thouſand Paces to eight Hours; than which kind of Argumentation nothing can be more abſurdly ridiculous, as any one may eaſily perceive. The ſame Perſon ſays in the Dialogues wherein he profeſſes to examine and amend the modern Mathematics (but I wiſh he had more diligently examined and amended his own; (g) *As the Quantity of a Weight will be to the Length of the Line which repreſents it, ſo will the Quantity of twice the Weight be to the Length of twice the Line repreſenting it.* And being reminded of this Error by his Opponent, inſtead of laying it aſide, he coined new Definitions and Acceptations of Words in his own Excuſe or Defence, as well leſs conſonant one with another, as more remote from common Uſe, and for the moſt Part repugnant to his own Concluſions, and deviſed ſtrange Pretences contrary to all pure Reaſon, which it will not be foreign to the purpoſe to ſhew, in a few Words, both for the ſake of illuſtrating the Matter in Hand, and to prevent others from falling unwarily into the like Faults, by ſhewing how circumſpectly all ought to behave in theſe Things. He defines *Meaſure* this Way; (h) *Meaſure is one Magnitude of another, when it, or its Multiple, being applied to another coincides with it.* And again in Words a little different, but in the ſame Senſe; (i) *Meaſure is a Magnitude of a Magnitude, a leſſer of a greater, or not a leſſer, when the leſſer being once or oftner applied to it is equal to it.* According to which Definitions it appears, that *Meaſure* is nothing elſe but ſome Part of a Thing meaſured, which being ſome Number of

(g) Dial 3. p. 80. (h) Dial 1. p. 11. (i) Dial. 2. p. 43.

Times

Times taken, ſo exhauſts the Whole, as to leave no Remainder, as the Words (*k*) μετρον, μετρεῖν, καταμετρεῖν are moſtly or always accepted in the *Elements*, as has been ſhewn. Moreover he defines (*l*) *Homogeneous Quantities to be thoſe, one of whoſe Meaſures may be applied to the other, ſo that they may be congruous: And whoſe Meaſures are accommodated to one another.* But Meaſures, as was juſt now ſeen, are with him, the Aliquot Parts of Quantities. Therefore to make him conſiſtent with himſelf, thoſe Quantities will be *homogeneous* whoſe *aliquot Parts* are capable of Congruence. But the *aliquot Parts* of a Quantity of Time are no other than Quantities of Time, nor of Weight than Quantities of Weight, nor of a Line than Quantities of a Line, nor of a Body than of a Body. Therefore ſince none can conceive how a Quantity of a Line can be applied to a Quantity of Time (*viz.* the Quantity of a Line of one Cubit to the Quantity of a Year of Time, or an Ounce of Weight) ſo as to agree or coincide with it; therefore Lines will not be *homogeneous Quantities* of Time and Weight, according to his own Definitions and Hypotheſes. Thus would common Logic infer, but with a ſtrange Sagacity he concludes the contrary; *Becauſe* (ſays (*m*) he) *a Quantity of Time may be meaſured by a Line, and a Line may be applied to a Line, therefore a Quantity of Time will be homogeneous to a Quantity of a Line.* Behold the Source from whence moſt of the Abſurdities flow with which theſe Dialogues abound. *Becauſe a Quantity of Time*, ſays he, *may be meaſured by a Line:* But pray, ingenious Sir, be pleaſed to look back at your own Definition, and ſee whether according to it, a Line can be a *Meaſure* of Time, or (becauſe you rather love to ſpeak more intricately) a Quantity of Time, *i. e.* whether a

(*k*) Pag. 110. (*l*) Dial. 3. p. 80. (*m*) Dial. 5. p. 110.

Line

Line can be any *Aliquot Part* of a Quantity of Time, or a Quantity of Time be made up of Lines, or a Line be a Quantity of Time (for an aliquot Part of a Quantity of Time is an aliquot Part of Time;) and by a like Reaſon whether a Line be an aliquot Part of a Superfice, of a Body, a Weight, or any other Quantity; or whether all Quantities may not be altogether compoſed of Lines, *viz.* whether or no the Quantity of a Year or a Month, an Ounce or a Pound, a Square or a Cubic Foot, are Lines, or conſtituted of Lines: Or if you advance any of theſe Things will you not juſtly make your ſelf ridiculous to him that hears you? But this learned Man has not conſidered enough how much he departs from his own Definition in the Uſe of the Word *Meaſure*, and thereby miniſters the Occaſion of his own falling; and when he calls a Line ſo often taken a *Meaſure* of Time, Weight, or of any other Quantity, he cannot mean that a Line is an *Aliquot Part* of a Time, a Weight, a Motion, or a Body, or that a Line can be congruous with theſe; but *Meaſure* is uſed in the more looſe Signification, according to which, as we have more diſtinctly explained heretofore, *Meaſure* does often deſign *any Thing, which may either conveniently repreſent or any Way notifie another.* In which twofold reſpect a Line (eſpecially a right or circular Line, becauſe of their Simplicity and Uniformity) is wont to be called the *Meaſure* of Time, Weight, Velocity, or of any Quantity whatſoever. For becauſe every *Reaſon* of Quantities may be expreſſed by *Right Lines*, therefore *Right Lines* are moſt commodiouſly applied for repreſenting them; as *ex. gr.* for two Solids, one of which is in Proportion to the other, as $\sqrt{2}$ to 1, or as the Diameter of a Square to its ſide, (when nothing is to be conſidered but their *Proportion*,) may be ſubſtituted two *Right Lines* exhibiting their Reaſon: And by like Reaſon

Reaſon may two *Right Lines* be aſſumed for exhibiting the *Reaſons* of two Times or two Weights; and ſo far may thoſe Lines in the wideſt Acceptation be called the *Meaſures* of theſe Quantities: In which Senſe Numbers are the *moſt common* and *uſual Meaſures* of *commenſurable Quantities*, expreſſing their *Reaſons*, and being ſubſtituted for them in a Courſe of arguing. And not only Lines, but even any Quantity whatſoever may be a *Meaſure* in Reſpect of any other: for as every Quantity may be repreſented by a Right Line taken at Pleaſure, ſo may it be equally deſigned by any Superfice, Body, Letter, Character, or Name. A *Right Line* then obtains, (and by like Reaſon every other Magnitude may obtain) the Name of a *Meaſure* ſtill more properly, though at the greateſt Diſtance from Mr. *Hobbs*'s Definition, as it may ſerve for determining or declaring the Quantity of other Quantums; as the Longitude of the Line, which any moveable Thing runs through in any aſſigned Time, declares and diſcovers its Velocity and conſequently its Meaſure; and a circular Arch intercepted between the Legs of a rectilineal Angle ſhews *i. e. meaſures* (according to this Acceptation of the Word *to meaſure*, which we have largely explained already) the Quantity of the Angle. If therefore he with whom we are contending had throughly perceived or weighed this Ambiguity of the Word *Meaſure*; or if he had ſtuck more conſtantly to his own Definition: I imagine he would not thus have confounded the Quantities of all Things and pronounced them *homogeneous* to one another in the Strength of ſuch an Argument. Becauſe a *Line*, he argues is a *Meaſure* of *Time*, the *Quantity* of *Time* will be *homogeneous* to the *Quantity of a Line*. But I anſwer a *Line* may be called the *Meaſure* of *Time* by taking a *Meaſure* for a Symbol, Argument, or Index of the Quantity which

which *Time* has; but taking *Meaſure* according to his Definition for an *Aliquot Part*, it ſufficiently appears, nor does he deny, that a *Line* is not the *Meaſure* of *Time*, and conſequently even according to his own Definition of an *Homogeneal*, the *Quantity* of a *Line* will not be *homogeneous* to a *Quantity* of *Time*. Nay by the ſame Argument with which he goes about to prove that the *Quantities* of *Time* and a *Line* are *homogeneous*, it is equally concluded that the ſame are *heterogeneous*, *viz.* becauſe a *Quantity* of *Time* may be *meaſured* (i. e. deſigned, declared, or notified) by a *Parallelogram* or a *Cylinder*; and a *Line* cannot be congruous to a *Parallelogram* or *Cylinder*, according to his Definition of *Heterogeneity*, therefore they are *heterogeneous* to the Quantity of a Line. Nay farther all Quantities whatſoever are both *homogeneous* and *heterogeneous* at the ſame Time: for *They* (ſays (*n*) he) *are homogeneous which are meaſurable by the ſame Kind of Meaſure*; therefore ſince all Quantities are menſurable by Lines, they will all be *Homogeneous*. And theſe Quantities are *Heterogeneous* (as the ſame Perſon teaches) *which are meaſured by a different Kind of Meaſure*: therefore all Quantities are *Heterogeneous*, becauſe they all may be meaſured by Lines, Superficies, or Solid Angles (moſt by rational or ſurd Numbers) *viz.* in the Way he takes *Meaſure*, when he is framing his falſe Arguments. And indeed all his Arguments relating to this Subject ſeem to labour under this one Fallacy of Ambiguity: for really thoſe Things are *homogeneous* that are determined by the ſame Kind of *Meaſure*, taking *Meaſure* for a Part or ſomething congruous to the Thing meaſured; but they are not always *homogeneous* which are meaſured by the ſame Kind of *Meaſure*, taking Meaſure for a Sign or Argu-

(*n*) Pag. 47.

ment

ment of the Thing meaſured; thus indeed there would be no *Heterogeneity* of Quantities, and the Controverſy would be eaſily put an End to.

But he expects to extricate himſelf out of theſe Difficulties by diſtinguiſhing very ſubtilly the *Quantities* of Things from the *Quantums* themſelves. *The Quantity* (ſays (o) he) *of every Thing in the abſtract is homogeneous to the Quantity of every other Thing, and therefore the Quantities of Lines, Superficies, Solids, Time, Motion, Force, Weight, Strength, Reſiſtance are homogeneous, though the Things themſelves are heterogeneous.* Again, *I ſee now, though it be abſurd to ſay a Line is equal to a Time, yet it is not abſurd to ſay the Quantity of a Line is equal to a Quantity of Time.* And in other Places here and there he inculcates this wonderful Comment. Whereby notwithſtanding he effects nothing; but only ſpends Words upon us, or rather upon himſelf. For I am pretty ſure that he can conceive nothing by that *abſtract Quantity* he ſpeaks of, which is different from a Line or a Time themſelves. What, pray, is the Quantity of a *Line*, but the particular and determinate Magnitude of that *Line*, or the *Line* itſelf whereby it is ſo determined? What the Quantity of a *Time* but a definite Extenſion of that Kind, or the Time itſelf, as ſo extended? Therefore if a *Line* and a *Time* are *heterogeneous*, their *Quantities* will be alſo *heterogeneous*. And that a *Line* and a *Time* are Things *heterogeneous*, not only as Phyſical Things, but as ſubject to Mathematical Conſiderations, himſelf, being conſtrained by the too great Evidence of the Thing, does ſcarce deny. But how are they *heterogeneous?* not as *Hot* or *Cold*, *Black* or *White*, but as *Great* or *Little*, *i. e.* as Quantities; for a Mathematician conſiders them no

(o) Dial. 3. p. 81.

otherwiſe;

otherwiſe; Why? becauſe they have no mutual Habitude or Relation, nor can be compared together, according to Quantity, as *Euclid* truly teaches, i. e. becauſe they are not Quantities after the ſame way, but have each a Quantity of a different Kind; or becauſe it cannot be ſaid without great Abſurdity, that ſo much of *Time* is equal to ſo much of a *Line*, or that a Year is as much as a Furlong. Therefore the Quantities of a *Time* and a *Line* are of a different Kind.

But he replies, *The Quantity of Time is meaſured by a Line.* Yes ſay I again, taking the Verb *to meaſure* equivocally; i. e. it *meaſures* not as a *Quantity*, but only as a *Cauſal*, or *Conſequential Sign*; from which nothing can be concluded for his Purpoſe. I add, that the *Quantity* of *Time* is not very properly meaſured, but rather the *Time* itſelf is meaſured as a Quantity, or as to its Quantity; Thus *Whiteneſs* is not ſo much ſeen as the Body as *White* or by reaſon of *Whiteneſs*; *i. e.* becauſe it is ſo diſpoſed as to affect the Thing ſeen, after ſuch a manner. From whence neither according to his Definition, that *Homogeneous* Things are ſuch whoſe *Meaſures* are *congruous*, are Quantities abſtractly taken well capable of *Homogeneity*, becauſe they are not meaſured themſelves, but rather the concrete Quantities by reaſon of, or in reſpect of them; and indeed by reaſon of them, things are even Mathematically *homogeneous* or *heterogeneous*.

Yet ſtill it is urged that the *Reaſons* of *Times* are rightly compared with the Reaſons of Lines: for it is ſaid, that as one Year is to two Years, ſo is a Line of one Foot to a Line of two Feet, why then may not the *Quantity* of a *Time* be compared with the *Quantity* of a *Line?* But how great is the Blindneſs of ſuch Arguments, to confound the abſolute Quantities of ſimple Things with the ſimilar Reaſons of a Plurality of Reaſons? Becauſe an Egg

Egg is to two Eggs, as an Angel to two Angels; or becauſe the Relation of one Egg to two Eggs is the ſame with that of one Angel to two Angels, can it be any way inſerred that the Quantities of an Egg and an Angel are ſimilar and homogeneous? or that the ſame Meaſure agrees with the Quantities of an Egg and an Angel? or that an Angel can poſſeſs any abſolute Quantity at all? But there is no Diſparity at all between this and the preceding Inſtance. An Egg, as it is ſaid, is not liker an Egg. Thus it often happens that they who are more deſirous to extenuate or defend their Errors, than ingenuouſly confeſs them, don't only decline them, but very often fall into much worſe than the former. That proverbial Verſe falls in very fitly here.

> Μὴ κινεῖν καμαρίναν, ἀκίνητος γὰρ ἀμείνων.
> *Move not that ill, 'tis better let remain.*

It follows then becauſe the Quantity of a *Time* (*viz.* of a Year, a Month, or a Day) cannot appoſitely be compared with the Longitude of a Line (*viz.* a Foot, a Cubit, a Furlong) according to Equality or Inequality, Exceſs or Defect, Addition or Subduction, that they are perfectly *heterogeneous.* And the ſame Way are all other Quantities affected, in which reſpect we are not to depart from the common Opinion and Speech of Mathematicians.

But if theſe Words do ſometimes occur in another Senſe; as if, becauſe of ſome ſubaltern Diverſity of Nature any ſhall call Curve Lines *heterogeneous* to Right, or gibbous to plane Superficies; as *Ramus* calls right rectilineal Angles *heterogeneous* to oblique rectilineal ones (and for almoſt the ſame Cauſe might the Quadrant of a Circle's Periphery be ſo called to a Sextant, a Line of one Foot to a Line of half a Foot;) or if, becauſe of ſome peculiar Agreement, Quantities different in Kind

are

are called *homogeneous*; as a certain Modern *(p)* Geometrician, not otherwise unlearned, does often call a Parallelogram and Cylinder *homogeneous* Figures, because Right Lines parallel to the Basis proceed with a like Tenour in this, as parallel Circles in that; which in his Stile is to proceed by *proportional Principles.* Such out of the Way Novelties of Words, I say, which induce Darkness and Confusion upon these clearest of all Sciences, it is better to beware of and avoid; and it would be much safer to refrain from all new Words in expressing our Sentiments, than to forbear using the ancient established ones. But I cease speaking any farther.

I thought to have subjoined some Things to these concerning the *Homogeneity* and *Heterogeneity* of Quantities, about their *Similitude* and *Dissimilitude*: But since the Keenness of my Pen has already overshot the appointed Bounds of Time, let so much suffice for paving the Way to those Disquisitions concerning the *Analogy* of Quantities, which are next to follow, when a fit Occasion offers. In the mean Time I bid you Farewell.

LECTURE XVII.

Of the Names and Diversities of the twofold Kind of Reason or Proportion, viz. *Arithmetical and Geometrical.*

PASSING by all prefatorial and circumstantial Speeches, according to my accustomed Manner (yet most candid Auditors, not without

(p) Ant. Farbius.

congra-

congratulating your present Health, and wishing it a long Continuance to you hereafter) I apply myself to the Business, and resume my too long intermitted Task. But, with your leave, permit me to stick close to my former Method, and finish out what remains of my Undertaking, concerning the Preparatives to the Mathematics, which I hope to effect with this Term; that after we have stuck so long upon the Shore, and cruised along the Coasts of these Sciences, we may at length be carried out into the Main Sea. Though in Truth the Subjects we are now undertaking to discuss, whether we respect their Subtilty or Utility, do seem not to be far from the very inmost and deepest Part of the Mathematics. For *Reason* or *Proportion* is first to be considered, then *Analogy* or *Proportionality*; about which the Whole of Mathematics is some Way or other employed either as its Objects or Instruments of Invention and Demonstration; and therefore the divine *(a) Plato* in his most divine Work (I mean his *(b) Timæus*) thinks it to be the *Chain and Bond of the Mathematics*, or rather *of all Disciplines*. Nor does the most illustrious Author of the famous Discourse concerning the Method of using Reason, differ from hence. *Because*, says *(c)* he, *I observed that those* (viz. particular Sciences called the Mathematics) *although conversant about different Objects, did yet all agree in this, in examining nothing but certain Relations and Proportions, which are found in them, I thought that these Proportions only are to be considered.* I add *Eratosthenes*, who pronounces, *That all Things in the Mathematics consist of the Proportion of certain Quantities.* Therefore the Consideration of *Proportions* pervades and

(*a*) Theon. Smyrn. p. 131. (*b*) Plato Tim. p. 1048.
(*c*) Pag. 18.

in

in a manner contains the Whole of these Disciplines: So that while we are contemplating the Nature of *Proportions* we ought not to think we are touching the outward Skin, but are entring their very Pith and Marrow. The Theory of the determinate Situation or Position of Magnitudes will succeed this, whereby the various Similitude and manifold Diversity of Figures appears, together with their *Proportion*; next, of the *Species* or *Specifical Agreements* and *Differences* of the Magnitudes consequent to these; lastly, of the Motion whereby Magnitudes are generated: I say, it will remain to consider these. Thus after we have examined the most, at least the principal of all the Properties of Magnitudes, which are laid down by Mathematicians or implied in their Hypotheses, returning into the same Track from which we first departed, we will produce certain Particulars worthy to be observed concerning the Hypotheses themselves and other Principals. Which Business being dispatched, we will apply ourselves to that which, I remember well, was heretofore promised, *viz.* to explain in the Method of Mathematical Invention. And I should be very glad if we could be able to finish this proposed Undertaking within the Course of the present Term. These Things being first spoken of let us first begin to discourse of Reason or Proportion.

As to what pertains to *Reason* and *Proportion* (for these Names are equipollent among most Writers) the *Greeks* design it by the Word Λόγος *Logos* Speech; than which scarce any Word in that Tongue occurs more ambiguous, and of more different Acceptations. *Theon. Smyrnæus* (*d*) thought it not amiss to recount most of its Significations in an Exposition of those, which are necessary for the

(*d*) Cap. 18.

reading

reading of *Plato*. But I ſhould ſeem too much a *Philologer* and ἔξω λόγȣ, *i. e. beſides the Purpoſe*, ſhould I in Imitation of him endeavour to reckon up the moſt of thoſe, and confirm them by Examples.

It is a known Thing that the Word *Logos* (as the modern *Peripatetics* diſtinguiſh it) does commonly denote both the *Internal Speech of the Mind*, and the *External* and *Enunciative Speech of the Tongue*, both the Faculty operating, and the Operations themſelves with the immediate Effects flowing from thence; and eſpecially whatſoever of theſe is joined with Diſcurſus or Ratiocination, which is proper to the Nature of Man; he being reckoned the only *Logical*, i. e. *ſpeaking* or *diſcurſive Animal* among living Creatures. Nor can any one who is moderately learned in the *Greek* Tongue be ignorant that every where among Greek Authors, not only particular Sentences conceived by the Mind or delivered by the Mouth are after a peculiar Manner called Λόγοι *Logoi*, but alſo different Mixtures and Syſtems of many Sentences; *viz. Fables* or *Apologies*, i. e. Words feigned at pleaſure; *Trifles* and *Querks*, *i. e.* mere Talk void of Senſe and Reaſon; *Adagies* or *Proverbs*, i. e. *Sentences* of common Uſe; *Rumours* of Fame, or popular Reports, *Stories* of all Kinds, *Orations*, and finally *all Letters*. Examples might be readily produced to confirm theſe common Significations of this Word, but I willingly paſs them by. Yet I know not but it may be of Uſe to glance at certain other Acceptations which do alſo obtain among the Vulgar, as coming nearer to our Purpoſe and the Senſe of Geometry. Such as when λόγος deſigns any Kind of *Reckoning* or *Compariſon of Things together*, as in theſe uſual Phraſes, Ἀποδιδόναι λόγον to *render an Account*, συναίρειν λόγον *to reckon or compare Accounts*, ὑπέχειν λόγον *to undergo Examination*

tion or *be called to Account.* Examples of which are in the Holy Scriptures, as that in St. *Luke,* (*d*), *Render (or give an) Account of thy Stewardship*; and in St. *Matthew* (*e*), *The Lord of those Servants cometh and reckoneth (or compareth Accounts) with them*: Where *Account* signifies the Account of the Administration of an Office, or of any Thing committed to Trust; which is nothing else but to compare Actions with the Rules prescribed by a superior Power according to which they are directed, or to compare Sums exhibited with those which they lawfully ought or are expected to be Also when λόγος intimates the *Value, Price,* or *Worth* of Things, as that is wont to be said, ἐν οὐδενὶ λόγῳ τίθεσθαι *to be placed in no Account*, which is neglected, less esteemed, and debased; and to be οὐδ' ἐν λόγῳ οὐδ' ἐν ἀριθμῷ *neither in Account nor in Number*, which is accounted as Nothing, no where taken Notice of, nor esteemed. Thus *Sophocles*,

Οὐκ ἂν πριαίμην οὐδενὸς λόγου βροτὸν,
Ὅστις κεναῖσιν ἐλπίσιν θερμαίνεται.

That venal Mortal is of no Account
Whose Breast is fired with every flatt'ring Hope.

Also Ἐν λόγου θεοὺς ποιεῖσθαι *to make Account of the Gods*, i. e. *to worship the Gods.* Λόγον δικαίου ποιεῖσθαι *to make Account of Justice*, is an Expression of *Demosthenes.* I add *Galen* (*f*), *That Name* (says he) *ought to be taken into Account* (εἰς λόγον) *in every Disquisition.* In these Expressions λόγος signifies some Magnitude, Force, or Power of the Things to be estimated. And it seems not much diffe-

(*d*) Luke xvi. 2. (*e*) Matth. xxv. 19.
(*f*) De Meth. Med. I. 5.

rent

rent when it is put for the Cauſe or Condition of a Thing, *i. e.* for that which ought to be conſidered and is required that ſomething may be done. Thus *Plato* in his *ſeventh* Epiſtle to *Dion*, *I promiſe*, ſays he, *to come hither on theſe Accounts or Conditions* ἐπὶ τούτοις τοῖς λόγοις. Δέχεσθαι λόγον *to agree to the Condition* is uſed by *Demoſthenes*. So, *to be rewarded on the Account* (or *for the ſake*) *of Virtue* εἰς λόγον ἀρετῆς, and *to be puniſhed on the Account* (or *for the Sake*) *of Vice* εἰς λόγον κακίας, are Terms of Speech in Uſe among the *Greek* Orators : *On the Account of Virtue or Vice*, *i. e.* from the Conſiderations of Virtue or Vice examined by *the Rules of Morality*.

I have produced theſe Inſtances to make it appear, that the Senſe of this Word as applied by Geometricians does not ſo far recede from its moſt received Uſe among other Writers, and the common Way of Speaking. The ſame might be ſhewn concerning the Word *Reaſon* which is here in the Sciences brought to expreſs the *Greek* Word λόγος, and borrows moſt of its Significations from thence. But becauſe of the exceeding Clearneſs of the Thing, and the too much Pains already beſtowed upon Appendices of this Kind, I forbear. I will only add that the Word λόγος ſeems to have taken both theſe foreign Senſes and the Senſe peculiar to Geometricians, from hence, becauſe in comparing different Things together, their determinate Value or Quantity is declared and expreſſed from a Reſpect which one Thing obtains to another. But *Reaſon* in Latin *Ratio* is derived from the Latin Word *Ratus* judging (or from *Reor* to judge, ſuppoſe, or think) and conſequently ſignifies a *Judgment*, *Account*, or *Eſtimation* of Things known from a Compariſon of them. As alſo the Latin Verb *putare* (in Greek λογίζεσθαι) with its Compounds *computare* and *ſupputare* do ſignify to *eſtimate* the Quantities

Quantities of Things (chiefly as to *Magnitude* or *Price*) by *numbering* or *comparing* them. But the Word *Proportion* is several Times used in *Cicero*, though in a Sense not exactly the same. For sometimes it appears to him to be of the same Importance with *simple Reason*, at other Times to design a *Similitude* or *Analogy* of *Reasons*; and he seems to be the first who invented its Use, at least the first who applied it to the Mathematics: Thus he intimates in the Fragment which is inscribed *Timæus* or *De Universo*. The Words may be thus rendered in *English*. *But that is the fittest and fairest of Ties which, from itself and with Respect to these Things that it binds, most especially effects one. And that, which by the Greeks is called Analogy, most completely reaches it, which in Latin*, (for we must presume, because these Things are first innovated by us) *may be called Comparison or Proportion. Moreover in that Book the Word Proportion is often used, yet in a Sense something various.* The Origin or Occasion of inventing which Term seems to be taken from hence. When in gathering Tributes and publick Taxes, every one had his Share to pay, according to the just Value of his Estate, which Share was called each Man's *rated* or *computed Portion*; hence every one was said to pay *pro Portione*, or *pro rata Portione*, *i. e.* according to his computed Portion: And hence proceeded the Word *Proportion*. This is the Opinion of *Cicero*, while he was studying to suit the *Greek* with his *Latin*, that he might express the Words λόγον and ἀναλογίαν, which are obvious to any one who looks into *Plato* and the other Greek Philosophers.

But let us remove our Hands from under the Ferula, and going out of the Schools of the Grammarians let us see what the Geometricians understand by λόγον, and the *Reason* and *Proportion* answering

ſwering to it (according to the more frequent and approved Uſe of *Proportion*, for ſometimes it ſignifies *Analogy* or *Proportionality* ;) And let us enquire what is the genuine Notion of this ſo common a Word. For it ſeems ſtrange that there ſhould be ſo great a Diſpute, among Men by no Means of the loweſt Rank of Mathematicians, concerning the Nature of that which every where occurs in the Mathematics, and well nigh makes the Whole of that Science. As if a Thing ſo plain, ſo uſual, and ſo diligently examined were not to be known. From whence can this proceed? I ſuppoſe from thence; that it is very difficult either diſtinctly to imagine, or accurately define Things very abſtract and univerſal, and eſpecially the Modes and Relations of Things. I believe that there are ſcarce any, at leaſt among ſuch as are ſkilled in the Mathematics, who do not ſufficiently underſtand what they mean themſelves when they pronounce this Word, and what others conceive pronouncing it; but they are not perhaps ſo ready to explain in other Words or define their own or other Peoples Conceptions anſwering to it. Hence ariſes a Cauſe of Diſpute in this, as in moſt other ſuch like Matters which are diſjunct from the Senſe: *Carteſius* has noted this, and thence eſteems that moroſe Curioſity of defining Words as a Fault in Philoſophers, in theſe Words; (*f*) *I do not explain many of thoſe Names, which I already have uſed or ſhall uſe in what follows, becauſe they ſeem to be ſufficiently known of themſelves. And I have often obſerved Philoſophers to err in this that they attempted to explain thoſe Things, which were moſt ſimple and known of themſelves by Logical Definitions; for thus they rendered them more obſcure.* Which Obſervation of this

(*f*) Princ. I. 10.

moſt

most subtle Person is most strongly confirmed from hence; because there is seldom any Agreement about these Definitions, at least among those who have given up their Name to no Sect; but what one approves the other disapproves, or judges less fit, or not sufficiently accurate: As also from hence; because the Definitions of those most abstract Names do rarely or never enter Demonstrations, nor serve for drawing Conclusions, which yet is the principal Use and Design of Definitions. For Instance, I observe by the Way, but very opportunely, that the Definition of the Word λόγος is no where to be found in the whole System of the Elements, nor is elsewhere cited (that I know of) in any Mathematical Book, for erecting any Demonstration, or deducing any Conclusion. The Word *Diastema* among the ancient Musicians may afford another Example, which they all defined, but all differed in Words, and varied something from one another in the Sense: This will appear to any one that pleases to consult *Aristoxenus*, *Euclid*, *Nichomachus*, *Bacchius*, *Aristides*, *Gaudentius*, *Capella*, &c. But to come nigher the Purpose.

First it is to be noted, that there is a certain Ambiguity or Distinction of the Words *Reason* and *Proportion*, even as they are used by Mathematicians, though not, I imagine, of the Greek Word λόγος. *Reason* or *Proportion* according to some is twofold, *viz.* *Arithmetical* and *Geometrical.* For the better understanding of which, it is first to be premised that each Kind of *Reason*, as it intimates any Comparison of *Homogeneous Quantities* belongs to that Classis or Category of Beings which *Aristotle* calls τὰ πρός τι; and others *Relations* or *Habitudes.* The two Correlatives of which Relation are by Mathematicians called *Terms.* *A Term* (says *Theon Smyrnæus*) *is that which expresses the particular*

particular Nature or Property of the Things mentioned, as Number, Magnitude, Power, Bulk, Gravity. Or elſewhere more clearly: (g) *We call thoſe Terms which, agreeing in Genus or Species, are aſſumed in Compariſon.* And the former of theſe two Terms in the Compariſon is called the *Antecedent*, the latter the *Conſequent.* This being premiſed, ſome, with the ancient Scholiaſt cited by *Meibomius*, call *Arithmetical Reaſon* or *Proportion the Relation of two Quantities as to Difference,* i. e. *as one exceeds or is ſhort of the other*: and it may be added, *as to Equality too*, i. e. *as they differ nothing from one another*; for there may be alſo a Compariſon made between *equal* Quantities, and this particular Relation of the ſame may be ſignified by having for their Difference *nothing*, which is the Middle Limit between Exceſs and Defect. By *Difference* I here do not underſtand any abſolute Quantity remaining after the Subduction of one Term from another (ſuch as indeed is generally called Διαφορὰ *Difference*) but the *Compariſon* or *Reference* in a ſingular Manner of this to that. *Ex. gr.* The Relation between a Line of three Feet and a Line of two Feet, according to which that is conceived to exceed this by a Line of one Foot; or inverſely, the Relation of two Feet to three Feet, as that is conceived to fall ſhort of this the Quantity of a Line of one Foot; theſe are called *Arithmetical Reaſons*, the former of *Exceſs*, the latter of *Defect*; yet the abſolute Magnitude of the Line of one Foot, though it uſually goes by the Name of Difference, is not the *Arithmetical Reaſon*; but this exceeding or falling ſhort is called the *Arithmetical Reaſon.* Such a *Habitude* (I ſay) of Quantities to one another do ſome call *Arithmetical Reaſon.* I will not now diſpute

(g) Cap. XX.

why

why they stile it *Arithmetical*, because the Thing is controverted; I only say that it seems to be thus denominated because the Ancients termed a certain *Analogy Arithmetical*, of which it will be proper to speak when we come to treat of *Analogies*.

But among the *Greeks* I no where find any *Arithmetical* λόγος; on the contrary they always distinguish the λόγος of Quantities from their *Difference* which they denote by the Words διαφορὰ and ὑπεροχὴ; and sometimes term διάστημα, *i. e.* an *Interval*, *Space*, or *Distance*, not thereby intimating any *Interstice* resulting from *Local Position*, but a *Diversity*, and as it were *Distance* in Quantity by which one cannot be equal to another, or a certain *determinate Removal* from *Equality*; but by λόγος they continually designed that *Habitude* of Quantities which is wont to be called *Geometrical Reason*, or simply *Reason*. For when *Reason* is put at large, always *Geometrical Reason* is meant, *i. e.* that σχέσις *Habitude* according to which one Quantity is conceived some Number of Times to contain or be contained in another. *Ex. gr.* the *Relation* of a Line of three Feet to a Line of two Feet (according to which the former is conceived to include the latter *once* and *half as much* besides, or is to the latter as *three* to *two*,) is called a *Geometrical Reason*, or particularly a *Sesquialter Reason:* and inversely the Relation of a Line of two Feet to a Line of three Feet (according to which the former makes *two third Parts* of the latter, or is to the latter as *two* to *three*) is called a *Subsesquialter Reason*. Whence it may appear how much Difference there is between these two *Relations* called *Arithmetical* and *Geometrical*. For it is very different for one Quantity to exceed another, and for one Quantity so often to contain another, or for one Quantity to fall short of another,

other, and for one Quantity to be contained in another. This Diverſity is commonly not ill explained from the *Manner* whereby theſe *Relations* are inveſtigated and known, eſpecially then, when the *Terms compared* are expreſſed in Numbers (I am againſt this Exception, becauſe by reaſon of that Neglect the Doctrine of *Reaſons* is either unadviſedly or obſcurely delivered :) But let us ſuppoſe the *Terms compared* to be expreſſed in Numbers ; then their *Arithmetical Reaſon* is found by ſubducting the *Conſequent Term* from the *Antecedent*, and the *Geometrical* by dividing the *Antecedent Term* by the *Conſequent* ; I ſay found, *i. e.* diſcovered and ſubjected to our Eſtimation. *Ex. gr.* by comparing two Quantities denominated by the Numbers *Three* and *Two*, ſuppoſe *three Feet* and *two Feet*, by ſubducting *Two* from *Three* there is left *One* for the Difference, or a Line of *one Foot*. But, the Terms being tranſpoſed, if the Line of *three Feet* be taken from the Line of *two Feet*, there remains *leſs one*, or the *Defect* of a Line of *one Foot* for the *Difference* ; and from theſe Remainders are known the *Relations as to Difference*, or the *Arithmetical Reaſons* of the propoſed Quantities ; ſince if the Reſidue found by both Subductions be added to the *Conſequent*, the Sum reſulting will be the *Antecedent* : For in the former Compariſon $1+2=3$, and in the latter $-1+3=2$. And this ſeems to be the Tendence of every Compariſon of Quantities, that other Compariſons may be reduced to, and ſome Way eſtimated by *Equality*, which is the moſt ſimple, conſtant and comprehenſible *Relation*. The *former Relation* from the *former Difference* is called the *Relation of the Exceſs of one*, the *latter* from the *latter Difference* the *Relation of the Defect of one*. But if two Quantities repreſented by the Numbers 20 and 4 be compared, by dividing the *Antecedent* 20 by the *Conſequent*

Consequent 4, the *Quotient* is 5; but inverting the Terms, by dividing 4 by 20 the *Quotient* is $\frac{4}{20} = \frac{1}{5}$. By which *Quotients* are declared the *Geometrical Reasons* of the proposed Quantities, because if the *Quotient* found be multiplied by the *Consequent*, the *Product* is equal to the *Antecedent*: for in the former Comparison $5 \times 4 = 20$, in the latter $\frac{1}{5} \times 20 = 4$; as Things again are referred to *Equality*. The former *Relation* by the *Quotient found* is denominated a *Quintuple Reason*, the latter *Subquintuple*. But I must now shew a Cause why I have explained *Arithmetical Reason* otherwise than it is vulgarly done, not by *subducting* the lesser Term from the greater, but indifferently the *Consequent* from the *Antecedent*. For which many Causes may be assigned; as

First because this Way is more commodious for shewing the Diversity we are insisting upon, of these different *Reasons* by *Subduction* and *Division*; because this Way the *Subduction* which signifies an *Arithmetical Reason* in every respect answers the *Division* which signifies a *Geometrical*. For according to us the twofold *Subduction* in the former is the same Way performed as the twofold *Division* in the latter: There the greater Term is improperly *subducted* from the lesser, as here the lesser Term is improperly *divided* by the greater: As the *Remainder* there is less than *Nothing*, so the *Quotient* here is less than *Unity*; and as the *Antecedent* there is always made by the *Addition* of the *Consequent* and *Remainder*; so the *Antecedent here* is formed by the *Multiplication* of the *Consequent* and *Quotient*: Therefore this Method is more commodious than the other, according to which the *Subduction* or *Difference* is of one Sort only, *viz. Positive* or greater than Nothing, and the other Properties do no how agree.

Secondly,

Secondly, this Way of explaining *Arithmetical Reasons* by *Subduction* is also more true in itself, and more agreeable to the *Reason*. For since a Transposition of the *Terms* in comparing two unequal Quantities causes a twofold *Relation* (for the *greater Term* is not the same Way referred to the *lesser*, as the *lesser* to the *greater*) by the Acquisition or Invention of *one only Difference*, from the *Subduction* of the *lesser* from the *greater*, therefore these two *Reasons* are not rightly and usefully explained; but it is better to express them by *two Differences*, the one *Positive* shewing an *Excess*, the other *Negative* signifying a *Defect*. *To lack* and *to exceed* are not the same, and therefore ought not to be denoted by the same Sign. This being unobserved by some, they asserted that there is no *Relation of Quantities as to Difference*; because if there be, it ought to be twofold; but a *Positive Difference* is simple and One. *Nichomachus* in his *Enchiridion of Harmonies* says: *They who account a Difference and Relation for the same, think Wrong*; *for lo two has the same Difference to one, as one to two, but not the same Relation.* Consequently he argues aright from the Hypothesis of one only *Difference*; but I answer that the *Difference* between 1 and 2 is —1, as signifying 1 to lack one of 2; but the *Difference* between 2 and 1 is +1, as signifying 2 to exceed 1 by one. Therefore since the *Difference* is twofold, nothing hinders, but there may be two *Relations*, as it were contrary to one another or universal. Therefore *Theon Smyrnæus* thinks wrong with *Nichomachus*, *That the Difference of two unequals, either to other, is one and the same, but the* λόγος, i. e. *Geometrical Reason of either to other is different and contrary.* Indeed I can hardly perceive why *Geometrical Reasons* which lie between two unequal Terms ought not to be equally confounded from a Transposition of the Terms,

Terms and accounted for one *Reason*, as the *Relations according to Difference* which lie the same Way between unequal Terms are vulgarly esteemed for one. Nor does any Thing hinder but there may be such an improper *Subduction of a greater from a lesser* and what perhaps seems difficult to conceive, *Something* less than *Nothing* itself. For the *Division of a lesser by a greater* is scarce thought less improper, nor is it easier to conceive how often a *greater is contained in a lesser*. It is enough that this Kind of *Subduction* is subject to Arithmetical Laws as well as that Kind of *Division*, and is not devised or applied without Cause.

It may be added that this Method of *Subduction* is very useful in other Respects, especially in the Comparison of *Geometrical Progressions* with *Arithmetical*; and chiefly of those *Progressions* which proceed on one side by *encreasing* and on the other by *decreasing* from *Unity*: For as *Positive Exponents* are assigned to the *encreasing Terms*, so *Negative* ones are attributed to the *decreasing Terms*. But here is no Place for speaking farther of this. I only take notice, that these *Negative Differences*, or *Terms less than Nothing* are easily exhibited in Geometry. For they are only computed from the same fixed Limit, in an Order contrary to those wherein the *Positive Terms* proceed, or such as are *greater than nothing*. As in a Right Line (FIG. V.) extended indefinitely are assumed the two Right Lines AM, AN, towards the contrary Parts, each being equal to any Right Line Z, and let the Right Line AM proceeding forwards be represented by $+Z$, then will the Right Line AN taken backwards be represented by $-Z$. As suppose one swimming forwards and aiming against the Stream towards M, be carried backwards by a double Force, then the Distance he has made will be $AM-2AM$ or $-AM$ to be computed from A backwards to N. These

These Things may in part ſuffice for illuſtrating the *Diverſity* between *Arithmetical* and *Geometrical Reaſons*, by *Subduction* and *Diviſion*. We will perhaps hereafter treat of the ſame Thing more opportunely and accurately, when their Opinion comes to be examined, who would confine the *Doctrine of Reaſons* and what belongs to that Diſquiſition to Numbers. We ſhall now only touch upon one or two Diverſities of theſe *Relations* drawn from their Nature. *Firſt* of all it is to be noted, that the ſame *Arithmetical Reaſon* is exhibited in *Terms* of one Kind only, but a *Geometrical Reaſon* may be fitly repreſented or expreſſed by Quantities of any Kind. The Reaſon is, becauſe an *Arithmetical Reaſon* is determined by ſomething abſolute within the Limits of a certain Genus *viz.* by the *Difference* of two *homogeneous Quantities.* which is always *homogeneous* to the *Terms* themſelves ſo compared: But a *Geometrical Reaſon* is determined from the *Manner* whereby one Thing contains or is contained in another, which *Manner* may be equally agreeable to the *various Conjugations* of *heterogeneous Terms*; whence it comes to paſs that every two Quantities are capable of expreſſing or ſubjecting to Eſtimation the Relations of any other two Quantities the ſame Way affected. *Ex. gr.* The *Arithmetical Reaſon* of two unequal Lines can be exhibited only by two Lines, not two Weights, Times, or Bodies; becauſe no Line exceeds another by any Weight, Time, or Body, but only by a Line determined according to its own abſolute Quantity: But the *Geometrical Reaſon* of the ſame two Lines may be expreſſed by two Weights, two Times, or two Quantities of any other Kind; as the *Reaſon* between a *Foot* and an *Inch* in Length may be repreſented by a *Pound* and an *Ounce Troy* in Weight, by a *Year* and a *Month* in Time, or by any other ſimilar Terms, of which

one

one contains the other *twelve Times*; becauſe the *Terms* of theſe *heterogeneous Conjugations* being compared together according to their abſolute Quantities do reſpect one another the ſame Way, and are the ſame Way affected towards one another. From hence a moſt learned (*h*) Man takes Occaſion to ſay that all *Geometrical Reaſons of whatſoever Quantities are homogeneous* to one another, *becauſe all are in the Genus of Number.* And afterwards he adjoins. *Where a Compariſon is made in reſpect of Reaſon, the Reaſon which emerges of the Things compared does not ſeldom leave their Genus and paſs into the Genus of Number; of whatſoever Genus the Things are, which are compared.* Which Words notwithſtanding I do not ſo well approve of, as well for other Cauſes not yet to be explained, as becauſe I know of no Genus either of *Reaſon* or *Numbers* comprehended under Quantity: For neither in my Opinion are *Reaſons* Quantities, nor capable of Quantity (as hereafter I ſhall endeavour to evince in its proper Place) but are *mere Relations* founded in Quantity; and Numbers I account only as the Names and Symbols of Quantities, which we have already ſhewn more than once. I add, it ſeems manifeſt, that when two Quantities are compared together (*viz.* to inveſtigate their *Reaſon* by certain artificial Operations Arithmetical or Geometrical, *i. e.* to render it comprehenſible or eſtimable) yet there is not thence framed any new *Reaſon* but the ſame exhibited in other *Terms*; nor does the Reaſon ever leave its Genus, but is exhibited in *Terms* of a different Genus, for the moſt part more ſimple and known; indeed generally in Numbers when it may be done, becauſe theſe are Symbols moſt accommodate to our Capacity for determining the Meaſures of Things, *Ex. gr.* to him that enquires what *Reaſon* a *Shilling* has to a *Groat* in

(*g*) D. Wallis's Arith. p. 226.

Value,

Value, or in Weight, he that anſwers, It has the *Reaſon* of 12 to 4, produces no other *Reaſon*, but explains what is ſought in *Numerical Terms:* and moreover he who aſks what is the *Reaſon* of the Number 12 to 4, and dividing the *Antecedent* 12 by the *Conſequent* 4 finds it to be *triple*, mentions no new *Reaſon*, but expreſſes the *Reaſon* propoſed in *Terms* more eaſy to be eſtimated, *i. e.* in the *leaſt Numbers, viz.* 3 and 1. For he who ſays that is *triple* to this, ſays and means no more than that is to this as 3 to 1; the *Antecedent* being expreſſed, and the *Conſequent* (which is always Unity in the Denominations of ſuch *Reaſons*) underſtood.

Hence may another *Diverſity* of theſe *Reaſons* be taken notice of, that a *Geometrical Reaſon* is always expreſſed by *two Terms*, at leaſt in the Underſtanding, and thoſe always *Poſitive*. For the *Reaſon* even of two *Negative Terms* is *Poſitive, ex. gr.* the *Reaſon* of —4 to —2 is *Double*, or as 2 to 1, becauſe multiplying each Term by —1 there is produced +4 and +2. But an *Arithmetical Reaſon* is expreſſed by only *one Term*, and that ſometimes *Negative:* as ſuch a *Reaſon* between 1 and 3 is moſt commodiouſly denoted by the *Negative Term* —2, as was juſt now ſhewn. Moreover an *Arithmetical Reaſon* is found between two *Terms* affected with different Signs; but there is no *Geometrical Reaſon* between ſuch. *Ex. gr.* the *Arithmetical Reaſon* between 2 and —2 is all one as the *Reaſon* betwen 6 and 2; for the *Exceſs* of the *Antecedent* above the *Conſequent* in both is 4; but 2 to —2 has no *Geometrical Reaſon*; for the former is to the latter, as ſomething is to what is leſs than infinitely little; nor is there any imaginable Number how great ſoever which is not leſſer in Reſpect of 1, than 2 is in Reſpect of —2.

Again the *Geometrical Reaſon* of *Equals* is always denominated by *Unity*, and the *Arithmetical Rea-*

ſon

ſon by *Nothing*; the *Geometrical Reaſon* of a *greater* to a *leſſer*, if explicable in Numbers, is denominated by a Number exceeding Unity, integer or mixed, the *Arithmetical Reaſon* by a Difference exceeding Nothing, which yet is not always as much as Unity; but the *Geometrical Reaſon* of a *leſſer* to a *greater* is always denominated by a Fraction or Number leſs than Unity, and the *Arithmetical Reaſon* of ſuch *Terms* is ſignified by a Number beneath Nothing, involving Negation, as we have already inculcated. But we have ſpoke more than enough concerning the *Differences* of *theſe Reaſons.*

Since therefore theſe *Relations* are ſo different by Nature, the ſame Name of *Reaſon* will not agree with both univocally; and conſequently it is better to appropriate that Word to *Geometrical Reaſon* alone. Therefore diſmiſſing that which is called *Reaſon* without Authority, let us come to examine the Notion of this *Geometrical Reaſon* a little nearer. Let it ſuffice to have cleared the Way at preſent which lay blocked up with Ambiguities; and in the next Lecture we will follow it more cloſely: In the mean Time, I wiſh you Farewell.

LECTURE XVIII.

A Defence of Euclid's *Definition of* Reaſon *or* Proportion.

LAYING aſide all Prefaces, and having diſperſed the Clouds of Ambiguities, which lay in our Way, we come now to enquire into and explain the Nature of *Geometrical Reaſon*. *Geometrical Reaſon* or ſimply *Reaſon* (for in this Senſe we we will always hereafter uſe this Word, as alſo its equivalent, *Proportion*) I ſay *Reaſon* or *Proportion* ὁ λόγος is defined by *Euclid* (or by *Eudoxus*, if he, as is ſaid, be the Compoſer of the fifth Book of the *Elements*) to be a *certain Habitude* (or Relation) *of two homogeneous Magnitudes to one another, according to Quantity.* About which Definition *two Things* may be enquired into and diſputed; *firſt* what is his genuine Meaning; and then whether it be ſufficiently juſt and accurate. I will endeavour to ſatisfy each Diſquiſition applying certain Obſervations to his Terms, that we may at the ſame Time interpret the Senſe, and defend the Authority, of our Maſter. Be pleaſed to pardon my Contentiouſneſs, and take it not for the worſe that being led with a certain Piety I ſtudy to vindicate the *Father* and *Prince* of Geometry from the undeſerved Reproaches, which are every where thrown upon him.

1. In every Definition, Care is to be taken that the Thing defined be reſtrained to a certain Claſſis of Beings; for that conduces very much to determine its Nature and diſtinguiſh it from others. Therefore the Genus is firſt to be enquired into, which in this Definition is (i) *Habitude*, or *Relation*, and that rightly; for ſince every Quantity may be conſidered two Ways, either as having a certain abſolute Extenſion of its Genus (abſolute, I ſay, and determinate from the intrinſecal Property of its Nature;) or as, in Compariſon with another Quantity, *it has itſelf in a certain Manner* towards that other: The Comprehenſion of which *Manner* is ſerviceable for the better Conception of its abſolute Quantity and the Declaration of others. I ſaid, *it has itſelf in a certain Manner*, *i. e.* as either wholly congruous and equal to it, or unequal in ſome peculiar *Reaſon*, which is rendered known

(i) Σχέσις.

and

and computable by Numbers, *i. e.* by Symbols of the Quantities divided into equal Parts, or by the Exposition of other Quantities which are to one another *in the same Manner.* I beg pardon for spending a little more Labour than ordinary in illustrating a Thing so very difficult to be explained, and well nigh too subtle for the most attentive Mind. But when a Quantity *has itself in a certain Manner to another, i. e.* is thus equal to another, or in a certain Reason unequal, it is said (by Agreement of the Masters who prescribe Names to the Things considered in this Science) *to have this or that Reason to that other*; and such very *Respect* abstractly taken is named *Reason,* which consequently is rightly added to the Classis or Category of Relations. For it is apparent that the Quantities thus considered are *mutually referred to one another,* and do undergo all Things which Logicians assign to *Relatives* or *Correlatives*; and *Aristotle* takes his first Examples of his τὰ πρός τι (*i. e.* Things referred to another) from hence both in his Logics and Metaphysics: *Those Things* (says he) *are said to be to one another* (i. e. to be Relatives) *which as to that very Thing which they are, are said to be of others, or are some other Way referred to another: as a Greater, whatsoever it is, is entirely attributed to another, for it is greater than something: and also a Double whatsoever it is, is attributed to another, because it is the double of something.* Nevertheless our Countryman the wonderful Corrector of Modern Mathematics is most unmerciful and unmannerly with *Euclid* upon this Account. *The Definition of Reason* (says (*k*) he meaning *Euclid*'s) *is sufficiently unapt.* Again, *As* Euclid *had insignificantly said.* Again, *It may be that* Euclid *himself did not sufficiently perceive the Nature*

(*k*) Pag. 44. 100. 88. 82.

of

of Reaſon ; *nay it could not be otherwiſe*, *ſince he defines Reaſon by* ποιὰ σχέσις, *i. e.* a certain Habitude or Relation. And again he reckons that *Euclid* has *coughed* in this Place, *i. e.* he has given us an empty Sound, becauſe he had nothing to ſay to the Purpoſe. But good Words I beg, what Reaſon is there for all this tragical Outcry ? Is it becauſe *Euclid* has defined Reaſon by σχέσις, *i. e.* a *Habitude* or *Relation?* Pray what can you conceive by σχέσις, or you would have it to ſignify Nothing ; what does the Man mean ? Himſelf like all others defines *Reaſon* truly and accurately thus ; *(l) Reaſon is the Relation of the Antecedent to the Conſequent according to Magnitude. Reaſon* is a *Relation*, and what elſe did *Euclid* think or mean ? Who ever conceived his Meaning otherwiſe ? But this Dictator, by his own Authority, will not only ſpeak himſelf, but underſtand others to ſpeak after his own Will and Pleaſure : he aſſumes to himſelf (for who may forbid him ?) as a moſt expert Inventor of Words, to declare the Senſe of his own Mind contrary to Cuſtom ; and not content with that he alſo arrogates to himſelf the Power of interpreting the Opinions of others, contrary to common Conſent and the moſt received Uſe. Σχέσις, when himſelf commands and permits it, ought to ſignify an *Habitude* ; but an *Habitude* Nothing, whatſoever moſt other Mortals ſay againſt it, when applying theſe Words to deſign their own certain Senſes. *Grammarians* call the *Agreement* or *Connexion* of *Nouns* between the *Subſtantive* and *Adjective* σχέσιν ὀνομάτων. *Divines* diſpute whether *Images* are to be worſhipped σχετικῶς, *i. e.* for the σχέσιν or *Relation* which they obtain to the *Originals they repreſent. Common Speech* deſigns the *Relations* of *Kindred* and *Affinity* ariſing from a

(*l*) Pag. 45.

Conjunction

Conjunction of Nature or mutual Agreement by the same Appellation of σχέσις. One might produce Waggon Loads of Examples, but the clear Testimony of one of the best Grammarians may serve. Ἡ σχέσις, i. e. *Relation* (says *Suidas*) *is said of Things which are referred to another, as the Son to the Father, a Friend to a Friend : for these both relate and are related to one another. and therefore are termed* σχέσεις *Relations. Again Things are said to be related according to Comparison as lesser, greater, double, also Science and Sense.* The Word σχέσις then is not altogether insignificant and void of Sense, but notes something aptly enough, and is the same with *Relation* itself. *(m) But I ask* (says our Adversary) *what is that which in this Place has, and what is that which is had? Is Reason called an* Habitude *because it has something or because it is had? If it have, what is it that it has, but if it be had, by what is it had? All which are trifling.* To which I answer, when *Reason* is said by him to be a *Relation, i. e. a Telling* or *Carrying again.* I also ask what is that which there is *carried* or *carried again*, from whence or whither is it carried? But we have no Leisure for Trifling, in being strict and severe to gather the Significations of Words from their Etymologies alone, which are rather to be taken and approved from Custom and Consent, to which they only owe their Force and Power of signifying. Albeit since τὸ ἔχειν, *i. e. to have* is used innumerable Ways, nothing is more customary with Philosophers than by it to denote *Relation* and *Respect*. *Aristotle* in his *Categories, The Essence of Relations consists in this* πῶς ἔχειν *that they have themselves in a certain Manner, or are in some sort affected, to something.* And to have that Foundation true and real inti-

(*m*) Pag. 45.

mates

mates what is had and found in the Terms of any particular *Relation*, by reaſon of which, or according to which, they mutually reſpect one another. *Ex. gr.* there is had (to anſwer our Adverſary more fully) a determinate Quantity in the *Terms* of every *Proportion* by reaſon of, or according to which, one is compared with another; from whence is the Form of Speech uſed by Geometricians (not unobſerved by himſelf) which explains the *Similitudes of Reaſons* thus. As *A* has itſelf to *B*, ſo has *C* itſelf to *D*. Therefore *Euclid* is not out of the Way (he who has had the united Voice of ſo many Ages,) but his Cenſurer inſolently wrangles; the former writes not inſignificantly, but the latter reads careleſly; the former has a right Perception of the Nature of *Reaſon*, but the latter perverts his Explication of *Reaſon*; laſtly, it is not *Euclid* that *coughs* but a certain Perſon that ſhameleſly boaſts: One to whom it is indeed juſt to make Retaliation, and reprove with that Saying of *Euripides*.

——Ἐπεὶ τὰ μὴ καλὰ
Λέγειν ἐτόλμας, πλῆθε ϗ τὰ μὴ φίλα.

Since you have dared to utter Things unkind
Expect to hear unkind Things in return.

But I trifle too much. I will only ſubjoin one Thing by the Way, that (*n*) *Nicomachus Geraſenus* in his *Muſics*, by what Authority I know not, has χέσις for *Species*, and λόγος for *Genus*, changing the Order.

Secondly, After the Genus in defining Accidents, the Subjects come next to be conſidered, which are called *Terms* in *Relations*. Hence I take notice next that *Euclid*, applying this (*o*) Book to Geome-

(*n*) Nicom. Muſ. l. 1. p. 24. (*o*) Μεγεθῶν.

 try,

try, undertook only to define the *Reason* of Magnitudes. Hence it is there Magnitudes, instead of which, to make the Definition of *Reason* as general as possible, it ought to be *Quantities* or *Terms.* As it is in *Theon* (*p*) *Smyrnæus*, *Reason is a certain Habitude of two homogeneous Terms to one another, according to Analogy*, And (*q*) *Nicomachus* in his Arithmetic: *Reason is the Habitude of two Terms to one another.* But *Ramus* blames our Author for this, because he has defined the *Reason* of Magnitudes separately, since *Reason* agrees with all Things. *The Sophistry* (says (*r*) he) *is perpetual through the whole Book of Logic and Arithmetic confined to the latter Subject concerning Magnitudes.* I answer *first*, that a greater *Sophism* is committed by this Censurer himself, who confines Reason to Numbers, a Subject equally particular and less apt. (*s*) *Another Comparison of Quantity is conjunct with Numeration, and is called Reason, which considers how often the Consequent is contained in the Antecedent.* As if every Comparison of Quantity were subject to *Numeration*, and every *Reason* agreed with Numbers, or might be expressed by Numbers. It is sufficiently apparent, nor does himself deny but there are certain *Surd Reasons* and such as are inexplicable by Numbers; but there is no *Reason* at all which cannot be exhibited in Magnitudes of every Kind. Therefore *Number* is unsuitably assumed for the adequate Subject of *Reason*; and *Magnitude* is much more suitable, since there is no *Mode* or *Species* of *Reason* but what agrees with it. I answer *secondly*, since (as I imagine it has been abundantly proved) Magnitude is the principal and only Genus, properly so called, of Quantity; and others only by Rela-

(*p*) Cap. 19.
(*q*) Lib. 2. p. 62.
(*r*) Schol. 13.
(*s*) Arith. 2. 2.

tion,

tion, Participation, and Analogy, and consequently challenge the Attributes of Quantity only secondarily; and since the (*t*) Philosopher teaches us well, that the Reason of such Analogies requires that the Things which are primary are separately and in the first Place to be defined, hence the *Reason* of Magnitudes is deservedly first defined and separately; and nothing hinders but the Definition agreeing to it may be transferred analogically to the *Reasons* of other Quantities. And indeed whatsoever is truly attributed to the *Reasons* of Magnitudes and demonstrated by them, that agrees exactly to the *Reasons* of all Quantums; seeing all Quantums, as they have their own absolute Quantity, so they have a respective Quantity also consequently dependent on and to be determined by Magnitude. I answer *thirdly*, that the Author of the fifth Element did enough, if he openly professed only to expound the Nature of the *Reasons* of Magnitudes. Since (as we have insinuated) he proposed with himself to treat of these as confined to Geometry. This is usual with the Masters of all particular Sciences: Grammarians only describe Moods and Tenses, as significative for the Declensions of Verbs: Rhetoricians Tropes and Figures, not as they agree with all Things, but with Words and Sentences: The Moralist defines Virtues, not as the Virtues of Horses and Dogs (which *Plato* so often predicates) are comprehended in them, but such as relate to human Practice only: Musicians explain the *Proportions* and Spaces not of all Quantities, but of Sounds: and not to mention more, all particular Disciplines are wont to assume this Authority to themselves; they deduce, adapt, and confine the Significations they use to their own particular Consideration; they define

(*t*) Met. III. 2. VII. 4.

or describe the Terms they apply especially studying Perspicuity, and as much as may be Brevity, avoiding being compelled by another either to repeat any general Doctrine for the most Part separate from their Purpose, or to omit any Explication which may conduce for understanding what is said. But if this be not so exactly agreeable to the Laws of *Ramus*'s Logic, yet it is not contrary to the Dictates of Reason itself, or worthy of Blame; for it is the utmost Injury to good Authors and the Arts themselves to act by the utmost Strictness from these, or any other Logical Prescripts. But it is one Thing to reduce the Whole of Philosophy into one Body, and another to treat of particular Sciences; in the former the Order of Things and an elegant Brevity, in the latter Clearness, Facility, Validity, are especially attended to, it being always of Moment to accommodate the Doctrine to the Capacity of the Learner. But I digress too far. Furthermore it may be answered with some that Magnitude may be so taken as to design every Quantity, by a very common Catachresis of that Word. For if Number, Weight, and Time be often said to be (*Magna*) great, why may not these Things as far as they are Quantities be called Magnitudes; and thus the Definition in the Elements may be extended to all Quantities? But enough has been said in the Defence of *Euclid* against the Opposition of *Ramus*. I proceed,

Thirdly to note, since even *heterogeneous Magnitudes* may some Way be compared together, or respect one another, according to something, *viz.* a Line may respect a Superfice, and a Superfice a Body as far as a Superfice may be applied to a Line as to its Side, and a Body to a Superfice as the Basis on which it stands; and as a Line is the Perimeter of a Superfice, and a Superfice encloses a Body, also a Line may be coextended with a Super-

fice

fice as to one Dimension, a Superfice with a Body as to two, and so far those may be compared with these: Also any sort of Comparison may be many Ways instituted as to the other common Affections, between such Quantities different in Kind; from which Comparisons notwithstanding, the Respects resulting are very different from this, according to which *homogeneous Magnitudes* are referred to one another in a manner which is here understood to be defined; therefore for excluding those whatsoever Relations there may be between *heterogeneous Magnitudes*, *Euclid* assigns the proper Terms of the Relation designed by it, and adequate Subjects of the Reason circumscribed within its Limits, by the Addition of (*u*) *Homogeneous. Homogeneous Quantities* alone are said to have *Reason*, because they alone are capable of Equality and Inequality, they alone admit of mutual Excess and Defect, and have the Properties adjoined to them subject to Geometrical Speculations. But we have treated enough of this before. Nor will I here dwell much upon *Ramus* blaming us with no shew of Reason: *That Reason*, says he, *of Equality and Inequality which* Euclid *proposes to define is common to all Things, a Line may be compared to a Superfice and a Body. Thus in the fourteenth Element, Bodies, Superficies, and Lines are compared together; so also* Hippocrates's *Lunula is squared, and oblique lined Angles are equal to rectilineal ones.* But who except this Censurer (that seems to catch at all Handles, and every where hunt for Occasions to abuse those ancient Masters of the Sciences, whom yet it were just not to reprehend without great Cause, and only where they manifestly are in the wrong; it would become us that are indebted to them for such great Inventions to act more mildly

(*u*) Ὁμογενῶν.

with

with them;) I ſay who, except this Cenſurer, thought that ſuch *Compariſons* of Lines with Superficies and Bodies as are handled in the fourteenth Element do pertain to the Nature of *Reaſons?* When it is inveſtigated how the Sides of a Pentagon or Decagon, of a Pyramid or Octoedron are ſo affected to one another, or towards the Radius of the Circle or Sphere in which theſe Figures may be inſcribed; who ever thought that theſe Right Lines or Sides of the Figures are compared with the Figures themſelves as to *Reaſon?* I believe none are ſo ignorant: Yet *Ramus* means ſo, or he means Nothing to the Purpoſe; at leaſt as far as I can perceive he can underſtand nothing elſe. Alſo who ever thought, that the Lunula of *Hippocrates* is a plane Figure terminated by a Square, or *heterogeneous* to every other plane Figure, that being ſuppoſed? Why could he not by a like Reaſon have produced a more obvious Example by comparing a Sphere with a Cone or Cylinder, *i. e.* a Body comprehended in one round Superfice, with a Body contained in a mixed Superfice? He is unwilling to underſtand what is *homogeneous* and *heterogeneous*, at leaſt what Geometricians continually ſignify by theſe Words; he is unwilling to diſtinguiſh *Homogeneity* and *Heterogeneity* from *Similarity* and *Diſſimilarity*. But I paſs from hence and note,

Fourthly, that ſince even *homogeneous Magnitudes*, as to many of their Accidents, may be compared (ſuppoſe as to ſome of their particular Properties, *viz.* their Situation, local Diſtance, or diverſe Qualities; I add, with the ancient Scholiaſt, alſo as to Value or Price;) *ex. gr.* two Lines as to Rectitude or Curvity may be to one another *Similarly* or *Diſſimilarly*, one may be at Hand, the other twenty Furlongs diſtant, one may be White, the other Black; yet ſince none of theſe Relations can

be

be ſignified here, ſetting theſe apart, here is adjoined (*x*) *according to Quantity*, ſignifying the Foundation of this Relation. For the Foundation is next to be ſubjoined which ultimately compleats its *formal Reaſon*, and what the Logicians call its *Eſſential Difference*, for explaining the Nature of the Relations after the Genus is expreſſed, and the Terms lawfully conſtituted. *According to Quantity*, *i. e.* according to the Determination of its Magnitude, or the determinate Magnitude itſelf, at leaſt as far as it is aſked how great Things are, and the Anſwer is made *ſo great*, by which he ſeems to ſignify nothing but the Magnitude itſelf, as it is determined in itſelf by its own Singularity (if I may ſo ſpeak,) and is diſtinguiſhed from other Quantities. Now the Cauſe by which a Magnitude, or rather a *Thing great* (for generally concrete and abſtract Terms are confounded,) is ſuch a Way referred to another, is conceived to be Nothing but abſolutely the having ſo great a Magnitude in itſelf, as univerſally every *Relation* is founded in *ſomething abſolute*. Therefore I do not well approve of that Expoſition of ſome, that *according to Quantity* means, according as one Thing is ſo many fold of another, or *according to Tantuplicity*; for they ſtick not to coin ſuch Words, ſignifying I do not know what by them. For beſides ſuch a Definition (*ex. gr.* of a *double Reaſon to be the Relation of two Quantities according to Duplicity*) ſounds not well, *Tantuplicity* ſeems intrinſecally to contain or denote a certain Relation; but the Foundations of Relations are not Relations, but are Things abſolute becauſe of, or according to which the Terms of the Relations are referred to one another. I ſuppoſe it would be wrong to ſay, This is ſimilar to that, becauſe it

(*x*) Κατὰ πηλικότητα.

is

is ſimilarly affected; but right becauſe it is hot or white, or by Reaſon of the abſolute Qualities Heat and Whiteneſs: ſo alſo this is ſaid to be equal to that, becauſe of, or according to the abſolute Magnitude of each, and becauſe of the ſame, this is ſaid to be ſo many Times that. Nor for the ſame Cauſe do I like that Interpretation of *Clavius*. *According to Quantity*, i. e. *according as one is greater than another*, *or leſſer*, *or equal*. Equality, Majority, and Minority are not Terms alſo relative, nor conſequently fit for founding a Relation. Moreover when *Reaſon* is defined, *Equality*, *Majority*, and *Minority* (as being comprehended under their Reaſon or Genus) are themſelves defined in Part and virtually. From whence they ſeem not to be well placed in the Definition of Reaſon itſelf. Yet I do not diſlike, nay I think the Obſervation very good, which is made by the Greek Scholiaſt who thinks it deſignedly put *according to Quantity*, rather than *according to Quotity*, becauſe all *Reaſons* are not capable of being expreſſed by Number, nor is every Quantity ſo many Times another in any comprehenſible Manner. According to him, *Euclid* would not found the Reaſon of Quantums in their *Quotity* or *Quotuplicity*, becauſe every Quantum is not a Quotum of another, *i. e.* it does not contain, nor is contained in, another ſo many Times, either perfectly or imperfectly according to itſelf, or to any of its aliquot Parts; but *according to Quantity*; becauſe every determinate Quantum has a Quantity in itſelf according to which it may be compared with another determinate Quantum.

But it is objected againſt this Definition ſo explained that it equally agrees with the *Relation of Quantums* which intimates their *Difference*. For that alſo is truly called a *Relation* of two Quantums of the ſame Kind *according to Quantity*. I anſwer

anſwer *firſt* that when it is here ſaid *according to Quantity*, it is underſtood according to the Quantity of the Terms themſelves. But the *Relation intimating Difference* ſeems not to be founded in the Quantity of the Terms compared, but in the Quantity of ſome third, *viz.* of the Exceſs, or of the abſolute Quantum whereby the Antecedent exceeds or is ſhort of the Conſequent; *ex. gr.* the Relation between 10 and 8 ſeems to be founded in the Quantity of *Two* and not in the Quantity of the Numbers 10 and 8. For that Term alone (*viz.* the Number *Two* repreſented) ſufficiently indicates and expreſſes that Relation; but a *Geometrical Reaſon* cannot be expreſſed but by two Terms expreſſed, or at leaſt underſtood. This that moſt learned Man acknowledges in his Diſpute againſt *Meibomius*. *We ſay indeed* (ſays he) *that that Difference is not an Arithmetical Reaſon properly ſpeaking, or even the Eſſence of that Reaſon, but the Foundation of that Relation which is called Arithmetical Reaſon.* By which Saying he ſolves his own Exception againſt *Euclid*'s Definition explained after our Manner. And *Ariſtides Quintilianus* ſeems to have obſerved this, when he diſtinguiſhes the Geometrical and Arithmetical Conſiderations of Quantities thus. *Geometrical Reaſon compares two unequal Quantums*, i. e. *the Whole and the Part, according to their Quantities; but Arithmetical Reaſon, which regards the Differences of unequal Terms, conſiders the Conſequent Term and the Exceſs as Parts of the Antecedent.* But I anſwer *ſecondly*, that perhaps *Euclid* with others of the Ancients before recited were not acquainted with the *Arithmetical Relation* of Quantities, at leaſt thought that there was no ſuch Reaſon taken notice of by Geometricians. For the Conſideration of that Relation ſeems to ſuffice for the Dimenſions of Quantities, and other Determinations as to Species and Situation, which are

the

the principal or only Scopes of a Geometrician. Nor does the very Vulgar hardly conceive any other Relation of Quantities: For when Men commonly ask how much this or that is, they only enquire how often it contains some stated Measure similarly known to us, or how often it is contained in it, *i. e.* they seek a *Geometrical Reason* to this Measure of it. I adjoin *thirdly* that *Relation according to Difference*, when it is expressed by a Number denominating any of the Terms compared, it scarce differs in reality from *Geometrical Reason.* As when I say B exceeds A by 3 A, it is all one as if I said B is four times A, or is referred to A as 4 to 1. Or if I should say B exceeds A by one third Part of B, it is all one as if I said B is three halfs of A, or is to A as 3 to 2. And perhaps they have an Eye to this, who say that (y) *Reason consists in the Difference of two Quantities compared with either Quantity*; which way of speaking notwithstanding is very difficult and obscure in itself, and productive of most grievous Errors; as may be seen from the Disputation of that learned Man against *Hobbs* and *Meibomius*; whose Methods therefore of explaining Reasons I neither approve nor defend. However, I say, the *Relation of Quantities as to Difference*, if at any Time it is considered by Geometricians for determining the Measures of Quantities, it for the most part intimates the same with *Geometrical Reason*, as applied by them. Wherefore *Euclid* neglected it, either as useless, or no way different from Geometrical Reason.

But I proceed to observe *fifthly*, that the (z) Words *to one another* in the Definition are commonly interpreted to signify a certain Reciprocation,

(y) Hobbs de Corp. c. 11. §. 3, 5. c. 12, §. 8. c. 13. §. 1
(z) Πρὸς ἄλληλα.

and alternate Permutation of this Relation, by ſuch a Tranſpoſition of the Terms, that ſometimes the Antecedent may be the Conſequent, and the Conſequent the Antecedent; which Interpretation I do not think to be good, as making the Definition itſelf abſurd. For if the Compariſon be inverted or changed by the Tranſpoſition of the Terms, there will ariſe two Relations very different from one another. As *ex. gr.* the Relation of a Line of three Feet to a Line of one Foot is the Relation of three to one, or a triple Reaſon; but inverſely, the Relation of a Line of one Foot to a Line of three Feet is the Relation of one to three, or a ſubtriple Reaſon; one of the Numbers denominating which Reaſons is nine times the other. $\frac{1}{3} = \frac{1}{9} \times 3$. Therefore I rather chuſe to interpret *To one another*, to mean *One to the other*. For without doubt he aimed to define, or certainly ought to define, one ſimple Reaſon of one Magnitude to another, not two inverted Reaſons to one another. But becauſe it is no Matter in this Compariſon whether Magnitude ſupply the Place of the Antecedent, or whether of the Conſequent (foraſmuch as every Magnitude indifferently obtains ſome Reaſon to every other homogeneous Magnitude,) therefore he put *to one another* to ſignify an Indifference, as to the Situation and Order of the Terms. If any two homogeneous Magnitudes were compared together as to Quantity, whatſoever Antecedent be ſuppoſed its Relation to the other is called *Reaſon*. Nor does the Word ἄλληλον even taken in the utmoſt Rigour of its Original Notion refuſe but rather favour this Interpretation, as ſignifying ἄλλο ἤ ἄλλο, i. e. *One or another* diſjunctively; and not ἄλλο ᾗ ἄλλο, i. e. *One and another* conjunctly. But I forbear to criticiſe any longer.

There

There remains in the *Sixth* Place only the Word (*a*) *Certain* to be examined, *a certain* (*b*) Habitude, Which Interpretation a certain great Mathematician of our own Country diſlikes, ſuſpecting I know not what abſtruſe Myſtery to lie hid under the Adjective ποιὰ. For *certain* (*c*) he would rather have ſubſtituted *qualitative*, i. e. as himſelf explains, (*d*) *which belongs to the Predicament of Quality*, becauſe *Reaſon* determines the Species and Quality of Figures with the Indication or Situation of their Parts. But he rejects the vulgar Interpretation, becauſe the Word ποιὸς always cuſtomarily reſpects *Quality*, nor does it here ſo much intimate a *certain* as a *certain Species*, or rather a *qualitative Habitude*, which belongs to the Predicament of Quality. To which he ſubjoins, *And indeed in an accurate Definition it is by no means excuſable, for Reaſon to be indefinitely defined a certain Reaſon, but it is to be determined what ſort of a Relation it is.* Farthermore ſince it might be anſwered that the Relation is ſufficiently determined from what goes along with it, eſpecially from the adjoined Condition according to Quantity ; he denies that this is ſufficient, becauſe there is another Relation juſtly belonging to Quantity, *viz.* the ſo often mentioned *Relation according to Difference*, which yet as he thinks is not ποιὰ σχέσις a qualitative Habitude. But I can't notwithſtanding be eaſily brought to believe that this ſubtle Expoſition is agreeable to the Sentiment of *Euclid* himſelf. For firſt it is ſomething hard for ποιὸς to ſignifie *belonging to Quality*, or rather *effective* or *determinative of Quality*, according to the Sentiment of that moſt learned Man himſelf. Indeed with *Ariſtotle* and others ποιός is every where of the ſame Signification with ſome Sort or

(*a*) Ποιά. (*b*) Ποιὰ σχέσις.
(*c*) Arith. c. 25. contra Meib. 7. (*d*) Ἑαυτοντιμ. p. 60.

endowed

endowed with *some sort of* Quantity, (as that which is affected with any sort of Habit, Power, or Passion is by him denominated ποιός τις) but no where, I believe, with *Qualificative* which had been better denoted by ποιωτική and more agreeable to his own Exposition than *Qualitative:* for ποιεῖν signifies to *make* or *render such.* Therefore he has attributed to our Author a Manner of Speech sufficiently improper, unusual, obscure, and consequently incongruous to the Laws and Nature of Definitions. I add that it seems sufficiently remote from the intrinsecal Nature of *Reason*, and only accidental to it, that it sometimes conduces to determining the Species and Quality of Figures. It is not considered in Figures only, but often without them, nor is it otherwise subservient for their Determination than by first determining the Quantities of certain Magnitudes, *viz.* of the Lines or Superficies by which they are included. It does not then seem likely that our Author here regarded Definitions, since Definitions ought only to contain such Attributes of Notions as are necessary, universal and primary. And as to the Predicament of *Reason*, it pertains simply to Relation; but, because of the Comparison of the Terms which are always Quantities, may respectively be reduced to Quantity, and rather because of its own Foundation, which is some absolute Quantity, as is said above. It is vulgarly reckoned among the Properties of Quantity that by it Things are said to be equal and unequal, *i. e.* one is equal, double, triple, &c. of another, or affected with such a *Reason* towards another. Therefore *Reason* is *rather* a *Quantitive Habitude*, as *Similitude* is wont to be called a Relation in Quality or *Qualitative Relation*, because it is founded in some Quality. But if I am not mistaken it would sound ill to most Ears to be called a *Qualitative Relation*

tion according to Quantity, therefore *Quantitative* is better than *Qualitative.* Moreover there are innumerable Examples among the ancient Mathematicians that the Word ποιὸς does not always design a Quality properly so called, even in Definitions, as is pretended, but *oftner* a mere *Particularity*, *i. e.* an indefinite Restriction of a general Word; the same Way, as when Man is defined *a certain Animal endowed with Reason*, where *certain* only intimates that the Name *Man* is contained under the Name *Animal* confusedly and indistinctly, assigning no certain Limits, and is not perfectly adequate, to it. Thus (*e*) *Theon* defines *Analogy* to be ποιὰ σχέσις *a certain Habitude* of *Reasons to one another*; and not as I suppose, a *qualitative Habitude*, for what *Quality* intervenes in that Place? *Aristides* (*f*) *Quintilianus* defines the Genus of *Music* to be ποιὰν διαίρεσιν *a certain* (not a *Qualitative*) *Division of a four stringed Instrument*: For a *four stringed Instrument* may be innumerable Ways divided, yet all these Kinds of Divisions do not constitute the Genus of Music, but some certain only; *viz.* one Kind is *Diatonic*, another *Chromatic*, a third *Enharmonic*. To which agrees *Euclid*, the *Genus*, says he, *is* ποιὰ διαίρεσις, i. e. *a certain Division of four Sounds.* And the same *Aristides*, *It is from Sounds and Spaces having* ποιὰν τάξιν *a certain* (not a qualitative) *Order*. *Nicomachus* in his *Enchiridion* defines a musical Space or Difference to be ὁδὸν ποιὰν *a certain Passage from Flat to Sharp*, or the contrary. And such is the Definition of *Thrasyllus. A Space or Difference is a certain Habitude of Sounds to one another*: Where it is to be noted that the Arithmetical Reason, or Difference which is between *two harmonical Sounds* is precisely called ποιὰ σχέσις a *certain Habitude*:

(*e*) Cap. XXI. (*f*) Page 16.

which the learned Man acknowledges to be only a *Quantitative Relation*, and reckons that a *Geometrical Reaſon* in Contra-Diſtinction to it is termed ποιὰ σχέσις, i. e. *a qualitative Relation.* But becauſe ſuch indefinite Words are thought not fit to be ſuffered in accurate Definitions, we muſt affirm that however the beſt Authors have admitted ſuch. And beſides thoſe juſt now appealed to, I will cite *Euclid* for one, who in his *Iſagogetharmonics* inſerts the Word τὶς in the two next contiguous Definitions, *A Tone*, ſays he, is τόπος τις *a certain Place of the Voice capable of Conjunction with another, without Latitude.* And again *Mutation is the Tranſlation* ὁμοίου τινὸς *of ſome like into an unlike Place.* He refuſed not, nor indeed in my Opinion ought he to refuſe, ſuch Words. For in every Predication of a more extenſive Word concerning a narrower, or of a more general Word concerning a more ſpecial, if ſome Reſtriction be not expreſſed, at leaſt it is tacitly underſtood. As when it is ſaid *a Man is an Animal*, it is underſtood a *certain Animal*, and that which is underſtood in the direct Propoſition is expreſly pronounced in the converſe *a certain Animal is Man.* But that which is always underſtood can never be expreſſed without Blame, wherefore I ſee not why ſuch Definitions as theſe ought to be diſliked, *A Man is a certain Animal endowed with Reaſon*; *A Triangle is a certain plane Figure comprehended within three Right Lines*; *Reaſon is a certain Relation of homogeneous Quantums according to Quantity.* But he thinks that this laſt Definition vulgarly taken agrees as well with *Arithmetical Reaſon*, from which notwithſtanding it ought to be diſtinguiſhed: to which it was anſwered by Way of Anticipation, when we endeavoured to explain what is meant by being *referred according to Quantity.*

I will

I will only now add, that perhaps in delivering this Definition *Euclid* designed nothing else but a Prelude for Method or Ornament's sake to those more accurate Definitions of *the same*, *a Greater*, and a *Lesser Reason*, anon to be subjoined, that he might insinuate a certain general Idea of *Reason* into the Minds of the Learners by this *Metaphysical* Definition: I say *Metaphysical*, for it is not properly *Mathematical*, since it has no Dependence upon it, nor is, or I believe can be, deduced in the Mathematics. Of which sort also may this Definition of *Analogy* be reckoned. *Analogy is a Similitude of Reasons*, which can be serviceable for no Mathematical use, nor I think is proposed for any other End, but that by it some general confused Notion of *Analogy* may be instilled into the Minds of Learners. And the whole Doctrine of Reasons, the whole Business of Mathematics depends upon the accurate Mathematical Definitions afterwards subjoined by him; to those therefore we ought especially to attend, by these the Doctrine of Reasons is perfectly explained; and these and the like cannot at all be omitted without a remarkable Detriment to the Mathematics: as we may see in the seventh Element, where the *Analogy of Numbers* is defined and treated of; yet without applying any Definition of *Reason* agreeable to *Number*, though such a Definition was as requisite and useful there, as here; but the Necessity in neither Place was great. Albeit I do not believe that a Thing in itself so general and abstract, and therefore more difficult to be conceived and explained, is capable of a more commodious Definition than this which *Euclid* has assigned, which I therefore thought fit to explain more fully, and vindicate against the Cavils of Opposers. Where I now fix my Foot, designing in my next Lecture to proceed to the Species, and more especial Properties of Reason.

LECT.

LECTURE XIX.

Of the Species and Differences of Geometrical Reason.

WE have in Part delineated the Nature of *Geometrical Reason* by explaining and vindicating its Definition assigned in the *Elements.* Which might have been otherwise declared by saying more generally and confusedly, but perhaps more agreeable to a common Capacity, that *Reason is the determinate Way or Manner whereby any one Quantity contains, or is contained in, another*, which is the same, or very like to that *Way* or *Manner* according to which one Quantity is said to be *so many Fold* of another, or to contain another *so often*, or to be *such a Part* or *so many Parts* of another, or to be *contained so often* in another: which *Manner* is easily comprehended, when the Quantities compared can be expressed in Numbers; as the *Manner*, whereby a *Pound Troy* contains an *Ounce*, signifies no more than that the former contains the latter twelve Times, or is to it as 12 to 1; whence a *Pound* is said to obtain a *Duodecuple Reason* to an *Ounce:* The *Manner* whereby a *Foot* in Length is contained in a *Geometrical Pace* is that the former is the fifth Part of the latter, or is to it as 1 to 5, which is signified by saying, that the *Reason* of a *Foot* to a *Pace* is *subquintuple:* Which *Manner* is expressed by the abstract Word *Quintuplicity* or *Quintuplity.* But when the Quantities compared, as to their absolute Quantity, are such as cannot be perfectly expressed,

preſſed, at leaſt they may be underſtood in Numbers; becauſe that contains, or is contained in this, after ſome *determinate Manner*, otherwiſe than it contains, or is contained in, any other Thing unequal to this; therefore this *Way* or *Manner of containing* is very like that, whereby the Quantities denominated by Numbers reſpectively do contain, or are contained in, one another, and may always be nearly expreſſed in Numbers ſimply, and on the Part of the Thing. As *ex. gr.* when the *Reaſon* of the *Periphery* of a *Circle* to its *Diameter* (though not exactly and perfectly known) is repreſented by ſaying that the *Periphery* by *Appoſition* is *triple* and *ſeſquiſeptimal*, *i. e.* contains the *Diameter* three times and one ſeventh Part of it nearly. So alſo the *Reaſon* of the *Diameter* to the *Side* of a *Square*, which the Nature of the Thing will not admit to be preciſely expreſſed in Numbers may yet be repreſented approaching the Truth, by ſaying that the *Diameter* is to the *Side* as 1.4 to 1, or more nearly as 1.41 to 1, or yet again more nearly as 1.416 to 1, *&c.*

But we will endeavour farther to illuſtrate the Nature of *Reaſon*, by exhibiting *firſt* its *Species* and *Differences*; for the Comprehenſion of the *ſubjected Species* conduces very much to a perfecter Knowledge of the *Genera* or *Kinds*, the *Genera* themſelves being conſtituted and as it were generated from the Argument of theſe as to ſome eſſential Property: then *ſecondly*, by exhibiting certain *primary Accidents* of *Reaſons* (expounding their *Compariſons* to one another, *Compoſition*, *Continuation*, *Addition*, *Subtraction*, *Diviſion* and *Reduction*) alſo in the mean Time examining, by the Way, ſome controverted Queſtions, which do not a little contribute to the Illuſtration of this Subject.

As to what pertains to the *Species* of *Reaſon*, its *firſt* Diviſion moſt naturally follows the different Affection

Affection of the *Terms* in this Manner: the *Antecedent* of the *Reason* is either *greater* than the *Consequent*, *Equal* to it, or *Lesser* than it, hence arise *three Species* of *Reason:* The *Reason* of *Greater* Quantity to a *Lesser*, of an *Equal* to an *Equal*, and of a *Lesser* to a *Greater*; commonly called a *Reason of greater Inequality*, *of Equality*, and of *lesser Inequality*; but they may be more simply and concisely named *Majority*, *Equality* and *Minority*, and by these Names for brevity's sake we will always design them. But some stile *Majority* and *Minority*, the *Reason of Excess* and *Defect*, which Words also we will perhaps sometimes use. And that *double Dichotomy* according to (*a*) *Nichomachus* comes to the same Thing, when *Reason* is first divided into *Reason of Equality* and *Inequality*; and *Reason* of *Inequality* again subdivided into *Reason of greater* and *Reason of lesser Inequality*. The Thing is too plain of itself to be illustrated by Examples; yet we will give one: For Instance, the *Reason* of a Pound Troy to an Ounce (or of the Number 12 to 1) is a *Majority*, or *a Reason of greater Inequality*, or *a Reason of Excess*, because the Antecedent is greater than the Consequent. The *Reason* of a Quarter of a Pound Troy to three Ounces is a *Reason of Equality*, because the Antecedent is equal to the Consequent: But the *Reason* of an Ounce to a Pound is a *Minority*, or *a Reason of lesser Inequality*, or *a Reason of Defect*, because the Antecedent is lesser than the Consequent. These by the (*b*) *Greeks* are sometimes called *greater*, *equal* and *lesser Reasons*, but improperly; for these Words do more frequently and properly design the Respects of the *Reasons* themselves compared together, and not the *Species* of *particular Reasons* absolutely taken. For instance, in comparing the *Rea-*

(*a*) Nicom. lib. 1, p. 24. (*b*) Theo. Smyr. cap. 22.

sons of nine Ounces to four Ounces, and of eight Ounces to four Ounces; the Reason of nine Ounces to four Ounces is *greater* than that of eight Ounces to four Ounces, *i. e.* the *Reason* of 9 to 4 is *greater* than that of 8 to 4. But the *Reasons* of nine Ounces to four Ounces and of eight Ounces to four Ounces simply referred to one another, are not rightly stiled *greater Reasons*, but *Reasons* of *Majority*, *Excess*, or *greater Inequality*, i. e. *Reasons* of *greater* Quantities to *lesser* Quantities. This is the first Division of Reasons.

Otherwise *Reason* (or *Reason* of Inequality, for it matters not whether *Reason* universally, or *Reason of Inequality* particularly, be so divided) otherwise, I say, *Reason* is divided by respecting those *Properties* already explained in Part, which I call *Commensurability* and *Incommensurability*. For because some of the Terms compared together are *commensurable*, *i. e.* are capable of being measured, compleatly divided, or quite exhausted by the same Quantity taken once or oftner, and consequently of being accurately expressed in Numbers; while others are *incommensurable*, *i. e.* are mensurable by no common Measure, have no Part aliquot to the same, and consequently, being so affected cannot be expressed or perfectly represented by any Number: Hence arises the Division of *Reason* into *Effable* and *Ineffable*. Where notwithstanding it is to be noted that these Words ῥητὸς *effable*, and ἄῤῥητος *ineffable* are very often used in the Elements. For when *Euclid* considered that, any Right Line being expounded (which he calls *effable*, as being denominable or effable by any Number at Pleasure,) the Lines compared with it are of three Kinds, *viz.* some are *Commensurable* with it in Length, others are *Incommensurable* in Length, yet so that their Squares are commensurable, and capable of being denominated by Numbers most perfectly exhibiting

their

their true Reasons to the Square of the Line expounded: Lastly, most others are not only *Incommensurable* to the Line expounded in Length, but also in Power, *i. e.* their Squares are also *Incommensurable* to the Square of the Line expounded: I say, when *Euclid* considered this, he named the Lines of the two former Kinds *Effable*, as capable of being some Way expressed; but the last Kind he called *Irrational* or *Ineffable*, as being no Way explicable, or capable of being expressed, by Numbers. Therefore according to *Euclid* some *Incommensurable Quantities* seem to have an *Effable Reason* to one another (for if the Quantities themselves are said to be *effable*, consequently their *Reason* will be *effable*) I say Quantities incapable of *Commensurability* in Length, Breadth or Thickness may have an *Effable Reason*; for albeit their *Reason* cannot be *immediately* represented by any common Numbers, yet it may in Part be so *mediately*, *viz.* by the Intervention of their Squares, when these are truly denominated and expressed in Numbers. For from thence they may be called the *Sides* or *Square Roots* of such Numbers; at least such an Expression suffices for determining their relative Quantity, and causing that the Quantities themselves may be both in some Measure subjected to our Estimation and easily capable of real Representation. But with some it seems most agreeable to Reason to have the *Reasons of Incommensurable Quantities* called *Ineffable*; because the Terms of such *Reasons* cannot properly and immediately be expressed in Numbers vulgarly known and received, and therefore we will retain this Sense; though the most learned *Borellus* (perhaps for avoiding Ambiguity) chuses to divide *Proportion* into *Commensurable* and *Non-mensurable*, devising new Words, and such as in my Judgment are not very suitable. For the *Proportions* of *in-*

commensurable

commenſurable Quantities are *menſurable*, as well as the *Proportions* of *commenſurable Quantities:* and in my Opinion he had ſpoke more accurately if he had ſaid *Proportion* is either of *Commenſurable Quantities* or *Incommenſurable Quantities.* But of theſe Things by the by, let us return to the propoſed *Species of Reaſons.*

An *Effable* or *Explicable Reaſon* is that which may be really expreſſed in common Numbers, *i. e.* in Integers, mixed Numbers and Fractions; or rather always in Integers, becauſe every *Reaſon of Numbers* however fracted or compoſed of Integers and Fractions may be always reduced to Integers by multiplying by the Denominators of the Fractions. Examples may be taken from all Meaſures of the ſame Kind, ſuch as a Finger's Breadth, a Span, a Palm, a Foot, a Cubit, a Yard, an Ell, a Pace, a Furlong, a Mile, a League for meaſuring Intervals of Longitude; a Grain, a Dram, an Ounce, a Pound for eſtimating Weights; a Farthing, a Penny, a Shilling, a Crown, a Mark, a Pound for computing Money; a Minute, an Hour, a civil Day, Month, Year; I ſay, civil, becauſe it cannot be known whether theſe natural Parts of Time are commenſurable or no. Theſe Quantities and the like have their *Reaſons* to one another *Effable* or *Explicable*, and are therefore ſuited to vulgar Uſes. For Inſtance the *Reaſon* of a Mark to a Pound is *Effable*, becauſe they are expreſſed by the Numbers $\frac{2}{3}$ and 1 or 2 and 3, or any other Number which are ſeſquialter to one another. So alſo the *Reaſon* of a Shilling to an half Crown is expreſſed by the Numbers $\frac{2}{5}$ and 1 or 1 and $2\frac{1}{2}$, or 2 and 5; which *Reaſon* is ſaid to be *ſub-multiple-double-ſeſquialter*, as we will ſhew anon.

An *Ineffable* or *Inexplicable* (or as ſome call it *Irrational*) *Reaſon* is that which is between *Incommenſurable Quantities*, whoſe Reaſon cannot be perfectly

perfectly expressed by any true and vulgar Numbers whatsoever. Such is the *Reason* in that most trite Example of the Diameter to the Side of a Square; for no two Numbers can be found in the whole Series of possible Numbers (integral, fracted, or mixed) whose *Reason* does exactly represent the *Reason* between these two Quantities. For since the Square of the Diameter (as is demonstrated in the Elements) is twice the Square of the Side, and there are no two Square Numbers the one double the other, in the whole Series of common Numbers, therefore there are no Numbers which can exhibit the *Reason* of the Diameter of a Square to its Sides. And innumerable such *Reasons* are found in all Kinds of Quantities, so that comparing together regular Figures, as well plane as solid, inscribed or circumscribed, in the same Circle or Sphere; scarce any will be found to have a *Reason* to one another *explicable* in Numbers, either as to their Sides or Perimeters, or as to their Areas, or as to their Solidities. Whence that the *Reasons* of these and most other Quantities may be some Way referred to Numbers (as being the most general, most known, and most commodious Symbols of Quantities) it was necessary to devise those Numbers called *Surds* or *Irrationals*, that the *Reasons* of these Quantities may be some Way expressed. And of these *ineffable Reasons* there are reckoned no *Species*, because the different Ways whereby their Terms contain, or respect, one another, cannot be well conceived to be distinguished, and no Method is yet invented for expressing them otherwise: But I will endeavour to reckon up the *Species* of the *Reasons* commonly called *Effable*, and explain them as briefly as I can. For why should I dwell upon Things sufficiently clear of themselves? It is rather my Design to offer those Things to your Consideration, which seem less common and more intricate,

intricate, every where paſſing lightly over ſuch Things as are obvious and plain.

Nothing, in the *firſt* Place, is more manifeſt than that the *Reaſon* of equal Quantities is always *Effable*, as being capable of Expreſſion by any equal Numbers whatſoever. *Ex. gr.* Every equal Quantity is to every other, as One to One, or Two to Two. Therefore the *Reaſon of Equality* may be ſaid to be the *firſt Species* of *Effable Reaſons*. And ſince the *Reaſon of Inequality*, as we have ſeen, is twofold, *viz.* of *Majority* and *Minority*, or the *Reaſon of Exceſs* and *Defect*, there are vulgarly *five Species* of *Effable Majority*, to which there anſwer univerſally juſt as many *Species* of *Minority*. Theſe we will recount and expound, yet ſo as firſt to inveſtigate the Foundation and Original of this Diviſion, which ought eſpecially to be regarded in every technical Diviſion. And this we undertake to do by noting that when we compare two Quantities, whoſe *Reaſon* to one another is *Effable*, or in their Stead the Numbers whereby they are repreſented, *i. e.* when we ſeek the *Manner* whereby the Antecedent contains, or is contained in, the Conſequent, we attempt to repreſent this *Manner* in Numbers as ſmall as poſſible; becauſe every *Reaſon* is more eaſily eſtimated and comprehended in the *leaſt Terms*. Therefore we endeavour that one of them, *viz.* the Conſequent be Unity, the loweſt and moſt ſimple of Numbers, which being laid down, we ſeek an Antecedent Term to Unity agreeing with the Conſequent. And *that* Term of the *Reaſon* to be eſtimated is called the *Denominator*, as denominating and expreſſing it moſt ſuitably to our Capacity. But becauſe ſuch is the Nature of Arithmetical Diviſion that as often as the Number to be divided contains the Diviſor, the Quotient found contains Unity; therefore that Denominator

minator (or Antecedent of the Reaſon whoſe Conſequent is Unity) is found by dividing the Antecedent of the Reaſon propoſed by the Conſequent. Moreover, ſince that *Denominator* or Quotient, becauſe of the *intrinſecal Diverſity* of the Terms themſelves, may be a Number of a different Species (*viz.* Integer, fracted, or mixed, and not the ſame Kind of Fraction or mixed Number) *ex. gr.* by conſidering the *Reaſon of greater Inequality*, the ſaid Quotient found by the Diviſion of the Terms may be either an Integer, or Unity with a Fraction whoſe Numerator is Unity, or Unity with a Fraction whoſe Numerator is greater than Unity, or an Integer greater than Unity with a Fraction whoſe Numerator is Unity, or laſtly an Integer greater than Unity with a Fraction whoſe Numerator exceeds Unity. From theſe *five various Ways* or *Species* of the ſaid Quotient ariſe five Species of *Effable Majority*, which are vulgarly called *multiple*, *ſuperparticular*, *ſuperpartient*, *multiple-ſuperparticular*, and *multiple-ſuperpartient*; to which anſwer the *Reaſons* of *Minority* named *ſubmultiple*, *ſubſuperparticular*, *ſubſuperpartient*, *ſubmultiple-ſuper-particular*, and *ſubmultiple-ſuperpartient*: which we come now to illuſtrate in their Order.

Firſt, The Reaſon of one Term to another is ſaid to be *multiple*, when the Antecedent exactly contains the Conſequent any Number of Times more than once; or when the Conſequent perfectly meaſures the Antecedent, ſo as to leave no Remainder. Or which is the ſame Thing, when the Conſequent is any Aliquot Part of the Antecedent, which being taken ſome Number of Times totally compoſes, equals, or compleats the Antecedent; and conſequently the *Denominator* of this *Reaſon* is always an *Integer*. Thus a Geometrical Pace is to a Foot in a *Multiple Reaſon* denominated

by

by the Integer 5; becauſe a Foot taken five Times exactly makes a Pace; or becauſe a Pace includes a Foot five Times without a Remainder. Hence it is apparent that this *Reaſon* has as many *ſubordinate Species* as there are Integers by which they may be denominated, and diſtinguiſhed which are infinite: *Ex. gr. Double*, *Triple*, *Decuple*, *Centuple*, *Millecuple*, &c. *Reaſons* are *Species* of *Multiple Reaſon. Submultiple Reaſon* therefore, which anſwers univerſally to *Multiple*, is when the Antecedent exactly meaſures the Conſequent, is an Aliquot Part of it, or is contained in it ſome Number of Times; and its Denominator is always ſome ſimple Fraction, whoſe Numerator is Unity. Thus a Foot to a Pace is in the *ſubmultiple Reaſon*, as being five Times contained in a Pace, and having for its Denominator the Fraction $\frac{1}{5}$. In like Manner this Kind of *Reaſon* has as many *Species*, as there can be ſimple Fractions denominated by any Number, whoſe Numerator is Unity: *Ex. gr. ſubduple*, *ſubtriple*, *ſubdecuple*, *ſubcentuple*, &c. *Reaſons* are *Species* of *ſubmultiple Reaſon.* For ſince theſe *Reaſons* cannot fitly be ſignified by Words of common Uſe, therefore Mathematicians deſign them by prefixing *ſub* to the Names of the *Multiple Reaſons* inverſed. For the Words *Second*, *Tenth*, *Hundredth*, *Thouſandth* (by which are expreſſed the Aliquot Parts of Unity) cannot be ſo fitly applied for denoting theſe *Reaſons*, becauſe they are moreover ordinal, and do not only ſignify a Diviſion into Parts, but alſo a certain Place of Things diſpoſed in ſome Order: as the *third King from* Romulus, the *eighth of the Wiſe Men*, the *hundredth Year hence*: Otherwiſe I do not ſee but the *Third*, *Fourth*, *Tenth*, &c. *Reaſons* might ſerve for denoting theſe *Reaſons*, as well as *Double*, *Triple*, *Decuple*, &c. for the Species of *Multiple Reaſons.* It appears then that the Correlative Terms *Whole* and

Part

Part are common to both *multiple* and *ſubmultiple* Reaſon, by taking the Word *Whole* according to its native Signification and the Word *Part* for an Aliquot Part according to *Euclid*'s Senſe and Definition. *A Part is a Magnitude of a Magnitude, a leſs of a greater, when the leſs meaſures the greater.* But I proceed to other *Species.*

Secondly, A Reaſon is ſaid to be *ſuperparticular* when the Antecedent ſo exceeds the Conſequent that ſome Aliquot Part of the Conſequent remains over and above, whence the Reaſon of the Name: Or when the Antecedent includes the Conſequent no oftner than once, and ſome one only Aliquot Part of it beſides: Or when the Antecedent divided by the Conſequent exhibits Unity for the Quotient, with Unity alſo remaining yet to be divided by the Conſequent: and conſequently the Denominator of this Reaſon is Unity with a Fraction annexed, which has Unity for its Numerator. Such is the Reaſon of a Cubit to a Foot, becauſe a Cubit exceeds a Foot by one half of a Foot; ſo alſo 9 Ounces is in a *ſuperparticular Reaſon* to 8 Ounces, becauſe 9 Ounces contains 8 Ounces once and an eighth Part of it more, or becauſe $\frac{9}{8}=1+\frac{1}{8}$. The *Species* of this *Reaſon* are alſo infinite, according to the infinite Multitude of Denominators; which in Latin uſe to be ſignified diſtinctly by prefixing the Particle *ſeſqui* to the Names of the Ordinal Numbers, as *Seſquialtera* (or *Seſquiſecunda*) *Seſquitertia, Seſquiquarta, Seſquidecima, Seſquicenteſima,* &c. which Words muſt be thus underſtood, *viz.* when the Antecedent exceeds the Conſequent by its half (as 12 exceeds 8) that is ſaid to be the *Seſquialtera* of this; when by one third (as 12 exceeds 9) *Seſquitertia,* &c. The Inverſe of *Superparticular Reaſon* is called *Subſuperparticular,* and its Species *Subſeſquialtera, Subſeſquitertia, Subſeſquidecima,* &c. The Nature of which *Reaſons* ſufficiently appears by by comparing them with their Opposites; for they differ from those only by a Transposition of the Terms, and their Denominators are to Unity, as Unity to the Denominators of their inverse Reasons. Concerning which we will yet remark this, that the Denominator of a *Subsuperparticular Reason* is always some Fraction whose Numerator is an Unit less than the Denominator. Thus the Denominator of a *Subsesquialter* Reason is $\frac{2}{3}$, of a *subsesquiterce* $\frac{3}{4}$, of a *Subsesquiquart* $\frac{4}{5}$, *&c.*

Thirdly, we proceed to a *Superpartient Reason*, which is when the Antecedent exceeds the Consequent by some Aliquot Parts more than one, whence the Name: Or when the Antecedent includes the Consequent once, and some aliquot Parts of it more, I say Parts to distinguish it from a *Superparticular Reason:* Or when the Antecedent divided by the Consequent exhibits Unity for the Quotient, with a Remainder exceeding Unity. Therefore its Denominator is Unity with a Fraction whose Numerator exceeds Unity. Thus 9 is said to be in a *Superpartient Reason* to 7, because 9 exceeds 7 by two 7th Parts. This Reason has also infinite *Species* from the infinite Variety of Denominators, which *Species* are so expressed in Words that both the Numerator and Denominator of the Fraction adjoined to Unity, are pronounced in the *Denominator* of the proposed *Reason*; *as Superbipartient Tertias, Quintas, Septimas,* &c. *Ex. gr.* The Reason of 12 to 7 is said to be *Superquinquipartient Septimas*; in which Expression the numeral *Septimas* distinctly shews by what sort of Aliquot Parts the Antecedent exceeds the Consequent, and *quinqui* (for the Adverb *quinquies*) denotes by how many of the said Parts it exceeds it. And the same Way in others. But (as we have said) an Exception ought to be observed, that the Excess of the Antecedent above the Consequent ought always to be more than one

Ali-

Aliquot Part, or that the Fraction annexed to Unity in its least Terms must not have Unity for a Numerator; for then the *Reason* will not be *Superpartient*, but *Superparticular*: As *ex. gr.* the *Reason* of 12 to 9, according to this Division will not be said to be *Superpartient*, but *Superparticular Sesquiterce*, because 12 exceeds 9 by one third Part. *i. e.* by 3. Though according to the Truth of the Matter, such Limitation being set aside, this *Reason* may be called *Supertripartient nonas*, as 12 exceeds 9 by 3, *i. e.* by $\frac{3}{9}$ or three ninths of 9, which Fraction is equal to $\frac{1}{3}$. But the Difference of these Reasons requires the Denominators distinguishing them to be expressed in the most simple and the smallest Terms, or otherwise a *Multiple Reason* will in some Measure coincide with a *Superpartient one*; for instance, the *Reason* of 9 to 3 may be truly called *supersextipartient tertias*, because 9 exceeds 3 by six thirds of three, *i. e.* by six Units; but it is plain that this *Reason* is expressed much more simply and fitly by saying that 9 is a *Multiple*, *viz.* the *Triple* of 3. And hence as in the foregoing, the Opposite of this Reason, together with its Species, is easily understood. For they differ only as to the Thing by a Transposition of the Terms; and as to the Name by prefixing the Particle *sub*: as, *Subsuperpartient*, *Subsuperbipartient tertias*, *quartas*, *decimas*, &c. therefore we will dwell no longer upon them. And these three are the Species of *simple Reasons*, when the Antecedent contains the Consequent only once. There remain other two Species resulting from the first conjoin'd with the second and third, *viz. Multiple-superparticular*, and *Multiple-superpartient*, with their Opposites.

Fourthly, when the Antecedent includes the Consequent more Times than one, and one Aliquot Part of it besides, (as 9 contains 4 twice, and a 4th Part of it more) the *Reason* of these Terms in general is said

ſaid to be *Multiple ſuperparticular*; in particular (as in the Example propoſed) *double ſeſquiquärt*, and ſo of others. The Inverſe Reaſon of which, ſuppoſe of 4 to 9 is in general ſaid to be *ſubmultiple ſuperparticular*, in particular *ſubduple ſeſquiquart*. But

Fifthly, when the Antecedent contains the Conſequent more Times than once, and more Aliquot Parts of it, beſides than one (as the Number 8 contains the Number 3 twice with two third Parts of it), the *Reaſon* of thoſe Terms to one another in general is ſaid to be *Multiple-ſuperpartient*; in particular (as in the Example propoſed) *Double ſuperbipartient tertias*; and after the ſame Manner in others. Alſo the Inverſe Reaſon of this, as the Number 3 to 8, is in general ſaid to be *ſubmultiple ſuperpartient*, in particular *ſubduple ſuperbipartient tertias*. I imagine there will be no need of inſiſting longer upon theſe Things which are ſufficiently manifeſt.

And thus we have briefly reckon'd up and expounded the Kinds of *Effable Reaſons* to be *five* of *Majority*, with the ſame Number of *Minority* oppoſite to them; nor is there any other *Reaſon of Inequality* expreſſible in Numbers, which may not be reduced to ſome of theſe; as every greater Quantity contains a leſſer either *(firſt)* ſome Number of Times perfectly, and conſequently is a Multiple of it, and this a *ſubmultiple* of that; or *(ſecondly)* once with one only Aliquot Part of it, and conſequently is a *ſuperparticular of it*, and this a *ſubſuperparticular of that*; or *(thirdly)* once with more Aliquot Parts of it than one, from whence it is a *ſuperpartient* of it, and this a *ſubſuperpartient* of that; or *(fourthly)* more than once, with one Part of it only, whence it is called a *Multiple ſuperparticular*, and this a *ſubmultiple ſuperparticular of that*; or *(laſtly)* more than once with more Aliquot Parts of it than one, therefore called a *Multiple ſuperpartient*, and this on the contrary a *ſubmultiple-ſuperpartient* of that; nor does the

the Nature of the Thing admit more Ways of containing. Consequently this Enumeration is perfect.

Notwithstanding in *Theon Smyrnæus* (*a*) I find yet another Species of Reason, by him said to be simply Effable, and its Terms to be as one Number to another, but distinct from the foregoing; which he therefore designs by the Name of *Neuter*, and, says he, *is the Reason of a Number to a Number*, when the Greater is to the Lesser in none of the aforesaid *Reasons*. For an Instance of which he brings the *Reason* which is between the Terms of the Musical Interval called a *Limma* the greater being to the lesser as 256 to 253. And *Meibomius* follows him in the *Dialogue concerning Proportions* for which he is reproached, as if he dreamed: And indeed not undeservedly. Yet *Meibomius*, we see, did not fancy this out of his own Brain, but is supported by the Authority of *Theon*. What then, Is *Theon* in the Wrong? So it seems, since the Reason of a *Limma* is entirely *superpartient*, viz. *superdecupartient ducentesimas quadragesimas tertias*, and therefore not distinct from the foregoing. I can't otherwise untie this Knot, nor excuse *Theon* of Error, but by saying that *Theon*, and perhaps other ancient Mathematicians, understood a *superpartient Reason* for such a *Reason* only, whose Antecedent so exceeds the Consequent that the Residue may be divided into two simple Aliquot Parts of the Consequent (I call those simple whose Numerator is Unity;) As in the Comparison of 11 with 6, the Residue 5 contains 3 and 2, of which 3 is one half, and two one third of the Consequent 6. From whence this Reason is superpartient even according to *Theon*, and the Interpretation he gives of a *superpartient Reason*. But according to this Ac-

(*a*) Cap. 22. 28.

ceptation,

ception, the *Reason* of a *Limma* will not be superpartient: for 13 the Excess of the Number 256 above 243, cannot be divided into two simple Aliquot Parts of the Consequent 243, as will be found by Tryal. *Bullialdus (a)* gives another Example of the Number 29 to 23, either not at all considering, or purposely dissembling this Difficulty, and subscribing to the Error of *Theon*, if it be an Error. For the *Reason* of the Number 29 to 23 is plainly *supersextipartient* 23as, taking a *superpartient Reason*, as it commonly is. But of this enough.

I might have added Rules for investigating any Terms of all these Reasons already expounded; but besides this would be difficult to accommodate to the Understanding of Hearers, and not very profitable, and requiring many Words, would take up much Time; *Clavius* in his *Precedaneous Works* to the *fifth Element* is ready for any who has a Mind; or among the more ancient *Nichomachus* in his *Arithmetical Works*. Here I rest for the present.

LECTURE XX.

That Reasons are not Quantities.

WE have explained the Nature, and reckon'd up the *Species* of *Reason* in our last; I come next to discuss some of its *Accidents*. It happens to *Reasons*, according to the common Way of Speech, as to Quantities, to be *added* or *subtracted*, *encreased* or *diminished*, *protracted* and *contracted*, *multiplied* and *divided*, and *compared together according*-

(a) Ad. Cap. 22. The. Smyr.

ing

ing to Equality and Inequality; which laſt, ſince it is the principal Thing in itſelf, and altogether neceſſary for underſtanding the reſt, as well as for illuſtrating the whole Doctrine of *Reaſons*, we will diſcourſe of it in the firſt Place. Yet ſo that it concerns me to ſpeak ſomething by way of Preface, before I enter upon a Thing ſo ſubtle and intricate, which, either by the Nature of the Thing, or thro' the Fault of thoſe that treat of it, is involved in a moſt thick Miſt; to clear up which I can neither hope nor promiſe from my poor Ability: eſpecially ſince I find it a very difficult Thing to expreſs the Thoughts which occur to me about it in ſuitable Words, and digeſt them in a clear Method. *M. Meibomius* declares that he ſpent five full Years in this Speculation, nor does all that vaſt Labour ſeem to produce any Thing ſound or ſolid, beſide ſome little Criticiſms. And that great Man *Gregory Vincentius* who is behind none of the modern Geometricians dwelt longer, and took more Pains upon the ſame, and yet in my Opinion left the Thing as obſcure as he found it. What then can be expected from the Study of a few Hours, what (to ſay no more) from this almoſt extemporary Writing, about ſuch a perplexed Subject? Nevertheleſs we muſt purſue our Method, we muſt proceed in the Journey we have begun, however rugged and impervious, and ſuggeſt ſomething, tho' rough and unelegant to be poliſhed and improved by your more mature Judgment.

Theſe Things being premiſed, I betake my ſelf to the Buſineſs in Hand. But firſt of all a Queſtion is to be decided conducing very much to the Underſtanding what is ſaid: *viz.* ſince Reaſons, no otherwiſe than all abſolute Quantities are ſaid to be *compared together*, *according to Equality*, *or Inequality*, *compounded or reſolved*, *added* or *ſubtracted*, *multiplied*, or *divided*; it may be doubted in what Senſe

theſe

theſe Things are to be underſtood, whether properly or improperly; or whether Reaſons accurately ſpeaking are *Quantums* properly ſubject to thoſe Affections of Quantity, *viz. Equality*, *Inequality*, *Reaſon*, *Compoſition*, *Diviſion*, and the reſt. Moſt of the Moderns are of this Opinion, and expreſly affirm, that Reaſon is a *peculiar Kind of Quantity*, and has the Attributes of Quantity rightly applied to it. This *Vincentius* lays as a Foundation to the whole Doctrine of his *Proportionalities*; and his aſſociate the learned *Tacquet* agrees with him: This Mr. *Hobbs* inculcates without Oppoſition from his learned Adverſary; and the famous *Borellus* owns the ſame, *We are now treating*, ſays (*d*) he, *of a new Species of Quantity*. Why ſhall I mention, *Merſennus*, *Meibomius*, and others, ſince all with one Conſent, eſpecially they who ſtudy to innovate about the Doctrine of *Proportionality*, ſeem to agree in this Opinion? Neverthele ſs I muſt preſume to oppoſe the illuſtrious Authority of ſo many great Men. Truth requires moſt of all to be defended againſt ſuch powerful Enemies. This Opinion to me ſeems not only falſe, but alſo very prejudicial, becauſe it begets and maintains uſeleſs Controverſies, and introduces very many Confuſions and Errors into the Doctrine of *Proportions*. Some few more Janglings will be ſilenced, ſome Difficulties taken away, Errors avoided, and Clouds diſperſed, by maintaining that *Reaſon* is not a Genus or Kind of Quantity, nor any thing ſubject to Quantity, or any where properly attributed to Quantity directly by itſelf, but agrees no otherwiſe with it, than by a *Catachreſis* or *Metonymy*. And indeed it ſeems ſtrange for any one to have thought otherwiſe; for ſince Reaſon is, and is acknowledged to be a pure perfect Relation, how can it

(*d*) Ad. 7. def. lib. 3.

paſs

paſs into another Category, and conſtitute a Genus of Quantity? Since it is nothing but a Reſpect of two *Quantums* founded in Quantity, how can it be conceived a *Quantum* of itſelf, or a Subject of Quantity? Since it is abſtractly a Relation how can it be concretely a Thing related? Is not this to confound Things abſolute with Things reſpective, and concrete Names with abſolute? Logicians have hitherto taught that *Relations are inherent to, are attributed, and depend upon abſolute Things*; but abſolute Things, I believe, are never ſaid nor heard by any to inhere to Relations. So neither does it ſeem plauſible to be ſaid, nor poſſible to be conceived, that Relations reſpect themſelves, that Habitudes have themſelves this or that Way, that Diſtances are diſtant, Similitudes ſimilar, or Compariſons compared. When *ex. gr.* it is ſaid this Reaſon is greater than that, firſt (according to the Opinion of our Adverſaries, taking that Expreſſion properly,) ſome Magnitude, or Quantity inherent to the Reaſon is attributed to it, becauſe of which Magnitude the Reaſon is referred to another, or in which is founded its Reaſon to another; then it is ſaid interpretatively and conſequently, *this Inequality* is unequal to *that Inequality*, this *Majority* greater than *Majority*: thus abſolute Things will be inherent to Relations, and Relations attributed to Relations; concrete Words predicated of their paronymous Terms, and paronymous Terms of abſtract Words. Moreover by what Cauſe and Right a Man in comparing Reaſons together, will pronounce them to be properly equal, or unequal, and to obtain a Reaſon to one another, by the ſame Cauſe and equal Right, in comparing the Reaſons of thoſe Reaſons, he may aſſign *Equality* and *Inequality* to them, and conſequently a new Genus or Kind of Reaſon: Nay more, he may yet frame other Rea-

ſons

ſons of theſe Reaſons, and ſo continually proceed *ad infinitum.* If Reaſon be a Kind of Quantity diſtinct from the Quantity of the Magnitudes compared, and if it obtain Reaſon itſelf, then this new Reaſon will by equal Right be a new Kind of Quantity, and the Reaſon of this Reaſon will make another diſtinct Kind, and ſo we ſhall have infinite Kinds of Quantity, hitherto never dreamt, nor thought of. But ſuch a liberal and eaſy Multiplication of Beings, which is neither neceſſary nor imaginable, is deſervedly rejected by Philoſophers. I add, that no Quantity of any Reaſon can immediately be diſcerned or eſtimated of itſelf, it occurs not to the Senſe, it ſhews not itſelf by its Effects, is not gathered or proved by any certain Reaſon, as we ſhall hereafter endeavour to ſhew. Therefore it is ſuppoſed, and affirmed *gratis*, and may with the ſame Eaſe be rejected and denied.

But I foreſee it may be thus objected againſt our firſt Argument: The Relation of a Father to a Son, is it not truly ſaid to be like to that of a Prince to a Subject, of a General to a private Soldier, or of a Paſtor to his Flock? And ſo a Relation is attributed and inherent to a Relation, *viz. Similitude*, or *Likeneſs* to *Paternity*. I anſwer briefly, firſt that ſuch Relations as *Paternity* and *Likeneſs* are of a very different Nature, nor when it is ſaid *Paternity is like*, is ſuch an inconſiſtent Reduplication and Confuſion of concrete Names with abſtract committed, as is incurred by ſaying a *Likeneſs is like*, or *Inequality unequal.* But I anſwer more fully *ſecondly*, when it is ſaid *Paternity is like the Principate* (or the Relation of a Prince to his People,) *Likeneſs* is not founded in the Relations themſelves, nor in any Thing inherent to them, but in the abſolute Things to which theſe Relations belong; or in other abſolute Things, which follow from theſe Foundations: becauſe caufe *ex. gr.* to beget a Son and gather together a People, to govern a Family and prefide over a City, are like; fince to be beloved, to advife, to punifh, to help, to provide, to defend, to require due Reverence, Obedience and Gratitude are common to both a Father and a Prince: hence a *Father* and a *Prince* may abfolutely be faid to be *like*, for many Caufes and Reafons, as being affected with *like Qualities* and doing or fuffering *like Things*. From whence by a Tranflation of the Name, the Relations themfelves of *Paternity*, and the *Principate* are faid to be *like*, not becaufe thefe Relations in Strictnefs of Speech are related to one another; (For fince a *Relation* is defined to have its whole Effence in Refpect to (or from the Confideration of) fome Kind or Kinds of Being as diftinct from all others, how can it be conceived that Relations which belong to two different Kinds or Species of Being (as that of *Paternity* and the *Principate*) fhould alfo be Relations to one another; which would be all one as to fay, that that which has its whole Effence with Refpect to certain Beings, as they are diftinct from all others, has alfo its whole Effence with Refpect to fomething elfe which in like manner has its whole Effence from other different Beings as they are diftinct from all others? The Inconfiftence of which, who does not fee?) but becaufe fuch Qualities or Actions are always conjoined with thofe Relations, by Reafon of which the Terms related are truly accounted to be *like*. Therefore this Relation of *Likenefs* is not fo much inherent to the faid Relations, as concomitant to them, and only therefore attributed to them. And fomething like this happens in the Subject we are profecuting. Whatfoever *Equality*, or *Inequality*, or particular Reafon does really agree with abfolute Quantums, is afcribed to their Reafons. *Ex. gr.* when a *fex-*

tuple

tuple Reason is said to be greater than (*viz. double* to) a *triple Reason*, nothing is meant but that the Thing denominated by the Number *six* is greater in a *double Reason* than the Thing denominated by the Number Three; or that the Antecedent of one Reason is *double* the Antecedent of the other; by Reason of which *Manner* of *Inequality*, one *Reason* may *metonymically* be said to be *unequal* to another. For any one will readily own, if he attentively consider the Matter, that a *sextuple Thing* may most truly and properly be said to be the *double* of a *triple Thing* (by applying concrete Words, and consequently involving certain absolute Things;) but it can never be truly and properly said that *Sextuplicity* (using abstract Names) is the double of *Triplicity*. Certainly a *Sextuple* may at any Time be divided into two *Triples*, and a *Triple* may be so doubled, and taken twice, as to compose a Sextuple. But *Sextuplicity* itself seems to be something indivisible, nor can *Triplicity* aptly go to a Composition. Indeed $3+3$ equals 6, but I cannot conceive what Sum can be made by *Triplicity* + *Triplicity*. Three Hours is the *Triple* of an Hour, and three Years the *Triple* of an Year, yet I understand not what Sum, mathematically computable, can be made by adjoining that *Triplicity* to this; but rather see that no *Sextuplicity* can emerge from those two *Triplicities*, which are *metaphysically* two. But that these Things may appear plainer, and because no Necessity requires any distinct Quantity to be assigned to Reasons, we shall more closely advert to some Things about the Comparisons of Reasons.

First, I observe, that no Reasons can be so compared together as to make any such Reason, as our Adversaries pretend, known or estimable, except they be first reduced to a *Common Consequent*, viz. *immediately*, or *mediately*, *actually* and *explicitly*, or

virtually

virtually and *implicitly*. *Ex. gr.* No Body can know, or conceive which Reaſon whether of the Number 12 to 8 or of the Number 4 to 2 is greater, or which Way greater, but by conſidering that 12 is to 3 as 4 to 1, and 4 is to 2 as 2 to 1: Or ſubſtituting any other common Conſequent, ſuppoſe 5, in the Room of Unity, by conſidering that 12. 3 :: 20 : 5, and 4. 2 :: 10. 5. This being conſidered and underſtood the Inequality, and *Reaſon* as it is called, of the *Reaſons* propoſed is known from the Compariſon of the Antecedents in thoſe new *equipollent Reaſons*. Therefore it appears alſo from hence, that *Reaſons have no Quantity of themſelves* at all imaginable or diſtinct from the Quantity of their Terms; but yet after they obtain a common Conſequent, they are denominated *Inequal* becauſe of the *Inequality* of the Antecedents.

In like Manner it may be adverted *ſecondly*, that when the Terms of any two Reaſons are heterogeneous, they cannot at all be compared or eſtimated, except they be firſt reduced to ſome common Genus. *Ex. gr.* let two Weights, and two Times be propoſed, it may hence, and ſcarce otherwiſe, be in ſome Meaſure known, which is greater, the Reaſon of theſe two Weights or Times, by this means. Let a Quantum of any Kind be aſſumed at Pleaſure, but generally a Right Line may be aſſumed moſt conveniently (becauſe of the Simplicity of Right Lines above any Thing elſe, and their Capacity for expreſſing any Reaſon,) let any Right Line, I ſay, be ſo aſſumed, if it can be done, that the firſt be to the ſecond, as ſome Line to the Line aſſumed; alſo that the firſt Time be to the ſecond, as ſome Line again to the ſame aſſumed Line; then as the former Line thus found is to the latter, ſo will the Reaſon of the Weights be ſaid to be to the Reaſon of the Times; I ſay, it will be ſaid to be ſo becauſe the ſaid Lines are thus to one another, borrowing their Denomination from their Reaſon. Inſtead of a Line, a Number may be moſt conveniently aſſumed, if the Reaſons propoſed be explicable in Numbers; but if they be not, which for the moſt Part happens, then is Number unfit for this Compariſon. Whence, I obſerve by the Way, that a certain great Man in his *(a)* Arithmetical Works ſeems not rightly to ſay *that all Reaſons exiſt in the Genus of Number:* as if other Quantities could not obtain Reaſon, and that ſufficiently knowable, without any Conſideration at all of Numbers. But what Way can this Sort of Reaſon be in the Genus of Number, which can be expreſſed in other Terms, and yet not in Numbers? In like manner, what he infers hence ſeems foreign to the Truth, *viz. that the whole Doctrine of Reaſons ſuits more with the Speculation of Arithmetic than Geometry*; for how ſo, are there yet many Inventions and Doctrines concerning Reaſons entirely general, and agreeing alike to all Quantities? Such Reaſons alſo as cannot be expreſſed in Numbers ſurpaſs the Limits of Arithmetic, of which there are innumerable, to which the Theorems of the fifth Element are adapted, as well as to *Arithmetical Reaſons.* But this by the Way: I do not know that it can be better explained otherwiſe. Conſequently it may be moreover obſerved,

Thirdly, that no Reaſon can be eſtimated or comprehended ſeparately, and by itſelf, nor is peculiarly capable of being expreſſed or repreſented by any determinate Quantity, but by all or any one indifferently; nor conſequently is it ſubject to any abſolute Quantity; for what Sort of Quantity can that be, which paſſes through all the Genera of

(a) Wallis Arith. p. 226.

Quantums?

Quantums? And if it have no intelligible Quantity of itſelf, how can it be conceived to have any, when compared with another Reaſon? How can a Compariſon of Quantities comprehenſible of themſelves be made without any Reaſon, or how can there be a known Relation of unknown Quantities? Moreover a Reaſon compared with another Reaſon obtains only a looſe and arbitrary Quantity; for as the common Conſequent is taken differently at Pleaſure, ſo what are called the Quantities of the Reaſons compared are different. Therefore theſe Reaſons have but a deſultory and indeterminate Quantity, *i. e.* none. For whatſoever is, is ſomething determinately; and that which is not ſo, is nothing. The moſt ſagacious *Vincentius* ſaw this, and plainly owned and declared as much; but whether being deluded by the Ambiguity of the Words, or ſomething elated with the Hope of being the Author of a new Science, he gives it another Turn. *I anſwer*, ſays he, *it is true, if the Reaſon, which cannot be expreſſed in Numbers, be taken ſolitarily, that its Denominator cannot be repreſented Geometrically.* But I here interpoſe that it may always be exhibited, by taking any Quantum for the Conſequent; which will perform the ſame Office that Unity commonly does in repreſenting or exhibiting the *Denominators* of *Effable Reaſons*; nor is there any thing peculiar in this Reſpect to Reaſons effable in Numbers. But *Vincentius* proceeds, *But if there be two or more given Reaſons, the Denominators of each may be aſſigned, which may demonſtrate what Proportion is between the Reaſons themſelves; and this will not only be performed by two certain Lines, but by any others, that are proportional to the former.* Thus he. Since therefore there can be no Quantities of Reaſons aſſigned, beſide ſuch Denominators; but if taken ſimply there can, though various; it follows, there

there will not be any Quantity of Reaſons abſolutely determinate: But *Vincentius* (as I ſaid) ſeeming to be deceived with the Obſcurity of certain Words, has turned theſe Things beſide the Purpoſe.

Wherefore I obſerve *fourthly*, that the only Foundation, upon which the Doctrine, we are oppoſing concerning the *Quantities* and *Reaſons of Reaſons*, depends and ſeems to be deduced, is the cuſtomary Manner of ſpeaking: *Theſe two Magnitudes are equally unequal with thoſe two*; *theſe are more or leſs unequal than thoſe*; from whence they infer there are *Quantities* and *Reaſons of Reaſons*. If this Reaſon be greater than that, then they are Quantums, and this has a Reaſon to that. *From whence* (ſays Mr. *Hobbs*) *it is underſtood that the Reaſon both of Exceſs and Defect are Quantities* (or Quantums) *as receiving* (*i. e.* as capable of being ſaid to be) *greater and leſſer*. And *Vincentius* in the firſt Demonſtration of his Book concerning *Geometrical Proportionalities*, argues thus: *Reaſon is a certain mutual Habitude of an Antecedent to its Conſequent, according to Exceſs and Defect, and Equality. When therefore the Antecedent of one Reaſon exceeds, or falls ſhort of its Conſequent, more than the Antecedent of another Reaſon exceeds or falls ſhort of its Conſequent; it is manifeſt that one Reaſon is greater or leſſer than the other, as much as one Quantity is greater or leſſer than the other.* But to this plauſible Diſcourſe I anſwer. In the uſual Forms of Speech we are not to regard the Sound of the Words, but the Meaning of the Speakers. And it was juſt now ſufficiently ſhewn that nothing can be conceived by this Sort of Words, but that when the Reaſons of any Quantums are reduced to a common Conſequent, their Antecedents exceed, fall ſhort of, or are equal to one another. For, as themſelves are forced to confeſs, no Rea-

ſons

ſons can be eſtimated or compared together, till ſuch a Reduction be made; and after they are ſo reduced, this, which they call a *Reaſon*, is only known and denominated from the Compariſon of the Antecedents. And theſe Antecedents are by themſelves called the Denominators of the Reaſons. Therefore nothing elſe is neceſſary to be deſigned or underſtood by the aforeſaid Expreſſions, but the *Equality* or *Inequality* (*i. e.* the *Reaſon*) of the *Antecedents*. Nor therefore is the Argumentation deduced from theſe Forms of Speech of any Force. I ſaid nothing elſe is neceſſary, but in Fact nothing elſe is conceivable; whence to put an End to this Diſſertation,

I obſerve *fifthly*, whatſoever is vulgarly attributed to Reaſons, that only truly and properly agrees with the Denominators of Reaſons, *i. e.* with the Antecedents of Reaſons reduced to the ſame Conſequent. The Quantity, they aſſign to thoſe, is nothing elſe but the Quantity and Reaſon of the Denominators; and when they would be thought to add or ſubtract the Reaſons themſelves, they only add or ſubtract theſe Denominators; alſo when they multiply or compoſe, divide or reſolve them, it is the ſame. This will appear to any who attentively examines the Propoſitions of *Vincentius*, which are indeed compoſed with exquiſite Labour, and are propoſed univerſally, and lawfully demonſtrated according to his Definitions and Hypotheſes; but if any one take them particularly, as meant concerning Numerical Reaſons, he will find his whole Doctrine to terminate in this, That the Addition and Subtraction, Multiplication and Diviſion, and Compariſon of Fractions as to Proportion, are delivered as numerical, or as they are Quotients found by Diviſion. And what a numerical Fraction, or Quotient of Diviſion is in Arithmetic, the ſame is the Denominator of any

Reaſon

Reaſon in Geometry; *i. e.* any Magnitude, ſo affected, is referred to the homogeneous Magnitude put in the Place of Unity, as a numerical Fraction or Quotient to Unity. Wherefore *Vincentius* ſeems to proſecute nothing elſe but Arithmetical Fractions, and the Denominators of Geometrical Reaſons anſwering them; to which he aſcribes all the Properties agreeing with Reaſons themſelves. *Ex. gr.* Suppoſe the two *Numerical Reaſons* of 3 to 5 and of 7 to 3, the Denominators of theſe Reaſons will be the Fractions $\frac{3}{5}$ and $\frac{7}{3}$ (ſince $\frac{3}{5}$ to 1 is as 3 to 5; and $\frac{7}{3}$ to 1 as 7 to 3;) or by reducing the ſaid Fractions to a *Common Denominator*, the Denominators of theſe Reaſons will be the fracted Numbers $\frac{9}{15}$ and $\frac{35}{15}$. Therefore when he added theſe Fractions to, or ſubducted them from, one another, when he multiplied or divided the one by the other, and when he exhibited their Proportion; he pretended to have added or ſubtracted, multiplied or divided the ſaid Reaſons themſelves, or to have exhibited their Reaſon. That great Man therefore, as *Tacquet* thinks, did not frame any new Science about Proportions, but only faſhioned the old Doctrine in another Model, and that not over appoſite, and delivered it in new Words; which yet he has enriched with many Theorems invented by himſelf. And as we have ſaid, it is common to him with the reſt, that embrace this Doctrine (*viz.* concerning the Reaſons and Quantities of Reaſons,) to confound Reaſons with numerical Fractions, while they are medling with Numbers; and to handle the ſame by their Denominators, while they are conſidering other Reaſons. Which they ſometimes do openly, and in expreſs Terms, but oftner otherwiſe. Mr. *Hobbs* does often take notice of this, and reprove it in his Antagoniſt, but it appears that he himſelf is not altogether free of the ſame Fault; for it is the ſame Thing to attribute Reaſon

to

to Reaſons, as to account Reaſons the ſame with their Denominators, or at leaſt to ſpeak nothing and inſignificantly; for they mean this or nothing. But this may ſuffice in ſome meaſure for explaining and confirming our Opinion, that Reaſons have no Quantity properly ſo called, nor are they truly compared together, as to Reaſon. From whence we will deduce ſome Conſectaries. As

Firſt, hence will be eaſily decided the Queſtion which *Euclid* terms *concerning the Compoſition of Reaſons*, whether it is more rightly accounted the *Addition* or the *Multiplication of Reaſons:* for from what has been ſaid, with Reſpect to the Thing itſelf, Reaſons, as void of Quantity, can neither be added nor multiplied; but as to the Manner of Speech, becauſe when Reaſons are ſaid to be compounded their Denominators are multiplied, it is manifeſt that Reaſons are more rightly ſaid to be multiplied than added. As alſo, when one of the Denominators divides the other, the Operation will be more juſtly called a *Diviſion* than a *Subtraction* of *Reaſons*. Though it has obtained, to have the former Operation called *Addition*, and the latter *Subtraction*.

Secondly, Hence is entirely overthrown, or fully decided the Controverſy, which ſome do agitate, and which ſeems to have been raiſed by (*a*) *Merſennus*, *viz.* Whether a *Reaſon of Equality refers*, or *is equal to nothing*, a Reaſon *of greater Inequality* is *above nothing*, and a *Reaſon of leſſer Inequality below nothing*. For in Truth ſince no Reaſon is a Quantity, the fundamental Hypotheſis of this Queſtion falls to the Ground, and the Queſtion itſelf along with it. But from the Hypotheſis, that the Affections of the Denominators are to be applied to their Reaſons, it alſo appears moſt evi-

(*a*) In Præfat. ad Cogit. Phyſico-Mat.

dently,

dently, that the Reaſons of *Minority* and *Equality* ariſe above nothing. For the Denominator of a leſſer Reaſon is always ſome Quantity leſs than the Conſequent; and conſequently in Arithmetic is a Part or Fraction leſs than Unity. And the Antecedent of an equal Reaſon being always adequate to the Conſequent, its Denominator in Arithmetic is denoted by Unity. Nor is any Thing farther required for the Deciſion of this Queſtion.

Thirdly, Hence is eaſily refuted all that *Meibomius* advances againſt the ancient as well as modern Geometricians, in a Stile but too indecent and unmannerly. As when he affirms, that a *ſubmultiple Reaſon* is the ſame with a *multiple Reaſon*, becauſe of the ſame *Diſtance from Equality*. For beſides that the Diſtance is not the ſame (for how far is a Defect from an Exceſs, or a negative from a poſitive Diſtance,) it will ſufficiently appear by reducing thoſe Reaſons to a *common Conſequent* (which we have ſo often ſhewn to be neceſſary for the Compariſon of Reaſons,) that the Denominator of a ſubduple Reaſon will be leſſer than a Denominator of a double Reaſon, by a quadruple Reaſon: For if the common Conſequent be 2, then will the Antecedents be 1 and 4. And when he concludes that Reaſons of Exceſs and Defect cannot be compared together, he is evidently miſtaken, for theſe as well as any other, may be compared by Help of the Denominators. Alſo, when he ſays, that a leſſer Reaſon only can be taken from a greater (he would have ſaid more rightly a leſſer divided by a greater, as was premoniſhed,) he is plainly in the Wrong: for what hinders the Denominator of a leſſer Reaſon to be divided by the Denominator of a greater, either *Arithmetically* or *Geometrically*? Again he miſtakes, when he pronounces the Reaſon of Something to a greater to be often greater than the Reaſon of the

ſame

ſame to a leſſer; as that the Reaſon of 4 to 7 is greater than the Reaſon of 4 to 5; and conſequently that the Names of *Greater* and *Leſſer Reaſon* are hitherto uſed amiſs by all Geometricians. For if we reduce theſe Reaſons of 4 to 7 and 4 to 5 to the ſame Conſequent, by ſubſtituting *ex. gr.* the Equipollent Reaſons of 20 to 35 and 28 to 35, it is apparent that 20 is leſs than 28, and conſequently the Reaſon of 4 to 7 leſs than the Reaſon of 4 to 5. And hence it appears univerſally that the Appellations of *Greater* and *Leſſer Reaſons* are moſt fitly applied by the Ancients; *viz.* becauſe they are lawfully derived from the Quantities of the Antecedents after Reduction, as the Reaſon of the Thing requires; from whence both the Reaſons themſelves are diſcovered, and receive their Denomination, and are at all capable of being any way compared or comprehended. Wherefore it is alſo abundantly clear, that the ſame Perſon has no ſolid Reaſon for oppoſing the Definitions of *Euclid* as falſe. For if any Reaſon be greater than another, which himſelf does not deny (and if none be properly greater, which I think to be the Truth but for Argument ſake will not inſiſt upon it;) I ſay, if any Reaſon be ſuppoſed greater than another, that ſurely will be moſt worthily called *Greater*, whoſe Demoninator is greater, and which is named ſuch by *Euclid*, and is notoriouſly circumſcribed in the Definition, and diſtinguiſhed from others. With the ſame Eaſe are all the Paradoxes diſpatched, which that Perſon has ſuggeſted contrary to the common Sentiments of Geometricians.

Nor *laſtly*, will that *Logomachy* that is ſo toſſed about be very troubleſome to us, about *Multiple* and *Multiplicate*, *Double* and *Duplicate*, *Triple* and *Triplicate*, and the like *Reaſons*. For from what has been delivered, it manifeſtly appears that *ex. gr.*

gr. what is called *Duplicate Reaſon* is not the Double of the Reaſon with which it is compared: As the Reaſon of the Number 9 to 1 is not double the Reaſon of 3 to 1, becauſe the common Conſequent of theſe Reaſons exiſting, the Denominator of the one 9 is not equal to double the Denominator of the other 3. From whence it appears that the Multiplication of ſuch Reaſons are named from another Cauſe, hereafter more conveniently to be ſhewn.

I will only add this, that if it be admitted, which I have been endeavouring to prove, *that Reaſons have no Quantity of themſelves, nor any Attributes of Quantity*, but as they are referred to their Denominators; hence very many of this Kind of Difficulties will immediately vaniſh, many Doubts be entirely taken away, or eaſily ſolved, and many Contentions and Strifes laid aſleep, which ſeem more to have proceeded from the Ambiguity introduced by this falſe Hypotheſis, than from any Thing elſe. Wherefore I thought it not foreign to the Purpoſe to handle this Queſtion ſo largely and fully.

But becauſe Reaſons commonly uſe to be compared together, and called *equal*, *greater*, or *leſſer*; nor does it ſeem that a Licence was ever denied the Teachers of Sciences for inventing and uſing ſuch Words for Clearneſs and Brevity's ſake, ſo they be proper, and give no Occaſion of Error For I am not willingly diſproving the Vulgar Ways of Speech, but am inveſtigating their genuine Senſe, that Words may not hurt Things, and the Truth not be impoſed upon by empty Sounds. Therefore we will enquire in the next Lecture what is diſtinctly ſignified by the Ways of Speech heretofore admitted, and long in Uſe not without ſome Foundation, and probable Cauſe, *viz.* we will ſeek what *Reaſons* are *Equal*, *Greater*, or

Leſſer

Lesser by expressing these Comparisons of Reasons in another manner briefly and not unelegantly; what is *Analogy*, what *Hyperlogy* or *Prology*, what *Hypology*, and how they may be rightly refined and distinguished from one another: Than which perhaps no Controversy disputed among Mathematicians is more subtle or of greater Consequence. In my Opinion these Definitions are best performed by *Euclid* (as far as the Thing itself will suffer) but to very many it now seems otherwise, and he is condemned and forsaken by almost all in this: Whether they do this for just Causes, and depending upon valid Arguments, it will be in your Judgment to determine from an Examination of what I shall say. In the mean Time, farewel.

LECTURE XXI.

A Defence of Euclid's *Definition of Proportionals in his fifth Book.*

IT seems to be sufficiently proved in the preceding Lecture, that *Reasons* truly and properly speaking do of themselves admit no Quantity, no Reason, nor therefore can one be predicated *greater*, *lesser*, or *equal* with Respect to another, because of any Thing inherent in, or agreeing with themselves; but these Attributes are derived from the absolute Quantums upon their Reasons. But because Custom has so long prevailed to have Reasons compared together like absolute Quantums, and the Names of an *Equal*, a *Greater*, or a *Lesser Reason* has obtained, and we do not unwillingly admit these Expressions with due Caution;

it

it next follows that we enquire by what certain Sign or Mark it may be known, when a Reaſon may be ſaid to be *equal* to another, when *greater*, when *leſſer*, *i. e.* how a Reaſon can be defined and diſtinguiſhed *greater*, *leſſer*, or *equal*. And indeed it ſeems plainly enough to follow from what has been ſaid, that, if two Reaſons conſiſting of homogeneous Terms have a common Conſequent, they may be moſt appoſitely defined by the reſpective Quantities of their Antecedents, *viz.* ſo that thoſe are to be called *Equal Reaſons* whoſe Antecedents are Equal, this *greater* than that, when the Antecedent of this is greater than the Antecedent of that, and this *leſſer* than that, when the Antecedent of this is leſſer than the Antecedent of that. But ſince it often falls out that Reaſons of a different Conſequent are compared, and conſequently this Condition fails, therefore ſome other *univerſal Sign* is required to diſcover the Relation of thoſe Reaſons, which may be ſufficient for determining the Habitudes of all Reaſons to one another. And we have hitherto found it a Thing of great Difficulty to find ſuch a ſufficient *Sign*; ſince various Cauſes hinder, eſpecially two, *viz.* the *Difference* between *Effable* and *Ineffable Reaſons* (*i. e.* the *Incommenſurability* of Quantities) and the *Heterogeneity* of the *Terms* of which different Reaſons conſiſt. For if all Reaſons were *Effable*, and only between commenſurable Quantities, an *Equal Reaſon* might be the ſame Way defined with the *Proportionality of Numbers* in the *fifth Element*, *viz.* by the equal Quotients of the Diviſions, and a *Greater* and a *Leſſer Reaſon* by the Inequality of the Quotients reſpectively: but the *Incommenſurability* of the *Terms* of moſt *Reaſons* hinders this from being univerſal, by which it happens that the Diviſion cannot be performed exactly, nor expreſſed in common Numbers, nor the *Manner* whereby the Terms

Terms reſpect one another clearly conceiv'd. Alſo the *Heterogeneity* of the Terms of the Reaſons compared exclude ſome other Ways deviſeable, whereby the Reſpect of the Reaſons might be otherwiſe defined, which perhaps ſhall be hereafter ſhewn. Hence it ſeems very difficult to exhibit any *Univerſal Mark*, by which it may plainly and certainly be pronounced concerning the *Equality* or *Inequality* of any two *Reaſons* propoſed, whoſe *Terms* are indifferently *commenſurable* or *incommenſurable*, *homogeneous* or *heterogeneous*.

Let us ſee then what ſort of *Marks* Geometricians endeavour to aſſign; or by what Means they attempt to define theſe Reſpects of Reaſons. And becauſe, if a good Definition of an *Equal Reaſon* could be conceived, it would not be difficult from thence to form Definitions of *Unequal Reaſons*, *greater* as well as *leſſer*, therefore we will firſt treat of the *Equality* of *Reaſons*, which is accounted the very Soul and Kernel of the whole Mathematicks, ay, as *Plato* ſays, *the Chain of all Diſciplines* (*a*).

We will begin then to handle a Matter of ſuch Conſequence from the very Foundation. An *Equality of Reaſon* in one Word (for Brevity and Clearneſs ſake) is wont to be called *Analogy*. Which Word, tho' it vulgarly denotes any Agreement, Conformity, or apt Correſpondence of certain Things with one another, foreign to the Mathematics; for Inſtance, the *Agreement of Speech with the general Rule* is by Grammarians called *Analogy*; and the Things that conſpire in any common Reaſon are by Logicians ſaid to be *analagous*. The Propoſition *ana* in the Greek ſignifies any ſort of *Identity*, *Equality*, or *Agreement of Things*. Examples are in the holy Scriptures. In the ſecond of *John*, verſe the ſixth, *Containing two or three Fir-*

(*a*) In Timæo.

kin

kins (ἀνὰ) *equally.* In the twentieth of *Matthew*, verſe the tenth, *And they received a Penny* (ἀνὰ) *each*, or *equally*. In the ninth of *Luke*, verſe the fourteenth, *Make them to ſit down by Fifties in a Company* (ἀνὰ) *equally*. And none are ignorant that it is preſcribed to the Students of Medicine in the Compoſition of their Drugs, to take ſuch Meaſures of ſuch or ſuch Things *ana* i. e. *equally*. The ſame Way almoſt are two Pairs of Quantities ſaid to be *Analagous*, when each Pair have their (*Logos*) Reaſon (*ana*) equal; and abſtractly ſuch an Agreement of the ſame Reaſons is called *Analogy*. The ſame is in Latin more commonly called *Proportionality*, becauſe *Proportion* in that Tongue for the moſt Part ſignifies the ſame with (*Logos*) Reaſon. Tho' *Cicero* in his Verſion of *Plato*'s *Timæus* tranſlates the Greek Word *Analogy* by the Latin Word *Proportion*. And *Fabius Quintilianus* (*b*) thought *Analogy* ought to be expreſſed by *Similitude* or *Likeneſs*: wherefore *Analogy* or *Proportionality* by *Euclid* is defined *a Similitude* of *Reaſons*; and by *Theon Smyrneus an Identity of Reaſons*. Tho' in my Opinion it would be better defined (but it is of no great Conſequence) *an Equality of Reaſons*, both becauſe the Word *Similitude* is too looſe and ambiguous, and *Identity* does not ſo well agree with Things actually different compared immediately as ſuch; and becauſe other Habitudes of Reaſons, viz. *Hyperlogy* and *Hypology* are not denominated *Majority* and *Minority* from *Diſſimilitude* or *Diverſity*, but from *Inequality*; and laſtly becauſe the *Denominators* of *equal Reaſons*, by which the Reaſons are capable of Compariſon, are not the *ſame*, or *ſimilar*, but *equal*. Yet theſe Definitions don't exhibit any certain eſſential Affection of the Thing defined, but only ſhew in Part, what the Word *Analogy* ſignifies; at leaſt they are ſuch

(*b*) Quintil. lib. V. H.

in

in *Euclid*, as appears from hence, becauſe he in his *fifth Element* ſubjects it to the Definition of Magnitudes having the ſame Reaſon; *Magnitudes*, ſays he, *having the ſame Reaſon are called Analogous* or *Proportional*; which is a meer Explication of the Word *Analogous*. And immediately after the Definitions of Magnitudes having an unequal Reaſon, *Analogy* (ſays he) *is a Similitude of Reaſons*. Wherefore *Borellus* does not well conceive *Euclid*'s Meaning, when he thinks that he propoſes this Definition as eſſential and ſcientific to *Analogy*, and imagines a *Similitude of Reaſons* to be here aſſign'd, as the known and firſt Property of *Analogy*. For he ſeems to have thought no ſuch Thing; but ſince often the Word *Analogy*, or *to be Analogous*, more elegantly and conciſely expreſſes an *Equality of Reaſons*, and ſometimes ſeems to be uſed, he was willing to explain it, that Learners might not be over much burthen'd with Labour, nor confounded with Obſcurity. Wherefore he does not deſervedly tax *Euclid* in ſuppoſing him to have delivered that Definition, as ſuperfluouſly and miſtakenly, exhibiting two Definitions of the ſame Thing. For he has really exhibited only one general Definition of Things having *the ſame* or *equal Reaſons* by one of their eſſential Affections; but what Cauſe pray ſhould hinder him from intimating beſides that Things having an equal Reaſon are called *Analogous*, and that the *Identity* or *Similitude* of Reaſons may be alſo deſigned by the Name of *Analogy*? He had Cauſe enough to declare the Force of a Word unknown perhaps to moſt.

But there ſeems to have been a Wrong done to *Euclid*, becauſe in *Clavius*'s, and moſt other Latin Editions of the Elements, the Deſcription of *Analogy* is put in the fourth Place, which ought to be in the eighth. Therefore that cenſorious Perſon rightly

rightly mistrusts that this Description is wrong placed, and perhaps he had not found so much Fault with it, if it had been otherwise. Albeit I don't deny, but to any one, who more attentively examines the Definitions of the *fifth Element*, something seems misplaced in the *Greek* thro' the Default of Transcribers; wherefore it is not now opportune to enlarge upon Conjectures. And the rather because we are engaged to find an apposite and accurate Definition of an *Equality of Reasons*, or *Analogy*, which is the principal Thing in this Subject. Which we will do after this Method. *First*, we shall explain *Euclid*'s Definition, and shew how it exactly agrees with all the Conditions of a lawful Definition: *Secondly*, we will observe and remove the Objections brought against this Definition: *Thirdly*, we will examine the new Doctrines and Methods of such as substitute in the Room of this Definition, and assay to shew what is deficient in them, and how far they give Place to, or fall short of, *Euclid*'s Definition.

As to the *first Head*, the Definition in the *Elements*, according to *Clavius*, is this: *Magnitudes are said to be in the same Reason, a first to a second, and a third to a fourth, when the Equimultiples of the first and third according to any Multiplication whatsoever are both together either short of, equal to, or exceed the Equimultiples of the second and fourth, if those be taken, which answer one another*; *i. e.* if the Multiple of the first Antecedent be compared with the Multiple of its Consequent, and the Multiple of the second Antecedent with the Multiple of its Consequent. Such is *Euclid*'s Definition of Proportions; that *scare-Crow* at which the over modest or slothful Dispositions of Men are generally affrighted: they are modest, who distrust their own Ability, as soon as a Difficulty appears, but they are slothful that will not give some Attention for the learn-

learning of Sciences; as if while we are involved in Obſcurity we could clear our ſelves without Labour. Both which Sorts of Perſons are to be admoniſhed, that the former be not diſcouraged, nor the latter refuſe a little Care and Diligence when a Thing requires ſome Study.

But this Definition may be conceived in other Words, a little more briefly, and perhaps more ſuitably to ſome People's Capacities. *Quantities are Analagous or Proportional Pairs to Pairs, when any Equimultiples of the Antecedents are together always either equal to, or greater, or leſſer than any Equimultiples of the Conſequents, ordinately. Or thus, Quantities are Analagous, when the Antecedents being any how the ſame Way multiplied, do perpetually keep the ſame Kind of Reaſon to the Conſequents being alſo any how the ſame way multiplied.* I have ſaid *the ſame way multiplied*, but by the Way, I might have ſaid *the ſame way divided*; *i. e.* for *Equimultiples* I might have taken *like Aliquot Parts*; that the Definition be render'd agreeable to *Euclid*'s. *Quantities are Analagous, when any like aliquot Parts of the Antecedents are always together greater than, or equal to, or leſſer than any like aliquot Parts of the Conſequents:* Or, *when the Antecedents, being any how the ſame way divided do together retain the ſame Kind of Reaſon, with the Conſequents, being any how the ſame Way divided.* And thoſe might be ſo coupled in the ſame Definition, as to contain diſjunctively both *Equimultiples* and *like Parts.* After this manner *Quantities are Analagous or Proportional, when the Antecedents being any how the ſame Way multiplied or divided have always the ſame Kind of Reaſon to the Conſequents, being any how,* &c. *Euclid*, I ſay, might have formed his Definition of Proportionals either of theſe Ways with equal Reaſon, as to the Thing. But becauſe Diviſion ſeems to be ſomething more intricate than Multiplication,

cation, and the Calculus of Integers is more ſimple, and eaſier to be conceived, than that of Fractions, and more readily diſpatched ; therefore he ſeems deſignedly to have ſelected and applied *Equimultiples*, rather than *like Parts.* And the Occaſion why he thus declares *Proportionality* is, becauſe he inveſtigated the general Definition as well of thoſe equal Reaſons which conſiſt of commenſurable Terms, as of thoſe, whoſe Terms are incommenſurable, and conſequently whoſe Reaſons themſelves are not *effable* ; alſo becauſe the Antecedents of *ineffable* Reaſons do ſo reſpect their Conſequents in an explicable Manner, that it can ſcarce be conceived how they do immediately contain them, or are contain'd in them ; therefore ſome univerſal Property of both Effable and Ineffable Reaſons, connected with Equality, and ſufficient for determinating it, ought to be fetched elſewhere, and not from the Way or Manner of containing, by which he might have eaſily defined the Equality of Effable Reaſons, and indeed actually has defined it, in the *ſeventh Element* ; which Property while he diligently ſought for, examining all, at length he conſider'd, that ſome Quantities are ſo combined, or connected together, or do ſo depend one upon another, as to the manner of their Quantity, either from ſome ſpecial Property of their Nature, or by Reaſon of ſome Condition aſſum'd, that both the Equality or Inequality of theſe do follow from the Equality or Inequality of thoſe ; and alſo every like Increment or Decrement of theſe, does carry along with it the like Increment or Decrement of thoſe. *Ex. gr.* any two Triangles of an equal Height by a certain particular Property of their Nature, demonſtrated in the firſt Element, are ſo connected with their Baſes, that if the former be any how encreaſed or multiplied, its Baſis will be alſo encreaſed or multiplied in like Manner : and as the latter is encreaſed or multiplied, ſo in like manner is its Basis encreased or multiplied: as also if the former Increment or Multiple be greater than the latter, the one Basis answering to it will be greater than the Basis of the other Increment or Multiple; if that be lesser this will be lesser; if that be equal this will be also equal. Again, any two Wholes, with their aliquot Parts, because of that assumed Condition of *Likeness*, are so connected, that all the Multiplications of the one do include and convey along with them, the like Multiplications of the other respectively; and if the Multiple of the former Whole exceed, fall short, or equal the Multiple of the latter; then the Multiple of the Parts of the former will also do the same with the Multiple of the Parts of the latter. This when our Author consider'd, and moreover found it to happen otherwise in Quantities otherwise affected, *ex. gr.* as we shall shew hereafter, in Triangles of a different Height, from the Excess of the one the same Way multiplied with its Basis above the Multiple of the other is never infer'd the Excess of its Basis above the Basis of the other the same Way multiplied with the other: neither if the Wholes be compared with their unlike Parts, from thence because the former equally multiplied with its Parts exceeds some Multiple of the latter, will it any Way follow that therefore the Multiple of the Parts of the former exceeds the Parts of the latter equally multiplied with its Whole? Those Things, I say again, when *Euclid*, or whoever else was the Author of these Definitions, observed and saw the said Property to agree with all Kind of Quantities promiscuously, whether commensurate or incommensurate, tho' no Consideration of any Commensurability or Incommensurability there intervenes; hence he thought that the mutual Respects to one another of the Reasons, happening to Quantities so affected, are to be estimated and defined from it. *Clavius* thinks that our Author,

when

when he firſt perceived this Propriety to happen to any commenſurate Quantities, at the ſame Time finding it to agree with any four incommenſurate Quantities, from thence by his own Authority reckon'd *Proportionality* in general to be determined from it. But I rather incline to think, when he found that to happen not only to *analogous Terms* of an Effable Reaſon ſo denominated according to ſome former Definition; but alſo, as I have hinted, to all that are connected together by the ſpecial Property of their Nature, or by an aſſumed Condition, he imagin'd that the Habitudes of Reaſons of this Sort were to be diſtinguiſhed by it from others; which he called the *ſame* or *equal*, becauſe if at any Time it happen'd for ſuch Reaſons to have or be capable of being any Way reduced to the ſame Conſequent, their Antecedents were always equal. Albeit perhaps the Author of this Definition reaſon'd thus with himſelf; it is ſeen from a confuſed Notion of Equality, as that ſeems to carry with it the higheſt Similitude of Reaſons, that the Antecedents in the ſame Kind of Reaſons are referred together to their Conſequents. But if the Antecedents be both multiplied by any one Number, it plainly appears that this *Likeneſs*, as to the Kind of the Reaſon, is never changed, ſince thoſe Terms encreaſe the ſame Way. And if the Conſequents be alſo multiplied by any one and the ſame Number, the ſame *Likeneſs* will ſtill remain, and the ſame Kind of Reaſon be retain'd on either Hand: tho', as the multiplying Numbers are aſſumed greater or leſſer, are the particular Quantities of the Reaſons thus unchangeable, varied, encreaſed and diminiſhed innumerable Ways; ſo that often the Antecedent Terms are equal to the Conſequents, often ſhort of them, or exceed them more or leſs. Perhaps that ſagacious Man has reached the bottom of this Affair, and from thence drawn us this Definition by this ſort of

Dif-

Diſcurſus, which is ſomething Metaphyſical, but not very obſcure. But by whatſoever Ways or Means the Author came to the Knowledge of this Property, however as its Invention was moſt ſubtle, ſo is its Uſe excellent and very opportune to the Matter propoſed; for from hence he deduces moſt of the principal general Affections of Proportionals moſt immediately, directly, briefly, and clearly; and alſo ſhews the *Proportionalities* of particular Quantities, which we ſhall ſpeak of hereafter.

But firſt of all let us explain the foregoing Definition. The appoſite general Condition is chiefly and eſpecially notable, *according to any Multiplication:* for it is not ſufficient for the *Equimultiples* of the homologous Terms, thus affected (*viz.* to exceed, fall ſhort of, or be equal together) to happen ſometimes, but it muſt be evinced by manifeſt Arguments to fall out always. It muſt, I ſay, be evinced, not from any perpetual Induction (Induction being a Thing of infinite Labour, and not agreeing with the Mathematics) but muſt be derived by an univerſal Demonſtration, from ſome eſſential Property of Particular Quantities or Uſe founded in ſome peculiar Conditions ſuppoſed or diſcover'd of ſome more univerſal Quantities. This *ſimultaneous Defect*, *Exceſs*, or *Equality* may in ſome Caſes happen to Quantities not proportional, but it happens to *Proportionals* alone univerſally, neceſſarily flowing from their Conſtitution, and conſequently may and ought to be univerſally demonſtrated of them, that their *Proportionality* and Agreement with this Definition may appear. But this Definition cannot be better illuſtrated than by Examples, by which Means it will appear moſt evidently, that this Condition really agrees to moſt Quantities, and that this Definition may be eaſily applied, as not being difficult to be underſtood, and yet apt enough for Uſe. We will begin with more particular Examples.

Let

Let there be two Triangles *(a)* ZAB and YMN of an equal Height, or between the ſame Parallels, upon the Baſes AB and MN. Here are therefore two Quantities; *viz.* Two Triangles ZAB and YMN and two Baſes AB, MN, to which I affirm the Condition of our Definition happens. For let the Antecedent Terms be any Way equally multiplied at Pleaſure, *viz.* the Triangle ZAB and its Baſis AB. *Ex. gr.* according to the Number *Three*, by aſſuming the Right Lines BC and CD equal to AB, and drawing the Right Lines ZC and ZD; for it appears from the Equality of the Baſis AB, BC, and CD, that the Triangles ZAB, ZBC, and ZCD are alſo equal. In like manner let the Conſequents, *viz.* the Triangle YMN and its Baſis MN be multiplied equally at Pleaſure, ſuppoſe with the Number *Two*, by taking the Right Line NO= MN, and connecting the Right Line YO. Then from what is demonſtrated in the firſt Element, it moſt plainly appears, if ZAD the *Triple* of the *Antecedent Triangle* exceed YMO, and the *Double* of the *Conſequent Triangle*, that AD the *Triple* of the *Antecedent Baſis* will alſo exceed MO the *Double* of the *Conſequent Baſis*; and if a Defect be there, a Defect will alſo be here; if an Equality there, an Equality will be found alſo here. Therefore theſe four Quantities obtain the Condition required in this Definition, nor is this drawn from any Induction, but from an univerſal Diſcurſus.

Again let there be a Circle whoſe Center is Z, *(b)* and two Angles at the Center AZB and MZN ſtanding upon the Arches AB and MN: it may be ſhewn that the Condition of this Definition alſo agrees with thoſe Angles and Arches. Let any Multiple of the Arch AB, ſuppoſe the Triple AD, be aſſumed, and let ZD be connected. It appears

(a) Fig. 6. *(b)* Fig. 7.

from

from the *third Element*, that the Angle AZD is alſo triple the Angle AZB. Then let any Multiple of the Arch MN be taken, ſuppoſe the double MO, and let ZO be connected. In like manner it appears that the Angle MZO is double the Angle MZN. But if the Angle AZD exceed the Angle MZO; from what is demonſtrated in the third Element, the Arch AD will alſo exceed the Arch MO; and if that equal that, alſo this will equal this; but if a Defect be there, alſo a Defect will be here. Therefore it is ſhewn that the ſaid Condition agrees with theſe Quantities by a certain univerſal Demonſtration.

Furthermore, for I ſhall add ſeveral Kinds of Examples for a more perfect Explication of this Subject; Let there be two Spaces ZA and XM (*a*) run thro' with an equal Velocity by a Body moved uniformly in different Times repreſented by the Line $\zeta\alpha$ and $\xi\mu$. I ſay the forementión'd Condition will agree with theſe Spaces and Times; for let any Spaces AB and BC be aſſumed equal to ZA, and as many Times $\alpha\beta$ and $\beta\gamma$ equal to $\zeta\alpha$. And let the Space XN be equimultiple of XM, and the Time $\xi\nu$ of the Time $\xi\mu$. It is plain that $\zeta\gamma$ is the time of the Paſſage through ZC, and $\xi\nu$ is the Time of the Paſſage thro' XN: *viz.* from the Definition of an uniform Motion, according to which the Spaces run through in any equal Times are equal; and contrarily the Times are equal in which equal Spaces are made. Alſo becauſe of the equal Velocity from the Hypotheſis, if the Space ZC be greater than, leſſer than, or equal to the Space XN, will the Time $\zeta\nu$ be in the ſame Order reſpectively greater, equal or leſſer in reſpect of the Time $\xi\nu$? From whence it is apparent that theſe four Quantities are to one another according to the Condition laid down in our Definition.

Again,

Again, if that be assumed, which is agreeable to Reason as well as Experience, that the Moments or motive Powers of Weights are so encreased or diminished according to their Distances from the Center of a Balance, that the equal Increments or Decrements of the Distances do superadd to, or deduct from, the same Weights, equal Moments; hence it will be proved according to this Definition, that the Moments of equal Weights are proportional to their Distances: As if the Point Z be the Center (*b*) of a Balance, upon which equal Weights are hung at the Intervals ZA, ZM and the Right Lines $\zeta\alpha$, $\zeta\mu$ do represent their Moments according to the said Distances; any Equimultiples being taken ZC and $\zeta\gamma$ of ZA and $\zeta\alpha$; it appears from the Supposition just now laid down, that $\zeta\gamma$ is the Moment of the Weight hanging at the Distance C. And likewise the Equimultiples ZN and $\zeta\nu$ being taken of ZM and $\zeta\mu$, it appears that $\zeta\nu$ is equal to the Moment of the same Weight hanging at N. But if ZC exceed, equal, or fall short with respect to ZN, also the Moment $\zeta\gamma$ will also correspondently exceed, equal, or fall short with respect to $\zeta\nu$. Therefore the Quantities ZA and ZM are *proportional* to $\zeta\alpha$, $\zeta\mu$, according to *Euclid*'s Definition. By like Means may this Condition be adapted to any particular Subjects, as far as, after this Condition is drawn from any Property of the Quantities proposed, their *Proportionality* may be demonstrated by it.

But more Examples may be suggested of universal Quantities, *i. e.* of such as are confined to no Species of Quantity, to which this Definition may be accommodated by reason of some Condition annexed. As if any two equal Quantities be taken A and B, and any other two equal to them C and D; it will be demonstrated that A and B are proportional to C and D. For it may be easily deduced from

(*b*) Fig. 9.

this

this Condition of Equality, either Way ſuppoſed, that this Property agrees with them. The whole *fifth Element* almoſt conſiſts of ſuch Examples; nor is there any other Thing handled there, but to the End that this Property may be ſhewn to agree with all Quantities endowed with a certain Condition, and from thence that the Name of *Proportionality* is due to them. Wherefore I will dwell no longer in bringing more ſuch Examples, after I have only added one, from whence it appears almoſt univerſally, that moſt Definitions ſubſtituted by others, *i. e.* the Properties by which others define the *Analogy* of Quantities may be deduced and demonſtrated from this Definition.

Let any two Pairs of Quantities A, B and C, D be *proportional*, according to this Definition, *i. e.* let the Reaſon of A to B be equal to the Reaſon of C to D: I ſay, it follows, that the Quantity A divided by B is equal to the Quantity C divided by D, *i. e.* that Affection agrees with them, from which *Euclid* in the *ſeventh Element* has defined the *Analogies* of commenſurate Quantities, and by which ſome alſo think the *Proportionality* of Incommenſurate Quantities may not be inconveniently defined. Foraſmuch as if A and B *ex. gr.* be ſuppoſed incommenſurate, then A cannot be ſo divided by B as to have a rational or effable Quotient, yet ſome ſuch Quotient may be really underſtood after a confuſed Manner, which may differ from a rational Quotient aſſigned by a Quantity leſs than the leaſt Quantity aſſignable, both as to Exceſs and Defect. Nor conſequently do we deny, but any Diviſion alſo of incommenſurate Quantities, and a Quotient not diſtinctly effable, may be conceived: nay we willingly allow this, that the univerſality of the ſubſequent Argument may appear the more. Theſe Things being noted, repeating the former Hypotheſis, I ſay, if according

to

to our Definition A. B : : C. D, then will $\frac{A}{B}=\frac{C}{D}$. If you deny it, let there be an Exceſs on either Hand; *ex. gr.* let $\frac{A+X}{B}=\frac{C}{D}$. Let X be multiplied by ſome Number M, till MX be more than B. Which may be done from that moſt clear Axiom, that Geometricians aſſume with *Archimedes*, *viz.* Any Quantity may be taken ſo often that its Multiple taken ſo often may exceed any aſſigned Quantity of the ſame Kind. It appears therefore that B may be ſo multiplied by ſome Number N, that NB cannot be exceeded by MA, but may be exceeded by MA+MX, becauſe MX is greater than once B. But becauſe $\frac{A+X}{B}=\frac{C}{D}$ from your Hypotheſis, then multiplying both Sides of the Equation by the ſame Number M, will $\frac{MA+MX}{B}=\frac{MC}{D}$: and again dividing both Sides of the Equation by the ſame Number N will $\frac{MA+MX}{NB}=\frac{MC}{ND}$. Therefore becauſe it was ſhewn that MA+MX $\sqsubset$ NB will MC be $\sqsubset$ ND. For when two Fractions are equal, if the Numerator of one exceeds its Denominator, the Numerator of the other will exceed its Denominator alſo, otherwiſe they will be unequal, contrary to the Hypotheſis; the one being greater, and the other leſſer than Unity. Becauſe therefore it is proved that MC is $\sqsubset$ ND, but MA is not $\sqsubset$ NB, it appears that according to our Definition, A is not to B as C to D: which is contrary to the firſt Hypotheſis. Therefore our Adverſary is wrong in denying that A divided by B is equal to C divided by D. Q. E. D.

And now from theſe Examples it evidently appears *Firſt*, that this *Definition* depends upon an Hypotheſis

Hypothesis clearly possible *viz.* such as is demonstrated by innumerable Examples, and is not feigned without Grounds, but actually is; or that the Condition of this Definition really agrees with many Quantities. *Secondly*, that this Property is so universally extended, as not to be hindered by any *Incommensurability*, or *Heterogeneity* of Quantities: since neither these, nor their Opposites, *viz.* *Commensurability* and *Homogeneity*, were at all considered in its Application. *Thirdly*, that this Property necessarily flows from Nature, or is intimately conjoined with the specifical Condition of the Quantities to which it is attributed, and consequently is not remote from their Essence, as *Proportionals*. For it is always shewn to agree with the Quantities proposed by their Definitions, as so conditioned, or by some principal and essential Properties. *Fourthly*, that this Definition is not barren, nor unprofitable, but the fruitful Mother of Conclusions about Subjects both general and particular. For the whole *fifth Element* depends upon it, and whatsoever is any where proved in the Elements of Geometry about *Proportionalities*. *Fifthly* I add, that neither is it troublesome nor tedious, but begets most of its Conclusions with a great deal of ease. For by it the first and principal *Proportionalities* of Quantities are drawn and demonstrated immediately and directly, without any unnecessary Circumstances. *Sixthly*, that from this Definition are easily enough deduced both those Affections by which others make their Definitions, and the remaining Affections which those draw from their own Definitions; and consequently again, that this Property is most intimately conjoined with the Nature of *Proportionality*. *Seventhly*, I add, because of the Calumny of *Induction*, that no *Induction* appears here; but the Discursus, which is here used, consists altogether of universal Propositions,

and

and flows from univerſal Principles. Nor do I ſee how any one, who will but moderately attend to ſo many clear Examples, can juſtly accuſe this Definition of *Euclid* not only of Incomprehenſibility, but even of the leaſt Obſcurity or Difficulty: But all Knowledge of all Things ſeems difficult to a lazy Mind, as far as it requires Attention. This is a common Vice to us, that we deſire to live void of Care, and eſpecially to obtain Knowledge without Labour. But what finally hinders but from a juſt Perception of theſe Things, notwithſtanding the Oppoſition of ſome, we may boldly pronounce, that the Mark and Title of the beſt Definitions agrees with this Definition of *Euclid?* For it moſt appoſitely agrees with the principal Laws of a good Definition, which are found agreeable to Reaſon and Experience. Since it depends upon an Hypotheſis moſt evidently poſſible, diſtinguiſhes its Subject from all others, exhibits an Affection of it as ſuch, neceſſary, eſſential, and reciprocal, from whence the other Affections may be deduced; and conſequently is uſeful for drawing Concluſions, and begetting Science; and laſtly, ſince it may be eaſily, clearly, and directly applied to Things, and transferred to Uſe: Beſides which, I have hitherto ſcarce obſerved any other Laws, Conditions and Properties of a good Definition; which becauſe they all agree with our Definition, I fear not to pronounce it very good. This will more plainly appear from repelling the Weapons with which our Adverſaries do angrily oppoſe us, which fly in ſo thick a Cloud, and are flung with ſo ſtrong a *force*, that the preſent Lecture not being ſufficient to receive them; therefore we will attempt them in the next.

LECTURE XXII.

An Anſwer to the Objections againſt Euclid'*s Definition of Proportionals.*

IN our laſt we endeavoured to expound *Euclid*'s Definition of *Proportionals*, and defend it with ſome preparatory Arguments. But becauſe moſt of the Moderns do either greatly oppoſe, or quite reject it (ſome indeed as a Propoſition ſimply falſe, but more as a bad Definition ;) it remains that I clear it from the Accuſations they bring againſt it.

And firſt of all *Ramus* has taken it in the worſt Senſe ; yet ſo as plainly to ſhew that he pronounced unadviſedly, and without a right Underſtanding of the Matter. *Firſt*, he ſays it is *very dubious and falſe* ; which indeed is a mere Calumny, proceeding from nothing, but a moſt groſs Error : *viz.* becauſe he does not rightly underſtand what is meant by *exceeding*, *falling ſhort*, or *equalling together* (or *ſimultaneouſly*) *according to any Multiplication*. Since *Euclid* moſt expreſly requires it, as a Mark of *Proportionality*, that a *perpetual Simultaneity of Exceſs*, *Defect* or *Equality* in all Reſpects be proved concerning the Equimultiples of the homologous Terms ; but becauſe it falls out, that Quantities not *Proportional* do ſometimes obtain certain ſuch like *ſimultaneities*, he therefore accuſes *Euclid*'s Propoſition of *Dubiouſneſs* and *Falſity* ; and what can be more ſpiteful or weak ? To produce ſomething parallel from a common Subject : Suppoſe any one ſhould define or deſcribe a *good Man*, for one who compoſes and conforms all

all his Actions according to the Rule of right Reason; does he weaken this Description because a *bad Man* does sometimes Actions agreeable to Reason, or sometimes acts justly and soberly? Nay it sufficiently distinguishes a good Man from a bad, to say, in a moral Sense, that the former acts according to the Prescript of Virtue constantly and perpetually, but the latter inconstantly and contingently. In like manner also here, a *perpetual Simultaneity* distinguishes *Proportionals* from *Improportionals* which do not obtain it necessarily or perpetually; nor does it any Way hurt our Definition, because it happens sometimes to them. But besides that *Archimedes*, and other most sagacious ancient Geometricians have not built their Demonstrations upon a false Foundation, most of the modern Impugners of this Definition, as such, do oppose it under this Pretence, that it is demonstrable, *i. e.* necessarily true: and consequently *Tacquet*, *Borellus*, and *Hobbs* have demonstrated it from their own Principles, and *Clavius* himself, as to Numbers, from *Euclid*'s Principles. So far is this Proposition from being false, or *Ramus*'s Accusation from just.

But *Ramus* insists upon these Words; *For Proportion* (says he) *is not accurately enough concluded from that triple Difference, since there is a most false Sophism in that Argument* (but you would do well to shew me where, O *Ramus*:) *An equal Subtense* (you say) *subtends an equal Periphery, a greater a greater, and a lesser a less. Therefore* (*viz.* according to *Euclid*'s Definition) *Subtenses are proportional. Which* Ptolemy (you say right) *Conjectures to be false.* But, O excellent Censurer, this Argumentation is as far from the Purpose, as the Heaven is from the Earth. For what Application is here of *Euclid*'s Definition? What mention of *Equimultiples?* What here has any Affinity or

Likeness

Likeneſs to theſe, to deduce the *Proportionality* of Peripheries with their Subtenſes? For no ſuch Thing either is or can be gathered from our Definition rightly underſtood. The contrary indeed follows, and is rightly gathered by *Ptolemy* himſelf from the Propoſitions of the Elements derived from hence, and from *Euclid*'s ſubſequent Definitions of kin to it.

But leſt we ſhould be thought to ſay this without Proof, we will give a moſt eaſy Inſtance (FIG. X.) Let there be two Arches ZA and ZM, the former a Quadrant, and the latter a Sectant of the whole Circumference. I ſay the Arches ZA and ZM are not proportional to their ſubtenſes ZA and ZM, according to our Definition. For let the Antecedents ZA be multiplied by the Number *Four*, and the Conſequents ZM by the Number *Six*; it is apparent that the *Quadruple* of the Arch of the Quadrant ZA is equal to the Sextuple of the Arch of the Sectant ZM, ſince each Multiple equals the whole Periphery of the Circle. But the *Quadruple* of the Chord ZA is leſs than the *Sextuple* of the Chord ZM, *i. e.* the Perimeter of a *Square* inſcribed within a Circle, is leſs than the Perimeter of a *Hexagon* inſcribed within the ſame: Therefore, according to *Euclid*'s Definition, the *Peripheries* ZA and ZM are not *proportional* to their *Chords*. Which was the Thing to be proved, together with the Weakneſs, and (pardon the Word) Impertinence of *Ramus*'s Inſtance. In the mean while we may wonder at ſuch a licentious Cenſoriouſneſs as this trifling Talkative Man, not to ſay worſe, is wont to uſe againſt the ancient Geometricians.

But he diſputes farther, *That ſhould there be no ſuch Sophiſm* (as indeed I interpoſe there is not) *yet nothing will be defined in this Definition* (Why ſo pray?) *for neither here* (ſays he) *will it be taught why*

why they are proportional, but an Alternation of Proportionals will be propoſed. Laſtly this Definition will teach that the ſimple Terms are proportional, whoſe alternate Multiples are proportional. Therefore the Hyſterologia is twofold, &c. But with what Eyes has he ſeen or read any *Alternation* of *Proportionals* propoſed here? Where is found the leaſt Appearance of *Proportionality* of Multiples? I ſee indeed an *Exceſs*, *Defect* or *Equality* of Equimultiples; but I can perceive no Mark, no Footſtep of Alternation or *Proportionality*. Is not this to treat, or rather dream of Things, in a diſorderly Manner? How comes he for ſuch poor Cauſes and falſe Arguments to brand thoſe venerable Perſons, with Notes of Fallacy, Sophiſtry, and Abſurdity, and defame thoſe Builders, and firſt Propagators of the Sciences with ſuch uncivil Contumelies; without whom perhaps this mighty Artiſt at Trifles had had nothing but Fables to apply his wonderful Logic in the Reſolution of? Which had been done more innocently and ſafely, than in inveighing ſo furiouſly againſt ſuch Men. Indeed I can ſcarce moderate my Indignation, but uſe him as he deſerves, and return thoſe Railings more ſtrongly upon his own Head, which he throws againſt the Ancients. It would be troubleſome to mention what he objects beſides, with the like Acuteneſs and Skill; which plainly proves nothing elſe but this, that it is entirely different to compoſe Logical Methods, and to judge of the Myſteries of the Sciences. But ſome he concludes peremptorily, and with the utmoſt Aſſurance, *Wherefore* (ſays he) *ſuch a Definition is quite taken away from the Mathematics.* I reply, Except it be ſhaken with ſtronger Machines, it will continue fixed to Eternity, and never be removed from the Mathematics.

But

But leaving him, let us encounter *Tacquet*, a Man of a more ſagacious Perception, who as he engages us more modeſtly, ſo, as it uſually falls out, more ſtrongly, and with a greater Shew of *Probability*. Let us then hear what he ſays; *Firſt* (ſays he) *it is certain, that the Nature of equal Reaſons is not explained by that Definition, but only ſome Affection.* I return *firſt*, that no Definition explains the *Nature* of any Thing otherwiſe than by aſſigning ſome neceſſary and reciprocal Affection of it, as is done here. If he can ſhew any ſuch, I ſhall not unwillingly give up the Cauſe; but if he cannot, as I am confident he cannot, then he involves all Definitions in the ſame Fault, and ſtrikes them with the ſame Weapon. He who defines a *Circle* from the *Parity of its Radii*, a *Triangle* from the *Concourſe of three Right Lines including Space*, a *Square* from the *Equality of its Sides, and Rectitude of its Angles*, what does he elſe but explain the Nature of thoſe Figures from certain of their Affections? *Secondly*, I ſay, that there neither is, nor can be conceived any ſuch *Nature*, as he feigns and ſuppoſes diſtinct from ſuch neceſſary Affections or prior to them. To have ſome ſuch Affection is the Nature itſelf of a Thing, is eſſential to it, and conſtitutes it. At leaſt, which is all one, to have a certain Complication of Affections ſo connected, as every one to imply and neceſſarily draw along with it the reſt, does truly conſtitute the Nature of every Thing. From whence, he, who ſays a Thing has ſuch an Affection, explains the *Nature* of that Thing. *Ex. gr.* a *Circle is a Figure having equal Radii*, or a *Figure of ſuch a Nature as to have equal Radii*: where *to have equal Radii*, is the very *Nature of the Circle*; or at leaſt *to have equal Radii, and other concomitant Affections* entirely contains and declares the *Nature* of it.

As

As alſo *to have right Angles at the Circumference ſubtending the Diameter*, or, any other reciprocal Affection, does equally expreſs the *Nature of a Circle.* They, who imagine or ſeek for other *Natures* of Things, do only impoſe upon, and delude themſelves, by purſuing after fleet and vaniſhing Chimera's, never to be perceived, or overtaken. Therefore *Euclid*, when he exhibited a *neceſſary Affection* of *Proportionals*, did abundantly declare and explain their *Nature*, as much as is uſual and capable of being done. And conſequently the Fact ſeems enough for this Objection.

Moreover *Tacquet* purſues us with another twofold Argument; *Next*, ſays he, *that Property of Multiples is brought, either as an infallible Sign of equal Reaſons, that whenſoever it is demonſtrated concerning any Reaſons, we may certainly infer that they are equal; or elſe that is his Senſe, that he would have Magnitudes bearing the ſame Reaſon to mean nothing but that their Multiples exceed, or are exceeded in the aforeſaid Manner.* I anſwer Both are true; it is both produced as an *infallible Sign*, and exhibited as an *eſſential* and *diſtinguiſhing Character* of *Proportionals.* Which two Things indeed have no real Difference, and do agree with every good Definition. For there is no *infallible Sign* of any *Thing*, but its *eſſential Attributes.* Every Thing may be ſtript of all Things, but its *eſſential Attributes*, nor conſequently can any Thing not *eſſential* indicate the certain Preſence of a Thing. But our Adverſary oppoſes both ſeparately, in theſe Words; *Albeit firſt it muſt be demonſtrated that that Affection is in all equal Reaſons, and them alone, that the Equality of Reaſons may be certainly inferr'd from it. But that Theorem is not common, which neither Euclid nor any after has demonſtrated.* I anſwer, that here is an unjuſt and impoſſible Law fixed upon *Euclid*, and other Authors of Definitions, *viz.* That they

demon-

demonſtrate the *Predicate* of a Definition to agree with its *Subject* ; which they are neither able nor obliged to demonſtrate, but to aſſume gratis, *i. e.* impoſe at Pleaſure the proper Name of the *Subject* upon the *Attribute*. Is it incumbent upon me to demonſtrate the Name of a Circle to agree only with Figures having equal Radii? No ſurely, but of my own Authority I aſſign the Name of a Circle to all thoſe, and them only. Juſt the ſame Way, at his own Pleaſure (tho' not raſhly, and imprudently, but for certain juſt and proper Cauſes, which I have mention'd more than once) does *Euclid* attribute the Name of *equal Reaſons*, to all Reaſons endow'd with the ſaid Property, and to them only ; he appropriates the Appellation of *Proportionals* to Quantities obtaining that Condition : whence becauſe of this Name of *equal Reaſons* and *proportional Quantities* it muſt juſtly be thought to agree with all thoſe, and thoſe only. For it is eſtabliſhed by a moſt juſt and neceſſary Law, that as it is a *Right* belonging to Teachers of Sciences to impoſe Names, ſo Learners are obliged to receive them. There is only one Thing that the Author of a Definition is bound to demonſtrate, (*viz.* by Examples clear to the Senſe, or by an evident Diſcurſus) which is that the Attribute of the Definition contain nothing impoſſible or merely imaginary, but that the Things endowed with the ſuppoſed Property or Condition, may really exiſt. As he that defines a Circle from the Parity of the Radii (for I purpoſely uſe the moſt eaſy and familiar Examples) is obliged to demonſtrate nothing elſe, but that it is not repugnant for ſuch Figures to exiſt wherein that Property agrees. Which he can moſt clearly ſhew from their Generation, by the Circumduction of a Right-line, or otherwiſe. Thus ſince it can be very eaſily and plainly proved, and is every where actually done by *Euclid*, where he applies this Definition to any determinate Subject,

that

that there are Quantities to which the Hypothesis of this Definition may agree, therefore nothing is required further; and it is supported by the best Authority, to affix the Name of *Proportionals* to all these Quantities, and to them only.

But because he subjoins, *this Property* to happen to *Proportionals*, that *that Theorem is not common:* I answer, repeating what was heretofore expounded, that in Reality every Definition is a Theorem; *viz.* a Proposition demonstrable from other Definitions of the Subject, or from other reciprocal Affections before attributed to the Subject: Also on the contrary, that every Theorem may be formed into a Definition, if it consist of a perspicuous Example, or include a possible Hypothesis. Wherefore because this Property may be infer'd from other Definitions of *Proportionals*, and a Theorem constituted from thence; nothing derogates or hinders, but that it may enter a lawful Definition: as neither permutably, because, as has been shewn from this Definition, the Property may be deduced, from which *Tacquet* himself rather defines *Proportionality*; and consequently because its Definition may put on the Form of a Theorem, does that any Way hinder, but its Definition ought to be thought just and lawful; tho' other Things perhaps may hinder. But if, by his saying the Theorem is not common, he intimate as tho' this Definition is drawn with difficulty from the Definition and Principles laid down by himself, he does nothing to the Purpose. For it is not requisite to the Perfection of a Definition that the Property applied in it do easily follow from other Principles however posited. For by the same Means will his own Definition merit the Title of a Theorem not common, because it will be no easy Thing to derive it from all other Definitions; in particular not from our own. Nor next is it strange that this Theorem is demonstrated neither by *Euclid,*

clid, nor any other, becauſe they have aſſumed it for a Definition, and accounted it as a Principle ſubſervient for demonſtrating other Theorems; for whoever attempted to demonſtrate his own Principles? Wherefore I make no Account of *Tacquet*'s Diſcourſe elſewhere in theſe Words; *The Demonſtration indeed*, ſays he, *of which Buſineſs, ſince it is ſufficiently difficult and prolix, as anon we ſhall find in Reality; it will eaſily appear that* Euclid *has acted prepoſterouſly, who would take the firſt and fundamental Property of the Equality of Reaſons from this Property of Multiples hitherto indemonſtrated, whoſe Connexion with the Equality of Reaſons is ſo remote and obſcure.* Which Words I ſhall ſo retort upon the Accuſer, as I doubt not, but caſt the prepoſterous Judgment upon him who makes it a Crime to have put an indemonſtrated Property in his Definition; as if the Property of the Subject in a Definition, could without manifeſt Contradiction be demonſtrated by him who defined the Subject by it. For as it is put in the Definition, it is aſſumed to be the firſt Property of all; but as demonſtrable, it ſuppoſes ſome prior Propoſition, and therefore cannot be the firſt. Wherefore our Maſter has not proceeded in a *prepoſterous* but a *moſt direct Order*. But when he exclaims that the Connexion of this Property with the Equality of Reaſons is remote and obſcure, he notoriouſly begs the Queſtion; for certainly *Euclid* ſuppoſes it to be moſt manifeſt, and therefore makes a Connexion of that with this in defining this from that.

But he goes on, as he thinks, to preſs hard upon us; *If*, ſays he, *Euclid, by Magnitudes having the ſame Reaſon, would only underſtand that their Magnitudes exceed, or are exceeded after the ſaid Manner, we ſhall be ſecure of the Things taken in the Senſe of the Definition concerning the Verity of the Theorems, but it will not appear to us from the Force of Demonſtrations*

strations concerning the absolute Equality of Reasons. To which place I have nothing more to answer, than that I am utterly ignorant what *absolute Equality of Reasons* he here dreams of, as pre-existent and distinct from the Affections by which an Equality of Reasons may be defined, which is here supposed without any Foundation. An *Equality of Reasons* (like all other Subjects consider'd in the Sciences) is no otherwise found than from its Agreement with their Definition, whether *Euclid*'s or any other Definition, that may be reckon'd lawful. Reasons are therefore most absolutely and formally equal, because they have the Property expressed in their Definition ; wherefore since this Property is demonstrated in *Euclid*'s Theorems to agree with any Quantities, an Equality of Reasons at the same Time appears to agree with them ; as when a Parity of Radii is shewn concerning any *Figure*, it is demonstrated that that is a *Circle*.

The *Epiphonema* therefore is weak and vain, with which he closes these Argumentations. *Howsoever then*, says he, *that Definition be taken, the Demonstration of the fifth and sixth Books do totter so long as it is not demonstrated that a true Equality of Reasons is connected with that Property of Multiples.* According to which Sentence indeed all the Demonstrations of every Science will totter. For if it must always be demonstrated that the Properties attributed in Definitions are connected with their true Subjects, there will be no End of demonstrating, or rather no Beginning, but every Argumentation must run backward *ad infinitum.* Besides since himself has assigned a Definition of *Proportionality*, the same Thing may be objected against him, in the same Words ; so that himself is bound by his own Law to demonstrate the Property, which he assumes to agree with equal Reasons ; *viz.* from some prior one, and that again from another, till being wea-

ried

ried with the endless Labour, he shall own his Error.

In Sum, I observe universally of those Reasonings of *Tacquet: First*, That he every where begs the Question, and commits vicious Circles, arguing thus, *A Property is not proximate, but remote, because it can be demonstrated*, i. e. *because there is another nigher*; *another is nigher, because it may be demonstrated that this Property constitutes not an Equality of Reasons* (i. e. cannot enter its Definition) *because it differs from it, is not clearly connected with it, or is very much removed from its Nature.* And so every where.

Secondly, I note that neither he, nor most others, as far as I can judge, do sufficiently perceive the *Nature* of a Definition; by whom nothing is really done, but a Name imposed upon a Thing, as it is the Subject of an Affection evidently discovered by Sense or Reason: but they devise I know not what abstruse *Natures*, *Essences* and *Formalities*, which can never be brought to Light. By which, if we search the Thing to the quick, it will appear that they understand nothing but some imperfect and indistinct Conceptions, or Significations, answering to the customary Name of the Thing defined, which are not to be received in the Sciences, and are unfit for Demonstrations; to which consequently no Definitions are requisite; nay Definitions are to be formed by secluding and banishing those, and substituting for them certain Distinct and clear Ideas of Things; appropriating Names to Things, as far as they are subject to certain Affections conspicuous to the Sense, or to the Understanding.

I observe *Thirdly*, That *Tacquet*, led by such Arguments, has assigned a Definition of equal Reasons very vicious and useless. For he says, *Reasons are equal, when the Antecedent of the one contains, or is contained in, its Consequent in the same Manner as the*

the Antecedent of the other does contain or is contained in its Consequent. Which Definition only begets a groſs and confuſed Notion of *Proportionality* unapt and unſuitable to beget any Concluſion. For the Phraſe, *to contain in the ſame Manner*, is dubious and obſcure, nor is it really limited to ſignify any Thing diſtinctly, but by another Definition. There are many *Manners of containing*, which may in ſome Senſe be ſaid to be the ſame; *viz.* every greater Thing contains a leſſer *in the ſame Manner of Exceſs*; and again any two unequal Things reſpect one another *in the ſame Manner of Inequality* with two other unequal Things. Therefore except a Mark be ſhewn by ſomething more ſtrict and certain, what it is *to contain after the ſame Manner*, any Identity of Manner may be here deſigned, and conſequently we ſhall be ignorant or Uncertain what an Equality of Reaſon is.

But to paſs by other Inconveniences to which this Definition is ſubject, one only Exception remains more plauſible than all the reſt, which I fear it will not be in my Power to remove; not that it carries any great Force along with it, but becauſe it is favour'd by the Prejudices of many, and encourages Idleneſs. It is propoſed by him in theſe Words; *Laſtly, that all Things might conſiſt with one another, yet that Labyrinth of Multiples has always been diſpleaſing to me and others, and has always created too much Trouble to Learners, whoſe Minds are for the moſt Part ſo embarraſſed by it as hardly to be extricated.* Which Capital Crime that I may in ſome Meaſure remove out of the Way, I anſwer, *firſt*, we are to ſeek from what Cauſes that Perplexity ſo diſcouraging to many can ariſe which they pretend; whether from the Thing itſelf, which can admit no Expoſition more commodious or clear; or from the Heedleſsneſs of Interpreters, who have not illuſtrated this Definition with Examples ſufficiently

per-

perſpicuous; or laſtly from the Default of the Learners, who imagine with themſelves that the Difficulty is inſuperable, and ſo are diſcouraged before they apply their Mind to it. If any of theſe Things be the Occaſion, as indeed I am perſuaded they all contribute ſomething towards the making this Definition ſeem more perplexed, the Author is to be pardon'd, and the Blame imputed to other Cauſes. The Thing itſelf cannot be quite excuſed, which, becauſe of the Incommenſurability of Quantities, labours under ſome peculiar Difficulty; ſo that no Body allows it not to be difficult to find out ſome Affection equally congruous with all *Proportionals*, or to exhibit ſome Definition comprehending all Equalities of Reaſons. Which alſo appears from hence, becauſe hitherto it ſeems to have befal'n the moſt famous Perſons who have attempted to apply a Remedy to this Diſeaſe, that either they have performed nothing at all ſufficient, or they have walked in Ways more prolix, and not leſs intricate and perplexed; or at leaſt they have deliver'd Methods worthy of ſome greater Blame, and conſequently the Thing itſelf is too ſtubborn to be handled in a very eaſy and ready Method. Nor do I wholly excuſe Interpreters from Blame, not even *Clavius* the beſt of them, who tho' he has both explained this Definition well, and ſtrongly defended my Opinion, yet he ſeems not to have illuſtrated it enough with clear and appoſite Examples. For the Examples he brings do rather explain the Senſe of the Words, than repreſent the Poſſibility of the Condition ſuppoſed, and its true Exiſtence in Things, which eſpecially recommends as well as illuſtrates any Definition; ſo that they confound the Imaginations of Learners, with their being too univerſal. Perhaps alſo he is not expreſs and clear enough (which is itſelf another Occaſion of Confuſion) to the Intent that he may prevent Learners from imagin-

ing

ing that an *Induction* is required, or that infinite Tryals of Multiplications must be run over in the Mind, at which it is no Wonder if they be also confounded and discouraged; though no such Thing is here requisite, as we have often taken Notice. And as to the Learners it appears they are generally too much wanting to themselves. For though the Words of this Definition are most clear, and void of all Equivocations, yet how few are they, who can have so much Patience as accurately to examine the Sense of three Lines? But I dare lay a good Wager, and almost engage my Word and Promise, that to him, who seriously reads over this Definition, and gives diligent Application to the last Proposition of the sixth Element, it will not appear perplexed, intricate, or difficult. These Things being premised, I answer the Words of *Tacquet* by plainly denying that here is any *Labyrinth* to render the Thing more intricate, than it is in itself, which a little Art of the Expounder may not extricate, and from which a small Share of Attention may not free the Learner. I add, where there is no double Meaning in the Words, no Prolixity, and where there is always applied a most direct Discursus (all which Things are found in this Case to concur,) there can be no great Obscurity or Difficulty. This Definition is especially used in a few Propositions of the fifth Element, but every where, as I remember, they are demonstrated by it directly and immediately. And where it is accommodated to particular Subjects in the other Elements, or in other Books of Geometry; it always concludes in the same most simple and direct Manner, and not as others do in their Methods, indirectly, or by reducing the Thing *ad absurdum*; which Manner of demonstrating, as all acknowledge is very obscure and ignoble. Moreover if with *Tacquet*, we may assume what we please,

please, as clear by its own Light, and (what the ancient Geometricians studiously avoided) heap together an immense Number of Axioms, indeed the Thing may be often very compendiously handled, but yet for all the Brevity it gains, and some Evidence arising from thence, it loses as much of its Strength, which is of much more Concern, and ought to be more regarded in the Sciences. Of which, as I remember, we have already treated. Wherefore *Tacquet* has no Reason to boast of the Shortness, or Evidence of his Method: especially since he has given no Definition of *Analogy*, or what is next to none, and has accommodated his Propositions, which are either taken *gratis*, or, as himself thinks, demonstrated, to an uncertain Subject. But we now seem to have sufficiently repelled this considerable Adversary.

Mr. *Hobbs* follows, whom we will very readily dispatch, because in the preceding Arguments, we have suggested Solutions, which may be adapted to his. Let us hear what he says, *But it is impossible to find four such Quantities by this Definition, because a Multiplication by all Numbers is impossible, since they are infinite*; *This is not then a Definition, but an Hypothesis.* To this Discursus I premise, that this Philosopher mistakes *Euclid* to have given him so much Labour in this Definition, as if he treated of the *Generation of Proportionality.* He neither thought nor aimed at any such Thing, but only to assign the *distinguishing Property* of *Proportionality*; as when he defines a Circle from the Parity of its Radii. Where perhaps it may be worth the while to take notice by the by, that though commonly such Definitions are best, which express the *Generation* of Things (nay indeed strictly speaking such only are good, when the Things defined are immediately, and as it were originally of themselves capable of *Generation*) yet such

ſuch Definitions are not agreeable with ſome Things, *viz.* with thoſe that are not *generated* by themſelves but, as ſecondary Affections, reſult from the Conſtitution of other Things already *generated*, and flow from their primary Affections. *Ex. gr.* He that undertakes to define the *Focus* of a *Parabola*, or *Ellipſis*, after he has obſerved that ſuch a Property is in a *Parabola* already conſtituted, *viz.* that all the Radii (or Rays) parallel to the Axis are reflected from the Curve Line of the *Parabola* to a certain determinate Point in the Axis; and that ſuch an Affection agrees with an *Ellipſis*, *viz.* that the Radii proceeding from one certain Point in the Axis are reflected from the Ambit of the Ellipſis towards another Point in the Axis; this Property, I ſay, being known (which flows from other primary Properties of thoſe Lines,) he may beſt define the Focus, not from its *Generation*, which would be a Thing of infinite Labour, but from the *ſaid Property found*, *viz.* to be a Point in the Axis, into which all Rays parallel to the Axis, or proceeding from one certain aſſignable Point in the Axis reflected in the Manner ſhewn, are gathered or do tend. So *Proportionality*, ſince it is not a Thing ſubſiſting primarily, nor immediately generable, but a certain *Affection* reſulting from ſome predeterminate Condition of Quantities, it is ſcarce poſſible, at leaſt not expedient, to be defined by any Generation. However it will be manifeſt to any one, who examines the Words of this Definition, that no Generation is here really hinted at, but only ſome Property often agreeing with four Quantities, which, from the Hypotheſis of having that Property, are ſaid to have the *ſame Reaſon*, or be *Proportional*.

I anſwer then to *Hobbs*'s Exception, that tho' it be allowed to be altogether impoſſible by this Definition to find four proportional Quantities (as it is impoſſible

impoſſible from the Parity of Radii to find a Circle, *viz.* by attempting and trying whether or no the infinite Radii in the propoſed Figure be equal) yet that which is here ſolely intended and is ſufficient, it is very eaſy to demonſtrate, that this Property univerſally agrees with ſome Quantities (*ex. gr.* with two Parallelograms of the ſame Height and their Baſes ;) as alſo from certain given Conditions, it will be eaſy to ſhew that ſome Figure has all its Rays equal. For this no Multiplication is required by all Numbers, no infinite Labour, as often has been ſhewn. Therefore this Objection effects nothing. But farther, *This*, ſays he, *is not a Definition, but an Hypotheſis, indeed a true one, but not a Principle, becauſe it is demonſtrable, and is demonſtrated by* Hobbs. I anſwer *firſt*, that neither he, nor any other has demonſtrated, or can demonſtrate, that thoſe Quantities which obtain the Property noted in this Definition ought by *Euclid* to be called *Proportionals*, or ſuch as have the *ſame Reaſon.* For this ſolely depended upon *Euclid*'s Will and Pleaſure. It is not therefore altogether true that this Definition was demonſtrated by *Euclid. Secondly*, I ſay, it is no Hindrance to any Definition, that the Property by which it is defined can be demonſtrated concerning the Subject defined by ſome other Property ; otherwiſe it would be no good Definition. Some Things indeed endowed with many Affections may be conveniently and rightly enough defined many Ways. An Inſtance may be brought from the *Conic Sections*, which ſince they may be generated various Ways (*viz.* by the Dependencies and different Compoſitions of Motions ; by the Sections of various Bodies ; and by the manifold Methods of deſigning infinite Points) and ſince they obtain infinite Affections intimately connected with them, and on the Part of the Thing equally original, and equally depending upon

upon clear Hypotheſes, they are wont to be defined many Ways; therefore I think none of them is to be rejected, though any one being choſen as the *firſt*, the remaining Properties may follow from that, and conſequently are demonſtrable. From whence it appears by the Way, that the Principle delivered by *Ariſtotle* in his Topics is falſe, upon which our Adverſaries ſeem chiefly to depend, *viz.* (a) *That it is not poſſible for more Definitions than one to be of the ſame Thing.* For it is poſſible for every Thing to have as many Definitions, as it has reciprocal Properties clearly expounded, and apparent to us. Therefore Mr. *Hobbs* ſays nothing to the Purpoſe againſt our Definition.

I ſhall only recite what the great and learned Perſon (b) ſays concerning this Definition in his Arithmetic, who partly favours, and partly oppoſes it. *We*, ſays he, *have thought fit to omit this Definition in our Demonſtrations, though indeed true, and apt enough for* Euclid'*s Purpoſe, nor do we accommodate Proportionals to this Criterion. But becauſe it ſeems ſomewhat perplexed, and perhaps not perſpicuous enough, eſpecially to Learners. Nor indeed does it ſo immediately reſpect the Nature of Proportionals, as ſome Affection of them, which is ſufficiently remote.* Theſe are his Arguments: Which or the like having been already ſufficiently conſidered, there is no Cauſe why we ſhould dwell longer upon them.

We have now come to the laſt Puſh, *viz.* to the moſt ſubtle *Borellus*, the moſt bitter Adverſary, and who above others has done this Thing extraordinary, that he has produced out of his own Store a new Doctrine of *Proportionality*, indeed elegant and ſolid; yet in my Opinion not on all Accounts to be preferred to this of *Euclid*. But

(a) Topic VI. 5. (b) Cap. 35.

neither

neither after a diligent Examination of his Disputation, do I find any Thing at all of Moment derogating from our Definition, to which abundant Satisfaction seems not to be made in what we have said already. Most Things rather touch *Clavius* than *Euclid*; and I do not look upon it to be our Business at present to defend *Clavius*'s Words, howsoever able. But since the present Dissertation has already exceeded its Bounds, whatsoever *Borellus* has produced new and worthy of Consideration, I leave to be examined hereafter, when I begin my Animadversion upon the Methods of him and other Moderns. In the mean Time, let it suffice to have proceeded so far.

LECTURE XXIII.

An Answer to Borellus's *Objections, and of the Insufficiency of the Definitions of Proportionality which are substituted in the Room of* Euclid's.

IN the last Lecture we have endeavoured to repel the Attempts of some principal Adversaries again *Euclid*'s Definition of *Proportionals. Borellus* remains, who, in my Opinion is by far his most considerable and powerful Opponent; and the more so, because he has devised of his own Head a new Method of resolving *Proportionality* in vain attempted by others, which we readily own to be a Work very elegant, laudable, and not unuseful; it being both pleasant and profitable to handle the same Subjects various Ways, and deduce the same Theorems from different Principles; yet, I think, he he was more happy in framing his own, than in opposing the common Method, as we shall next attempt to shew.

Let us hear what he objects, *It cannot*, says (*c*) he, *be said in Reality that the Property assigned declares the Nature of the Thing, and distinguishes it from every Thing else: so far from it, that it renders a difficult Thing more obscure.* So he judges, but, I suppose we have shewn in what went before, that these Things are spoke at Random, *viz.* that the Nature of *Proportionality* is nothing else but to have some such Property, which other Properties follow; and consequently that its Nature is as abundantly declared in this Definition, as it can be in any other: and that this Property distinguishes *analogous* Things from Things not *analogous*, since *Analogy* reciprocates with it, and to be *analogous* signifies nothing but to have this Property, at the Designation and lawful or reasonable Pleasure of the Definient. Lastly, I deny that the Thing is rendered more obscure by it: For also (as himself confesses in express Words) the Words of the Definition do expound without Ambiguity, what such a Property is: And (I add) it most clearly appears that it exists in very many Things; also its Application is not difficult, as Experience plainly shews; and nothing hinders, but the Name of Proportionals, or some other may be attributed to Quantities having this Property; at least no Obscurity can arise from the Assignation of that Name. In what then pray does this Obscurity consist, where is it, or from whence does it result? Why it is no where at all. Except we dream of I do not know what mysterious Nature of *Proportionality*, which is prior to every Property entering that Definition.

(*c*) Pag. 125.

But

But he ſubjoins the Reaſons and Foundations of his Opinion, *It is unknown*, ſays he, *whether four Quantities having ſuch an Affection can be found in Nature*; *becauſe if infinite Equimultiples of the Antecedents be compared with infinite Equimultiples of the Conſequents, they muſt exceed together, fall ſhort together, or be equal together.* I anſwer, this is not unknown, becauſe it may be ſhewn by clear Examples, that there are many four Quantities endowed with the ſaid Condition. And if there were not, this Definition could by no Means be applied to Uſe. For as often as it is applied, ſo many Examples of Quantities having this Property are added to the Number. It is the ſame Way unknown, that there is ſuch a Figure as has equal Radii, till that is made plain to Senſe by Generation, or to the Mind by ſome Diſcurſus ſufficiently evident. Therefore this firſt Argument is of no Force.

Again, *Thoſe infinite Compariſons*, ſays he, *cannot be comprehended, and therefore this Affection will not be moſt evident, as that ought to be, which conſtitutes the Principle of a Science.* In the *firſt Place*, I admire that ſuch Arguments are uſed by a learned Man; then (not to repeat what I have before anſwered to the like Arguments) he enquires whether or no Experience teaches, that it is eaſieſt demonſtrated by *Euclid*, *Archimedes*, and moſt other Geometricians, that this Property agrees with many Quantities, *viz.* Triangles and Parallelograms of equal Heights with their Baſes; alſo Pyramids, Priſms, Cones, and Cylinders with their Baſes; Circles and Spheres with their ſimilar Sectors; Angles with the Arches on which they ſtand; Spaces run through by an equal Velocity with their Times; the Moments of Weights with their Diſtance from the Center of a Balance; and innumerable ſuch like. How then can it be *incomprehenſible? Secondly,*

condly, I ſay, here is no Infinity of Compariſons ſuppoſed more than in any general Propoſition, where the Univerſality of the Terms ſuppoſes Infinity. For that which is reckoned in Definition *by any Multiplication*, what elſe does it intimate but the Univerſality of the Condition laid down; proved not from a Viewing of all the Particulars, or any inductive Inference, but from an univerſal Argumentation? It is only required that all the *Equimultiples* of the Antecedents be in ſuch wiſe affected towards all the Equimultiples of the Conſequents; be in ſuch wiſe, I ſay, affected, *i. e.* obtain the ſame Kind or Manner of Reaſon, Exceſs, Defect, or Equality. If any Infinity be here *incomprehenſible*, alſo all Theorems of all Sciences becauſe conſiſting of univerſal Terms, muſt be equally *incomprehenſible*. Nor will the Propoſition be comprehenſible, *Every Man is an Animal*, becauſe the Property of Animality is affirmed in it, which may agree with innumerable Men. *Thirdly*, the very Application of this Definition moſt manifeſtly refutes this Inſtance, which only proceeds by ſubſtituting any one indeterminate and arbitrary Multiplication of the Antecedents, and one of the Conſequents for all their Multiplications which can be imagined; entirely the ſame Way as all other univerſal Propoſitions are wont to be applied. Here no Infinity is diſcovered, no Ambages, or idle Circumſtances, but the moſt ſimple Argumentation. Neither therefore does this Reaſon affect any Thing.

But *thirdly*, he ſays, *Though hypothetically it be granted*, *yet it is unknown*, *what ought to be gathered from that Ambages of infinite Compariſons.* I anſwer that there is no need of any Thing to be granted *Hypothetically*, for it may be aſſerted poſitively, it may be wreſted whether you will or no, that there are really Quantities endowed with ſuch a Cona Condition, as we have often ſhewn. Next, I aſk, what he means, when he ſays, it is unknown what ought to be gathered? Here is not any Thing gathered; but at leaſt, it happens, as it uſes, in every Definition, a Name is impoſed upon Quantities endowed with ſome Condition or Property, *viz.* the Name of *Proportionals*, or Quantities having an equal Reaſon is impoſed upon Quantities ſo conditioned or affected. From which it is afterwards gathered, if at any Time it appears by Argumentation, or otherwiſe, that this Condition agrees with any Quantities, that thoſe Quantities are Proportional.

But, he again makes a Noiſe with the *Ambages of infinite Circumſtances*, when no ſuch appears. For he inſiſts farther, *For neither* Clavius *himſelf could expeditely and by the Light of Nature gather Proportionality from the Affection of Equimultiples in Commenſurable Magnitudes, but he was forced to demonſtrate this in thoſe four Propoſitions of his own. But how will that be a moſt evident Affection, which cannot be accepted in Commenſurable Magnitudes without Demonſtration?* I anſwer, to the End that a Property may rightly enter a Definition, it is no Matter how it is, or may be demonſtrated from any other preſuppoſed Property; otherwiſe, as has been ſhewn, no Definition is good; for all may be thus demonſtrated. *Secondly*, *Clavius* deduced this Property from another Definition of commenſurable Proportionals, not indeed in four Theorems, but in one of four, and that not very intricately or prolixly demonſtrated; which I ſuppoſe he did not, becauſe it was neceſſary to demonſtrate that Property to make it reciprocate with this, or manifeſt its Evidence, but to ſhew the Conſent and Connexion of this Affection of Commenſurables with the other Affection which is well known. For the performing or effecting of which, he prejudges nothing

nothing of this Property from elsewhere by Examples of a known or knowable Evidence. Moreover, *thirdly*, we will allow him this, that albeit this Affection of Commensurable Quantities, as such, having the same Reason, be not the most noted; yet it is no Hindrance, but it may be the most noted of the general Affections agreeing with all Proportionals both commensurable and incommensurable; and Experience seems to persuade us that it really is most known, because, though many have attempted it, yet no one that I know of has assigned any genuine Property more known. Nay lastly the Possibility of no Hypothesis can be more evident than that which this Definition depends upon. Therefore no evidenter Affection of Proportionals can be demonstrated; nor therefore does this Reasoning succeed.

But at length he gives *Euclid* a most cruel Blow, so that he not only vanquishes him (as he thinks) but condemns him out of his own Mouth. *It was judged*, says he, *insufficient by* Euclid *himself, when he again defined commensurable Proportionality* (the Proportionality of Commensurables he would say) *in his seventh Book.* I answer this Scandal by utterly denying that *Euclid* therefore judged this his Definition insufficient, because he uses another in the seventh Element; for if himself had judged this insufficient, he would not have used it at all, but either have given none, or have investigated another. To publish Things not approved, much less Things disapproved by himself, was neither agreeable to *Euclid*'s Genius, nor his Intent; as if so knowing and prudent a Person would undervalue his own Work with insufficient Principles. On the contrary rather because he found the Definition of the seventh Element not to agree with every Kind of Proportionality, as being only adaptable to the Proportionalities of Commensurables;

rables; and found this to agree with all univerſally, therefore when he here entered upon a general Treatiſe of *Analogy*, rejecting that, he rightly embraced this. But he applied that (I will not ſay after or before) to commenſurable Proportionals, not ſo much for the ſake of Neceſſity as Convenience, that he might ſeem the ſimpler and eaſier to a vulgar Capacity with Reſpect to that particular Subject. Nor is it much to be wondered at, that he choſe the moſt ſimple Property for determining numerical Analogies, ſince he undertook to treat of the Theory of Arithmetic ſeparately and independently from others, though it agreed not with other Analogies, nor was ſufficient for the general Doctrine of Proportionalities. Albeit for a full Defence of *Euclid* we might prove that it is lawful and ſometimes expedient (for Variety and Facility's ſake,) to raiſe particular Doctrines from particular Principles (however oppoſite it be to the common Rigour of Logic) but this being beſide the Queſtion we will not now touch upon it. Let it ſuffice to have ſhewn, that, as our Adverſary pretends, it does not follow from hence, becauſe *Euclid* has elſewhere accommodated a particular Definition to a particular Subject, that therefore himſelf has diſapproved, or judged inſufficient, this his general Definition adapted to a general Subject.

From all which it appears that the Concluſion, which *Borellus* ſubjoins, depends upon weak Premiſes; *Therefore*, ſays he, *it is certain that the Property of the ſixth Definition of Proportionals is obſcure and difficult*, *becauſe it not only evidently declares the Nature of incommenſurable Proportionals*, *as does the twentieth Definition of the ſeventh Element*; *but again*, *which is ſtrange*, *he does not explain thoſe Things*, *that we have required the Foreknowledge of concerning the Thing itſelf to be defined.* (I interpoſe,

interpoſe, as has been often inculcated, that there is no ſuch Thing as a Nature of Proportionals prior to the ſaid Property, nor is it needful for us to know any Thing before that Definition concerning them, at leaſt diſtinctly and certainly. But he goes on, *For from hence, becauſe four Equimultiples of Magnitudes have that Condition of Exceſs or Defect, it is not perceived when, or how, they are Proportionals, if the Antecedents do together exceed, or fall ſhort of their Conſequents, neither if the Exceſſes be equal to one another, or no.* Which Words of *Borellus* ſeem very obſcure and ambiguous; but whatſoever they ſignify I am certain they can no Way hurt us. For from hence, becauſe four Equimultiples of Quantities have that Condition, it is plainly perceived that the Name of Proportionals agrees with them, nor is it any Matter, what elſe is perceived.

There remains one Objection to be removed after all Theſe, which is the moſt weighty of all the reſt, if it do but depend upon a true Suppoſition. *Nor finally (*ſays he*) can the leaſt Knowledge be gathered from the ſaid Property,* viz. *that to make four Magnitudes proportional, when the firſt exceeds the ſecond, the third Magnitude muſt neceſſarily exceed the fourth, as* Clavius *confeſſes in Prop.* XVI. *lib.* 5. *Elem.* I anſwer, *Firſt*, That this Confeſſion ſeems to be falſly fixed upon *Clavius*, for in the Place cited I can find no ſuch Thing. *Secondly*, How has *Euclid* demonſtrated, if not from that Property, having premiſed no other Definition of Proportionals? Certainly he has demonſtrated by it, though not immediately. And who knows not that in moſt Demonſtrations the Property of the Subject is not deduced immediately from its Definition? it being ſufficient to be done mediately by other Properties before derived from the Definition of the Subject. *Thirdly*, I add, though *Clavius* did

did not gather that Knowledge from this Property, yet it may be gathered, immediately and not difficultly: Which I thus prove by an indirect Discursus. Let A. B : : C. D according to our Definition, and let A ⊏ B, then I say C ⊏ D. If you deny, let C = or ⊐ D, and let all the Terms be multiplied by any one Number M; then because A ⊏ B by the Hypothesis, also MA ⊏ MB; and because C ⊐ D will MC ⊐ MD. Therefore according to this Definition A will not be to B as C to D, which is contrary to the first Hypothesis; and our Adversary wrongly denies that by supposing A ⊏ B therefore will C ⊏ D. So the said Knowledge (as he calls it) is deduced from our Definition, and the Objection of our Adversary answered.

Who then (says the Objector) *will say that the sixth Definition is good and a Principle of Science, if it affords a Knowledge obscure and imperfect?* To put an End to this prolix Disputation, I deny not myself to be one who will positively affirm (whatsoever he or others say in Contradiction) that it is one of the best of Definitions, a Principle most suitable to this Science, suggests a Knowledge most evident and perfect, and consequently, in my Opinion, overthrows all the Assaults of its Adversaries. And therefore I defend *Euclid*'s Definition and the Doctrine of Proportionality depending upon it, as much by the Probability of the Thing, as out of a Reverence to Antiquity.

In the next Place it follows for me to dwell a little (as I promised) upon the Definitions and Methods substituted by others; by which the Excellence of *Euclid*'s Doctrine will farther appear, with what Necessity he is bound, and for the avoiding of what Inconveniences he is led to own the Property so often mentioned.

The

The *first* is the Method of thoſe, who think a *Similitude or Identity of Reſpect* to be the moſt known Affection of Proportionals by which it ought to be defined. According to which they imagine that ſome principal Propoſitions of the fifth Element are to be put for Axioms, becauſe they are perſpicuous from their own Light, and need no Proof; and therefore they deduce the other Affections of Proportionals from thoſe. That learned Man *Johannes Benedictus* is long ago ſaid to have embraced this Opinion; which (or at leaſt ſomething like it) the moſt acute *And. Tacquet* has very lately reduced into a Form and embelliſhed. Which Method is accuſed of Inſufficiency by *Borellus*, and in my Opinion labours under many Defects. As *firſt*, in ſuch Definitions a fooliſh Tautology ſeems to be committed, and Propoſitions altogether identical put for Definitions; as in this, *Quantities obtain the like*, or *the ſame Reaſons, which have like Reſpects in Quantity*; *i. e.* (for what elſe can be here meant?) *which have the like or the ſame Reaſons.* Is not this to define a Thing by itſelf? Is this to explain the Nature of the Thing propoſed, or to lay down a Principle of Demonſtration? At leaſt, which is all the ſame, This ſeems to be nothing elſe, but to define by a Genus alone, without applying any Difference, in this Manner, *An Identity of Reaſons is an Identity of Reſpect. Thoſe Things have the ſame Reaſons, which have the ſame Reſpect:* Do ſuch Definitions, I beg, deſerve to be accounted perfect? *Secondly*, a *Similitude* or *Identity of Reſpect* are Words very equivocal, and of an uncertain Signification, impreſſing no diſtinct Conception on the Mind of the Hearer. For there are many Species, and many Degrees of *Similitude* and *Identity*. Therefore except ſome further Diſtinction be invented (*i. e.* except ſome Affection be applied, which is more known, and more

particular

particular than this) nothing will appear from this Word. Wherefore Definitions confifting of fuch lax Terms explain nothing, are unprofitable, and not at all fcientific. *Thirdly*, it can hardly be comprehended or explained in what Manner incommenfurable Quantities refpect one another; and therefore it cannot be perceived immediately what it is for them to refpect one another, in a like or in the fame Manner, nor when they are affected with fuch a Similitude of Refpect. Thus far *Borellus* feems to oppofe *Tacquet*; from whence it follows, *Fourthly*, that they who proceed in this Method do neither rightly affume Axioms, nor demonftrate Theorems concerning *Proportionals*. For how can any Thing be affumed or proved to agree with Proportionals, when it does not yet appear, or is not clearly conceived, what it is to be Proportional? Wherefore this Method has no Foundation. Not to infift upon this, that to take, and as it were beg many Things *gratis*, or indemonftrated, is derogatory to the Dignity of Geometry, and introduces too great a Licence into the Mathematics. To which I add *fifthly*, that fuch Definitions cannot be adapted to particular Subjects, but the *Proportionality* of fuch Subjects is demonftrated by intermediate Conclufions, and thofe depending upon Arguments fufficiently prolix and intricate. As will appear to any one who looks into *Tacquet*'s Demonftration of the firft or laft Propofition of the fixth Element. The Definition of *Proportionals* there cited does not appear, but another Propofition of *Tacquet*'s that he elfewhere proves in a long and indirect Difcurfus. Which feems a certain Sign to me of the Unaptnefs and Imperfection of the Definition laid down, and that the Method is not fcientific. To all which Defects does *Tacquet*'s Method feem obnoxious, none of which can be objected againft the Doctrine of *Euclid*; where nothing

nothing is trifling, ambiguous, or incomprehensible, but all Things proceed directly, are supported firmly, and the fewest Hypotheses are supposed; and lastly (which is the best Judgment of a most excellent Definition) where Analogies of particular Subjects are derived out of its very Bowels by an immediate and direct Discursus; as will appear to any that consults all its Applications in the Elements, or elsewhere; and particularly the Propositions alledged in the sixth Book.

But I here note by the Way, as to *And. Tacquet*'s Method, that, in my Opinion, he would have done far better if he had defined *Proportionals* by that Mark of *Proportionality*, which he brings, and in some sort demonstrates; and if by the Help of that Definition he had demonstrated the other Affections, which I judge (as himself professes) he was able to do. For by so doing he would have emulated *Euclid* and have proceeded in a *scientifical Way*; he would have avoided most of the Inconveniences we have mentioned, and might have been defended the same Way with *Euclid*. To which I exhibit this cognate and seemingly easier Affection of *Proportionals*, on which such Definition depends, *viz. Quantities are said to be proportional, when the Antecedents are equally contained respectively in the Equimultiples of the Consequents, or the Consequents in the Equimultiples of the Antecedents*; or *when those may be taken just so often from these*, or *the contrary*. From which Definition it would not be difficult to raise the whole *Doctrine of Proportionals* in a Procedure very *like Euclid*'s, but in my Opinion by no Means more short and clear. Against which however all may be objected, that has been objected against *Euclid*'s Method, and perhaps something besides from the Incommensurability of the Quantities, from whence *Euclid*'s Doctrine is most clear: Wherefore I do do not think it worth the while to innovate any Thing.

Having diſmiſſed *Tacquet* and his Fellows, I will give a Glance at Mr. (a) *Hobbes*'s Method, who thus defines *Analogy*, (as he thinks very accurately) *A Geometrical Reaſon is the ſame with a Geometrical Reaſon when the ſame Cauſe producing equal Effects in equal Times may be aſſigned determining the Reaſons of both.* Concerning which Definition I cannot forbear ſaying, that if any one turn over all the Writings of both the Ancients and Moderns, I believe he will no where find any Thing, which is undertaken to be illuſtrated, to be more obſcure, or to labour under more and more unpardonable Errors. For it is both hard and difficult to be underſtood (in my Opinion indeed it is not perfectly underſtood by its Author,) and contains Things very much from the Purpoſe; and I do not know whether it can be accommodated to any Subjects, at leaſt to very few, the whole Doctrine which is built upon it being ſo weak, confuſed, and prepoſterous (alſo in ſome Things of great Moment, falſe) that I never ſaw any Thing like it performed in the Mathematics. While I am examining this (which indeed is rather a *Phyſical* than *Mathematical*) Definition, I find Nothing that I can approve, or ſcarce any Thing that I can diſprove, conſequently it contains no Explication or Evolution. It explains not what it is for a Reaſon to be determined by ſome Cauſe, which is ſufficiently obſcure of itſelf. It is not apparent why it puts in *the ſame Cauſe*, ſince often even the homogeneous as well as heterogeneous Terms, of particular Reaſons are produced by different Cauſes, and conſequently do ſeem determinable by no Cauſes: Nor does it appear why

(a) De Corp. 13. §. 6. Dial. 2. p. 49.

that

that determining Cauſe is by a ſtrict Law confined to act uniformly, or to produce *equal Effects in equal Times*, ſince the Reaſons of Quantities produced by any unequal Impetus may be equal; therefore here is nothing explained. Again it cannot be conceived why a particular Conſideration of Times ſhould intervene with a general Expoſition of equal Reaſons: Certainly theſe can be no Way neceſſary to *Analogy*. *Ex. gr.* When I ſay two Quantities are proportional to their Equimultiples; what mention, I aſk, can there be of any Cauſe producing equal Effects in equal Times, unleſs very impertinently and out of the Way? When I ſay a Sphere and its Circumſcribing Cylinder are proportional to eight Ounces or a Pound Troy, do I ſpeak of performing equal Effects in the ſame Times to determine thoſe Reaſons of Bodies, Weights, or Numbers? Nay, even when I am deſirous to ſhew that two Times may be proportional to two Spaces, what Cauſe performing equal Effects in equal Times will ever determine thoſe Reaſons? Will the Reaſon of the Terms propoſed be determined by theſe or by other Times? But I am hoodwinked, and grope in Obſcurity.

Neither as to the Application of this Definition, do I find any Thing but mere Darkneſs, Confuſion, and Diſcord. The firſt Propoſition founded upon this Baſis, is as follows. (FIG. II.) *Let there be two Lines* AD *and* AG *deſcribed uniformly from a moveable Point* A; *then all the contemporary Pairs of their Parts will be proportional to one another*; *i. e.* if AB and AE, or AC and AF, be deſcribed in the ſame Times, then will AB and AC be proportional to AE and AF, or AB. AC : : AE. AF. Which he thus infers from this Definition, if we repreſent his Reaſoning more ſuccinctly and clearly: Becauſe the Velocity in AD by Reaſon of the Uniformity of the Motion, is always the ſame, there-

like

fore the Reaſon of AB to AC is determined from the Difference of the Times alone. Alſo from a like Cauſe the Reaſon of AE to AF is determined from the Difference of the Times. But the ſame Times are both here and there, and conſequently the ſame Difference of the Times. Therefore the ſame Cauſe determining thoſe Reaſons may be aſſigned. So far I underſtand ſomething; but he ſubjoins farther. And the Cauſe which thus determines the Reaſon of both effects equal Things in equal Times; for the Motion is uniform; here I begin to be blind and to ſtumble; the former Difference was aſſigned for determining the Cauſe of the Times; but now, becauſe it ſeemed inconſiſtent for the Difference of the Times to effect equal Things in equal Times, another Cauſe of the uniform Motion is ſubſtituted; tho' here is not one only, but at leaſt two uniform Motions. Do theſe agree with one another? Do they effect any Thing? or does himſelf underſtand his own Definition, or know how to apply it? But however he concludes; therefore by the next preceding Definitions AB. AC : : AE. AF. From this particular Theorem thus demonſtrated, he would ſeem to deduce, as Corollaries, general Theorms concerning *Proportionals*, which comprehend the general Affections of *Proportionals*, and moſt of them the ſame contained in the fifth Element. Who can ſuffer this, that from one Example a general Doctrine ſhould be drawn; or that thoſe Things may be immediately extended to all Subjects, which can be ſhewn of any two Lines and two Times? As if all *Proportionality* conſiſted in Times only and Spaces performed with an uniform Motion.

But to paſs by all other Faults of this Method, it ſeems to have happened to this Man, as it uſually does to thoſe, who, when they have looked ſomewhat long intently upon any Thing of a lively Colour,

lour, do seem to see all Things tinged with the same Colour: thus this Philosopher seems more intent upon what *Galileus* has writ concerning equable Motion, or is otherwise fixed upon the Contemplation of Physical Motions, when he refers all Things belonging to Magnitude and Quantity to certain preconceived Species concerning Motion. But in every Thing as it is said, *He who has respect to few Things judges ill.* Therefore Things being so, there is no Reason for us to tarry longer upon this new Method. For it is an Affront put upon *Euclid's* Doctrine to compare it with this.

Next we will concisely handle what a most learned Man proposed in his Geometrical Works. Who assumes it for a Definition, *That Reasons are equal, when the Antecedents divided by the Consequents make equal Quotients.* Which Definition differs nothing from that which *Euclid* uses in the seventh Element for the particular Doctrine of Numbers. But these Things seem to hinder it from being a just and accurate Definition of *Proportionality* taken universally. *First*, because antecedently to the Doctrine of *Proportionality* (*i. e.* that being not yet constituted) it is difficult to conceive what that Division of Quantities is, or how it is performed; *viz.* what it is for a Line to be divided by a Line, a Body by a Body, a Weight by a Weight, or a Time by a Time. There are indeed a certain Division and Multiplication of Lines and other Quantities, which are of Affinity to those Arithmetical Operations from whence they receive their Name, but these are defined and performed from the Invention of *Proportionals*, and consequently suppose *Proportionality* to be foreknown. Moreover Division is commonly by Arithmeticians defined by the Analogy between the Divisor and the Dividend, Unity and the Quotient.

tient. Therefore the Diviſion or Equality of Quotients reſulting from it does not ſeem ſo fit for a general Explication of *Proportionality.* Perchance you will ſay, it is eaſy enough to conceive what it is for a Line to be ſo often contained in a Line, a Weight in a Weight, or Time in a Time, nor is any Thing elſe meant here. Very true; but it is here required for the Terms of the Reaſons compared to be repreſented in Numbers; which raiſes another Argument againſt this Method, *viz. Secondly*, becauſe it ſeems to confine *Proportionality to Numbers alone*; and intimates as if the Reaſons of Quantities are only comparable with one another, as far as the Quantities themſelves are denominated by Numbers. For to conſider how often one Thing is contained in another, is the ſame as to exhibit the Proportion of thoſe Things, or denominate them in Numbers. But though Quantities neither be, nor perhaps can be repreſented or expreſſed in Numbers, yet their Reaſons may be exhibited, and their *Proportionalities* known, by *Euclid*'s, or a like, Method. And ſince it happens immediately to Quantities as ſuch, and not as they may be ſignified by Numbers, for Reaſons to relate to one another, and conſequently to be compared together, therefore it ſeems more agreeable to the Nature of the Thing for them to be determined in one general Manner, rather as Things abſtracted from Numbers, than ſubjected to them. Moreover, *thirdly*, when the Terms of the Reaſons compared are incommenſurate, neither the Conſequents nor any aliquot Parts of them, can be contained a juſt Number of Times in the Antecedents, and conſequently accurate Diviſions cannot be performed, nor any Quotients diſtinctly comprehenſible exhibited. For it is not eaſy to diſcern, or demonſtrate, when or how Quotients confuſedly imaginary are equal to one another.

Where-

Wherefore this Definition can hardly be accommodated to particular Uſes, which is almoſt the principal Imperfection of a Definition. In ſhort what was ſaid againſt *Tacquet*'s Method, is equally againſt this, which in Reality is ſcarce any Thing different from it.

But the ſame great Man hints at another Definition; Yet if any (ſays he) would rather call in the Aid of ſome Affection for the more convenient Procedure of Demonſtrations, I know none better than this; *If four Quantities be proportional, the Product made by the Extreams is equal to the Product made by the Means*, and the contrary. Concerning which I will ſay nothing further, but that that Affection propoſed is not general and adequate to *Proportionals*, according to the received Name. For the drawing or Multiplication of Numbers into themſelves, or into other Quantities is proper to Numbers alone; the Multiplication of Lines being performed by Similitude, if it be of one into another, or by a Parallel Motion if into Superficies. But who can conceive Lines to be drawn or multiplied into Bodies, or Weights into Times? Let the two Weights A and B be proportional to the two Times Y and Z, tell me what can be produced from the Weight A drawn into the Time Z; why nothing imaginable. Therefore this Affection is not ſtrictly ſuitable for a general Definition of *Proportionality*; at leaſt it will not any Way ſerve for determining the *Proportionality* of Numbers and Lines.

But laſtly it now remains for us to paſs our Opinion concerning *Borellus*'s Method; and leſt we ſhould ſeem to detract from the Merits of ſo great a Man, we readily acknowledge *firſt*, that his Doctrine, as far as we can ſee, is very firm, and built upon a good Foundation. We confeſs that the principal Affections of *Proportionals* are rightly

rightly deduced and demonſtrated by him from his own Definitions and Principles. We deny not but his Method is ſufficiently neat and elegant in itſelf, and if there were no other might by candid Judges be accounted as ſufficient and abſolute enough: But yet in Compariſon with *Euclid*'s it will be found faulty, and though it contains in it moſt Things well, yet theſe are not ſo excuſable.

Firſt, that ſince Equality is equally agreeable with all Reaſons of Quantities both Effable and Ineffable, and certain univerſal Properties are congruous with that, yet here every Equality is not defined univerſally and together, but particularly and ſuccceſſively. For the *Equality of Effable Reaſons* is firſt defined from ſome of its own particular Attributes, their *Greater* and *Leſſer Effable Reaſons* from that, and laſtly the *Equality* of *Incommenſurable Reaſons* from theſe. But to what End are all theſe Diſtractions of a general Subject, and Goings about by Inferiors, if there can be a general Property (as is exhibited by *Euclid*) of all Kinds of equal (as alſo unequal) Reaſons from whence they may be univerſally defined? If any eſſential Property can be found in the Genus of Animality, is it not more agreeable to the Nature of the Thing, the Genius of Science, and the Rules of good Logic, to define Animality entire and at once, than the Animality of a Man, and the Animality of a Brute ſeparately? It ſeems ſo to me.

Secondly, it is not ſo well to define the *Equality of Ineffable Reaſons* negatively, and ſo as to ſuppoſe the Definitions of *Unequal Reaſons* foreknown. For poſitive Definitions are univerſally reckoned preferable to negative ones, as begetting a more noble and clear Knowledge of Things. Then it ſeems prepoſterous to determine any Thing concerning *Equality* from *Inequality*, that ſeeming prior, more ſimple and more ſtable than this, and entirely indiviſible

indivisible in itself. Thus the Ancients; *Equality* (says (*a*) *Nicomachus*) *of itself is inseparable and indivisible.* Damascius, *Equality is analogous to any Station.* (*b*) Theon Smyr. *The Reason of Equality is the chief, the first and the principal of all the said Reasons, and of the Analogies according to the same.* Therefore the *Equality of Reasons* seems wrongly to be put after their *Inequality.* Has not *Euclid* then done better in defining *Equality* first by a positive Affection, and *Inequality* correspondently from another contrary Affection?

Thirdly, I observe the Prolixity of this Doctrine, which scarce performs that by an Ambages of long Definitions (*viz.* to distinguish the *Equality of Reasons* from their *Inequality*) which *Euclid* effects in only two, and those, if we weigh the Matter well, much shorter and more simple. The same might be observed in the whole Process of their Doctrines, that *Euclid* every where does the Thing with much fewer Syllogisms.

Moreover *fourthly*, I note that whosoever inspects *Borellus*'s Propositions and Demonstrations, he will find that the principal Properties of *Proportionalities* in that Method of his are not drawn but by indirect and oblique Argumentations; which too much argues them to be none of the best Principles. *Aristotle* teaches, and all Men allow, that not so clear and convincing a Science is produced by such Reasonings. Nor is it strange that winding and crooked Demonstrations should flow from the Fountains of negative Definitions. Is not *Euclid* then to be preferred, who gathers the same Things from positive Definitions by an immediate and direct Discursus?

Fifthly, what displeases me most, and is in my Opinion most faulty, is the Accommodation of these

(*a*) Nicom. l. 2. Vide Bull. Notis in Theon. p. 273.
(*b*) Theon. c. 51.

Definitions

Definitions to particular Subjects, or rather they cannot be fitly so applied. For the *Proportionality* of Things is neither quickly known by the Help of Definitions, nor readily deduced from thence, but is demonstrated from such intermediate Propositions, as are not so easy to be comprehended, being proved by an indirect Argumentation. Look, if you please, into the Demonstrations of the first and last Theorems of the sixth Element (which with *Borellus* are the first of the fourth, and second of the fifth) and you will find it as I say; and perhaps will subscribe to my Opinion, that *Borellus* has no Cause to boast of the Evidence of his Doctrine above that of *Euclid.* For the Evidence of a Doctrine appears chiefly in Use, and an easy Aptness to the particular or special Subjects of the first Definitions; nor is there any greater Virtue in these, than as it immediately appears they agree with the Things subjected. This *Euclid* has most clearly shewn of his, but not *Borellus* of his. Why may we not then pronounce that the Performances of the former are preferable to the Endeavours of the latter however excellent in themselves?

I have briefly taken Notice of these Things, not to derogate any Thing from the Praise of this great Man, but to shew the Excellency of *Euclid*'s Doctrine, and at the same Time defend the ancient Geometricians following and submitting to him, especially *Archimedes*, the most august Prince of Mathematicians, who subscribes to him, as often as Occasion requires.

I add, and close up this designedly limited Disputation, with this Attestation, that, in my Judgment, there is nothing extant in the whole Work of the Elements more subtilly invented, more solidly established, or more accurately handled than the *Doctrine of Proportionalities.* Which was chiefly in in my Mind to declare, when I entered upon this Contemplation and Theory concerning *Reasons* and *Analogies*. Of which Work I must now take my Leave, but am sorry it has fallen out contrary to my Hopes and Intentions, that I can neither compleat this whole Subject of *Proportionality*, nor propose what follows concerning the Determination, Similitude, and Generation of Magnitudes: Things perhaps neither unprofitable nor unpleasant. Therefore these are to be reserved or suppressed, as we shall see Cause hereafter. In the mean Time, most candid Auditors, I leave you to the Protection of the good God.

FINIS.

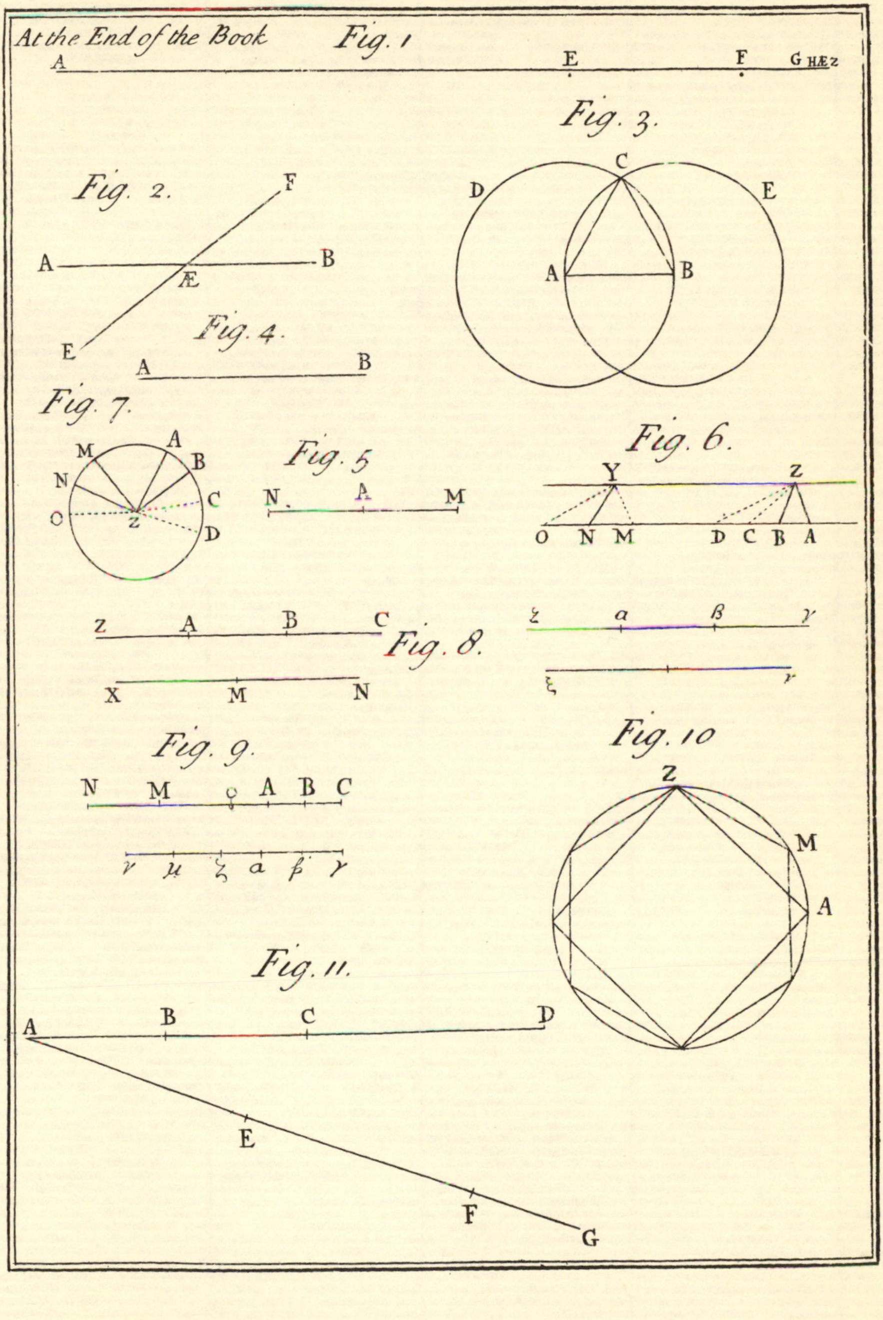
At the End of the Book
Fig. 1
A
E
F
G HÆZ
Fig. 2.
F
A
B
Æ
E
Fig. 3.
C
D
E
A
B
Fig. 4.
A
B
Fig. 7.
M
A
B
N
C
O
Z
D
Fig. 5
N.
A
M
Fig. 6.
Y
Z
O
N
M
D
C
B
A
Z
A
B
C
Fig. 8.
X
M
N
ζ
α
β
γ
ξ
r
Fig. 9.
N
M
ϙ
A
B
C
r
μ
ζ
α
β
γ
Fig. 10
Z
M
A
Fig. 11.
A
B
C
D
E
F
G

An Alphabetical

I N D E X

OF THE

Principal Matters

Contained in this WORK.

A.

D.

Lesser,

N.

Q.

NAMES

Made Use of in this

WORK.

Names.	Years before and after Christ.	Countries.
	A.	
Adrastus.		
Michael Angelo.		
Apollonius.		
Archimedes.	A. C. 220.	*Sicily.*
Archytus.	A. C. 400.	*Greece.*
Aristotle.	A. C. 350.	*Greece.*
Aristoxenus.	A. C. 320.	*Greece.*
	B.	
Bacchius.		
Johan. Benedictus.		
Blanchanus.		
Boethius.	P. C. 500.	*Italy.*
Alphonsus Borellus.		
Bullialdus.		
	C.	
Capella.		
Renatus Cartesius.	P.C. 1630.	*France.*
Cavallerius.	P.C. 1640.	

Chrysippus.

NAMES, *&c.*

Names.	Years before and after Christ.	Countries.
Chrysippus.	A. C. 330.	*Asia the lesser.*
Cicero.	A. C. 60.	*Italy.*
Clavius.		
Copernicus.		
	D.	
Damascius.		
	E.	
Epicurus.	A. C. 310.	*Greece.*
Eratosthenes.	A. C. 240.	*Greece.*
Euclid.	A. C. 410.	*Greece.*
Eudoxus.		
Eutocius		
	F.	
Ant. Farbius.		
	G.	
Galen.	P. C. 130.	*Lesser Asia.*
Galileus.		
Gaudentius.		
Geminus.	A. C. 60.	*Italy.*
Guildinus.		
	H.	
Petrus Herigonius.		
Hippocrates.	A. C. 380.	*Coos in lesser Asia.*
Hobbs.	P. C. 1650.	*England.*
	L.	
Longomontanus.		
Lucretius.		*Italy.*
	M.	
Meibomius.		

Mersennus.

Names.	Years before and after Christ.	Countries.
Mersennus.		
	N.	
Nichomachus.		
	P.	
Pappus.	A. C. 380.	*Egypt.*
Peletarius.		
Dr. *John Pell.*	P. C. 1660.	*England.*
Pererius.		
Plato.	A. C. 380.	*Greece.*
Plutarch.	P. C. 100.	
Proclus.		
Ptolomy.	P. C. 130.	*Egypt.*
Pythagoras	A. C. 540.	*Samos.*
	Q.	
Aristides Quintillianus.		
	R.	
Ramus.		
Rivaltus.		
	S.	
Seneca.	P. C. 60.	*Italy.*
Willebrord Snellius.		
Socrates.	A. C. 440.	*Greece.*
	T.	
And. Tacquet.	P. C. 1650.	
Theoaosius.		
Theon Smyrnæus.		
Thrasyllus.		
Torricellius.	P. C. 1640.	

Fran.

NAMES, &c.

Names.	Years before and after Christ.	Countries
	V.	
Fran. Vieta.	P. C. 1590.	*Switzerland.*
Greg. Vincentius.		
Vitellius.		
Vitruvius.		
Vossius.		
	W.	
Dr. *John Wallis.*	P. C. 1670.	*England.*
	X.	
Xenocrates.	A. C. 340.	*Greece.*
	Z.	
Zeno.	A. C. 360.	*Cyprus.*

FINIS.